New Toddler Taming

A parents' guide to the first four years

DR CHRISTOPHER GREEN

with illustrations by Roger Roberts

Vermilion
LONDON

First published in Australia and New Zealand in 1984 by Doubleday
This revised edition first published in Australia and New Zealand
by Doubleday in 2006
This revised edition published in the UK by Vermilion,
an imprint of Ebury Publishing, in 2006

Ebury Publishing is a Random House Group company

The Random House Group Limited Reg. No. 954009

Addresses for companies within the Random House Group can be found at
www.randomhouse.co.uk

A CIP catalogue record for this book is available from the British Library

The Random House Group Limited supports the Forest Stewardship Council® (FSC®), the
leading international forest-certification organisation. Our books carrying the FSC label are
printed on FSC®-certified paper. FSC is the only forest-certification scheme supported by the
leading environmental organisations, including Greenpeace. Our paper procurement policy
can be found at www.randomhouse.co.uk/environment

Printed and bound by CPI Group (UK) Ltd, Croydon, CR0 4YY

ISBN 9780091902582

Copies are available at special rates for bulk orders. Contact the sales development
team on 020 7840 8487 or visit www.booksforpromotions.co.uk for more
information.

To buy books by your favourite authors and register for offers, visit
www.randomhouse.co.uk

*To my wife, Dr Hilary Green, without whose inspiration,
support and encouragement this book would
never have happened.
She believed that life is too short for squabbling, holding
grudges or fighting with children; instead she showed
us all the importance of understanding, love
and warmth, and that life is for enjoying.
Sadly, for Hilary life was too short and she never saw the
completed new edition of this book, but through it her
ideas will be remembered.*

Contents

Acknowledgements

Thanks to:

My wife, Dr Hilary Green, who had a natural instinct for 'toddler taming' and whose clever ideas, found throughout this book, make parents feel valued and understood.

My boys, James and Tim, who in their toddlerdom taught me to expect the unexpected. Without their inventiveness this book would have contained much less practical wisdom. Now grown up and always much loved.

Jon Attenborough, a publisher who believed in *Toddler Taming* from the very beginning and whose vision and encouragement gave me the opportunity to change parents' lives.

Michael Morton-Evans, who gave me the confidence to write in my own style and shaped my original manuscript into a bestseller.

Dr John Yu, Prof. Kim Oates and Dr Peter Procopis, my bosses at the Children's Hospital, Westmead, for their support of my work which gave me the freedom to talk to parents all over Australia and around the world.

My team at the Children's Development Unit, who taught me so much in my day-to-day work: Neralie Cocks, Kate Watson, Janis Mendoza, Dr Paul Hutchins, Dr Natalie Silove, Pam Joy, Polly Pickles and the late Joye Downes.

The children and their parents at the Royal Belfast Hospital for Sick Children, and the Royal Alexandra Children's Hospital, Sydney (Westmead), for being the 'test subjects' of my techniques and ideas over many years. They provided me with a unique education and this book would have been impossible without them.

Dr Henry Kilham, John Coveney, Jayne Hyde, Lorraine Partington, Dr Michael Green and Vanessa Hill for their kind assistance with various chapters of this book.

And finally Leonie Waks, my gifted editor, who encouraged me to start writing again after my wife died and I felt like giving up. Her belief in my work and heartfelt desire to make this a better book spurred me on. By persistently asking me the questions 'What are you trying to say?' and 'What is the solution?' she patiently helped me to reinvigorate the *Toddler Taming* message.

In the beginning . . .

There was a time when I was as confused as any parent when confronted with typical toddler behaviour. Twenty-five years ago, training as a paediatrician, I had no interest in children's behaviour and I certainly had no earth-shattering ideas about how to manage their more challenging moments. Like all trainees, I had been put into psychiatric rotation for half a year. Not only did I not want to do this, I thought that psychiatry was a pretty lame area to be working in. I was a 'real' doctor, interested in serious, life-threatening problems and could think of better ways to spend my time.

In those six months I learnt many things – from how to interpret Oedipus complex to all about castration anxiety, repression and projection. My supervisor was one of Australia's top academics, an internationally renowned child psychiatrist. Most of my time was spent observing other psychiatrists and psychologists but I was given a few cases to cut my teeth on. Every week, the professor would go over these cases with me and give me his learned opinion, but I was still far from becoming the Toddler Tamer. Then everything changed with one problem toddler and two exhausted and confused parents.

The child was 2 years old and having major tantrums. His father was a long-haul airline steward who, together with his wife, consulted me in the hope of putting an end to these embarrassing outbursts. Every time the father returned from a few days in London, the tantrums would make him wish he was 30,000 kilo-metres away again.

In the first consultation I started out just as my esteemed professor had instructed: getting a thorough case history, with details of the toddler's behaviour and the parents' lives.

One week later, the couple returned with their troublesome tot. The professor had listened to my case and commented that I required more information about the mother's relationship with her mother, as I didn't know enough to figure out why the toddler was having tantrums. So in the second consultation, I questioned her endlessly. Clearly puzzled, the father asked me, 'But what about the tantrums?' to which I replied that I needed to know more before we could do anything.

I took the new information to my supervisor, who listened to the details and remarked that I needed to find out more about mum and dad's sex life. Keen to solve this family's toddler problems, I dutifully enquired in this vein when they came in to see me a week later. They answered my probing queries, but again dad kept saying, 'But how do we stop the tantrums?' I wasn't any closer to an answer, so I went back to my professor and explained: 'Here's more case-history information, however the parents are getting annoyed. What will we do to cure the tantrums?' His reply? 'You have to get more history.'

So I went back to the parents, week after week, hoping to find the key to the tantrums in the stories they were telling me.

As the weeks wore on and the toddler's tantrums continued, the mother reached her wits' end and the father became ropeable. After another particularly useless consultation, I went back to my professor.

'These people can't cope any more; the toddler throws himself on the ground and screams at the drop of a hat. They don't care about more history, tell us what to do!' The professor didn't answer, so I petitioned again, and again he didn't answer, so I tried one more time: *'How do you cure the tantrums?!'*

After a considered pause, he gave me the answer I'd been waiting for: '. . . Hmmm . . . hmm . . . mmm . . .'

A light went on in my brain. I realised I didn't have the answer and neither did the experienced expert! Then and there I came to a conclusion: I wanted to be good at curing the common problems. I set out to find ways to make life easier for these desperate parents.

I got off the couch and out into the real world. A community paediatrician pointed me in the direction of the Early Childcare Clinics. Toddler behaviour is often at its worst when a new baby arrives, so while mum was having the baby's weight checked, I would check out her toddler. I began to consult with the mums about the behaviours that were bothering them. I would give them ideas and these mums would go home and see if they were useful and if they fitted into their lives. Some on their return said I was brilliant, and couldn't believe how easy it was. Some blithely told me my ideas hadn't made a scrap of difference. Others were rather less complimentary, going into great detail of how I had actually made life worse. I would make adjustments and modifications based on the successes; it was a slow process.

I completed my training and joined the rarified ranks of specialist consultants. Over the next three years, in the clinics and the wards, my everyday work was looking after very ill children, but my interest, sparked by the airline steward and his family, kept being drawn to behaviour. As the years passed, parents started to seek me out and I realised that I was beginning to have the answers that I had searched for from my professor.

I started to get invitations to speak to parent groups about my solutions to sleep, feeding, toileting and behaviour problems. Soon I was talking on radio and one morning was heard by a father suffering the effects of a sleepless night, thanks to his toddler. He thought that I knew what parents were on about. As luck would have it, he was also an international publisher. He camped out on my doorstep until I agreed to write a book. And so *Toddler Taming* was born.

The past two decades have seen many changes but one thing remains the same: toddlers are still toddlers. They may wear different clothes, have pull-up nappies, three-wheeler jogging prams and a complete collection of the *Tweenies* DVDs, but essentially toddlers haven't changed. As any parent will tell you, time has not dimmed their enthusiasm for creating chaos; it hasn't dented their unthinking and often unreasonable behaviour, nor muffled their noisy demands for attention. Toddlers are just as full of life and magic as they always have been.

So the same things that worried parents 21 years ago, when this book was first published, continue to worry them today. Modern parents are still confused by how to get a fussy toddler to eat his dinner, and exasperated at the seemingly endless phase of potty training. They remain at their wits' end due to their little insomniac's pre-dawn activity, shell-shocked by explosive tantrums and perhaps faintly appalled by the toddler's personal habits – little digits are permanently docked up otherwise cute noses and toddlers make an art form of stickiness.

No wonder parents are struggling. 'What am I doing wrong?' they ask. Nothing! You don't have to make such hard work of it. There are answers to even your most troublesome toddler tribulations. Toddlerdom should be enjoyable and, with my help, it will be. Put up your weary feet, pour yourself a double espresso, and get ready enjoy your toddler.

Author's note: For ease of writing I have used 'he' and 'his' when talking about all toddlers.

1
Toddler taming

For most parents, life as they know it changes with the arrival of toddlerdom. Suddenly – at times seemingly overnight – their compliant baby is transformed into an unpredictable toddler. It's a nasty shock to the system.

Toddler behaviour fluctuates wildly from minute to minute and day to day and can be confusing for even the most experienced expert, let alone novice parents.

In this chapter I outline the *Toddler Taming* message. Most of it will seem like simple commonsense and with trial and error you would no doubt have stumbled across these pearls of wisdom yourself. But I want to give you a headstart on the challenging toddler years that lie before you. If you were to read only one chapter of this book, this is the one I'd want you to read,

What's important:
the *Toddler Taming* message

After 25 years of hands-on work with troublesome toddlers, of all the ideas and solutions I've gathered for those common toddler problems that challenge most mums and dads, some stand out. I've come to see these as the bedrock on which to build strong parenting for the toddler years and beyond.

Unlike a whodunnit novel, where it's all a mystery until the big revelation on the last page, I want to give you the goods right at the start. These are the things that I believe are really important.

What toddlers want

- Attention
- Time
- Love and affection

Attention is the mainstay; I can't stress this enough. Toddlers need lots of attention, more than most parents realise. Basically, you can never give them too much.

The key to toddler behaviour is giving lots of the best, Grade A attention: undivided, uninterrupted, one-on-one interaction. When they can't get this premium type, toddlers will go for whatever they can.

Too often busy parents are distracted, thinking about the ingredients for dinner, their beeping mobile phone or the project that needs to completed for work. Left without his adoring audience for even a short time, the toddler becomes interrupting, noisy and demanding. We see bad behaviour, when in fact he's sending you the message, 'What about me? I'm important and I'll hijack your attention any way I can if you won't give it to me.' Lack of quality attention is the root of so many behaviour problems and parental headaches. If you give toddlers attention before they grab it, it won't get to that stage when they are demanding it.

Attention is also about being noticed – toddlers need a positive connection. The quieter, more placid child won't cause a ruckus to gain your attention, even though they need it just as much as the little terror methodically destroying the living room. They live with the paradox of being too good for their own good: they don't get enough attention because by behaving well, they don't draw enough attention to themselves.

Closely linked to attention is time. Working parents often feel guilty that they are not spending enough time with their children. There never seem to be enough hours in the day and a busy toddler can eat up an awful lot of them. Toddlers have a completely different sense of time from adults and they aren't interested in clock watching or time management. They live very much in the present; they want someone to play with *now*. Fortunately, at some point they go to bed, but nothing can replace time spent together.

Toddlers need to be given love and feel they are loved. I'm not being soppy or obvious – I'm talking about making sure that the toddler knows that his parents love him. Whether right or wrong, many people in loving relationships aren't secure in this knowledge. As for affection, again it may seem obvious but you need to demonstrate it. When in doubt, give your toddler a cuddle.

Parents' problems become toddler problems

- Stress
- Tension
- Upset

Children are sensitive – like a good antenna, toddlers tune into what's happening in their surroundings. So we really can't underestimate the impact of their environment, good or bad.

Whatever affects the parents affects the toddler: you may not be able to see the vibes, but that doesn't mean they aren't there. What they *don't* see and what they *don't* hear, they still feel. For instance, the toddler may not understand your dispute with your partner, or even hear you arguing, but they can feel the tension radiating through the home. Even if you think you're hiding the worst of it from the toddler, they can still sense uncertainty.

You unwittingly transmit what you're feeling, which is picked up by the toddler, who then makes life even more difficult. The toddler becomes clingy, stalls his toilet training or shows his distress through vocal tantrums. These then come back and hit you where it hurts, making you feel even more stressed and adding to a rapidly increasing vicious cycle.

A new baby, travel, illness, moving house, emotional baggage or money worries are all obvious causes of stress. At times like these, behaviour problems are normal and to be expected. In these situations, toddlers don't need more discipline – they need more understanding.

As a guiding rule, if mum or dad are stressed, then so is the toddler. I know life is stressful, and I won't tell you to not worry or be uncertain. But we need to be aware of how this affects the toddler and go gently.

You can't do it on your own

- Families
- Grandparents
- Support

So many young parents feel clever making a baby. And they think that because they have a career, a driver's licence and a mortgage, surely they can handle one small child all by themselves. Thankfully, after the first few sleepless nights, they realise they do need help. And hopefully, by the time the baby has become a toddler, they've realised that they need to accept help and support wherever they can get it.

Trying to raise a toddler on your own is possible but you don't need that kind of pain. Getting the support you need is essential so that you can give the toddler what they need.

Support comes from many sources and the most obvious is family. Families give a sense of security and, more importantly, a feeling of belonging which helps to build a child's confidence. The value of having family support is priceless. Nowadays, thanks to the technology of the internet and with satellites beaming phone signals around the globe, even living half a world away you can easily stay in touch with distant family.

I think that some of the very best support on offer is grandparents. Some still have a stereotypical view of grandparents as old people shuffling around in slippers, out of touch with the world today, but modern grandparents are a different breed. Many have as much energy as parents and being around the toddler seems to keep them young. Plus grandparents have the wisdom and experience of having been there before.

Unfortunately, family and grandparents are our most valuable but least used assets. These days, when there are fewer extended families and relatives living nearby, it's even more important to create a support network around yourself – through mothers' groups, neighbours, friends and baby clinics. Of course you can do very well by yourself when things are going well, but life isn't always on an even keel. Supportive people, whether relatives or not, provide essential backup for difficult times.

Discipline is a rewarding exercise

- Rewards
- Consistency
- Limits

Discipline doesn't have to be a drama but it is one of the biggest stumbling blocks for many parents. Figuring out what to do in the face of militant toddler behaviour strikes fear in their hearts and causes many parents to give up hope of a peaceful life.

Discipline can be a very rewarding experience – it is not about control or punishment, it is a positive thing. In this book, my aim is to gently steer behaviour in the direction that you want by encouraging the toddler when they're doing the right thing. This gentle way works 95 per cent of the time, which means you can leave the stronger techniques for when it's really necessary. However, there is no place for force: threats, shouting and smacking may belong in the wrestling ring, but they are not part of raising toddlers.

The most powerful way to discipline the toddler is using rewards. I'm not talking about bribery but the subtle use of attention to mould the child's behaviour. We use eye contact, our tone of voice, our touch and being noticed as rewards to praise good behaviour. This encourages the behaviour we want and discourages the behaviour we don't, and the power of the reward pretty much guarantees that the good behaviour will be repeated the next time. Most of our success comes from this simple approach. With this as our main course of action, we can then use good old-fashioned techniques such as diversion, and selective deafness and blindness to get ourselves out of trouble. For those times when our backs are truly against the wall, Time Out is a rapid way of diffusing an escalating problem.

Everyone feels happier with some discipline in their lives and this is especially true of the impulsive, unthinking toddler. Discipline creates guidelines and sets boundaries, giving a sense of security and consistency. A child needs to know what's expected of them, and that what stands today will still stand tomorrow. With positive, consistent discipline the toddler sees what behaviour is encouraged, what is allowed, and what are 'no-nos'.

You can see why the best kind of discipline is about guiding, rewarding and gently moulding the toddler's behaviour. I don't like being forced and I don't like being threatened; I have no doubt, however, that I like being gently guided and I love being rewarded. The toddler is equally fuelled by encouragement.

The solutions are simple

- Sleep problems
- Feeding
- Toilet training

It's fair to say that every parent will encounter difficulty with at least one of the Big Three of sleeping, feeding and toileting. But the solutions really are simple as long as you don't try to change everything at once. You have to start with the basics.

When it comes to sleep, all children have different needs, often not what suits the parents. Setting habits with a good bedtime routine is the place to start. For repeated middle of the night waking, we use the controlled crying technique and to keep them in their rooms, there is the Green patented rope trick.

As for feeding dramas, don't fight over food; the only thing it achieves is to raise your blood pressure. Trust me: no child has ever starved from stubbornness. Our most important concern is to make sure the toddler is getting adequate nutrition.

Toilet training creates trouble when you start too early, frustrating yourself and confusing your toddler. At 1½ years of age it's a long shot; at 2 years, the odds are favourable; by 2½, success is a deadset certainty. Three-year-old toddlers are mainly arid, but there will still be the occasional leak, which is normal.

Exhausted parents become overwhelmed and feel as if *everything* is wrong. When working with parents I'd ask them: 'If I had a magic wand and could solve one problem, what would you like to fix?' The key is to focus on the main area that's bothering you. Then, by using the techniques in this book, you will get quick results. Solving one problem builds your confidence and has a ripple effect. Like any good miracle, once you've seen one, you believe in more.

Different strokes for different folks

- Temperament
- Tolerance
- Competition

People used to think that all children were created with a 'blank slate' and that all bad behaviour was solely the fault of the parent. We now realise that every child is born with his or her own unique temperament and personality. Some are destined to be easy going; most will have the odd moment or two, while the remaining few will become hair-raising terrors.

Because of these innate differences in temperament, you can't raise toddlers 'by the book'. You'll never turn a noisy, sparky hothead into a placid little angel no matter how hard you try, and nor should you. You have to accept that your child is unique and find what works for you and your toddler.

The tolerance of parents is another important ingredient in the mix. Different people have different levels of tolerance and different views of acceptable behaviour. There are those parents who are more laid-back and others who are inflexible and easily inflamed. Added to this are various attitudes to parenting that parents absorb from their own parents.

Instead of making life interesting, all this difference leads to competition, guilt and the feeling that you are doing something wrong, as you compare your toddler to others at preschool or day care. Your toddler won't have an afternoon nap while the other 2 year olds snooze for hours. One toddler is tackling Harry Potter while yours is satisfied that books are for chewing not reading. You're not doing anything wrong, you just have a different child.

You can't change the temperament your toddler was born with, you can't change their genes, but you can change their behaviour. You can achieve this by adapting your approach to suit your child.

It's the difference between off-the-rack parenting and tailor-made for a perfect fit for your toddler.

Don't go looking for trouble

- Know what's normal
- Decide what's important
- Have sensible expectations
- Don't poke the lion

An awful lot of things that bother parents are what I call non-problems. These behaviours are so common in toddlers that we can actually consider them to be normal. And while that doesn't mean that you will like or even be able to live with all of them, to survive, it helps to realise that some things are just not worth getting worked up about.

When confronted by these normal – if not particularly nice – toddler trademarks, you have to pick your battles and decide what's important. It's easier to sidestep unwinnable wars than escalate a small skirmish into a conflict of intergalactic proportions.

So many parents prod their children and get themselves into trouble when they don't need to. If I was to find myself in the jungle with a lion blocking the path, I'd have two ways to deal with it. I could tiptoe past, or I could aim a well-placed poke at Mr Lion's posterior. The same goes when dealing with toddlers – it's a brave parent who decides that normal toddler antics need taming.

This is why having sensible expectations is one of the keys to surviving toddlerdom. Unfortunately most parents don't realise how unrealistic they are being until they are up to their necks in conflict and chaos.

As you read this book, you're going to find that I am an unashamed pacifist. The least inflammatory course of action brings about the most peaceful coexistence.

When in doubt, remember...

Take a step back

When things are tough, ask yourself, 'Is the toddler having a bad day, or am I?' Sometimes the toddler is less in need of an attitude adjustment than the parent.

Take a step back and consider why he is behaving this way. Could this be classed as normal toddler behaviour? What does he gain? Usually the toddler is telling you that he is in urgent need of an attention top-up.

Stop and look at it from the toddler's point of view

Toddlers aren't little adults. They have limited sense and attention spans. They don't think like we do – in fact, they rarely think before they act. When another toddler takes his toy, he doesn't understand that it is just being borrowed. He hasn't discovered the adult value of sharing, he just wants it back.

There's not a bad bone in their body

Toddlers aren't malicious and they aren't out to try your patience or punish you, even if it sometimes feels that way. It can be easy to start thinking that children are the enemy, when even the worst toddlers are good 95 per cent of the time.

Little children want to be good, which they'll show us if we give them even half a chance.

They'll probably grow out of it anyway

Whatever it is that your bundle of joy is doing that seems horrifying right now, it will often simply disappear one day, without any warning. This thankfully includes many of the behaviours that define toddlers. By school age, much of this will be a distant memory. You may even mourn the very things that had you climbing the walls.

The secret to your success

I want to let you in on a secret: I don't tame toddlers. Taming is not what bringing up a toddler is all about and it's certainly not what I'm about. Taming suggests that toddlers need to be brought under control, and while it may seem that way on the surface, that's not the answer to your toddler problems.

Understanding and sensible expectations will get you much further than control ever will. Success lies in knowing what makes your toddler tick and then using this to sidestep trouble rather than confronting it head on. This approach doesn't mean giving toddlers a free rein. It really is about saving your energy for the things that really matter.

In choosing this quieter, more peaceful way, that's not to say it will all be easy sailing. Even the most saint-like child has their moments and there will still be times when you wonder what you've got yourself in for. Ruling children with military zeal may produce a perfectly behaved child, but in the long run I believe that the gentler approach enriches your relationship with your toddler, rather than making it a casualty.

I'm confident that my ideas will make life easier for you – and, speaking of confidence, that's what we're going to look at next.

2
Confident parenting

This book is for parents with feet firmly on the ground, who want practical ideas to make their child-rearing both successful and enjoyable. But it appears that the more complicated child care theory becomes, the less we are prepared to trust our natural instincts. We all start our parenting journey with incredibly high ideals, but as tension and tiredness take their toll, we thankfully lower our sights to a more down-to-earth position. It can seem like you're the only parent with doubts, feeling inferior and unconfident. In fact, most people pretend they are in complete control when really their trouble-free life is just an act.

Confidence is what makes parents positive, powerful and puts them firmly in charge. It means having an 'I can do this' attitude. What does it take to be a confident parent? Some are swamped by the slightest wave, while others are buoyed by confidence even in the heaviest weather. This chapter is about protecting your confidence so that it helps you through the inevitable ups-and-downs of toddlerdom.

Snakes and ladders

When confidence is high the trivial hassles of our day-to-day lives seem like molehills. But as soon as confidence crumbles, we quickly lose all perspective for what's important and those same molehills become as towering as Everest. This leaves us vulnerable to outside influences that further erode our confidence.

Life is like a game of snakes and ladders – just as you get your foot on the top rung, a snake bites you on the backside. Confidence comes and goes as we journey through life, and even the most positive people have moments of doubt. Luckily, confidence-building ladders are plentiful and there are also ways to snake-proof your life.

Ladders

These are the things in life that build your confidence. The more you have and the stronger they are, the easier it is to be confident in your parenting skills. Some of them are like 10-metre extension ladders, others are more like stepladders, but they all help you to get over the next hurdle.

Security

When you feel secure, you can focus on being the best parent that you can be. If you spend all your time worrying about your job, your relationship or your mortgage, you will have little emotional energy left over for the demands of a toddler.

A sense of security comes from having a nest to come home to at the end of the day, from having enough money for the necessities in life and from stable and helpful relationships. Your confidence will grow when you know you can count on these things rather than adding them to the snake basket.

Whether your nest is a two-bedroom flat or a 20-room mansion, you draw strength from it. It is your base, and a springboard to help you bounce through life. When our relationships are healthy, we feel we can conquer the world. This is where it all begins for parents, with our 'team' that provides essential backup. The security we get from healthy, supportive relationships is priceless.

Support

As I've mentioned before, support is essential to parenting. Confident people look to others for support and advice, comparing notes on what works for them. They don't see this as being weak, merely sensible. On the other hand, lack of confidence usually causes parents to try to go it alone.

The more support you have, the easier parenting will be and the bigger your support network, the better your chances of success. These days there are often great distances between parents and their extended families, who were the original scaffolding propping up confidence. There is no need to struggle through on your own, so becoming one of those people who ask for help is the healthiest option for you and your toddler.

Experience

Because parenting is full of firsts, just as you've got babies sorted, you get a toddler. For first-time parents, it can be a rude shock. Here is a whole new world of interesting experiences – the first time you're faced with a toddler tantrum is a little like the first time behind the wheel of a car: full of drama and wobbles. But by the twentieth time, you negotiate the turns with barely a blink of an eye.

It's true that the more experience you have, the more confident you are. Many new parents have never encountered a behaviour problem before their toddler's charming displays. But rest assured that your toddler will provide you with lots of opportunities to develop your confidence!

Knowing what's normal

Often we feel we are the only ones with troubles when, if only we knew it, everyone else is in the same boat. Normal toddler behaviour is certainly character building but it does little for your confidence.

Getting to know what's normal is one of the biggest confidence builders around. It stops you wearing yourself down with non-problems, and allows you to relax and focus on what's important. For example, at 18 months, toddlers have little sense and unaware parents wail, 'What am I doing wrong?' when their creative little bundle of energy performs some act of senseless toddler perfection. If they only realised that this is normal, their confidence wouldn't suffer a blow.

A good book

Sometimes all it takes is a good book. There are two main sorts of books, fact or fiction. When dealing with parenting manuals, it's important not to choose reading material that is better suited to the fiction shelves.

A good book can be relied on for easy, on-hand advice. It helps you to navigate a safe passage through toddlerdom without mishap and provides markers on the way to show you're on the right course. If you're lost, it tells you how to get back on track. I know I'm a little biased, but I've been known to rely on a really good book by a man called Green.

Snakes

As a parent, it can feel as if there are snakes lurking at every turn. These confidence killers strike us when we're least expecting it. There are some parents who seem to be wearing snake repellant, never taking a wrong step. But the rest of us frequently find ourselves sliding down the slippery, reptilian slope. Some of these snakes are very poisonous, others only mildly annoying, but when we're stressed they all begin to look the same. However, we can avoid them all if we know what to look out for.

Competition

We live in a very competitive world and we can't help noticing how other people manage their homes, relationships and children. Soon our lives are lived constantly looking over our shoulder to see if we are performing up to scratch. This is made worse by the media which presents a strange slant on reality. Many popular magazines overtly promote 'The Perfect Marriage', 'Perfect Sex', 'The Perfectly White Business Shirt', 'The Perfectly Balanced Breakfast Cereal', 'The Perfect Child-Rearing Method'. When it comes to raising children, competition is often at its fiercest.

As you wait in the baby clinic, you may wonder why all the other children seem bigger, stronger, toothier and more advanced than your own. At preschool you may feel embarrassed when your little one fails at cutting-out or romps around when the core of children are pasting, painting and listening to stories.

If you already doubt your ability, competition only makes it

Knowing your competition

Parents' vulnerability is only made worse by those painful parents who boost their egos by boasting about their child's brilliance. As you gather at the preschool gate, some doting mum brags: 'My boy is four and recites Shakespeare sonnets with passion.' Before you can catch your breath this is trumped by another, who says: 'My girl is three-and-a-half and plays the violin perfectly by the Suzuki method.' All *you* can think is: 'My little one is almost five and still wets the bed every night!'

much worse. Parenting is never easy, but if you're constantly comparing everything your toddler does, you can easily end up feeling like a failure. Remember, competitive parents tend to cloud the perspective by boasting about the rare and clever while keeping quiet about those normal, annoying behaviours that all toddlers have in common.

Interference

Mother-in-laws – I'm sure that's what first springs to mind when I mention interference. But interference can come from various well-meaning, nosy sources: your own parents, siblings, mothers' group, friends, neighbours – the list is endless. Interference is advice that wasn't needed in the first place.

What is it about interference that is so damaging to your confidence as a parent? If you spend all your time worrying about what other people think, you begin to doubt yourself. You wonder, 'Am I doing a good job or am I a second-rate parent?' The reason that interference gets up people's noses is its message of 'You can't do it as well as me, so listen up: here's what you *should* do'.

Grandparents find it particularly difficult to not interfere in the raising of their grandchildren. They can recall having been through all this with their own children and they don't want the ones they love to stumble into the same traps. But like toddlers, parents learn by experience and no matter what grandma tells them, they have to work it out for themselves.

There is a fine line beyond which advice becomes a hindrance rather than a help. Nobody likes being told what to do. Most people react by blocking it out while quietly simmering inside. As they become more resentful, the interference blocks communication and fuels arguments.

There are ways to win without losing confidence and being drawn into battle. Our number one priority is the wellbeing of the child, followed by that of mum and dad. They are the majority shareholders and if interference is causing stress to them (and by default the toddler), it's time to exercise their options. There have to be some rules and boundaries if you are going to maintain your sanity. It's lovely to listen to what grandma has to say if she's being helpful, but you may need to filter her advice. I'm not suggesting a contract of informed consent before loved ones dare to offer their opinion, just some awareness of the no-go zones.

Stress and tension

How do you go from one day feeling like you can handle your energetic toddler, to the next doubting your every move? Stress and tension are so common that we certainly don't see how they affect our confidence as parents. Day-to-day stress has a direct relationship to our inability to cope with the demands of parenting. When times are tough, it's hard to keep your chin up. We begin to believe that because we can't deal with one aspect of our lives, we are failing in all of them.

I could fill a book with all the ways that life winds us up but no matter what the cause, it all has the same end result. When you let stress rule your life, the toddler will quickly pick up that you're losing ground. As they commence an all-out assault on your weakening defences, your confidence takes a nosedive. This vicious cycle will escalate until something snaps – usually the parent's patience.

When you realise that you're wound tighter than a spring, try approaching the problem from a different angle. We have to target what we can fix, be realistic rather than expect miracles. These are found in a much older book!

Depression

It is impossible to be a confident parent when you are depressed. Depression often goes unnoticed, unseen and undiagnosed, either because the sufferer is hiding their misery or because the people around them aren't paying attention. Thankfully, these days depression is much more talked about and even celebrities are openly discussing their own struggles.

It is said that one in five people suffer from depression at some point in their lifetime. Depression is more common in women than men, and approximately 14 per cent of new mothers will suffer post-natal depression. Post-natal depression is by itself a problem, and, unfortunately, for a significant number of women it doesn't resolve itself once the pregnancy hormones have returned to normal. This makes looking after an infant (or a toddler, if the condition goes on that long) especially difficult.

The problem with depression is it's a family affair. If mum is depressed she will have little energy to get through the day. Worse still, the toddler doesn't understand this tepid atmosphere but still feels it. They don't get a sense of connection from the depressed parent and desperately try to get their attention. Parents can start to see the toddler's behaviour as naughty, when in fact it is the parent with the problem.

Depression is a common reality, but is treatable once it is recognised. If you think that depression may be affecting you, don't let it drag you down any further. Go and get some help. (See 'Where to get help' in the Appendices.)

Guilt

Is there anyone who doesn't feel guilty about something? This is the oldest (and perhaps most famous) snake in existence. Parents suffer guilt about many things: not spending enough time with their children, being a working parent, not being able to breast-feed – we even feel guilty if we take time to enjoy ourselves. We feel guilty that we don't have more to give our children and we torment ourselves with 'If only I had . . .' and 'I should . . .'

It's pointless to suggest that you shouldn't feel guilty, because most people do. But life is a balance and guilt gets in the way. Guilt is immobilising and takes the joy out of life. We can all take a lesson from a pastor I know; last Easter, he decided to give up guilt for Lent.

Being unaware of individuality

Every child is born an individual, and we all have to learn to accept the child we have been given. But some parents try to force their children to be something they were never designed to be.

The child with an active temperament will never sit still long enough to learn to read at the age of 3, any more than the gentle boy with the quiet nature of St Francis will be suitable for the front row of the All Blacks rugby team.

Individuality is what makes us, *us*! Don't fall into the confidence-busting trap of trying to change the unchangeable. We must have the confidence to do our own thing and not be discouraged by those who do things differently.

As you've seen, remaining confident is a tricky business. Sticking to the ladders and avoiding the snakes is difficult but not impossible. Now you know what to look out for, it will be much easier.

Overwhelmed by experts

It may seem strange to many that in these days of TV and the internet, when there is almost an epidemic of child-care gurus and bookshops are overloaded with how-to-do-it manuals, parental confidence appears to be sinking rather than rising. In my more sombre moments I often wonder: if all we experts were to be blown from the face of the earth, would parents be any the worse off?

As I set out to demystify child care and boost confidence, it seems that a hundred others are out there hell-bent on making it all much more difficult. Life is tough enough without these smart philosophers producing learned treatises that make parents feel as though they are second class citizens. These theories do nothing but generate fears and create feelings of parental inadequacy. I sometimes think the books that contain them should be pulped and recycled to save some of the world's trees!

Parental confidence is fragile enough without being confused by some of the way-out, often incorrect, ideas I hear. Some of the more 'popular' examples are:

Every mother should want to be a 24-hour-a-day parent. Rubbish. It's OK for Supermum but all mothers need some space. We don't expect fathers to be 24-hour-a-day fathers, so why would we expect that from mum? Taking time out for herself is the healthiest thing for everybody.

Working mothers harm their children. Not true. Working mums are now the norm and though they may feel guilty that they are short-changing their children, it's not the number of hours spent away from home that is important. What makes the difference is the quality of the child's day care, and the richness of the time spent together. Warmth, attention and noticing the toddler when you are home from work has the greatest effect.

Dummies should never be used. Dummies may be my pet hate – I think they make children look stupid – but that doesn't mean they can't be used. If you have a child who is irritable and a dummy does the job, let's be realistic and buy a box of them! If they keep children and parents happy, use them.

Watch out especially for experts who assert that unless you bring up your children 'the one and only right way', some form of permanent, psychological damage will ensue. There is *no* one right way to bring up children. Childcare fashions come and go with the regularity of Parisian hemlines. *Vive la différence*!

'To be sure, it's going to be fine'

The helping professions should be good at helping, but unfortunately this is not always the case. Some professionals are still steeped in prehistoric ideas. They find it difficult to give any practical advice on toddler behaviour without looking at the past and psychoanalysing the parents.

I call this approach 'the Irish weather forecaster technique'. They can tell you every detail of what happened yesterday, the day before and right to the day the toddler was born, but when it comes to helping with today, tomorrow and the future, they turn mute.

While I am interested in how the problems start in the first place, I am *more* interested in solving them. I'm allergic to those experts who are so involved in where you've come from, they're unable to look forward to how they're going to help you.

Confidence is the key

Most mums and dads score nine out of ten for parenting, but many do not realise it. What they need are words of encouragement and support but what they get is criticism and comparison. Because they listen every time someone gives their two pennies' worth, their confidence quickly evaporates.

Confidence has a spin-off in almost everything we do as parents. Confident parenting promotes effective discipline, which improves children's behaviour. Children learn that you 'say what you mean and mean what you say'. In the long term, parental confidence forms much of the basis for the child's own self-confidence.

Confidence is such a valuable asset. Do everything you can to nurture yours and protect it from those things that crush it. Now, gather up your confidence, I'm about to introduce you to The Toddler.

3

Toddler trademarks

The toddler is an interesting little person, aged between 1 and 4 years. Some people call this stage the 'terrible twos', but it's not terrible – it's really a time of sweet innocence, dependence and a magic mind. Toddlers are so alive, so full of fun, and what's more they see life with innocent eyes and the most vivid of vivid imaginations. Toddlers are built to a design that is perfect in every detail, but for one small defect: they simply lack sense. They have all the activity of an international airport, but the control tower doesn't work. This explains why life with a toddler never runs to schedule. There's no way to predict what they will do next, and parents spend much of their time bewildered and frustrated. Years down the track, I know that you will see this as one of the most enjoyable stages of childhood. But to enjoy toddlerdom, you need to know what to expect. Then you can tuck some toddler-taming techniques up your sleeve and go for it.

What makes toddlers tick?

Toddlerdom starts at around the first birthday. You are in no doubt of its arrival when one day you put the dinner down and instead of the usual appreciation, your littlie takes one look and says 'Yuck!' You take this badly, jump up and down and in fact have a tantrum of your own. The toddler looks up, sees his power and thinks 'Wow! Look at what I can do!' Now you have a problem.

Whether you think of your bundle of joy as 'a little treasure', 'an ankle biter', or 'a terrible 2 year old', all toddlers have in common an interesting collection of behavioural traits that are their trademark. Let's see what makes toddlers tick.

Little sense

The most defining feature of toddlers is that they lack sense. I'm going to be a bore and repeat this many times because understanding this is so important. If you were to list the attributes of the toddler, it is unlikely that sense would immediately spring to mind.

It is my belief that between the ages of 1 and 2 years, most toddlers have zero sense. From 2 to 2½ years a delicately calibrated instrument might raise a flicker of a reading, but it is often hard for us parents to see this with the naked eye. Fortunately, from this time on sense starts to grow, with a significant amount present by 3 years. By the time they have reached their fourth birthday, most little ones are reasonably sensible.

When people talk of the 'terrible twos' I believe it is really the 'terrible one-and-a-halfs to two-and-a-halfs' that they refer to. **This short period is a time of minimum sense with a maximum of mobility.** You don't need to be called Sigmund to know that this combination is going to be psychologically upsetting to someone and that someone is likely to be you, the parent.

Toddlers can argue, fight and get into no-win situations but they don't have the sense to know when to stop. This is the age of unthinking behaviours (such as temper tantrums). Toddlers also have a complete disregard for danger. They live in the moment with no idea of the problems this causes. They can't see what's coming until they stumble into it.

Tick
Tick
Tick

Plenty of power

Toddlerdom may be an age when children show little self-control but it doesn't stop them trying to control those around them. Toddlers are contrary, show little sense and totally lack appreciation of the rights of others. (This combination of power without sense characterises toddlers – and many of our politicians.) **Small toddlers can exert an amazing amount of power over adults.** If they don't get what they want, such is their protest that parents often buckle under the onslaught.

It is not the power that causes the problem but rather whether it is used for good or evil. They can harness it with determination to dress themselves, or exploit their seeming bottomless reserves to complain, scream or throw a tantrum. With such a strong hand, all they have to do is dig in their heels and shout, and adults jump to attention.

Attention-grabbing

Toddlers love to be centre stage at all times as they really are attention addicts. If you don't give them the goods, they'll demand it. They resent it if others steal the limelight – whether it is a friend dropping in for a chat, a lengthy phone call or when your partner comes home from work.

Toddlers want attention 24 hours a day and if you give them this, then they will want 25 hours. Part of the reason it's so important to give toddlers attention is that they don't store it up for later – they need some now and will need a top up in half an hour.

After a day of play, answering incessant questions and trying to keep one jump ahead of such inventive and imaginative little people, mums are exhausted. This is not only physical exhaustion but a special sort of tiredness that leaves you numb from the neck upwards. Now dad swans in exclaiming, 'Gosh I had a tiring day at work!' He knows nothing of that numbness that leaves you in a state closely resembling brain death. Attention is important but it does take its toll.

Self-centredness

Most toddlers have tunnel vision, which focuses only on their own needs and happiness. It never occurs to them that other people may have rights too. **They think they are the most important person in the world.**

When a toddler is playing and wants a particular toy, it is unlikely that he will ask politely for it when 'smash and grab' is more effective. The idea of taking turns and thinking of another's point of view is not their strong suit, and sharing is quite a foreign concept.

Young toddlers enjoy being with other children but tend to play beside them rather than with them. This self-centred behaviour is normal for most toddlers, although it has been known to extend into adulthood! Some of the world's most notable dictators have shown skills that leave the toddler looking an absolute amateur.

Ten-minute time frame

Parents may be planning for the rest of the day, but not the toddler. The young toddler lives only for the here and now, with an interest in time that extends little past the last ten minutes and the ten to come. One of the great problems is that parents think their toddler thinks the same way they do. But their brains are very different from adults' and consequently, so is their thinking.

At this age, praise and rewards must be immediate, while discipline must happen now or not at all. It is pointless waiting to discipline the 2 year old once dad has returned home in the evening, hours after the event. It is equally foolish to expect the toddler to understand that being good today will be rewarded by going to the zoo next week.

You can use this to your advantage. One of the best discipline techniques to use for toddlers is diversion. With a short attention span, you can recycle methods and items of distraction over the course of a day. What you try early in the morning will be long forgotten by lunchtime and the toddler will be hooked just as easily.

Negativity

Children learn to say 'No' long before they learn to say 'Yes'. At the age of 3, this simple little word flows out with the clearest articulation, due mainly to two years of non-stop practice. **A contrary attitude is just part of being a toddler.** They can be incredibly stubborn and some parents decide that they'll attempt to *make* the child obey, but as we'll see, it's often more effective to go with the flow.

Some experts say that toddlers only copy their negative parents who say 'No, No, No' constantly from the child's earliest age. This is an interesting explanation, but I think the trait is inbuilt and can also be seen in the children of the most positive parents. They are really just winding you up and there's no point analysing it or getting into debates, as this only prolongs their fun.

Go with the flow

So toddlers have little sense, are self-centred, attention-grabbing, negative . . . but they are marvellous! These traits can all be seen as terrible but really it is our expectations that cause the problems. Many of the things that seem 'naughty' bring colour to our lives. While the next three years may feel like they go on forever, in a short time you'll look back and realise it was a special time – a time of closeness and wonder like no other.

It always saddens me to see parents who make very heavy weather of bringing up their children. They misread their toddler's behaviour and feel that the child is deliberately trying to upset them. They start believing their child is malicious – almost the enemy.

As a parent, stop getting bogged down by toddler trademarks. Instead, use your knowledge of what's normal, apply some common-sense and a dash of cunning, then go with the flow. Don't forget that having children is supposed to be fun. Welcome to toddlerdom.

4

Normal toddler behaviour

When life is going well, our toddlers bring us joy and we can laugh at their antics but on rotten days, a little toddlerdom goes a very long way. Much of what burdens us in these moments may just be toddlers behaving like toddlers but that knowledge doesn't make their exploits any easier to stomach.

The more I worked with toddlers, the less surprised I became at the displays of behaviour that I saw. There is an immense breadth of behaviour that I think can be confidently classed as normal, though I am less certain of what could be considered average, and when it comes to tolerable, this definitely lies in the eyes of the beholder.

Whether you live in Alice Springs or Palm Springs, your toddler will have a repertoire of antics that are practised by toddlers the world over. This chapter is about all those annoying normal toddler behaviours, and will help you to see that living with your toddler is possible, even on those bad days.

How behaviour develops

In the first eight years of life, a child's behaviour, demands and needs will change dramatically. These changes often catch parents off-guard, sending them into new, uncharted territory just as they thought they had everything under control.

Before we can understand normal toddler behaviour, we have to understand the changes that take place as they mature. In simple terms, we can expect our children to go through four very different stages of psychological development between birth and 8 years of age. Within this loosely-based order, as our children grow in size and cleverness, their behaviour will alter accordingly.

The baby: birth to 1 year

The baby from birth to 1 year is a cuddly little article who spends most of the time getting to know mum and dad, while they get to know him. This is the important process of bonding. **The aim of this stage is to develop a secure and trusting child, who has a secure and trusting relationship with his parents.**

The views of child care change regularly, but I firmly believe that you cannot spoil a newborn. When hungry, they should be fed, when frightened they should be comforted, when crying they should be cuddled, and when just being a nuisance, they should be given the benefit of the doubt anyway.

Create close bonds

Babies do not need discipline – the focus for parents is on care and comfort. Babies need to be showered with love, have regular routines and most of all, be enjoyed.

The younger toddler: 1 to 2½ years

Toddlerdom starts gradually after the first birthday when little ones discover that they have the muscle to manipulate and challenge.

Although it begins at around 1 year with senseless and unthinking acts, it is really 18 months before toddlerdom gets going in earnest and more considered forms of manipulation take over.

Between these ages there appears to be a sort of no-man's-land, with some children behaving so well that they need no discipline, while others have already morphed into fully-fledged toddlers and show all the attendant difficulties. Toddlerdom hits a peak at about 2 years and then gradually eases. I say it 'eases' because the behaviour challenges do not disappear, they just take on a more artistic form.

At playgroup, parents are embarrassed when their 2 year old is rough with other children, grabs, bites and won't share toys. He has no malice or aggression – there's not a bad bone in these little bodies. **The young toddler's main problem is simply an under-developed control system.** For them there is no waiting – they interrupt, won't take turns and when they need a wee it has to be in *this* flowerpot.

Some of the biggest developmental changes occur at this age, with the child learning to walk and talk. The toddler is alive and

Deeply meaningless

The brain is a wonderful gadget in which self-monitoring and sense are housed up top, in the frontal lobes. These are the bits that check behaviour before it happens and, below the age of 3, frontal lobe function is limited.

Some parents expect adult attitudes from their 2 year olds, but at this age the 'sense centres' aren't yet on line. Parents who are unaware of this conduct deep and meaningful debates with their toddler. The child may look interested, but this is about as useful as discussing the positive qualities of postmen with a rottweiler. When Fido sees a blue trouser leg, he'll forget philosophy and think with his teeth. The same is true of your spontaneous tot – anything goes in the spur of the moment!

There would be fewer stressed parents if it were universally understood that these innocent little people are not capable of adult logic.

alight and, with their newfound mobility, getting into everything. They are like a sponge for learning and every day they have added something that they couldn't do yesterday.

Here is the classic toddler and the peak time for parents needing help. This age group is what this book is mainly about.

Savour the magic

This is probably the most challenging stage for parents, but also the most rewarding. During the toddler years, savour the magic that they bring to new experiences. The aim is to steer them away from trouble and leave introducing adult attitudes to when the child's brain is good and ready. Don't let other parents make you feel guilty about your toddler's antics – believe me, even the most unsharing, shoving 2 year old can turn into a polite, loving grown-up.

The preschool toddler: 2½ to 4 years

Somewhere after 2½ years, children start to control their impulsive toddler behaviour. They learn to wait – though not for very long. They can control their tantrums, and they can separate from their mum and be left with friends. At preschool they begin to play together instead of side-by-side as the younger child does.

The toddler's imagination goes into overdrive and they see the world in Technicolor. Every day is exciting and wondrous, even though to the outsider it may seem the same as yesterday. They interact more with people and things around them, and they become much more creative and switched on. Another great development is their language skills. At this stage children have a lot of words but not much logic. They debate and argue because they can, not to drive you mad. Honesty, as far as toddlers are concerned, is the only policy – they know nothing yet of the diplomatic mistruths we adults use to avoid giving offence.

Enjoy their creativity

This is one of the nicest stages of toddlerdom. The preschool toddler is incredibly imaginative, verbal and cuddly.

Stealing my thunder

I remember one 3 year old I was treating for a sleep problem – she woke every night for no apparent reason. 'Why do you wake up every night?' I asked her, pen poised to write down her answer.

'I wake at night because of the thunder,' she replied. (She was a very verbal little girl!)

'But there isn't any thunder,' the clever Dr Green pointed out.

'I wake at night because the ships keep going up and down the harbour blowing their horns,' she said next.

'But you live a long way from the sea in Canberra,' I objected, scribbling notes.

Then she said with an air of finality, 'And anyway, I can't sleep because the horses keep galloping up and down outside my window.'

That stumped me! I wrote busily away, thinking to myself, *this is great, I'll put it in my next book*, and just then the little monkey looked up at me and said, 'Are you getting this down OK?'

The early school-age child: 4 to 8 years

Somewhere around the fourth birthday the child gradually slips out of toddlerdom to become an early school-age child. There is no firm developmental age for this – with some it may be as early as 3 years, and others 4½.

This fourth behavioural stage is once again quite different from all that has gone before. **We now have a child who thinks of the repercussions of his actions and exhibits quite a bit of sense.** He is interested in rules and, what is more, will often obey them. At school, many 5 year olds will sit at their desk, not only obeying the class rules themselves but seeing that the laws are applied equally to all. They take on the role of the class policeman, reporting the slightest transgression to their teacher. This is the age when it is fashionable to 'dob on your mates', an activity which becomes unpopular after the age of 8.

Encourage their maturity

At this stage of development, the child can be treated more like a little adult, with increased trust, democracy and reason. The senselessness of the toddler years is long past. You can cash in on their obsession with rules and at last you will be able to lay down the 'laws of the house' (with a fair chance of being obeyed!). They are now beyond the scope of this book and you'll need to read *Beyond Toddlerdom: Keeping five- to twelve-year-olds on the rails*.

Each of these stages provide different challenges to the growing child and his parents. Each child will behave individually based on his temperament – some will be easier for parents to manage through the changes and others will be more difficult. A behaviour problem is diagnosed when a child is acting in a manner that is inappropriate for his stage of development.

It helps to know what to expect in each stage. If you can recognise when your littlie slips from one stage to the next, you can be more prepared for unfamiliar behaviours lurking around the next corner. You will need to adjust your expectations as each stage passes and remember, they are going to go by in the blink of an eye – before you know it, your toddler will be off to school.

Toddlers are not mini-adults

Trying to make toddlers grow up before their time is painful and pointless. **Little children under 2 years just don't have the capacity to think about the possible outcomes of their actions.**

Toddlers understand nothing of adult values – if you leave an open box of chocolates on the table, they will be eaten; there is no deception or dishonesty here, they just have no idea of the concepts of ownership.

All of this is a common cause of friction. With time, little ones eventually conform to our strange adult attitudes. What happens in the meantime, however, should not be construed as naughty behaviour. What they require at this stage is understanding and gentle guidance, not heavy-handed punishment.

Taking control

As children move from being babies to being toddlers, they are excited by the unexpected freedoms that appear. Suddenly they can stand, walk, climb and run. They have the ability to manipulate objects, touch, take things apart and fiddle. They are amazed and overawed at their powers – it is almost as if someone had left open the door to a mighty arsenal of behavioural weapons, but unfortunately they forgot to leave the instructions behind. The toddler doesn't know how to use them wisely.

For the children, toddlerdom is all about control – learning to control their bodies and behaviours. There are six cardinal controls they will grasp:

- *Control of bodily functions:* Grasping the basics of bowel and bladder training.
- *Control of impulses:* Learning that their demands cannot be met immediately.
- *Control of frustration:* Knowing they want to do something themselves but accepting that they can't do it successfully, for example feeding or dressing.
- *Control of behaviour:* Learning that tantrums are not an appropriate way to influence people.

- *Control of separation anxiety:* Moving from the close clinginess usual at 1 year to becoming able to separate for preschool and later for school.
- *Control of selfishness:* Learning to share attention, share belongings, not interrupt and realising that others also have rights.

The toddler will learn these controls during the course of these three years and even take onboard a smattering of commonsense and something that vaguely resembles a conscience.

Heading for trouble

Toddlers are often confused by their parents' reactions. 'Why is Mum so angry, when last time she seemed really impressed with my finger painting?' Well, this time it's on the wall, not in a colouring book.

This is an exciting time for toddlers, but not without its fair share of confusion and frustration. They are frustrated as their little brains run hot with good ideas that the immaturity of their bodily co-ordination prevents them from seeing through.

They also find that by using their new-found weapons they may get lots of attention, but that this more often than not backfires. The angry reactions their new behaviours sometimes provoke can rob them of the closeness and love they enjoyed as babies. They feel your displeasure, yet they cannot grasp why.

Parents faced with this confusion and frustration need to set limits, avoid confrontation and be 100 per cent firm when required. Toddlerdom is a time of guiding the toddler gently through the rough waters of change.

Figuring it all out

All parents have moments of self-doubt but it's a different matter when we spend all our time feeling we are the only ones who cannot cope in the face of toddler behaviour. Life is tough enough without immobilising ourselves with such ill-founded guilt. To put our struggles into perspective, we can turn to research that has been conducted on toddler behaviour. The facts and figures we glean from these studies show us that raising toddlers is challenging for everyone.

Interesting research has reported that nine out of ten parents experience some behaviour difficulties with their toddlers. In fact, the researchers determined that one in four parents find toddlerdom quite tough. These figures were similar for parents attending the education programme I ran at the hospital, where in addition we found that 77 per cent have serious doubts about their parenting abilities. Which goes to show if you're struggling, you're not alone – toddlerdom is hard work.

For further figures it is best to look at a couple of old but good studies. While the following two studies were performed decades ago, the conclusions they reached are still relevant today – toddlers are still toddlers with similar traits.

The New York Longitudinal Study

This study began in New York in 1956 and followed 133 children from birth to adulthood. Researchers were most interested in the links between temperament and behaviour. The study showed that children have individual temperamental traits at birth. These traits affected their behaviour right through toddlerdom and into adulthood. They also had an impact on how parents coped and how far their sanity was stretched in the process.

When the results of the study were analysed, they found that while some children were a breeze to parent, more than half of the children were not so easy to handle.

Angels: Forty per cent of the group fitted into the 'easy child' category, being a joy to look after as babies and usually throughout childhood.

Parents, teachers and paediatricians all found this group easy. Whether the mother was competent or hopeless and the father a saint or Jack the Ripper, children of this group would probably do quite well.

For parents of these types of toddlers, every conceivable moment is so wonderful, they can't wait to have another child.

Little terrors: Ten per cent of the study group were little terrors from the word go. They were difficult as babies, often difficult as toddlers and their difficulties frequently accompanied them into school.

Parents, paediatricians and teachers all suffered under the strain. These children tended to be particularly negative, extremely loud in both voice and crying, and easily frustrated; they had irregular sleeping and feeding habits and showed great difficulty adjusting to any change. They were hard to handle, disputed decisions and had tantrums like infant McEnroes.

Such children quickly knock all confidence out of their parents and if the problems continue through school, a trail of teachers will sign off on sick and recreation leave. Though saint-like parents have less chance of producing – and more chance of managing – children like these, this group would be extremely difficult in anyone's hands. These children can make parenting so hard, they act as a very effective form of contraception!

Semi-impossibles: A further 15 per cent of the participants were described as 'slow to warm up'. They had many of the same characteristics as the 'little terrors', but these were not so severe. The difference was that when handled with care, understanding, persistence and patience, they had a sporting chance of doing well.

Parenting this group was a major challenge, with 'super parents' managing and normal parents struggling.

Intermediates: The remaining 35 per cent were an intermediate group that was neither very easy nor very difficult. Ease of handling this group depended on the parents and on the blend of temperament characteristics inherited by each child.

This study shows us temperament has a huge bearing on behaviour. We know that all toddlers have a tendency to be negative and stubborn, to have more power than sense, to live for today and to be short on humanitarian skills. All toddlers will have a smattering of these but some will have been dealt a weak hand while others will present with all the trump cards. We can say that all toddlers demonstrate the same, normal behaviours, but the temperament that a child is born with has a huge impact on their everyday demonstrations. The odds are rigged from the outset, and we don't all start the race with the same chances. Understanding the temperament of your child lets you set the bar for their level of 'normal'.

The Chamberlin study

Another New York study followed up 200 children from age 2 until school age. It demonstrated the main behavioural worries for parents at different ages (see table opposite) and set out to stir up specialist paediatricians into giving more help. A number of parents were interviewed and asked to describe their children's behaviour at three different ages. The behaviours commonly seen at ages 2, 3 and 4 were listed and then ranked in the order that caused greatest concern.

At age 2, many parents said 'He doesn't do a thing I tell him'. Not surprisingly, these stubborn and wilful characteristics were top of the list. Second place was shared equally between tantrums and 'getting into everything'. Continuing these behavioural Olympics, at age 4, the gold medal was still awarded for stubborn, wilful behaviour, although now verbal abuse and 'talking back' were also included as problems. The silver medal went to whining and nagging and the bronze was taken easily by lack of sharing and frequent fighting.

Even though more than 30 years have passed since this study was done, the perceptions of the parents who took part in the study are familiar to all of us. What I see when I look at the table is normal toddler behaviour! If well over half the children displayed almost every behaviour at age 2 and 4, surely it just shows that this is what toddlers do. This is one of my most important messages to parents: it's not about how children behave but how you accept and deal with them that will determine your sanity at the end of toddlerdom.

What about paediatricians' children?

Being both a paediatrician and a father, I am often asked: 'What problems did *you* have with your children when they were toddlers, or were they model children?'

When I wrote the first edition of *Toddler Taming*, I surveyed 28 paediatricians, all specialists at our hospital, about their own children. The questions covered a wide area, with behaviour featuring quite strongly. There were also general questions which yielded some astonishing answers. For example, four of the experts did not know the date of their children's birth, three were

Mothers' description of their children's behaviour at ages 2, 3 and 4

	Percentage of age group		
	Age 2	Age 3	Age 4
Behaviour	%	%	%
Eats too little	50	26	37
Doesn't eat the right kinds of food	64	43	54
Resists going to bed	70	46	56
Awakens during the night	52	52	56
Has nightmares	17	18	36
Resists sitting on toilet	43	2	2
Has bowel motion in pants	71	17	1
Wets self during day	75	14	7
Wets bed at night	82	49	26
Curious about sex differences	28	45	75
Rubs or plays with sex organs	56	49	51
Modest about dressing	1	7	26
Fights or quarrels	72	75	92
Jealous	54	47	42
Hurts younger sibling	44	51	64
Hits others or takes things	68	52	46
Stubborn	95	92	85
Talks back (behaves cheekily)	42	73	72
Disobedient	82	76	78
Tells fibs	2	26	37
Constantly seeks attention	94	48	42
Clings to mother	79	34	26
Whines and nags	83	65	85
Cries easily	79	53	58
Temper outbursts	83	72	70
Active, hardly ever still	100	48	40

uncertain whether their children were fully immunised; and 19 stated that their storage of drugs and medicines at home would be seen as negligent by our hospital's child safety centre!

In the behavioural area, about 10 per cent of the paediatricians had a child with breath-holding attacks; about 15 per cent had found toilet training a struggle and about 30 per cent had been troubled by feeding difficulties. About 40 per cent of these experts had also experienced at least one child with sleep problems and nearly half considered that their discipline was often far from effective.

As a last comment, most suspected that at some time their children would have been of interest to our child psychiatry colleagues. While of course this is a tiny sample, it goes to show that toddler behaviour is a worry to most parents, whether they are panel beaters, piano tuners or paediatricians.

What is normal?

I've said it often enough in this book, I don't want parents to worry about non-problems. Non-problems are those toddler behaviours that are so common that we can consider them normal. Don't get me wrong, by normal I don't mean likeable. They are however a part of life with a toddler that we are unlikely to escape.

Below is a list of what constitutes normal toddler behaviour; you will be familiar with many of them and you'll soon realise you are far from alone.

All toddlers...
- *Crave attention and hate to be ignored:* Some are quite satisfied with their parents' best efforts, others would grumble unless 25 hours a day, 8 days a week were devoted solely to their care.
- *Tend to be stubborn and wilful:* Some toddlers are quite militant but others will eventually bend to reason.
- *Have little sense:* Toddlers are impulsive and unpredictable and have little sense of danger, which is a hazard even in the apparently sensible child. All toddlers need close parental protection, particularly when it comes to roads.

- *Separate poorly from their caregivers:* In the first 3 years, a toddler prefers to play near his mother and does not like her to be out of his sight for long. For most, an unfamiliar child-minder causes initial problems, while being locked in a room or becoming separated when out shopping constitutes a major trauma.
- *Are busy little people:* Some are extremely active and hardly ever still; others are just active.
- *Show little respect for other people's property:* Their fingers are drawn as if by magnetism to everything they pass. Ornaments are broken and cupboards rearranged. Those ten active little digits have an amazing power to spread a sticky, jam-like substance over every surface they meet – rather like a small bee distributing pollen.
- *Tend to be blind to mess:* The tidy toddler who is neat and even picks up his own toys is the exception rather than the rule.
- *Ask endless questions:* Toddlers often ask the same question again and again, with little interest in the answer. This especially applies to the over-threes.
- *Change their minds every minute:* One day your toddler says, 'I like Weetabix'. When you are at the supermarket, they are on special and you buy a month's supply. Next day, 'Don't like Weetabix! Don't like Weetabix!' squawks the mind-bender. This is brainwashing, toddler style.
- *Constantly interrupt adults*: It is not that toddlers want to be rude, but they believe that what they've got to contribute is much more important than the irrelevant ramblings of their parents. This trick of skilfully interrupting mid-sentence everything that mum or dad says really jars the nerves.
- *Know how to hit a raw nerve with perfect aim:* Toddlers have an incredible ability to demoralise their mothers. Many will act as complete angels when in the care of others, reserving their demonic side exclusively for their parents. Other toddlers are difficult for their mothers and behave perfectly for their fathers. This is because they have long studied mum's vulnerabilities. There is no point telling anyone – who would believe you?
- *Are extremely sensitive:* Toddlers are easily affected by any tension, upset or excitement in their environment. Their sound sleep pattern can be disrupted by stress, illness and holidays. Often quite a minor event can make the child who was fully toilet trained start to leak.

Many toddlers...

- *Are determined and independent:* Some become so belligerent that they refuse to be fed or dressed, even though they are far too young to do either task unaided. Other toddlers are passive, dependent and quite happy to be pampered and directed.

- *Are compulsive climbers:* At an early age they will organise an expedition to the summit of the settee and once this has been scaled, will set out to conquer the bench tops, tables and anything that happens to be there. Other toddlers are more sensible and have a healthy fear of the 'painful stop at the end of the drop'.

- *See food as a bit of a joke:* Toddlers find food an interesting plaything and refuse to take it very seriously. This is a pain to the parent committed to delivering them a perfectly balanced diet. The toddler hasn't read chapter 14 of this book!

- *Go off their food:* This is common around their first birthday and a proper eating pattern may not return for anything up to a year. Some will only tolerate a narrow, unimaginative diet. Some eat main meals; others were born to be snackers.

- *Have something vaguely resembling a sleep pattern:* Many toddlers continue with a daytime sleep until the age of 3 years. Others discard this at about 18 months and nothing the parents do will bring it back. Most toddlers go to sleep before 8 o'clock each night, but others stay on the rampage until close to midnight. Some are lazy in the morning, finding it hard to get out of bed; others wake at an ungodly hour and disturb the whole household. With busy children who are on the rampage from dawn until after dusk it is often hard to change their pattern with any technique less powerful than a general anaesthetic!

- *Have fears:* Dogs, loud noises, new situations and strange objects and people cause distress in over half of this age group.
- *Have irritating habits:* This of course is not only a problem with children.
- *Have behaviour which fluctuates:* Toddlers' behaviour can vary considerably from day to day and week to week. Some parents tell me that their little children seem almost schizophrenic, with wild alterations in behaviour. Bad days are usually blamed on teething, lack of sleep or 'something they ate'. These all make good scapegoats but it never seems to occur to parents that adults can have good days and bad days and we don't blame this on teething. Even trainers allow racehorses the odd off day.
- *Are restless:* Some toddlers will sit and concentrate briefly to draw, do puzzles or attend to pre-reading tasks. A minority will settle for a long time but most become restless in about five minutes and look for a means of escape. Quite a large proportion of active little children will not sit even for the shortest of periods.
- *Are cuddly:* They are affectionate, 'giving' children. There are, however, a minority who resent handling, are distant and seem to give a poor return of love to their parents.

It's easy for me to call these behaviours normal, but they cause great pain as parents struggle at the battlefront of toddlerdom. Whether they are normal or not, you're probably sick and tired of many of them.

It is possible to encourage more acceptable behaviour in the toddler without having a nervous breakdown in the process. In the following chapters you'll find sure-fire ways to mould these normal behaviours into something you can co-exist with peacefully.

A perfect specimen

A docile, compliant, non-whingeing, non-stubborn toddler: a rare specimen indeed! The more common variety can be seen in homes and preschools, shopping centres and playgrounds all over the world.

You have probably got one of these normal types, and you're probably a normal mum or dad. Which means that it's normal to experience rough patches as your toddler passes through each stage of toddlerdom; it is also normal for you to find ways around them and focus on the delight that toddlers bring to our lives.

It's upsetting that so few parents realise that the toddler they have got *is* the perfect specimen. No matter what, it seems that most toddlers will cause us some behavioural bother – and a rare few will probably age us by years. Toddlers don't have sense but parents need sensible expectations. We are not aiming for perfect children, and your toddler is flawed just enough to make him imperfectly perfect.

5

Behaviour: where does it come from?

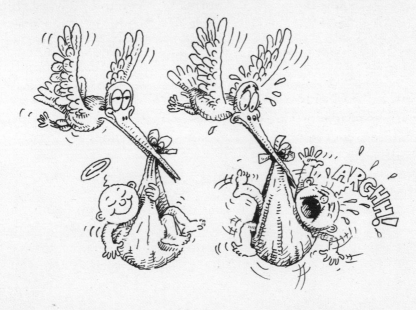

Here we come to an interesting question: Where does our children's behaviour come from? When it comes to the good points, all seems clear. Parents are quick to own up to giving their children beautiful eyes or a happy, sunny nature. 'Oh, she gets that from me!' proud mums and dads beam. It's a different story when we're talking about behaviour that makes us cringe. All of a sudden it's a mystery and no one has any idea of the true source of the toddler's dynamite outbursts. Is your toddler born with this behaviour or is it created?

Difficult behaviour causes guilt and frustration for parents, adding to the already considerable demands of parenting. We search for answers but the nature/nurture debate has raged for years and we still don't seem any closer to a definitive answer. So, are toddlers made good or bad?

Genes and environment

In the nineteenth century, thinkers were in no doubt that the cause of all deviant behaviour was bad breeding. Some put forward the notion that the born criminal and lesser sinners were beyond help due to their 'abnormal' make-up. Basically, you were born good or bad and there was nothing you could do about it.

As the twentieth century dawned, this view gradually changed, and environment was thought to be the major influence on behaviour. This of course also applied to children. By the 1950s the theory had become highly refined: all behavioural blame was laid squarely on the shoulders of inadequate parents, particularly mothers. It seemed irrelevant whether marriages were stable or parents exceptional. Mothers still collected the blame, regardless of the true offender, causing untold guilt and suffering. The role of breeding was largely ignored.

An unwanted inheritance

Often adult relationships fall apart because one or both parties have always had a way of behaving that is far from easy to live with. These behaviours have a definite chance of being transmitted through the genes to the children, who freely express them with their own difficult behaviour. The parents' behaviour also upsets the home environment and the end product is a complex coalition of heredity and handling. Take the following example:

Two parents have very different temperaments: mum is easygoing while dad has a fiery personality and a short fuse. After a few years in a tense and stressful relationship they split up amid much drama. Mum gets sole custody of their toddler. With little money and life dragging her down, she struggles as her toddler displays fiery, uncontrollable behaviour.

It would be easy to think that the toddler inherited this streak from his dad, but it would be just as easy to think that he had learned it from his home environment. Figuring out which is the cause would take the wisdom of Solomon, as when it comes to behaviour, the causes are a complicated mix.

Today's view is justifiably more balanced. We now know that both genes and the environment play a role in behaviour and temperament. For my thinking, the genes are responsible for more than 50 per cent and much is already set at conception. But while hereditary influence gives us the basic material to work with, the final product depends very much on environmental factors, which is a polite way of saying it's up to our standard of parenting.

The genes your toddler was born with are now well beyond your control, but you *can* change the environment you create with your parenting. There is no doubt that environmental characteristics play an enormous part in a child's behaviour. We have to smarten up our acts.

Like father, like son

Many children are just like their parents. I see busy children who can't sit still with bemused mothers who say, 'How on earth did I ever get a child like this?' Then out of the corner of my eye I see her jiggling the car keys and tapping her feet, and it's plain to me where the activity comes from. Some children who are sent to me because they are unenthusiastic and have little drive to do anything much in life, arrive in the company of equally boring parents.

Born to rock

Overactive, impulsive, intolerant fathers frequently produce active children. Some years ago I was brought 3-year-old twins whose mother complained that they would never sit still and were forever rocking and head banging. In my office I watched them rock, foot to foot, always slightly out of time, like defective windscreen wipers on a car.

When dad arrived a little later he burst into my office like a police raid. It was apparent within a minute that he was someone who had never sat still from birth. The longer he stood before me, complaining about his children's overactivity, the more I noticed him swaying, kicking his feet and rocking – a dead ringer for his twin boys.

The expression, 'like father, like son' is a familiar truth. **Parents would prefer their children to copy all their best points and bypass their weaknesses.** In reality, the reverse is more likely to be true, with our children seeking out our worst qualities and displaying them to a similar or greater degree.

Don't blame the milkman

It may seem a strange observation but sometimes a family gets a child that doesn't suit them. When a peace-loving, polite, quiet, obsessively tidy family is hit by a toddler-sized human tornado, the equilibrium is shattered. A similar upset occurs when a famous heavyweight football hero spawns a docile, passive boy who prefers picking flowers to jumping on people in the mud.

If you put a busy, noisy toddler in with a busy, noisy family, he will not be noticed, whereas a quiet, violin-playing, well-mannered child would stand out like a vegetarian at a butchers' picnic.

When a child seems out of place in a family, don't blame the milkman. Nature has a habit of doing this to nice parents, to bring a bit of interest to their lives. Even if our children do not suit us, the spark they provide certainly enriches our lives.

They're not all the same

Any person who views life with even partly open eyes could not help but see the immense variation based on simple hereditary in all aspects of human nature. Such variations cannot possibly be accounted for by the different standard of care each person received in childhood.

Parents would often say to me, 'I must be doing something wrong' when what worked with their first child was an utter failure with the second. **But the truth is children are not the same, and we have to adapt our parenting to suit.** When we are dealing with more than one child, we don't necessarily approach discipline the same way for each. We fine tune ideas and techniques to fit each child.

Stork surprises

One place where genetic influence stands out is in the newborn nursery of any hospital. Here we have babies who have as yet hardly been touched by their mothers, already demonstrating their different personalities. In one cot there might be a quiet, loving baby exuding affection, cuddling in tightly and feeding with ease. In the very next cot could be a child in an identical state of health, who is irritable, arches his back, cries most of the time, dislikes being handled and forever spits out his milk. You don't need to be steeped in the psychiatric tradition to know that one would be a joy for any parent, while the other would be a trial for even the most well-intentioned family.

The difficult child

I remember asking one mum who had brought her troublesome toddler for consultation, 'When did you first know you were having problems?' She told me of a difficult labour, with an epidural and an emergency caesarian section. When the baby was delivered, with the first ear-splitting scream the obstetrician said, 'I think you're going to have some trouble with this one.' As time went on, mum realised that he had hit the nail on the head at that very first breath. Some of the most difficult children I care for started life this way, their hereditary load bringing problems before they even left hospital.

It is not a nice thing to say, but there is no question that some children make themselves harder to love and get on with than others. These children are born with a difficult temperament, generating tension and upset in their environment which then rebounds onto them.

I am not naïve enough to believe that all parents are without fault, but I do resent out-of-date experts blaming parents for temperament and behaviour that is not of their making. Some children are born to be easy and some are born just plain difficult. **We can't send our little ones back to their manufacturer for a genetic tune-up, but we can smarten up our act as parents.** Improved handling will make a major difference. For example, if an extremely difficult child comes from a home filled with fighting, tension and parental conflict, he will only become more difficult.

If you are lucky enough to have been sent an angel, please don't get swollen-headed and hold up this child as the perfect reincarnation of a perfect parent. On the other hand, if you have a really difficult child, I do sympathise and I hope this book is of help. If you are fed up with criticism from parents showing off their child's perfect behaviour, let's jointly hope that next time round they get a proper little terror. Then we will know there is some justice in this world.

Babysitter ban

A mother explained to me just how difficult her toddler was proving to be. She and her husband arranged a much needed night out, booking dinner at a nearby restaurant and engaging the services of an experienced, highly-recommended babysitter. On their return they met the lady at the front door, hysterical and clutching her handbag ready to bolt. 'I don't want any money, I just want to get out of here!' she sobbed. This was the only time they used a babysitter.

Is behaviour worse these days?

It seems that there are now more behaviour problems among today's children than in the past. The current increase has been blamed on everything from preservatives in food to the watching of too much junk television. I think that there is a much more plausible explanation.

Maybe it's not so much an increase in the problems themselves, as an increase in the awareness of them. Fifty years ago, if you sought help from a doctor for your child's behaviour, you knew that the mother would be blamed for the problem. Even worse, long-term therapy for both parents was seen as the solution and there would be nothing quick about the fix. This in itself must have been a major deterrent for seeking help. Surely this prevented most troubled parents admitting to anyone but their closest family that they could not handle their offspring.

Now that parents realise that criticism will not be levelled at them, they are talking more openly about their problems and coming for help earlier. Behaviour may seem worse, when in fact parents are simply getting better at bringing it out into the open.

Genes and genius

There's more to the genes v. environment issue than just toddler behaviour, and it is decidedly more positive. It is about nurturing your child's god-given talent and helping them to excel.

Tiger Woods became the Number One golfer in the world; Mozart wrote music that is still popular today and Einstein discovered the Theory of Relativity – each of them was born with superhuman talent, but it's how they developed that talent that made them rise to the top.

Every child is born with a scattering of ability, dictated by their genes. How someone uses what he or she is born with is what's interesting. Even though people have these 'pre-set' levels, there are many things that will affect their potential. While geniuses start life with a genetically stacked deck, none of them will become icons if they aren't also shaped by their environment.

In this case when I say 'environment', I am talking about those things a child encounters as he grows. There are three in particular that as parents we can focus on to give our children the best chance in life. The first is opportunity, which includes time, teachers, tools and instruments. The next is encouragement, necessary to help their talents go from one stage to the next. Finally there is practice, without which none of us master any new skills. Add to these a little good, old-fashioned luck and the sky's the limit.

When we look at this potent combination of what the toddler is born with and the environment they are raised in, we see how we truly can help them make the best of what they've got.

Nurturing nature

I hope my message is coming across loud and clear: no matter what sort of temperament and behaviours your toddler was created with, what will ultimately make the difference is how you, the parent, approach them.

You can choose to see it as a challenge, fighting their nature all the way. You can be angry, hurt or resentful, and in the process create the worst kind of environment, making life for the toddler and yourself painful.

Or you can go with the flow, accepting the toddler's true nature and embracing it. By focusing on the good points and not getting worked up over things that you can't change, you create the very best kind of environment – loving, nurturing and warm.

Remember that behaviour results from both genes and environment. Of these, environment is the one we can change.

6

Toddler triggers: what sets them off

'**O**h why me?' you moan, your head in your hands, as junior puts on yet another Oscar-winning performance for the supermarket crowd. 'I've given him a ton of love and still he insists on embarrassing me with these painful performances.'

As a tired parent, it becomes easy to believe that your little loved one is out to punish you in every way possible. But it's not like that. In reality he is just an interesting little person with absolutely no sense, being triggered by life in a way that most parents either don't see or can't understand.

It appears to me that almost all behaviour stems from only a handful of these triggers. If you can spot them and understand their likely outcome, it can help you stay on top of 90 per cent of the behaviour that follows. This chapter will help you ride the waves of toddlerdom without being dumped.

The five triggers of toddler behaviour

When we parents are having a bad day, our toddlers' repertoire of behaviour may seem extensive but in fact almost every performance comes from one of five very predictable origins. These triggers are:

1. Attention seeking
2. Jealousy and competition
3. Frustration
4. Fear of separation
5. Upset and illness

1. Attention seeking

Just like pop stars, politicians and other adult exhibitionists, toddlers need to be the centre of attention all the time. This is a demand that many parents find hard to understand. Why do toddlers have to behave so badly to get attention when they are getting masses of it already? It may not seem very sensible to you, but for the toddler it makes perfect sense. Toddlers are attention addicts, and this is one addiction that we don't want to cure. In fact, cutting off their supply pretty much guarantees bad behaviour, and the emotional wellbeing of all involved suffers.

If you ignore toddlers they will hijack your attention. With attention-seeking, the toddler is trying to tell you: 'Hey, watch me!' He isn't greedy, he just wants to be noticed.

Solution: This is by far the most unrecognised but powerful trigger of toddler behaviour problems. I can't emphasise this enough: if parents were to understand only two things about toddlers – that they have little sense and that they need copious amounts of attention – the game would be won.

Stand back and deliver

At one stage in my career, I undertook some formal training in child psychiatry, during which I was taught how to interpret behaviour in psychodynamic terms. I have since learnt to interpret toddler behaviour in a much simpler and more practical

Made for television

About 15 years ago, one of the TV networks for Australia filmed a segment for their *60 Minutes* programme called 'The Terrible Twos'. For weeks they advertised for the worst-behaved toddler in Sydney and, surprisingly, hundreds of parents put their hands up for their children to be exhibited.

The segment that went to air was a classic example of toddler behaviour. A 2½ year old is seen romping around his backyard, while his mother and grandmother are sitting on the back verandah, having a cup of tea and chatting. The boy keeps coming up and wanting to talk to them, but they are having a great conversation and keep ignoring him. Finally the little boy goes to the edge of the yard, picks up a great big broom and, holding it above his head, starts back across the garden as the TV cameras slow down the motion and start playing the theme music from *Jaws*. Then he whacks the old lady across the head with it.

At this point the action stops and the interviewer asks me: 'Dr Green, how would you deal with that delinquent behaviour?' I'm not advocating hitting the older generation with gardening implements but the answer was simple: the toddler just needed a little bit of attention and he was getting none. The child was saying: 'Hey, you two, don't ignore me!'

way. **When a little child performs some particularly antisocial act, stand back and ask yourself why.** 'If I was doing what that little terror is doing, what would be in it for me?' For toddlers, the answer is nearly always the same: 'to gain attention'.

While attention seeking may well be at the root of most behavioural problems, the trouble is that we parents are often too tired and tense to realise what is happening before our very eyes. From where they stand our friends can see that we are being utter twits, but we are too close to the game to see which side is scoring the points.

The attention spectrum

- **Grade A** (the best): This is undivided, uninterrupted attention. It includes all those close parent–child interactions like talking, reading books and playing together, accompanied by warmth and cuddling. With this type of attention, the toddle thrives.
- If parents have their hands full and are feeding the baby or opening the mail, toddlers will drop down a grade or two, to **Grades B or C**. They will probably start asking endless questions even though they are clearly not in the slightest bit interested in the answers. At least it keeps the lines of communication open and gives them some sort of attention. These are often the times when parents think they're giving undivided attention, but the toddler knows better.
- **Grades D and E** is where a bit of arguing and debating is often seen as good value by the toddler. They can argue that black is white, give you a most plausible explanation of why the world is flat and debate with all the skill of a lawyer pleading his client's case. As far as toddlers are concerned, the topic is irrelevant as long as the parents take the bait.
- Now down in **mid-alphabet**, toddlers find that saying 'No!' to everything will regain Mum's attention.

Solution: The secret is to stand back a pace and ask: 'What is going on here? What's in this for junior?' If your toddler's anti-social actions are grabbing attention, then it's time to look at the quality of the attention you are delivering.

Grades of attention

Attention is deceptive; it comes in many grades and guises. Every parent should aim to give their children as much high-quality attention as they possibly can; it is extremely important to the happiness and emotional wellbeing of the child. **Quality attention is what your child craves and giving it will only benefit you, too.**

If by some mischance this doesn't work they can always climb on top of the baby, turn off the TV halfway through *Oprah*, or investigate the contents of mum's handbag. These all work to stir up lots of attention.

■ Around **Grades P and Q**, verbal abuse is a great way of guaranteeing a rise out of mum or dad. 'I hate you, Mum! You love Jack more than me.' Such statements will be delivered again and again, just as long as the target audience responds with the necessary attention.

■ By now we are descending into the **lower letters of the alphabet** of attention. These are the ones which harbour the really big-gun stirrers. Tantrums, breath-holding and even vomiting on demand lie in this nether region. Their pay-off may be a long way from Grade A but when top quality attention is not on offer, that's all the toddler's got.

■ By the time we get to **Grades Y and Z**, attention is of the very poorest quality. Parents shout angrily at their child and some may even deliver a few well-aimed smacks. While it may be difficult to understand why toddlers would actively seek pain and punishment, bear in mind that even a smack can hurt a child less than being ignored altogether.

But what exactly is this 'high-quality' attention I'm talking about? If we visualise attention as a spectrum, graded from A to Z, we see two colourful extremes with many shades in between – just take a look at the box above.

As we move down the spectrum, the reward for the child gets progressively less attractive. Our children will usually aim for the best level of attention (Grade A), and if the best is not on offer they will descend through the grades until they find one that gives them the attention they crave.

Solution: When you provide your toddler with lots of Grade A attention, you will have a well-behaved child; as you slip down through the grades, the toddler's behaviour worsens and you end up with unhappy children and frustrated parents.

You might as well resist giving poor quality attention as there's nothing in it for either of you. Giving attention of any kind is tiring – at the end of the day, most parents are exhausted. Since you'll be tired one way or the other, you can at least choose to avoid being angry, frazzled or resentful by steering clear of the middle and lower grades where your home turns into a battle zone. Grade A attention is the best you can give, so give plenty!

2. Jealousy and competition

At around 2 years, little children are not richly endowed with the values of sharing and seeing another person's point of view. They like to be the star of the show no matter what and when they are dispossessed of this role they can get mighty upset. A few toddlers are pretty laid back and humanitarian in their attitudes but most are downright possessive and resent intruders on their patch. Jealousy and competition are major triggers of toddler behaviour that cause problems for parents and often arise from some quite predictable situations.

Nose out of joint with the new baby

The arrival of a new baby threatens the toddler. On the one hand, it's fun to have this interesting, animated little doll around to play with but the sudden change in attention causes competition and jealousy. Usually toddlers and new babies settle in well together but there can be problems if parents don't consider the toddler's view.

It's quite natural for new mums to be overprotective of the new baby, just as the toddler will be protective of the baby butting in.

- If a tense mum overreacts every time the toddler approaches the baby, soon the toddler registers the negative vibrations and associates them with being near the child. This will damage the developing sibling relationship.
- Another hazard is the discovery that a quick poke to baby will ensure a fireworks display worthy of Sydney New Year's Eve proportions. Now all the toddler has to do is poke, prod or pinch to have mum's undivided – if somewhat bad-tempered – attention. It can be a powerful weapon.
- Tensions can also arise when friends visit the new arrival and tactlessly by-pass the sitting tenant. The toddler was there first and he's going to make sure you remember that.
- There is another potential for problems when tired parents feed, change nappies and give the baby comfort, forgetting that there is another little person who is in need of some attention.

Solution: Avoid trouble by making sure the toddler is involved with the new addition to the family. Toddlers like to think of themselves as grown up, so they love to help as it makes them feel important. By giving the toddler little tasks, they get attention and you avoid attention seeking.

Sibling rivalry

Parents who have only one child rarely realise just how much their life will change when they have a second. Two children together are usually the best of friends but they can also be fierce rivals. Toddler behaviour can be at its worst when competing.

- Toddlers compete for attention and object when they think they have been given less. It doesn't matter if the attention on offer is love or a serving of ice cream, they think they need the majority share.

- Younger siblings can become frustrated by not being able to do things as well as their older brother or sister.
- Some feel that others are getting privileges they don't. The toddler isn't quite sure why his big sister can go on the swing when he can't, he just knows it looks like fun.
- Little ones taunt older ones and older ones taunt the littlies, who retaliate by taunting the older ones . . . this cycle keeps tension and competition on the boil and isn't very relaxing for mum and dad.

Solution: Sibling rivalry is a form of competition and it is behind many an annoying display of bad behaviour. It is quite normal in toddlerdom, and it will probably continue until they leave home. Don't get drawn into the squabbles and fights, keep them all busy and make sure all children get enough Grade A attention.

Adults are in the way

It's not just other toddlers and siblings that stir up jealousy and competition in your little one, adults are often seen as being in the way too. When toddlers are taken out shopping they may resent the delays that occur when you stop to chat to friends. They wriggle, run off and tell you that it's time to get the show back on the road again.

- During a session on the phone, don't be surprised if your toddler generates just the right amount of noise to have you running to see what's up every two minutes. When the noise stops, the sounds of silence are even worse. It's the *potential* destruction that haunts parents, and the person who designed cordless phones is guaranteed a place in heaven.
- When dad arrives home, it may be hard for parents to chat about their day or impart important news to each other as toddlers interrupt. Even a simple cuddle between husband and wife is often out of the question, as the toddler will squirrel his way in between to get his share of the action.
- When good friends drop round for a deep and meaningful discussion, most toddlers will regard this as unfair competition. Asking to be taken to the toilet, or clambering all over you, ensures that coherent conversation is quite impossible.

Solution: You will only cause needless frustration trying to explain to the toddler or getting them to understand. Be selective and brief when interacting with other adults when the toddler's around. Try to give your message quickly and quit while you're ahead. Discussing the mortgage is best left until your toddler is happily dreaming.

Time-share conversations

Your friend comes round – her marriage is breaking down and she wants to talk to you. 'Sit down, here's a cup of coffee, tell me all about it,' you say sympathetically.

'Well, I think my husband is about to leave me,' she begins.

Within 30 seconds your toddler will be standing between the two of you or trying to get up on your knee, as you launch into counselling mode.

With little children, especially under the age of 3, I'm afraid you're either going to have to share your attention or have your conversation completely disrupted. So the talk may have to go something like this: 'So, you think your husband's going off with her then? *(Oh well done, that's a good drawing.)* And how long do you think it's been going on? *(Yes, he is a lovely teddy, isn't he!)*' – and so on.

It's either that or don't even attempt to have a sensible adult conversation with a toddler present.

Competition caused by other children

Toddlers generally enjoy the company of other littlies but they can still be very selfish when it comes to sharing their possessions or their parents' time and attention. Any attention given by mum or dad to another child is seen as competition. The toddler thinks he owns everything: 'this is *my* toy, this is *my* house and this is *my* mum'.

■ Many toddlers resent others touching their toys. This is a quite normal reaction at this age and doesn't mean that you've bred someone who is destined to grow up to be a mean and selfish adult.

- When another child comes to visit and is made a fuss of, your littlie thinks, 'What about me?' When you don't read the signs, he'll create a scene to regain his authority.
- Mothers who provide family day-care services can find they are sabotaged. Their own toddler's jealousy interferes with the work of looking after other people's children. As far as the toddler is concerned, these interlopers need to 'Back off!'

Solution: Time will soon cure this behaviour; six more months can make all the difference. When another child visits, you need to keep in mind that the toddler has some rights. You can encourage your child to share but by no means start a Holy War over the matter. Tricks like diversion and keeping them busy can smooth over these situations. Always remember that toddlers are just toddlers acting the way that toddlers do.

3. Frustration

Tiny toddlers have ideas way beyond their abilities and when things don't go as they have planned they can become mighty frustrated. The growing toddler is trying to come to terms with his limitations. Frustration brings out the worst in anybody, adults

and toddlers alike. In toddlers it can be a big trigger for bad behaviour. It's tough being a toddler.

- The 15 month old loads food onto his spoon but the cargo shifts on the circuitous route to the mouth and next thing you know the bowl's on the floor.
- The 2½ year old's almost completed construction falls apart and blocks get hurled around the room.
- The militantly independent 3 year old gets both legs stuck down one leg of his pants and he chucks a wobbly as he wobbles to the floor.

Solution: As parents we should accept that a certain amount of grizzling and tantrum-throwing is due to frustration and not just bad behaviour. Learning is about pushing our limits to succeed but sometimes it creates stress when our goals are out of reach. At this stage, understanding and encouragement is what the toddler needs. When things don't work out, it's a cuddle that's called for, not punishment.

4. Fear of separation

Toddlers usually want to be close to their parents and get upset when separated. Anxiety over separation starts at about 7 months of age, intensifies to a peak just after the first birthday, and gradually wanes over the next three years. This is a normal stage of development and not a behaviour problem even though it is a trigger for many a scene. See it from the child's point of view: every time you leave, even the most secure toddler is thinking, 'Is she coming back?' **Toddlers are always checking that you're still around and need to be near you where they feel safe.** This fear of separation is at the heart of many fairytales of children lost in the forest but you don't have to wander into the woods to frighten the toddler – just losing sight of you from the kitchen to the lounge is enough.

During this time, fear of separation can be the trigger for what is mistaken as bad behaviour.

- Many toddlers are hard to leave with babysitters or in day care. Their protesting is not naughtiness, they are just telling you

that you are important and they would prefer you to stay close.
- When life is stressful – for example, if dad is away on business or there has been a split in the family – toddlers may wake during the night to check that things haven't changed even more while they're sleeping.
- Even when everything is going well, many toddlers wake and call their parents in to check they are still there and to get a bit of a cuddle.

Solution: Problems with separation are part of toddlerdom and toddlers need understanding, not scolding and punishment. Between the ages of 7 months and 3 years, be especially forgiving. This is something that will sort itself out at the right time, when the toddler is ready. For the next 80-odd years they will have to go it alone – a few months is a small price to pay. The situation eases every week and you can gradually loosen the ties and let them go a little further. No one should rush a child; that time will come quickly enough.

5. Upset and illness

When the home is unsettled and routines disturbed, the toddler's behaviour may also take a turn for the worse. Toddlers don't like change and quickly pick up on any stress or tension in their environment. They don't have to understand what's happening for this to be a trigger of bad behaviour.

Families feel things together and what one person goes through will affect the lot. We can sometimes forget that our littlies are just as susceptible to this as the adults in the household, despite their lack of maturity.

- Moving house, new babies, illness or death in the family, visitors, late nights, holiday travel and family fights can all cause upset. In times of seemingly even minor change, expect a little bad behaviour to rear its head.
- If the toddler is sick, teething or has a temperature, it is unreasonable to want them to behave. They feel uncomfortable and irritable, so why shouldn't they grizzle and make a big drama out of life's trivial events?

Solution: Toddlers can be irrational, irritable and hard to handle when their environment is unstable or they are unwell. In times of change, turmoil and sickness, it is best to freewheel for a while and take things as they come. Recalibrate your expectations and be prepared to put up with more than usual. You can regain a firm hold once things are back to normal. If anything, give the toddler even more time to adapt than you think they may need.

What a handful

The bad behaviour of toddlers doesn't just happen – its causes are right there before our eyes. If we just step back and look at the big picture, we see that five predictable triggers are at the root of almost all of their antisocial antics. The catch is that inventive toddlers take this handful and produce hundreds of variations on each theme. No wonder parents struggle for sanity as they focus on these decoys instead of the main targets.

If you look carefully, you'll probably see that your toddler is being fired up by the same trigger every day and, as a result, so are you. Once you have this clearly in your sights, you can get a handle on your little one's behaviour.

7

Discipline, not punishment

'Here it comes,' you're thinking, 'he's going to tell us about smacking, locking them in their bedrooms, and taking the front wheel off the tricycle – all that sort of nasty stuff.'

Well, I'm not; that's not discipline. You don't have to be a control freak to raise happy, well-behaved children. Discipline is not about punishment or pain, it is about rewarding and encouraging the good behaviour you want to see. Young children want to be good and are happiest when they know what is expected of them. When I talk about discipline, I mean something very positive.

In this chapter we're going to look at the foundations for effective discipline and the traps that desperate parents fall into. There are times when you have to show your troublesome toddler that you're the boss and are firmly in control. Ninety per cent of the time, though, you can just go with the flow; it's only for that other 10 per cent that you'll have to stand your ground and tame your toddler.

Changing attitudes towards discipline

Attitudes towards discipline have come full circle over the past hundred years. At the beginning of the last century, life was pretty harsh and almost one in five of all infants died before their fourth birthday. Attitudes towards child rearing were equally severe. Babies were fed and handled with rather rigid routines and children were brought up on a brand of discipline that focused on rules and obedience. Little children were 'seen and not heard' and this is the era when discipline became associated with punishment.

After World War II, most people wanted peace on all fronts but even then, discipline of children still involved smacking and Granny's wooden spoon. By the 1960s and '70s, the pendulum had started to swing towards permissiveness. Everyone was pretty mellow. I think it had something to do with the music and it pretty much carried through into all aspects of life, including parenting. Around this time it was thought that babies should be fed, lifted and comforted the moment they cried. The older child was allowed greater freedom, while home became a democracy where adults and children were almost equals. As expectations changed, some parents began feeling guilty and apologetic if they dared to use firm discipline.

This gentle, more permissive 'Let it Be' attitude continued to be promoted until the 1980s. By the time I wrote *Toddler Taming* in 1984, people had started debating that we needed to go back to keeping children in line. The old-fashioned ideas of smacking and marching Junior off to his bedroom were dragged out again, and suggested by some as better methods to get children to behave.

Now the buzz word is control. We have swung all over the place in the past century, from strictness, to extreme permissiveness, to a strange form of democracy, up to a point where parents are so confused, they don't know which approach to take. I believe it is time for a more balanced position.

We start by understanding why behaviour happens, and then try to steer around most of the trouble. Discipline is then about guiding with gentleness and love but knowing exactly what you will and won't put up with. You know your limits as a parent and what to do when your back is against the wall.

What is discipline?

When the word 'discipline' is used, many parents still associate it with 'punishment'. But I want to show you that this is *not* what it is all about. **The word 'discipline' has a Latin origin which means 'teaching' or 'training'.** The similar-sounding word 'disciple' comes from the Latin for 'a learner'. Discipline is a far more attractive concept for both parents and toddlers when viewed as a learning experience. I like the idea of little children as disciples, learning through love and example – but in the background there are clearly defined rules.

Every one of us – whether school child, toddler or adult – needs discipline. We all feel much happier and more secure when we know exactly where we stand. If you have ever worked in an office or been in a relationship where there is constant uncertainty or unreasonable rules and limits, you will be able to understand how some children must feel.

Where does discipline come from?

Discipline can be imposed on us from outside or it can come from within as self-discipline. Obviously young toddlers have no idea of self-discipline and at this tender age all direction must come externally from us, the parents. Good discipline starts in the home and spreads, eventually preparing our children for a smooth passage through school. When they start their education they will be expected to sit, settle, share and behave. It will impress no one if their academic performance is like an infant Einstein but their behaviour like an infant raver.

By preschool age, children are ready to start taking some responsibility for their own affairs and this process can be helped if we loosen the reins and allow a little freedom of choice. This lets the toddler feel the repercussions of his right and wrong decisions. By school age this loosening up process can be extended, putting the child more and more in control of their own decisions. The ultimate aim is to have self-discipline firmly established by the time they up and leave home.

Styles of discipline

There are many ways to discipline our children. There are those parents who keep a tight rein and those who hold the reins loosely, giving just a bit of guidance. It doesn't much matter which way you choose, just as long as you don't go to the extremes of absolute strictness or permissiveness.

When to start

Starting discipline is a very individual decision but the main message is to go gently.

Babies in their first year certainly do not need discipline; they need love, routine and comfort. The overall aim is to establish the security and closeness that glues parent and child together with an epoxy-like bond, the earlier the better. Some of the older generation say that babies who get all this attention are destined to be more demanding, but these days we know that it actually makes them more secure and independent. Basically, you cannot spoil an infant.

Toddlers most certainly need discipline, the amount of which depends on the temperament of the individual child and the tolerance of the parents. Those of us who have been blessed with an infant like a living saint will have little need for discipline before the age of 20 months. Even then, an occasional soft whisper will produce a disgustingly well-behaved child. For those who have a toddler with the temperament of an urban terrorist, it is not as easy. Parents will need to keep a copy of this book within arm's reach at all times, with a spare in the car and in their briefcase.

Before the age of 2 our children do little that is devious, aggressive or nasty. Their actions just lack thought. Gentle, firm guidance is usually sufficient, leaving the wrath-of-God-descending-like-a-thunderbolt under lock and key.

Strict or permissive?

Parents who are excessively strict and punitive believe in the old saying 'Spare the rod, spoil the child' and that a home run on authoritarian lines can create a perfectly behaved child. On the surface this may appear to be the case but underneath such forced compliance lies resentment and potential for rebellion. These parents treat their home and family like a police state, where members are told exactly what to do and how, when and where to do it.

Model children produced through intimidation continue to behave well only as long as the threat is present. Once it is lifted they rebel, going wild, getting boozed up or having super orgies when their parents go away for the weekend. They usually leave home at the first possible opportunity, making a rude departing gesture as if to say 'Thanks for nothing!' Like government by intimidation, discipline of children by the same method never creates respect, long-term stability, independence or happiness.

At the other extreme, there is excessive freedom, where no limits are imposed and the child is free to do whatever he likes. Anything and everything is OK and no one encourages, notices or seems to care. These types of parents mistakenly think that if

The honeymoon is over

No matter which style of discipline someone was raised with, they will have carried into adulthood attitudes to child care which will surface when they themselves become a parent.

When getting married, a lot of thought and discussion goes into the dress, cake and honeymoon location. But rarely are the excited couple thinking about the children they'll have and how they'll raise them. Will they be strict within reason or favour a more laid-back approach?

As each adult enters the marriage with some undisclosed but quite set attitudes to child care, it is only a matter of time before diametrically opposed views collide. Life will get interesting when children arrive on the scene and sparks will fly.

they set any ground rules, they will lose their child's love. But children need limits to feel secure and this approach does not buy love, it loses respect. With this overly permissive style, children may feel that their parents do not care enough about them to care what they do. Children who have experienced little discipline before school also find it hard to change overnight and fit into the limits of a preschool class.

A happy middle ground

If we keep away from the punitive and permissive extremes, this leaves a very broad middle ground on which to base discipline. You're going to need more than bits of advice, you're going to need a plan. As you struggle at the coalface of child care, you don't want more philosophy, you want strong techniques that work.

If you are one of the lucky few who have been rewarded with an easy child, you may just be looking for a few new ideas in case the climate changes. But if you have scored a stubborn, determined, wilful toddler, then by now you are probably tearing your hair out. As your own discipline attempts falter, you begin to worry that you'll never survive toddlerdom. You don't want to screw up your toddler by doing the wrong thing.

So where do you start? What's the best way to discipline your toddler? We have a little way to go before we talk turkey – first we have to look at what I believe are the foundations for all discipline.

Foundations for discipline

This is where the story really begins. The elements I'm about to discuss are what you'll need to keep in mind before you even begin to discipline your toddler. These four elements provide the foundation for whatever style of discipline you choose combined with the techniques that work from the next chapter.

1. Clear communication

This is at the heart of positive parenting and effective discipline. Before you can get results you have to communicate clearly. Parents of unruly children frequently complain: 'He isn't doing

what I want!', but often they weren't clear about what it was they wanted. What's more, they weren't communicating in a language that the toddler could understand.

Here is a perfect example: On an otherwise unremarkable, bright, sparkly day in Sydney, I was waiting to take a ferry from the Opera House and observed a family nearby. They were tourists also killing time, looking in the souvenir shops while they waited. Their toddler was being a toddler and excitedly touching anything within reach while mum got more and more agitated. 'Honey, don't touch the merchandise. Sweetie, I said *don't* touch the merchandise!' As I looked on bemusedly, the 2 year old looked up at her, clearly thinking, 'What the hell are you on about? I'm playing with the toys.' The stuffed koalas were making more sense, for as far as the toddler was concerned, mum may as well have been speaking in Swahili.

For our discipline to be effective, we have to be clear and we need to let our toddlers know exactly what we want from them. Clear communication is about using your eyes, your tone of voice and getting down to the toddler's level. When you make eye contact, they know they are getting your undivided attention which, as we've already seen, is so important. Using a firm tone of voice instructs the toddler that you mean business. By not towering over them and getting down to knee-height, you give your message not through intimidation but by effective communication.

It is also about the language you choose to get your message across. Don't bury them in an avalanche of words; rather, convey just the important information in a few clear, simple phrases. Make sure there can be no mistake what you mean. Rules and limits have a better chance of working if the easily distracted toddler can understand you!

2. Be consistent

It would be an unusual family in which both parents agree completely about child rearing but despite this, we need to present our children with a united front. **Consistency is the key and in each home there can be only one set of rules.** Toddlers need to know what the rules are and that each day they'll be the same. If the speed limits on our roads changed every day and you never knew when the police might pull you over for speeding, you would quickly become confused, insecure and angry. The same goes for toddlers living in an environment of inconsistent, rapidly changing rules.

Present a united front

In some families, one parent is so determined to get their way, that each occasion of discipline becomes a dispute. Where there is such major disagreement, trying to improve toddler behaviour won't work until the warring parties can reach a truce.

At its extreme, I have seen parents use these disputes in their most sinister form. They deliberately inflame their partner, using their children to do their dirty work. This is a form of legalised child abuse. It may be a lot to ask, but parents need to show a united front even if a different story exists behind the scenes. For the sake of the children, be a pacifist.

If your toddler is allowed to get away with murder one day but is punished for a trivial offence the next, they will soon become unmanageable. They also cannot live happily in a home where messages are conflicting; when one parent says 'Do this' and the other immediately countermands the request, then you have just witnessed the end of effective discipline.

Being consistent lets toddlers know where they stand and the expectations you have for their behaviour. While tiredness, a mile-long to-do list and an inventive toddler are a challenge to any plan of attack, the more consistent you can be, the less trouble you'll have.

3. Structure and routine

Little children tend to be better behaved when they live in an organised, structured environment. They need to know the behavioural limits that their parents expect and will tolerate.

Most children thrive on routine and they will be thrown out of kilter by the smallest things, like disrupted mealtimes, unexpected visitors or a late bedtime. A simple daily routine of getting up, having breakfast, playing at playgroup, eating lunch, having a nap, playing some more, having dinner, then a bath and reading stories before bedtime gives a consistent framework for the toddler as they grow.

It isn't just toddlers that thrive on structure. Every day I get out of bed, do some exercise, then get to work writing for a few hours. When I have written enough, I reward myself with a coffee and keep going until lunch. By the end of the day, I've achieved much with little stress. If it wasn't for this routine, this book may never have been written.

Sometimes parents fall into the trap of thinking that structure and routine are boring and that, in order for life to be interesting for the toddler, every day has to be different. But toddlers are fascinated by the simplest things and we certainly don't have to fly them to Disneyland to light up their lives. What they do need is to feel secure.

Building a routine supports your discipline attempts and makes life easier for toddlers as well as parents. Disorganised parents produce equally confused children (and the combined effect is a sure recipe for chaos).

4. Act positive

Discipline techniques are most successful when they are delivered with a positive attitude. First you must believe in what you are doing, then communicate that clearly to your children. I refer to this brand of positive parenting as the 'evangelical approach'.

In my office I would see parents who had so little 'oomph' their manner seemed just shy of comatose – and they wondered about their toddler's lack of enthusiasm! Energy and motivation are powerful allies in your journey through toddlerdom – a little enthusiasm goes a long way. If you are positive, they are; it's infectious. Your confidence and belief in your ability to make it work transmits to the toddler – 'This is the way it is going to be!'

If at any time your discipline seems to be slipping, stand back and check your delivery is strong and confident. **Remember, positive parents are powerful people!**

Beware the traps

Now you've got the foundations, but before you race ahead to the next chapter, which is full of techniques, I want to point out a few traps that swallow up many eager parents. These are hazards best avoided in any relationship, not just between parents and toddlers.

Don't nitpick

Some adults never seem to get off their children's back. In my office, these parents would nitpick non-stop. 'Look at Dr Green when you talk to him!' 'Say please.' 'Use a tissue.' 'Don't touch that toy.' 'Sit up straight.' There can be no peace in an atmosphere where every little gesture is dissected and used to generate tension.

Nitpicking is a kind of over-disciplining and is counter-productive. Even adults don't like people to fuss over every move we make, it makes us stressed.

Solution: When every single movement a child makes is commented on, they quickly become numb to the constant background noise and tune it out. Parents make the mistake of thinking volume equals good discipline and that it will make the toddler behave. When disciplining we need to notice what matters, concentrate on that, and selectively screen out the rest.

Avoid escalation

Many parents seem to seek out some minor incident and go over it until it explodes into something much bigger.

A tired mum sits at home and junior drops a crumb on the carpet. Mum says 'Pick it up, please!' and the toddler ignores her.

Mum then says, 'Pick it up this instant!' as her blood starts to boil. 'I'm warning you, you will be in big trouble!' Within a few seconds, Mum is apoplectic.

How can a tiny incident ever justify such drama? The dog would probably have eaten it anyway. Escalation is how wars begin. What starts off as a small matter gets bigger and bigger until it is blown out of all proportion.

Solution: Take a deep breath, stop for a second and let the trivial pass.

Once finished, forget it

Children forget quickly but some parents just cannot let a matter rest. Parents who are slow to forgive their children write off days of their lives with ongoing psychological warfare, quickly draining their emotional reserves. Lack of forgiveness also ensures that tensions remain high and maximum home unhappiness is guaranteed.

Solution: Holding grudges only produces parents with hypertension – not stable, loving children. This is a major trap that parents fall into, so after each incident, forgive your little one and start again with a clean slate. A misbehaving child should be disciplined then and there, and the episode followed immediately by forgiveness.

Beware the negative rut

From time to time everyone hits a bad patch and with this, 'No!' can become a much over-used word. When things get really bad, each day becomes a constant battle of 'No', 'Don't', 'Stop it!', leaving parents demoralised and numb behind the eyeballs.

As they crawl into bed at night, these parents think, 'What good thing have I said all day? Is this what the joy of parenting is all about?' Next morning you greet the chirping birds with a sigh and the thought 'What awful thing will he do first today?'

Solution: Sinking into a negative rut alters our attitude to everything. Even the worst child is well-behaved 98 per cent of the time, but parents become so focused on the bad, they forget to see the goodness. When everything at first appears to be nothing but bad news, look carefully for that special kind of toddler magic and build on it. And if there doesn't seem to be any good, start by rewarding the 'nearly good' to build up a more positive attitude.

It takes two to tango

So often parents would tell me, 'He keeps fighting with me', to which I invariably replied: 'Surely you mean *you* keep fighting with him?' With toddlers, even the fight you win you lose. After 10 minutes the child has forgotten all about it, yet as much as an hour later steam is still gushing from the victorious parent's ears.

You only have to go to the complaints counter of a major department store to find out what truly calm, collected people are like. As the customer's voice ascends in octaves of rage, the only reaction coming from the other side of the desk is unswervingly serene: 'Oh, I'm sorry the blade flew off your new food processor and cut off your finger. That certainly has never happened before with this model. I'll draw it to the manager's attention for you.' Parents too, believe it or not, have the power to encourage or prevent fights, depending on their reaction.

Solution: Toddlers argue to gain attention and also just because they can. The responsibility lies with you, the adult, to put an end to disputes. It takes two to tango and if either party stays calm, there will be peace. Even the most gifted toddler can't fight by themselves.

Don't take it to heart

'He's deliberately disobeying me!' you fume. 'I told him just a few minutes ago not to do that.' Parents forget that they're dealing with a toddler and take their actions personally. Most toddler behaviour is not disobedience. It's just a very short attention span; and they're not really quite sure what you're on about anyway. The danger is seeing a child as naughty when they're just being a toddler.

Solution: This is a good time to remember all the 'normal' things that toddlers do. When it comes to discipline, don't try looking for logic in a toddler's behaviour because you won't find any. There's no point saying, 'He's doing that deliberately to annoy me,' because the chances are he isn't doing anything of the sort. The debate about good and evil is an utter waste of time at this age. Leave it until they're over 5.

Domino effect

Your toddler starts acting badly the day dad gets fired, or begins throwing magnificent tantrums the month interest rates go up. But these aren't examples of bad behaviour, they're examples of the infectious nature of tension.

So many behaviour problems are due to stress. 'My toddler isn't stressed' you say. Maybe not, but you are. Life isn't always easy and parents have many worries: jobs, relationships and money. Each family is like a group of delicately balanced dominoes: if one is rattled, they all topple.

Solution: As parents we can't stop the stress and tension in the outside world, but we can stop them entering our homes. While there is no miracle cure for our troubles, we can work on minimising the damaging effects they generate. Every one of us needs to become aware of just how infectious tension can be, then do our best to prevent it stirring up our children. While the only real solution of living in a bubble isn't practical, don't mistake the acting out of children as bad behaviour.

Don't stir up the animals

So many parents seem to be fighting battles that aren't worthwhile. But as I have often explained to parents, when you meet a lion, you don't take a stick and poke it in the backside. Instead, you tiptoe carefully past, because you aren't looking for trouble.

Solution: It's the same with little children: don't go stirring up the animals – it doesn't get you anywhere! Don't go looking for trouble because chances are you'll find it. Life with a toddler is exciting enough without poking lions.

Change comes gradually

When some parents left my office with a behaviour plan, they seemed convinced that it would work within the hour. But there is no point expecting that a child will leave my presence and be instantly cured. After all, the toddler had been practising their particular performance for months and it seems reasonable to allow them a few weeks to smarten up their act.

Sensible expectations are important for yourself and what you want from the toddler. It is time, attention and consistency that bring results. Don't get me wrong, I often see miracles – but of the slow and gradual kind.

Things may get worse

Before embarking on any major behavioural change, be sure you have the strength to handle that darkest hour which comes before the dawn. Things may get worse before they get better.

For some time now, your child has studied his parents well, knowing your every raw nerve and point of vulnerability. If you suddenly smarten up your act, close the chinks in your armour and cease to respond to his usual tricks, he will feel he is losing his touch. All he can do is turn up the pressure and try more of the same but with even greater persistence.

If your defences are strong, and remain that way, your toddler will go back to base to re-plan the campaign and attack on a different front. But now mum and dad are ready for any little skirmish. When you show clearly that there is a new you who is in charge and really means business, you can donate your armour to a museum and let it quietly rust.

Ready, set...

You're ready to go! Now that you understand why you have to have a strong foundation before using discipline techniques, you can get on with disciplining.

As you will have gathered, discipline is a very positive thing: it's about encouragement and guidance. Much can be achieved without recourse to raised voices, tantrums, force, threats or parental insanity. If you communicate clearly, are consistent and stay positive, you're more than halfway there. Look out for the traps and you'll set a course for success.

This approach is not only very powerful, it is also the most effective. In the next chapter I'll show you the techniques that put it into practice.

8

What works

As a parent, you learn by trial and error what works and what doesn't while raising your wilful toddler. Well, this chapter will give you a head start, because it is filled with discipline techniques that are guaranteed to work. The solutions to all the behaviour problems that you thought were insurmountable are in here.

We start with the foolproof, best way to discipline your toddler, by encouraging good behaviour; then follow with some tricks to have on hand for challenging moments. Finally, we'll look at your safety valve, the Time Out technique.

If this is the chapter you've been waiting for, dive right in. Leave what doesn't work as a thing of the past – life with your toddler is about to get much, much easier.

Encouraging the good, discouraging the bad

This is the most effective, most powerful way of disciplining your toddler. It uses a combination of what you have learned so far in this book about toddler behaviour mixed with a bit of amateur psychology.

So far we know that toddlers aren't intentionally bad, they just lack sense, and that they are fuelled by attention – the higher octane, the better. You can use this need for attention to your advantage when it comes to discipline. If you shower attention on the behaviour you want them to display, the toddler will do more of it, because they want to be good and seek your approval. If you encourage lots of good behaviour, there's much less room for the bad.

This technique has two parts: the encouraging part where we use rewards to show the toddler what we want from them; and the discouraging part, where we withdraw our admiration and attention from what's going on. Compared to the tropical, balmy atmosphere that is around when the toddler is behaving the way you want, when they're not behaving, the temperature is decidedly cool. Not frozen, just a little bracing.

While the theory sounds complicated, in practice it is remarkably simple. Any behaviour that is reinforced by rewards will tend to be repeated. You can use voice tone, actions and attention to reward desirable behaviour or discourage unwanted actions. It's just like at the end of a concert when the audience's enthusiastic applause results in an *encore* – you get a repeat performance. Everybody wins: the orchestra feels enlivened and the concertgoers are relaxed and happy. On a different night, however, the concert finishes but the audience is bored senseless and the applause absent – there will be no *encore*. So too with toddlers: any behaviour that is either not noticed, encouraged or reinforced generally disappears.

The example opposite shows how easily a behaviour you don't want is reinforced; all it takes is one time. So once you start using this technique, it's important to keep asking yourself, 'Am I giving the right message?' A behaviour which pays off for the child will generally be repeated. So what we want to make sure of is that pay-offs come for the right behaviours, not the wrong ones.

What a bummer!

The 2½-year-old toddler stands up, smiles, then in front of the visiting church committee, with perfect articulation, says 'Bum!' Mother blushes and explains, as all eyes turn to the toddler, that this isn't a word we use in this house. With such reward and reinforcement, before long all she will hear is 'Bum!' 'Bum!' 'Bum!'

If mum had been using the 'encourage the good, discourage the bad' approach, she would have handled it very differently. When the child said 'Bum', mum could have remained distinctly unimpressed, yawning quietly and continuing to chat. Junior would probably have just stomped off. No audience, no show.

A rewarding experience

Rewarding children for performing is not degrading, it is part of our way of life. I get rewarded with money for working, and I get no pay if I don't. If I give a successful lecture people thank me and before I know it I have agreed to give another.

There are two types of rewards that can be used effectively for disciplining your toddler:

1. *Hard rewards* are 'in your hand', tangible items – things your toddler can touch. A smiley stamp or a 'Thomas the Tank Engine' sticker are both hard rewards. Then there are all those sweet rewards, like ice cream, that tend to turn both your child's teeth and the dentist's bank balance black.

2. *Soft rewards* are more social, more emotional. A tone of approval in your voice or the twinkle of pride in your eyes are both soft rewards.

When deciding whether to use soft or hard rewards, the child's age is an important factor. Most toddlers are very happy with soft rewards, particularly attention, whilst older children are more aware of the value of objects and prefer hard rewards, especially those that jingle in the pocket.

Rewards are not bribery

Some of you will read this talk about rewards and think, 'Oh, I get it; it's all bribery.' But I need to point out that there is a very subtle but important difference between reward and bribery.

A *bribe* is when the child is told that he will be given something once he has performed a certain task. It is perhaps a form of blackmail, as you dangle a carrot to get what you want.

A *reward*, on the other hand, is given when there is no talk beforehand of what will happen after the good behaviour has appeared. Then the reward comes out of the blue as an unexpected bonus.

The eyes have it

Giving attention, praise, smiles and touch are all soft rewards. Of these, attention is the main reinforcer and when used wisely it can be very powerful. Both children and adults are very sensitive to soft, subtle boosting of behaviour by being noticed, by the warmth in a voice or twinkle in an eye.

When the toddler is behaving the way you want, offer these soft rewards to encourage more of this behaviour. Transmit love and approval in your eyes and the tone of your voice. Brush by them as they play, giving them a little pat on the shoulder and saying quietly, 'I love you', 'That's right', or 'Well done.'

When they aren't behaving the way you would like them to, then you can transmit that message, using the same approach. You use a firmer tone, one of disapproval. The twinkle in your eye is replaced by a deadpan look on your face. You move away from them, signifying that they have done something you don't like and you don't want to be a part of it. The toddler will instinctively know that they have done something wrong. They may not understand what, but they know you are not pleased. In this way, you are subtly moulding their behaviour.

Very often the difference between bribes and rewards is far from clear and though I would prefer you use rewards, if a bit

of good old-fashioned bribery achieves the desired effect, then go for it.

Behaviour modification

When we use this technique of encouraging the good behaviour we want from our little ones, we are employing a form of behaviour modification therapy. Parents often cringe at this term as it suggests some sinister brainwashing technique used by the secret police on unwilling dissidents. Even worse, some have heard that behaviour modification has been used to train dogs, pigeons and all sorts of circus animals.

Don't panic, this is not some animal trainer's trick. It is proven, it is effective and I am sure that, even though your parents never heard of behaviour modification, it was the way you were brought up.

Quick smart

In young children this technique will work best if the good behaviour is rewarded quickly. Remember, toddlers have a very short span of attention. Even a minute after the event the reward will have lost some of its power at this age. Withholding some treat until tomorrow is both unfair and ineffective.

Discipline for the toddler must also be immediate. If the toddler has to wait until the evening, he will have long forgotten his misdeed and the delayed discipline will come as a thunderbolt from the blue. This will do more to frighten and confuse the child than it will to improve his behaviour or act as a long-term deterrent.

Removal of privileges is an equally pointless exercise, as young children do not think much about the future or future events. By the age of 4 or 5 the situation will change, and a clear statement can be made as to the standard of behaviour expected and what will happen if it does not occur. Until then, do it right away or not at all.

The technique must be used consistently if it is going to be effective. If a behaviour is going to be ignored and underplayed, this must happen five out of every five times it occurs. If the ignoring is restricted to four out of five occurrences, it will always be worth trying you out. This is one instance where being pedantic will show big rewards.

Getting it back to front

Though we use rewards for behaviour modification every day, many times we unknowingly get it so reversed that it becomes an enemy, not an ally. It's an easy technique to master but it's also easy to create more problems than you started with, by rewarding behaviour that you don't want. So many behavioural difficulties are actually created by us parents.

An example of getting it back to front would be with feeding. You put food in front of the toddler, he takes one look at it and says 'Yuck!' To entice him to eat your delicious efforts, you decide he needs a little encouragement. Mum makes aeroplane noises, dad juggles oranges and the dog probably performs circus tricks – going completely overboard to at least get him to take a bite. With so much reward for *not* eating, the toddler's mouth remains firmly shut. Now you have created a feeding problem.

So to get it the right way around, you'd proceed something like this: He looks at the food: 'Yuck!' You ignore this. He either eats or ends up with hunger pains, but you maintain your sanity and have no future fights over food. Remember, toddlers may be stubborn but they won't go hungry for long.

Attention is one of the best rewards you can give a toddler, and something he craves from you. Paying attention to any behaviour, whether you do or don't want it, reinforces it.

Ignorance is bliss

Some years ago I was examining a little boy as he lay on his mother's knee. When I felt his tummy, he quite involuntarily straightened one leg and kicked me. As a bit of a joke I jumped back, holding my knee and made a great fuss. A few seconds later my foolishness was rewarded by a sharp kick on my other knee and this time it really did hurt. Again I jumped and by the end of the interview the little terror was tramping on my toes, kicking my shins and having a ball. A week later as I was working quietly at my desk, my office door burst open and before I knew it, the little devil dashed in and gave me another bruising kick.

Now admittedly this seems a particularly silly way for a paediatrician to behave, but it illustrates clearly what happens when we make a fuss over some trivial event. If the first unintentional kick had been ignored, that would have been the end of it. I should have ignored it, or purchased shin guards.

Tricks to keep up your sleeve

Even with all your dedicated encouraging of good behaviour, you will still need a few more tricks up your sleeve. You don't need a magician's wand to vanish unwanted behaviour when it pops up, just one or two techniques that will bring equally spectacular results.

Diversion

Diversion is one of those good old-fashioned remedies that has stood the test of time and still comes out with flying colours. Think back some years ago to when you were a child at granny's, just about to defoliate her pot plants more effectively than a dose of Agent Orange. She would say quietly, 'I just remembered I have some lollies in the big jar in the kitchen.' With this your hands disengaged from the plant and you were off to the kitchen with the speed of Phar Lap from the gate. Through all this never a voice was raised, peace was restored and the plant continued to do its bit to combat the Greenhouse Effect.

Today's parents can use the same technique with equal success, and it is particularly useful with toddlers. **When it seems you are about to run headlong into a bit of bother, it is often easier to quickly divert the child's attention before the obnoxious behaviour has time to take hold.** If a clever parent can sense and grasp the psychological moment, the situation is saved before control has been lost.

Imagine the scene: your talented tantrum-thrower is just about to stage yet another amazing Oscar-winning performance. He enters stage right, finds his spotlight, takes a deep breath for his first line: '*Sesame Street* is just about to start,' you say. With this the faint-hearted performer retires.

Some parents take exception to the use of diversion as they believe it deceives children, is dishonest and even downright degrading. My answer is simple – it works. Remember that one of the toddler trademarks is a very short attention span. Diversion has been used and proven effective for centuries. It prevents fights and helps families live in peace.

Selective deafness and selective blindness

To keep sane and happy it is best to install a sort of filter in front of your eyes and ears, one that lets you see what matters and shuts out all the rest. This technique to add to your repertoire is called selective deafness and selective blindness.

Selective deafness is of particular use when our little ones abuse us verbally or try out some of those words that were heard, but not taught, at preschool. A 3-year-old toddler who is not getting everything his own way, turns to his mother and utters the common toddler phrase, 'I hate you.' Mum gets upset and worries that the hate is genuine. She responds with such effusive assurances of love that it is like a soap opera.

The best response is to hear nothing, and stay calm. If a reply is needed, it's best to keep it short – such as 'Well, I love you' – and then leave it at that. You know that the toddler really does love you; remember who he wants close by him when he is sick or frightened.

Of course it is a big call to ignore all irritating behaviour but we can try. This is helped along by a bit of selective blindness. For example, a 2½-year-old boy wants to overdose on chocolate biscuits, but after scoffing three, his mother tells him, 'That's enough!' He knows she is a softie and puts on an interesting bit of theatre.

Despite the huff, puff and stamping of feet, mum must stand firm and put on an even better act. Play this one completely serene, like the Mother Superior in *The Sound of Music*, as you take a pile of washing, walk out and hang it on the line. There are few actors who like seeing the audience walk out in mid-performance and even the most thick-skinned toddler will tend to get the message.

Deaf husbands

I first discovered selective deafness while watching how husbands reacted when their wives asked them to do something. It seemed that a line like 'Did you put the garbage out?' often failed to register while 'Would you like a can of beer?' seemed to squeeze itself along the hearing nerve and be clearly registered by the brain.

And I have to admit that I was once troubled by this problem but my wife (also a doctor) soon sorted it out in her own quiet way. She just booked me into the Hospital Hearing Clinic to get my ears tested. At that point I most certainly heard what she was trying to tell me!

Keeping the show on the road

When I finish a family session my door opens and I send them all out and away immediately. Now this is not because I have another appointment waiting. It's that the parents need to take their new ideas and positive attitudes and put them into practice immediately. Yet I watch many parents move from a position of power to one of definite defeat, often within the space of a few short minutes at the end of a session.

At the end of a lengthy interview with a family, all their tired toddler wants is to be shot of my office. At this point there is peace – but then the parents blow it. 'Shake hands with Dr Green. Say thank you to the nice doctor. Now, pick up all the toys. Park the tricycle over there – No! move it next to the table.' After this the parents fiddle about looking for their car keys and chat to the secretary about the weather before they leave. By this time the toddler is protesting, the parents rise to the bait and the air becomes full of tension. Just like that, they've undone all our good work.

When you are handling material that can sometimes be unpredictable or highly explosive, you don't hang around looking for trouble. Don't release your grip; keep little ones interested and on the move. Sensible parents don't dally, waste time or stuff around. They realise they need to keep the toddler on the move in order to keep one step ahead of them.

Time Out

When all your best discipline has been tried and is getting you nowhere, when you've tried diversion, other tricks and your back is against the wall, it's time for Time Out. This is a technique which quickly brings an escalating situation to an end. It is a safety valve, gives rapid results and calms everything down.

The term comes from the sporting arena, and refers to a brief break in play that allows competitors to catch their breaths, collect their thoughts and regroup. In the family arena, the basic method is to remove the child from a deteriorating or stalemate situation and place him, for a short time, in another room. This takes the child from his position on centre stage to a less prominent place, where his antics pass unnoticed. He has time to cool off and this also permits the parents to calm down too. This is an important aspect of Time Out – it is designed for both child *and* parent to get some space. There may be times when it seems the parent benefits more than the toddler!

The main purpose of Time Out is not to punish the child but to separate the warring parties. This technique is not the same as the old 'Go to your room!' which was punishment for bad behaviour. Time Out is about peace. As said many times in this book, big bangs start with little triggers and it is much easier to use a method like this to defuse the situation in its infancy, than wait so long that you have to mop up after an incident of international proportions.

Time Out is probably most effective in the 2 to 10 year olds but it still can be helpful in those who are very much younger. I know there are children who never need Time Out, and their parents should be aware of how blessed they are. But the reality is that many parents have moments when they feel they will explode.

When you are rapidly losing control and your little one knows it – don't snap, use Time Out. Don't forget: real parents with difficult children do have their breaking points and it is never smart to see how close you can get to such a dangerous situation. Salvage the situation before the game is lost.

The Time Out technique

The child has reached a pitch of aggravation or limit-testing that can no longer be discouraged, ignored or diverted:

- Clearly tell the child that they are going into Time Out and why, even if they are too young to fully understand. Communicate clearly, use your tone of voice, eye contact and get down to the toddler's level to let him know you mean business.
- Calmly take him by the hand or carry him, then decisively put him in the Time Out room. This is the point where you might want to give up, particularly if he's throwing an award-winning tantrum. But be firm or the toddler will think he's on a winner.
- Be gentle, there is no need for harshness or roughness. At the same time, leave him in no doubt that you are going to see this through.
- Once inside the room, state positively in your best 'this is the way it is going to be' voice that he will stay there until he has calmed down. Don't get drawn into debates or arguments.
- Then shut the door and move quickly away from the scene. Don't lock the door; don't hover.
- Leave the child in Time Out for a length of time appropriate to his age. This is 1 minute for every year of their age; e.g.: a 3-year-old child stays in Time Out for

3 minutes. For children over the age of 3, a kitchen timer may be useful to show the child how long they are to remain in the room.

■ As important as how you put the child into Time Out is how you bring them out. You don't want to undo your good work, so don't hold grudges, don't threaten with repeat sessions and don't assume that it will be called for again in five minutes. Get on with life and get back to having fun with your toddler.

Points to remember

If you need to use Time Out, there is no need to feel like a failure, or guilty that it has come to this. Parents are the ones in these situations who have enough sense to know what's needed and create the necessary distance. The toddler doesn't know that the only solution is to get out of each other's hair. He relies on you to know best.

Do a mental dry run so that you are clear about the steps you will take. In the heat of the moment you might not be able to think clearly enough to decide what you'll say, which room you'll use, how long for, and so on.

Don't feel the need to constantly remind the toddler how naughty he has been after Time Out is over. Move on with life.

Don't lock the door. Time Out in the bedroom must never be mistaken for that unfortunate carry-over from the early 1900s of locking children in their room. This is more likely to terrify than help.

Unrealistic expectations

Many parents expect the child to walk out of Time Out, head bowed, stand before them and say, 'Dear mother, I have done wrong and will behave perfectly for the rest of the week.'

The purpose of Time Out is to allow both parties to cool off and thus prevent major fights. Time Out is often said to have failed when, in fact, it is the parents who have simply failed to realise what they are trying to achieve. Five minutes in a bedroom does not guarantee angelic behaviour for the rest of the day. No method I know, other than possibly a straightjacket, could ever produce such an outcome.

The child does not have to apologise. The only expectation is that he should re-enter in a more reasonable frame of mind. Unrealistic expectations maintain a high level of tension which is guaranteed to destroy everyone's ongoing happiness.

Other parents claim that Time Out does not work because the child repeats the original behaviour. If he walks straight out of Time Out and immediately and defiantly re-offends, then he must be put straight back into Time Out. However, when parents complain that their child repeats the same behaviour they usually mean that it recurred an hour later. Time Out is a technique that defuses a rapidly escalating situation at one particular time. Once this has passed and peace is regained, the method has shown itself to be effective.

Which room?

Many supporters of this method argue that the most important point is where Time Out takes place. The ideal Time Out room would be a dull, quiet space, of easy access but far from all excitement, for example, a spare bedroom. Nowadays we don't always have the luxury of a spare room to use for Time Out and in practise the nearest we can provide is often our child's bedroom.

The experts are quick to tell us that use of the bedroom is a mistake. They believe that the child will develop fears resulting in sleep problems. But if putting a toddler in his bedroom will put him off sleeping, then presumably putting him in the dining room will put him off eating, the kitchen off dishwashing (though who isn't allergic to that!) and so on. Parents might worry, too, that the child's room is full of toys and other distractions. I choose the bedroom because it is sufficiently soundproof and far enough away from the rest of the living area to give both parties the space they need to calm down. Attention is more valuable to the toddler than truckloads of toys. It is less important where they are than the distance you've created between the toddler and the other members of the family. As long as the child is safe, and there are no dangerous objects lurking in the area, the Time Out room can be any room.

If space is limited, use a corner of the lounge room, or even the front hall, to isolate the child. Making a child sit on a cushion in a corner is not ideal but some parents have no other choice. One of the problems with this is no sooner than your back is turned, the child increases his attention-grabbing behaviour with a flow of rude noises or gestures. Remember, the other half of Time Out is the parents getting space as well. Leave the room and keep yourself busy elsewhere for a few minutes.

Who's that jolly toddler?

Some parents feel they have been cheated when the child goes into his room in mid-tantrum and remains there to play happily with his toys. I must repeat that Time Out is not a punishment; it is a technique aimed at separating two people who are hell-bent on a 'barney'. Whether the child plays with his toys, stands on his head or sings 'Waltzing Matilda' in his room is utterly irrelevant, just as long as he cools off and parents are allowed a little time to relax.

Common mistakes

Sometimes when I suggested Time Out, parents returned saying that it did not work. When I heard this, I knew that it failed for one of a few reasons:

Immediate reappearance: One of the main complaints I get is that of rapid escape. The child is put securely in his room and before you have taken five paces he is out the door like a bullet from a gun. When I ask the parents where they were at the time of the child's reappearance, I usually discover that it was directly outside the door. Children are not stupid. If they know there is a welcoming party ready to greet them, of course they will come out – anything for a bit of fun and attention.

Other parents complain that the child is out of the room before they have even turned their back. It seems unbelievable to me that a 2 year old can run across a room, manipulate a door handle and escape faster than a fit adult can sprint from the scene. If this is the case it might be better to stop complaining and enrol immediately in a fitness class.

Solution: In my experience, if the parent puts the child in the room with commitment, closes the door firmly then clears off quickly, reappearance is extremely rare. I find this can usually be achieved if the parents harden their hearts and are 100 per cent firm at the time of banishment. Little children are very quick to sense when disobedience or a course of whingeing will get them what they want and they are equally aware of when their parents are serious and not about to give an inch.

Occasionally an escape artist does need some heavier guidance. At the first escape he must be put back with complete firmness. The next time the door may need to be immobilised for a short period. It sounds tough but remember, Time Out is the bottom-line safety valve. This is where we go when everything else has failed.

Getting a handle on it

Now and then I hear that Time Out was unsuccessful because the toddler forced the door handle. 'What were you doing at the time?' I ask the unenlightened parent. 'Oh, holding the other handle!' Toddlers just love this contest; it's like being a big game fisherman and hooking a whopper.

Screaming and kicking: 'Oh, I put him in his bedroom and he screamed and screamed until I had to let him out,' is something I often hear. When I ask where the parent was standing at this time, again the answer is 'outside the door'. Your toddler may be only 2½ but he is exhibiting considerably more intelligence than the parent who hangs around in such a position.

Cleaning up the mess

One wilful 4 year old in my care had long studied the art of tantrums and was now practising it with gusto. When put in her room she would cool off but then she would systematically pull the room apart. When I heard that the very necessary Time Out was being so effectively sabotaged, I started by getting the parents to clear the room of all breakable objects, pens, paint and any other messy substances.

The next time she was placed in her room she did not bother to cry as she knew that a little rearranging of her belongings would have much more impact on her mother. Ten minutes later she came out of the room in perfect control, looking extremely pleased. Her mother steadied herself as she glanced in the door to see the bed wrecked and clothes out of every drawer spread on the floor. But mum had got the message and as she walked past merely remarked, 'Oh dear, that looks a bit of a mess.'

Solution: Obviously if there is a captive audience listening to every whimper there will be a Royal Command Performance inside. Put him in the room, close the door, go away quickly.

Sometimes parents complain that their very young children lie against the door and kick. Generally they only do this if you are within earshot and anyway, if a bit of paint is displaced, this is always easier to repair than a parent's shattered nerves.

Wrecking the room: Many parents tell me that they cannot put their child in his room because he is liable to wreck it. In fact most are speculating that this will happen and it is extremely unlikely that they have put it to the test. Over the years I have seen very few children do this when their parents act as though they are in charge.

When a child shares a bedroom with a brother or sister, parents may find it hard to relax, fearing that the angry, attention-seeking toddler will reorganise the other child's property.

The little madam was taken aback as she was sure this would have scored a direct hit on mum's rawest of raw nerves. As she sensed a change in the balance of power, she was extremely careful to avoid any tantrums for the rest of the day.

Now when bedtime arrived she was sent in to get her pyjamas but returned complaining that she could not find them. 'I think they may be under that pile of clothes,' said mum helpfully. The toddler then asked how she was going to be able to sleep in her unmade bed. 'No problem,' said mum, plucking one blanket from over there and another from that pile in the corner and tucking them over her. The same procedure was followed the next morning, when the girl looked for her clean clothes. Again the untidy pile of clothes was pointed out and a message came across in the clearest of terms: wrecking one's room got no major reaction from mother but was a complete pain to the wrecker.

Solution: It is important not to have dangerous or destructive items left about. Anything that makes a mess should be put away.

When a shared bedroom is a problem it may be necessary to use another, 'neutral', room. When the captive child does wreak havoc in his own bedroom, you are left with three options: You can pretend (with great difficulty) to be completely unimpressed with what has happened and later, when the air is calm, tidy up together. Or you can pass a firm comment that you are far from happy, and then insist that he should tidy up. Finally, the wrath of God can descend on Junior and a message is firmly engraved which states that this is not acceptable behaviour. I would favour the first option.

Time Out is an extremely effective last-resort technique but it needs to be used properly, with a clear aim and insight. You hopefully won't need to use it too often but when all else has failed, know you have something to fall back on that never fails.

A bag of tricks

So there you have it. This is all you're really going to need – along with obligatory patience and sense of humour!

There is no question that the techniques in this chapter work. You now have a handful of techniques to use, from the everyday, to the ones to pull out on special occasions. In the next chapter, we'll look at the approaches to discipline that guarantee failure.

9

What *doesn't* work

By now you should have an understanding of discipline and what really works, but there is another side to the picture – the methods that just don't work. Threats, shouting and trying to negotiate with a toddler, are all common ways that parents try to discipline but they won't help your children's happiness or bring peace to your home. None is as effective as the techniques in the previous chapter and indeed often they make life worse.

Threats

Thinking back to my student days in my home town of Belfast, two things stick in my mind. I will never forget the winter rush hour with its overcrowded buses, their interiors smoky and thick with brown globules of condensation dripping from the roof. The occupants only took their pipes or cigarettes from their mouths to embark on a spasm of coughing that would have done credit to a tuberculosis ward.

Equally vivid is the memory of mothers on buses with their uncontrollable offspring. The trip from the city centre was punctuated with 'Stop that!' 'Do that again and I will smack you!' 'I am warning you!' 'I'll get the conductor to put you off!' Empty threats are a common and usually futile attempt at discipline.

On those Irish buses, the children knew their exhausted mothers were all talk and no action. They had heard the threats often before, it was all water off a duck's back, a daily ritual that stirred up the mother and did nothing for the child. When you tell a child that something is going to happen, it's important that it's carried out as promised. This consistency helps children know what is expected of them.

Standover tactics may be necessary in the realm of underworld crime, but they have little place in a household aiming for peace. **Children need to know the limits of acceptable behaviour and the consequences if they overstep the mark, but threats focus more on punishment than on teaching acceptable behaviour.** Constantly threatening your children only creates fear.

There is a difference between a warning, which lets children know what will happen, and a threat. One type of warning that good parents find useful is the 'I'll count to three' method. This only works with older toddlers and school-age children, and again you have to follow through. Continuing to count to four of five won't get you anywhere.

The wooden spoon

This form of discipline is too close to child abuse for my liking and must not even be considered. It is similar to smacking in that it can too easily escalate into something much worse. Using a wooden spoon was in vogue in the 1950s but thankfully it's no longer popular.

In Australia, the fly swatter was almost as popular as the spoon. Parents would tell me it made a most impressive swish as they waved it about but it does little other harm, unless you are a fly. However, while it may seem harmless, it is still a threat. There are so many better ways of helping behaviour without descending to this level.

Shouting

We all know that we shouldn't shout at our children, but we still do it. You don't need to be the town crier to see that a bit of volume helps grab a toddler's attention. The trouble is that shouting stirs toddlers up and often makes behaviour worse.

Young children are extremely easily wound up by noise, activity and tension in their environment. Preschool directors often tell me that their class becomes almost airborne with the noise and movement of a windy day. At home, the tenser we become and the more we shout, the worse our children behave.

More mind-boggling are the parents that ask me, 'Why does my little one shout all the time?' If they just stopped for a moment and considered when was the last time their toddler heard shouting and who was doing it, the answer would be clear. Toddlers mirror the behaviour around them, and if you shout to get their attention, this is what they'll learn.

Toddlers don't think before they open their mouths, but parents should. Communicate important messages clearly and firmly but don't get into a shouting match. **Calm is infectious and spreads to those around, so for peace in life, let us aim to keep the decibels down.**

I have to admit that there is an opposite extreme of controlled communication that makes me cringe. Some parents talk to their children with every word carefully articulated, considered and brainlessly boring. It is almost as though they are afraid to relax and act naturally for fear of dislodging a suppository.

Smacking

Australia and the UK are legislating to make smacking our own children an offence. Yet these same two countries do not mind using force against other nations instead of negotiating for peace. I would like to make it quite clear: I believe that using force against countries is wrong, and I certainly don't believe in forcing compliance on children. As parents we don't have to follow the example set by our vote-grabbing politicians.

Having said that, there are many good parents who may resort to the occasional smack. I feel that we must understand the difference between an occasional smack in a happy home environment and frequent beatings in a dysfunctional family.

We all know that children are very sensitive to the emotional happiness of their home. And it is well known that children of emotionally unhappy homes are much more frequently exposed to excessive corporal punishment, child abuse and domestic violence. There is now a proven link between excessive beating of children in one generation and pathological relationships, with abuse, in the next. I believe, however, that beating is not the cause, but rather the symptom of this, and it is the pathological relationship which goes from generation to generation in a disturbing vicious cycle.

In the big picture, while the occasional corrective smack may be pretty harmless, I am firmly anti-smacking. It is a form of discipline that doesn't work. And the danger is that the occasional can become the everyday and soon escalate out of control. The other problem with smacking is that parents start resorting to this as a form of discipline without trying other things. I can't say it too often: there are so many better, more peaceful ways.

Why smacking doesn't work

If you aren't yet convinced that smacking isn't a good form of discipline, here are a few examples of how the message gets confused for the toddler.

Parents lose the plot: Most smacks seem to descend when we parents are angry. This may make us feel better at the time, but it is often ill-aimed discipline, both badly timed and inappropriate. The problem for most of us comes about two minutes post-smack, when the child is in a flood of tears, our anger turns to guilt and then the game is lost.

Imagine the scene: You have had it up to the back teeth, but John still persists until – smack! He starts to cry; you feel bad. John knows you feel bad, so cries louder – you feel even worse. He knows how you are feeling and cries louder still, sensing that victory is within his grasp . . . you give up and John gets a cuddle. You end up teaching him that if he makes you feel guilty, he gets away with it.

The last straw smack: Most of the smacks we parents dole out are at times when we have had a gutful and can take no more.

Often the smack arrives after a long series of annoyances and is precipitated by some trivial, unimportant event which becomes the straw that breaks the parent's back. This certainly releases a lot of frustration for the parent, but it tends to confuse the child who thinks, 'What did I just do?'

There are better ways of handling situations like these than to become so worked up that we need to smack the child for a trivial misdemeanour. After all, we adults are supposed to be more intelligent and in control than the average toddler. Confusing them by exploding over a minor infringement will only cause you both stress.

Smacking back: Another occasion when smacking gets you nowhere is when the smacked child immediately smacks the parent back. The blow is returned and again the toddler reciprocates. Soon you have been drawn into a minor war that will be much harder to get out of than it was to get into.

As the battle heats up, the parent gets increasingly angry but for the toddler it becomes the greatest game for weeks. Toddlers are stubborn and have little sense. If their parents are even better endowed with these qualities, the fight can go on endlessly. Remember: you don't have to cast the last blow.

I never felt it!: Some 3- to 4-year-old toddlers have the most amazing theatrical talent. When smacked they stand stoically like Rambo under interrogation, look you straight in the eye and, with the dumbest of dumb insolence say, 'That didn't hurt!' Of course, it really did hurt, but they know that this reaction will infuriate the smacker (and besides, thinks the toddler, how dare someone lay a hand on me!).

Believe it or not, I once had a child referred to my clinic with a note saying, 'Please investigate the nerves in his legs. He appears to feel no pain!' It turned out that what was insensitive was the parents' brains!

One case for smacking? Life-threatening danger

After going into examples of all the reasons why smacking doesn't work, I want to say that there is only one possible excuse for smacking: if the child is in danger and won't listen.

I believe that smacking might possibly be a worthwhile deterrent to ensure that a dangerous life-threatening act is never repeated. Cats may have nine lives, but this does not extend to children. Children only escape once or twice when dismantling electrical appliances, playing with fire, climbing on high balconies or running across busy roads.

Motorway madness

Imagine your toddler opens his seatbelt while you're driving home on the motorway during peak hour. You have taught him the rules and he knows that you can't drive unless the seatbelt is done up. Yet on this otherwise normal day, your toddler decides to test you. He of course can't see the danger, but as a responsible parent you can. Not only will you be fined if caught by the police but in the event of an accident your toddler could be killed. So you pull over and refasten the seatbelt before driving off. But even though you give him a warning to keep it closed, he re-opens it again. After pulling over another time, you make it very clear that if the belt is undone again he will be smacked.

This sort of smacking is done out of love. We want to teach the child a lesson, and reinforce the message that what he did was dangerous. In those terrible moments when you see your child's life flash before your eyes, there doesn't seem to be anything else you can do. We feel powerless and frightened and have to do something to ensure that this doesn't happen again.

Even if a painful smack did produce minor emotional trauma, this may be a small price to pay if it prevents the major pain of injury and keeps our children alive and healthy. Smacking only ever has its place in averting danger, where our children would otherwise have been injured. Our aim is to protect our children, not harm them.

Is there a place for democracy?

With the modern move towards democracy for children reaching epidemic proportions, many of today's parents believe that every little detail of life must be explained to their toddler. While this is commendable, it often leads to trouble as egalitarian parents are unaware they are being manipulated by an infant, barely the height of their kneecaps.

An amazing amount of parental energy can be consumed each day being democratic with little children. Many of our toddlers are at this moment playing games with their unaware parents.

One of a toddler's main ploys to guarantee a constant flow of the attention they love is to ask endless questions. When you examine closer what is asked, you will find that their range is remarkably small and little interest is shown in the answers. The same question is often repeated again and again, as long as we parents rise to the bait.

All this verbal incontinence does nothing but stir the home. Asking questions should be encouraged up to a point but when this goes on and on, bearing no relationship to the quest for knowledge, parents must ask themselves, 'Is this getting us any-where or is the real reason for the exercise to stir us up?'

I believe the question 'Why' can be answered once and after this it is better to divert, become selectively deaf or pull rank and say 'Because I say so!' Educate and listen to little people but when the sole object of the exercise is to wind you up – drop democracy.

Because I say so!

Take for example the case of an acrobatic toddler who bounces up and down on your new coffee table. You communicate clearly and convincingly that he must get off but he immediately asks, 'Why?'

If you are more into democracy than preservation of property, it is all too easy to embark on a long dissertation concerning the lack of strength of modern chipboard furniture, or possibly mention Mrs Smith who lives in the unit downstairs, outlining the characteristics of her nervous disorder that account for her intolerance for loud overhead noise and her sensitivity to large sections of plaster landing from the ceiling onto her lounge room carpet. All this will avail you naught, when the sole object of the question was to hijack your attention.

Negotiated settlement

The technique of negotiated settlement is common in sorting out industrial disputes when the union members may agree to build an extra car a day in exchange for say, longer coffee breaks, and ten weeks' holiday a year. It may also be useful in dealing with school-age children, but bargaining with toddlers is usually a complete waste of time.

Despite that, I once saw a girl of 3 years whose parents were greatly upset that she still liked using a dummy during the day. Now they could have just taken it from her but instead, at their urging, we negotiated a settlement.

She was a bright little girl and clearly aware that we live in a consumer society, so the contract was drafted as follows. Her beloved dummy would be handed over in exchange for a doll she had spied at the local chemist. The doll would be used as a sweetener for giving up her dummy. With the deal struck, the family proceeded to the neighbourhood pharmacy, and with the pharmacist looking on as adjudicator, the trade took place. At this point it looked like we were on to a winner.

Everything changed with the dawn of a new day. The little lady woke up and felt that the new doll was no compensation for the surrendered dummy. The whingeing started, 'I want my dummy.' Mum and dad tried to placate her, 'But you have your lovely new dolly, you don't need a dummy.' The response was an affirmative 'I want my dummy!' An emergency trip to the chemist took place as the crying escalated in volume. Waiting for the doors of the shop to open did nothing to temper her performance. Once admitted inside, she headed straight for the rubbish bins, searched through them and abused the pharmacist when she discovered her dummy had gone for good!

Basically, negotiating with toddlers doesn't work because they have short attention spans, live only in the moment and the future is a foreign concept. It's best to leave it out.

This smacks of commonsense

Of course you know that threats don't work and smacking gets you nowhere, it's all commonsense. But when you're tired, demoralised, busy, distracted, overwhelmed or just plain fed-up, commonsense isn't very common.

Trying to get your toddler to behave using strongarm tactics is not the answer. Save your energy for the methods that work and leave those that don't in the past where they belong.

10

Tantrums and other tricks

Disciplining toddlers is a little like juggling with sticks of gelignite: you are never quite sure when things will go well and when they will blow up in your face. By the end of toddlerdom, many parents discover that they are qualified explosive experts.

There are definitely some moments of life with an erratic toddler that are more nerve-racking than others. How do we stay calm as the toddler performs theatrically on the lounge-room floor or spectacularly in the supermarket? How do we cope with a toddler who resorts to tears to get his own way? How do we deal with a toddler who turns deaf the minute we say 'No!'?

In this chapter we'll tackle those discipline situations that stump parents the most, starting with the example of toddler explosiveness that every parent knows well: the tantrum.

What is a tantrum?

Tantrums are one of the trademarks of the toddler. In the hands of a skilful toddler, the tantrum is an art form which can rival a Broadway show: every detail is designed to elicit the very best audience reaction. Once the tantrum starts, its length and intensity depends almost entirely on the sort of feedback the actor receives from the audience.

On centre stage is a wilful toddler who is being prevented from doing something that seems immensely important to him. He quickly sizes up the situation and makes instant preparation for a spectacular tantrum. First he takes a quick look over his shoulder to check that the proposed area for a crash landing is clear of hard and potentially hurtful objects. Next he takes a look at the audience, checking that they are well positioned and watching and that the lighting is adjusted to the best effect. Then quick as a flash, he is off. Crash! He hits the floor and the performance has commenced.

Tantrums start around the first birthday and are regular occurrences in the younger toddler age group. Tantrums in younger toddlers are mostly a combination of lack of sense and large amounts of frustration. They are sparky little things and very easily get wound up. In older toddlers – the 3 to 4 year olds – tantrums can be more intentional, used as a way to nettle mum and dad. While the younger ones run out of performance material quite quickly, the older toddler can perform epic-like tantrums that seem to only build in intensity. By the age of 4, however, most children have learnt that there are better ways to get what they want.

Tackling tantrums

Tantrums send parents into shock as their little one explodes with great force and very little warning. Once they have stumbled into this minefield, parents become frustrated and feel helpless at their inability to reason with the toddler and make him stop. What's worse is that tantrums often occur in public and embarrassed parents have to deal with not only their own reaction but that of the avid audience. In this setting, even the most serene and best-adjusted parents become severely stressed. Hands tremble, palms are sweaty, blood pressure surges, and they are close to having a stroke.

The treatment of the tantrum depends on the age of the child, the reason for the behaviour and where the performance is being staged. Before the second birthday when behaviour often just happens without much thought or reason, it is best to divert the toddler's attention and get through the drama as quickly as possible. It is different when you have a 3 year old who uses a tantrum to openly defy his parents' authority. This is absolutely not on and parents must stand firm, using discipline to diffuse the situation.

Not all tantrums are caused simply by a parent thwarting a wilful child mid-activity. Some come from the inner frustrations of

The tantrum-taming technique

■ A 2½-year-old music lover decides he wants to reprogram big sister's iPod. You can see this is not a good idea so you take it gently from him while explaining calmly, clearly and in three words or less why he can't have it, and place it safely on a high shelf. The toddler is not satisfied with the situation. He ignites his engines and they start to rev up in preparation for take-off.

Diversion
■ The first thing to do is divert his attention. 'Look! Dad's home early!' you say hopefully as you point out the window. 'Oh no, it was another white Ford.' With luck, this is enough to abort the mission.
■ Diversion hasn't worked so now a tantrum is inevitable. The toddler is now revved up almost to full thrust – CRASH! – he hits the deck, arms and legs going with all the grunts, groans, hype and genuine hurt of a professional wrestler.

Ignoring
■ You should now ignore the tantrum, but this is not easy. Luckily it is sufficient to pretend to ignore.

- Stay calm, don't fuss, don't argue; just go about your business. Move away to a different room. Wash the dishes, peel the veggies, hang out the laundry or get outside for a breath of air.
- *Note: Stop and think for a moment what is going on in the mind of a tantrum-throwing toddler. Here he is, having put on his best Oscar-winning performance and in mid-act the audience has upped and walked out. If this happened, most adult actors would stop there and then, but of course they are not toddlers.*
- Now that the audience has moved away and is ignoring him, the faint-hearted toddler gives up, waves the white flag and with a sniff and sob, goes for comfort. If this happens, forgive and forget. Don't lecture but don't be over-effusive either; after all the victory is yours and the tantrum-thrower must not be given a great reward.
- Back on the loungeroom carpet, the more determined toddler is still in full flight. 'This is a bit off,' he thinks as mum exits the scene, stomping out after her and putting on twice the tantrum at her feet.

Time Out
- The volume is now rising, your shins are being kicked and you are rapidly losing your grip. Don't forget that we parents are the big people and are the ones in charge. While still on top, use Time Out.
- Lift the little one gently, without anger or hate, and put him firmly and decisively in his room. Do this with complete conviction, leaving him in no doubt that you are 100 per cent serious.
- As you leave, say very firmly in few words that he must stay there until he has calmed down, then extract yourself rapidly to a distant part of the house.

Forgive and forget
- Once he has calmed down and the storm has passed, forgive and forget. Don't point score and don't hold a grudge.
- Get him moving along to some new and interesting activity and leave the tantrum and tension in the past.

the toddler himself, who is being stirred up or is impatient with his limited capabilities. If a young one becomes frustrated and throws tantrums because he has plans and designs which are way ahead of his abilities, then it is not punishment he needs but a helping hand and comfort. Any child who is sick or in a home that is upset also needs the gentle approach.

Tackling tantrums can be tricky but isn't impossible. The box starting on p. 112 outlines my winning way for dealing with the typical toddler tantrum.

Points to remember

As with dealing with other unwanted toddler behaviour, solving tantrums is quite straightforward. The technique uses the basics of diversion, selective deafness and blindness and Time Out that you have already been introduced to in greater detail in the earlier discipline chapters.

How many of the steps you use will depend on the degree of the tantrum that is being performed – sometimes you will be able to halt the initial volcanic grumblings; at other times you will be faced with an eruption that brings everything to a halt.

One reason this technique is so powerful is that it leaves no room for escalation, which quickly turns happy homes into war zones. The toddler will soon realise that his performances no longer score good reviews from the audience and brings the season to an end.

The biggest mistake you can make is to give in to the child's manipulation and dramatic skills. You end up reinforcing the very behaviour you want to change.

The 'firm cuddle' method

Some experts view tantrums in a different light. They don't see them as symptoms of militant little people trying to challenge the umpire's carefully considered decision. They believe tantrums are a sign of children trying to find their 'inner selves'. Instead of ignoring all the flailing limbs, rolling around, stamping and wailing, they recommend that children should be held close to their parent's body until the 'inner rage' subsides.

Of course, holding your little one close has a place when they are frightened or frustrated, but in the deliberate limit-testing tantrum, it is not only useless but also potentially dangerous. Few mums who are tired, run-down and well past contemplating scientific child care are capable of staying closely locked to a wriggling, high volume, angry child. It won't take long before you have two angry parties and the last thing you want is to bind them together in the hope that one will magically calm down. In real life there is the very real danger that someone will snap.

With major tantrums, it is best to separate the warring parties so that each has a chance to cool off. Parents need to remain calm, sane and emotionally in control, and this works best with a little distance.

Public tantrums

There is a distinct type of tantrum that strikes fear in the heart of many parents – the public tantrum. Tantrums are a different matter altogether when thrown in some prominent public place. Our Achilles heel is bared, leaving us feeling exposed, vulnerable and extremely guilty. After all, we are supposed to be able to go out in public with our children and remain in charge.

When outside your home, there always seems to be crowds of onlookers, watching to see how you will extract yourself from a sticky situation. What is worse, no matter what you do, half the people who are watching will think you have got it wrong. A rare few may think, 'Oh, poor mum, I know what it's like', as you visibly deflate before their eyes. But most of your audience judges you and decides you must be a second-rate parent.

When you are confronted by a public tantrum, whatever you do, don't feel guilty about your toddler's behaviour or be fooled into thinking you are the only parent this ever happens to. Your toddler may appear the worst behaved in the shop, the mall or even the entire city but there are always many more difficult little ones, whose mothers have learnt from experience not to take them shopping. While you are being embarrassed by your toddler in

public, crowds of similar children have been left with a neighbour, in casual care, or maybe even in a heavily fortified room at grandma's place.

Attention shoppers

The threat of tantrums while out shopping are a particular torture, as you find yourself in an environment perfectly designed to bring out the worst in a difficult toddler. Tantrum throwing toddlers and shopping just don't mix. Once inside the shops, the noise and bustle stirs most children up in an instant. There are people buzzing around everywhere, so many things to look at, and around every corner you are greeted with another surprise. This is exciting stuff. Shopping also means long waits and queues.

The most obvious solution to public tantrums is to plan ahead and avoid them in the first place:

- Use grandma, a neighbour or occasional care, to allow tantrum-free shopping. With some toddlers, the only way you are going to win is to not take them with you.
- Use late night shopping (again minus the toddler) or try internet shopping with home delivery.

If the toddler must come along, there are a few things you can do to make the trip go more smoothly:

- Bring your partner on a Saturday or Sunday as a minder, entertainer and an extra pair of arms.

- Choose to shop at those times when your toddler is well-rested, happy and grizzle-free (such as after, rather than before, his nap or once he has recovered from his cold).

- Try to find a less busy time of day to shop. After-school hours may be convenient times but most supermarkets look more like playgrounds as mums descend with their hordes in tow.

- Take a different approach to the weekly supermarket ordeal and turn shopping into a learning experience. Talk to the toddler and involve him in purchasing decisions. 'Will we buy apple or orange juice?' 'Show me: which is the green one?' Harness the twin powers of attention and entertainment.

- Each child has an individual time limit for shopping and once it has expired, don't stop to chat to friends, or take hours to decide what to cook for dinner while standing in front of the meat cabinet. Every effort must be made to finish your business and get out of there with all the speed of a military withdrawal. Some aisles are more treacherous than others and should be avoided – believe it or not, you don't have to explore every aisle, so give the junk food section a miss. The checkout can't be dodged but, with the inevitable queue and the rows of sweets on display, must be classified as a danger zone.

- Set up a distraction before you get to the section of the supermarket where you know the main temptation lies. 'Look, there's a man with funny-looking hair!' is always a good ploy.

- Opt for 'Smash and Grab' shopping. The S&G shopper knows exactly what she wants to buy before leaving home. She enters the supermarket, toddler in tow, with sparks flying from the trolley wheels. She speeds round, scooping products off the shelves with direction, determination and not a shred of hesitation; then she zips through the smallest checkout queue, pays and is away before you can say 'overly inflated profit margins'. This leaves the stunned little spectator still revving up for his usual supermarket performance, but it is all too late.

Stylish performance

Sometimes, even using all your best steering-around-trouble tricks, a tantrum is unavoidable. Perhaps the toddler is tired, or just having a bad day. For that matter, you may be stressed and feeling hassled, and the toddler is sure to pick up on it and help you along. The following example is a classic checkout clash.

After an agonisingly slow wait, you and junior are finally number two in the checkout queue. The management, it seems, has taken great care to leave rows of sweet stuff beside the queue, strategically placed at toddler height.

As you wait, it is not surprising that junior grabs a Mars Bar. He may not know that it is new, improved and 15 per cent bigger but he is quite convinced that he wants it, and wants it 'Now!'

You say, 'No – put it back!' He glances at you, at your most vulnerable with arms full, purse open and surrounded by an audience holding their breath just waiting to see what will happen next.

He grizzles a bit and you repeat, 'No!' CRASH – the toddler launches into a full blown tantrum and if the other shoppers held scorecards it would rate at least 7.6 for style.

You react predictably – wishing you were anywhere else but right there. While trying to appear calm and in charge, inside you are trembling and thinking, 'Help! What do I do now?'

Believe it or not, when all seems lost, there *are* things you can do. There are a number of strategies to choose from:

- Divert the toddler's attention. Just like a tantrum at home, this is always your first plan of attack. In this case, it will have to be something more enticing than a Mars Bar.
- You can try hard to ignore the extravagant goings-on. However, it is a big ask to calmly flip through *Good Housekeeping* and pretend that you unimpressed and quite unmoved by the toddler's huffing and puffing. You will probably hear half the audience mumble, 'I wouldn't put up with behaviour like that!'
- Take charge and set some limits to bring the tantrum to a halt. Crouch down to toddler level, get eye contact and make sure you have 100 per cent of junior's attention. Then say, 'That's enough! I love you but I will NOT take any more of this behaviour.' If doing this in a cramped checkout queue is not appealing, reverse out, take your toddler to the least busy place in the shop and proceed from there.
- Cut and run. In rare cases, you may have to leave the shopping, grab the toddler and get out of there. You may come off as a wimp to your audience because you won't tough it out but there is no point letting the toddler get

hysterical if none of your tricks are working. The audience may think you've thrown in the towel but their eardrums will thank you.

- I strongly advise against giving in to blackmail and buying the coveted chocolate bar. Toddlers learn quickly and if you weaken, each visit that follows will cost you.

In my experience, most children who throw a tantrum when out do the same at home. It is sensible to focus first on solving the tantrums at home, where you have a home-ground advantage. Once these have been defeated, tackling the 'away' tantrum will be easier. Of course you could always suffer stoically, buy a rinse to hide the grey hairs and wait for age and maturity to bring about some better behaviour.

Peak hour performances

'Dr Green, what do you do with a toddler throwing a tantrum in the car in rush hour on the Sydney Harbour Bridge?' This is the sort of impossible question that exhibitionist parents ask in a crowded meeting, knowing quite well there is no easy answer.

Driving with a irritable toddler takes its toll in more ways than one. Instead of focusing on the untreatable, keep between the white lines, turn up the radio to drown out the dramatics in the backseat and marvel instead at the engineering masterpiece that is the Coathanger. This is not the time to have a tantrum of your own!

Toddler tricks

Unfortunately, once you've got tantrums under control, it's unlikely you can rest there. Toddlers are inventive and they find many ways to put your best discipline efforts to the test. Below are some of the more common questions that parents would ask me about disciplining their toddlers. Here's the real test of all that you have learned so far. Can you keep it together when the going gets tough!

He did it again

'I tell my toddler "No". He stops momentarily, then when I have turned my back, he does it again.'

It can be extremely difficult to get your message past the toddler's innate wilfulness – they can be extremely single minded when they want to be. How you handle this scenario depends very much on the age of the toddler involved. A 1½ to 2 year old is probably just being a toddler – they can't see what's important from the parents' viewpoint, often forget within minutes what they've been told and are easily distracted.

But by the age of 3 it can be less innocent, and winding you up by ignoring your requests has become one of the best sports around. Toddlers at this age will goad their parents, testing how far they can stretch the limits. It is fun and rewarding to watch us grab the bait.

- Check why you are saying 'No' in the first place. If it is to stop the toddler hurting himself or causing damage, fair enough. If it is because he is getting on your nerves as he tries like mad to get your attention, then give him what he really needs.
- With the younger toddler, ask yourself if it is really important before making your next move. Are you prepared to let it go, saying to yourself: 'This is a toddler being a toddler'?
- If it is really important for him to stop what he's doing, you have to gain the toddler's attention, and be convincing. Make eye contact and transmit a clear, concise instruction.
- Don't make a fuss or you'll reward the wrong behaviour.
- Steer clear of overkill. Don't nag, otherwise nagging will always be needed to get action.
- Diversion is one way out of a stalemate, so move him on to something else and keep little bodies busy.
- If the scene deteriorates into a complete no-win situation, then use Time Out.

If you set clear limits, with consistent discipline, the toddler will learn what is allowed. If they are winding you up, it is important to send a message to the toddler that you are in charge and won't play these sorts of games.

Hear's the answer

One of the most common complaints I hear from parents is, 'When I ask him to do something, he doesn't seem to hear. Could he be deaf, Dr Green?' Well, if he is deaf he seems to be able to become 'undeaf' again with ease. Though he doesn't hear what is being asked, he has no difficulty picking up the hiss of an opening soft drink bottle at one hundred paces. This is not the case of him needing a hearing aid – and he most certainly doesn't need lemonade either!

Selfish and unsharing

'My two year old screams and pushes if any visiting child dares touch his toys.'
Parents get upset when their toddler won't 'play nicely' with other children. They worry that not sharing is a sign that their toddler will grow up to be selfish, rude and antisocial. While toddlers are very talented in many ways, sharing isn't one of them. Young toddlers are not heavily endowed when it comes to socialisation and they react badly when someone takes what is theirs.

- Don't make the mistake of having too high expectations of your toddler for this stage of development. Be more reasonable and allow him to be a toddler.
- Mention sharing when he plays with other children and make an effort to do this every time. Let the toddler know that sharing is something you would like him to do but don't force the issue.
- Notice and praise any sharing that does take place. When the behaviour we want does happen, rewarding it is a powerful reinforcement.
- When a squabble breaks out, very quickly divert the attention of *both* toddlers involved. Make them a better offer than the toy in contest – put on a *Tweenies* DVD or offer them a healthy snack.

Unless there is a repeated heavy assault on the visitor, Time Out is not appropriate here. Time and maturity will bring about a more considerate, egalitarian approach.

Turns on the tears

'Every time I discipline my toddler, she bursts into a flood of tears.'

You don't have to be making a lot of noise for some toddlers to turn into sprinklers whenever you show your displeasure. This is a common situation where discipline backfires leaving parents feeling confused and guilty.

I'm aware there are a few children who are truly sensitive and must be treated with gentle discipline. Others are little Mata Haris who use their seductive talents for reasons of subversion. They know they have a losing hand but use tears to trump their parents.

- With genuinely sensitive children, go gently. Let them know what you expect in the most compassionate way, while still setting limits. This doesn't mean no discipline, only that you need to take into account their uniqueness. Sensitive children are usually more attuned to what is happening in their environment and you can use this to your advantage – they will gain more from soft rewards like praise, and also sense very quickly your displeasure. We tend to think of being sensitive as a bad thing but I think the world would be a much better place with a few more feeling people in it.
- Check how you're delivering your message – every parent raises their voice from time to time but shouting, as we've seen, only frightens children instead of encouraging them to your way of thinking. Get down to her level, make eye contact and tell her what's required in a positive, determined tone.
- Open your eyes and check that the toddler isn't just trying it on. If you discover a pattern of major manipulation, using tears to get what she wants, you have to stand your ground. Show that you're unimpressed with the flood and wait for the deluge to pass. If she sees that this behaviour gets her nowhere, she will quickly stop.
- Tread carefully in times of separation, family stress, or if the toddler is out of her comfort zone. In times like these you need to give the toddler a little latitude. Set your sights lower.

Where parents go so wrong with this scenario is when they see the tears and let all their good discipline fly out the window. If the tears are more crocodile than genuine, all your good work is undone if you comfort the child. On close inspection, most parents can tell the difference between real and pretend tears.

Ban all pokies

Some toddlers play their parents like poker machines – as long as there is a pay-off or even a hope they might score the jackpot, they continue to play. They figure the next win, mum or dad's attention, is just around the corner.

If the parents can rig the odds so the toddlers never win, they may crank away all they like but they'll never hit the jackpot. By being firm and not being swayed as they push your buttons, the house is a sure winner. It won't take long for even a 2 year old to see that it is time to fold.

Barefoot in the park

'Our 2½ year old grizzles, kicks and complains when putting on her shoes to go out.'

Some toddlers are budding Imelda Marcoses but there are a few to whom shoes are more of a chore than a necessity. If your little one has decided that shoes aren't important right now, no amount of coaxing or reasoning will change her mind.

There are times when refusing to co-operate becomes a game to the toddler, as last time she got a rise out of her mum or dad. It may not be as much fun as being read to or cuddled, but at these moments she still has 100 per cent of your attention. The trouble comes when you have a different agenda and don't want to play.

- Be organised so you can get the task over quickly. Don't spend precious minutes searching for socks that match or the left shoe in the pair. Remember your aim of getting little feet shod and out the door.
- Move gently but with single-minded determination – transmit clearly what is going to happen: 'OK Sophie, we're putting on shoes and picking up Sam from school.' Be decisive, produce her shoes and put them on.
- Don't get into arguments or debates, allowing your blood

pressure to climb and your patience and confidence to plummet. If mum or dad show they are getting frustrated, upset or angry, the toddler will latch onto the stalling technique.

■ If it all gets too hard and you don't have time for drama, act like Cinderella and leave the toddler barefoot for now. Take the shoes with you, and put them on later when the diversions of the big wide world have captured her attention.

Remember that toddlers don't view time in the same way as you or I – they are innocent of the adult notion of being on time. The toddler isn't trying to stall you in order to make you late. It is your rush and the toddler doesn't share the need to be somewhere else immediately.

When ignoring is impossible

'You tell us to ignore undesirable behaviour but I can't ignore him when he is fiddling with the TV or stereo.'
There are some behaviours that you just can't ignore, and I wouldn't expect you to. No one wants to find a piece of toast where their DVD should go. Often this fiddling is just natural curiosity – toddlers see adults adjust their electronics and as apprentices to the big people, copy what they see. Most warranties don't cover 'toddler damage' – for obvious reasons – so in order to protect your property, you need more strategies than just ignoring.

■ The best way to prevent breakages is to keep vulnerable valuables secure and out of reach. The biggest difficulty here is that most entertainment equipment works best at toddler height.

■ With older toddlers, those 3 to 4 years old, let them know what you expect. Explain that touching dad's DVD is not allowed.

■ For a younger toddler this is unlikely to work and a little creative thinking is your best bet. Use a playpen but put the DVD – not the toddler – inside, as a palisade to protect your property.

■ Diversion works to avoid damage and to take the toddler's focus away from your brand new hi fi.

- Where touching is obviously being done as a deliberate attempt to defy your authority, you may have to use Time Out as the bottom line.

Toddlers are fiddlers and it is unfortunate that their fingers are drawn like magnets to those items we least want them to touch. Ignoring is designed for those behaviours that really don't matter, like playing in the dirt. It is not intended for when their activity may damage something or themselves.

Divide and conquer

'When I say "no", he goes to his father hoping to be told "yes".' Every toddler will have a go at this behaviour at some stage. Limit-testing is quite normal and no problem if both parents stick to the same rules of discipline. Toddlers sound out their territory to see how much convincing each parent will take before they capitulate. Over time they may learn that one parent is a softie who will cave in and say yes in the face of their appeals. All it really takes is one surrender and a lot of good discipline goes out the window.

- If the toddler gets wind of a split in the leadership, he will home in on this and prise it wide apart. Like political parties close to election time, there is room for different opinions in private but the public profile must always be one of complete unity.

- Formulate a solid game plan and make sure both you and your partner are on the same team. If some adjustments are necessary, regroup and refocus; don't let the side down.
- The toddler is happiest when he knows where he stands so make sure that the rules are consistent. Don't be afraid to enforce your limits.

If mother and father are united, no toddler will bother to play this game for long. Remember, united we stand, divided we fall.

Non-problems need no discipline

As I have talked to parents over the years, many of the questions they asked me turned out to be non-problems. Mostly they were about toddler behaviours that were so usual, parents needn't worry about them. There are enough real worries in the world without getting ourselves twisted up over these sorts of things. Here follows a list of quick questions, most of which are best answered with understanding, not discipline:

'My toddler won't say please or goodbye and cringes when kissed by grandma.'
That all sounds pretty normal; they are a bit young to understand the need for these adult utterances, and kissing probably spreads germs anyway.

'When my husband comes home tired my 2 year old won't let him watch the evening news in peace.'
Why should he? Toddlers see the affairs of the family as more important than the affairs of the world. What's more, they are right.

'When visitors come I cannot get my child to go to bed.'
This seems very reasonable. When there is so much excitement around, they want to be part of it. A later bedtime once in a while or a babysitter will do the trick.

'My 3 year old is not as tidy as his twin brother.'
Even twins have differences, so don't compare children. If they were all the same, life would certainly be pretty boring. And who ever heard of a tidy 3 year old?

'How do I take comforters and cuddly toys from my toddler?'
Why should you take comfort from a toddler? There are a number of parents, members of the 'toughen-up brigade', who move to prise thumbs, pacifiers, cuddly toys and comforters away from children at the youngest age to 'strengthen their character' and promote independence. We all need our comforters; why rush children and rob them of their childhood?

'At the end of each meal my toddler throws food on the floor.'
The key word here is end. This is toddler semaphore-speak for 'I've had enough, I'm full, now let me down from here!' The toddler is sending you a clear message but you have to receive it. If you can't interpret this behaviour for what it is, you deserve every aerial food drop you get.

'On a wet, miserable day my toddler's behaviour is unbearable.'
Active little children cooped up with tense parents in bad weather are notoriously hard to manage. Crank up the entertainment, and when it gets too difficult, defy the weather and get outside.

Just because you now know how to discipline effectively doesn't mean that every problem you face needs discipline. Sometimes all it takes is being more sensible. As I've said before, a vast majority of problems could be averted if parents held more reasonable expectations of their little ones.

A tricky business

Well, that's it. You've made it through some of the worst behaviour tricks that a toddler can throw at you and you've survived. Hopefully you will see that even the most challenging toddler behaviour is surmountable. Of course I can't guarantee that your toddler will never have another tantrum ever again, but at least now you know how to keep your cool when one strikes.

Being prepared is a good motto for parents as well as Boy Scouts. Discipline is such an essential part of the business of parenting that we have to make sure we are ready with a range of techniques for all occasions.

11
Making life easier for yourself

Our children's behaviour depends on two competing factors: their God-given temperament and the environment they inhabit. While we are stuck with their temperament, environment is something we can always modify as we try to handle day-to-day situations better.

Many parents seem hell-bent on making their lives as difficult as possible. I can't believe that there are that many masochists in the world, but I'm happy to leave them to their deviations. There has to be a less painful way.

This chapter is an analgesic for the everyday headaches most parents face. It is about toddlerproofing your home and above all, ensuring your expectations of parenting are sensible. There are some extremely simple ideas, which we can all use to make life more comfortable.

Sensible expectations

I believe that most of the major problems we experience would never surface if we had more sensible expectations of our children. As I've said before, no 2 year old is going to think or behave like an adult. As you'll read in this book over and over again, toddlers have no sense.

We have already discussed toddler behaviour and by now you should be an expert in what is normal. The main trick to making life easier for yourself is to readjust your approach to everyday situations. **Decide what's important and what isn't, and then quietly smile and think 'He's just behaving like a toddler'.**

Some of the more common areas of conflict are mentioned below. If you have realistic views about what happens in toddlerdom, your daily frustration levels will plummet and you will be able to see toddler antics, which really are quite funny when you stand back, for what they really are.

Life is messy

Toddlers by nature are noisy, dirty and messy. Not only that but they are also impulsive and accident-prone. If allowed to pour their own drinks, a good proportion of it will inevitably land on the floor. In wet weather, mud and dirt walk into the house with your toddler, and they are rotten judges of the dirt-resisting properties of your best quality Berber carpet.

They have absolutely no sense of the adult monetary system and our strange values, failing to realise the difference between breaking a jam jar and a priceless Waterford crystal vase. Animals they fondly cuddle yelp for release and ornaments they handle in genuine interest seemingly disintegrate in their fingers.

Solution: Toddlers aren't malicious, they are merely un-thinking. If you leave anything of value within their reach, you have only yourself to blame if it is broken. Hopefully, they will improve with age, but in the meantime, it's wise to toddlerproof your home.

Give them a break

If you give a toddler an expensive toy, there is a sporting chance that it will be broken before the sun sets. Toys do get damaged and it is useless to blame the toddler; it is probably you who should be reprimanded for spending too much money in the first place or not buying Made in the UK!

Solution: Little children manage fine without the latest toy with the most bells and whistles. And little children do not need expensive, easily broken toys either. They have such an imagination that an old cardboard box or the tube from the middle of a toilet roll can give hours more creative fun. And all the toys in the world won't compensate for someone to play with.

Happy hour

By evening, the toddler is bored with the parent who has remained at home. As he hears the other parent's (usually dad's) key turn in the lock, he happily comes to life with renewed energy, the stereotypical second wind. The returning parent is viewed as an exciting new entertainment-giver and the toddler eagerly looks forward to happy hour.

Dad is tired after a long working day and all he wants to do is sit down, put his feet up and watch the evening news. But the toddler has little respect for the parent's needs, he is raring to go and would rather play than sit and have a quiet catch-up.

Solution: Tired though you may be, you must try to see it from the toddler's point of view. Accept that relaxation time will be delayed until the toddler gets his dose of attention and fun. The child will expect it and is unlikely to accept rejection without a fight. Your toddler isn't greedy and only wants half an hour of your attention and time. You'll be just as tired whether you give in or fight it!

Honest to goodness

Children of this age have not yet developed the quality of 'social dishonesty' which is expected of any of us who wish to succeed in the grown-up world. Toddlers are not backward in pointing out different skin colours and people's disabilities, as well as informing complete strangers of their disastrous hairstyles or ugly features. When out visiting, if the cooking tastes rotten, the toddler will not beat about the bush. Instead of using the 'white lies' of an adult, he will say 'Yuk!' plainly for all to hear.

Solution: Whether we should change the toddler's honesty or the adult's dishonesty is an interesting philosophical point that we will not argue here.

Accept the inevitable

Some things happen, to both us and our children, that are just inevitable. They are going to occur whether we burn ourselves out with worry and tension, or lie back and adopt the philosophical approach of an Indian guru. **Part of having sensible expectations is not getting yourself worked up about things that are out of your control.**

A perfect example of this wisdom was taught to me by my wife. When little ones are sick, they usually wake many times during a night, whether we accept it as inevitable, or fight it. The wise approach is to salvage what sleep you can with thanks; the foolish approach is to so resent the situation that when at last your head hits the pillow, you find you are too keyed up to sleep anyway. As my wife pointed out with our two boys, we were in for sleepless nights anyway, so we might as well embrace it.

In child rearing it is fairly challenging to view life from a calm plane of philosophy but on the other hand, beating your head against a brick wall is a futile exercise. For parents, the calm approach is not gained by sitting cross-legged, chanting mantras and chewing vegetarian delicacies. We don't need to join an ashram to take a leaf out of the gurus' books. All we need is to stop blowing our tops and start using our brains. Taking the path of least resistance is the real key to a peaceful life!

Don't overdo it

Activity is contagious and winds up all those around. Toddlers love rough play and get very excited when springing around with a parent. A child who comes straight from frantic horseplay to the dinner table will not display the manners taught at finishing school. Similarly any child who is overexcited and over-exercised just before bedtime is unlikely to calmly fall asleep.

Likewise, children's parties are dynamite to the active youngster.

Parents assure me that this is due to the soft drink, chocolate and sugar in the birthday diet, but their bounce comes from being so close to activity, not food. Their behaviour would be just as over-the-top even if all they got was preservative-free rice crackers and pure spring water.

Toddlers will also become greatly stirred up in a noisy situation. Loud music is known to make spotty teenagers want to dance, and a mere fanfare of trumpets can move great armies to march off and fight. **It is hard to discipline the young in a home where the television set of life is going full blast.**

If you spend time stirring them up, you must also allow for time to let them unwind. Don't 'hype up' little children. Calm and peace are highly infectious qualities. Toddlers think and behave best when volumes are low and there is little distraction around.

Avoid no-win situations

If you seek a peaceful existence, it is wise to reserve time and energy for the worthwhile causes and avoid at all costs those that cannot be won. The clever parent is quick to spot when they are on a losing wicket and extract themselves gracefully.

The main no-win areas involve feeding, toileting and sleep. We also find ourselves losing ground when time is limited, the venue is very public or there are too many interfering adults around. You can't make a toddler do something he doesn't want to do.

Feeding: I am sure there is a Nobel Prize awaiting the person who discovers the switch that makes the reluctant toddler eat. It is easy to sit a child at the table and place food in front of him. What is difficult is to get him to eat it if he has decided it is not going to happen. You can't avoid mealtimes, but you can avoid them becoming battles.

While fighting over food entertains children, it ages their parents. Remember that no toddler has ever starved to death through stubbornness.

Toileting: You can take your child to the toilet, you can encourage him to sit there, but no amount of parental jumping up and down will make something drop out if junior has decided it is not going to happen. This is yet another case when you must accept that he may be small but he has the ultimate veto.

Sleep: In exactly the same way as you can lead the proverbial horse to water but cannot make it drink, parents can put a child to bed but there is no way to make him go to sleep. The little rascal can generate unbelievable powers of wakefulness when required.

Parents can put them in their beds, keep them in their bedrooms, but have to accept that they cannot make them go unconscious. Firing tranquillising darts through the keyhole, while tempting, is most certainly not an option.

Special occasions: We parents have to be sensible. Sometimes our children chuck a boulder before us as we go down the highway of life and when this happens, it is easier to steer around it than hit it head on and cause a major confrontation.

When toddlers are out of their comfort zone or feeling below par, such as when they are in a strange environment or are sick, large rocks will crop up with alarming regularity. These are the times when we don't push our luck. We accept that the toddler is stirred up and will not behave as a model citizen.

Time waits for no toddler

It's a hot summer day and your 2½ year old is splashing around naked in the backyard paddling pool. In exactly ten minutes you need to have him dressed, in the car and up at the school to collect his big sister. He's having a lot of fun and has no idea or need for deadlines; you need to get him dried off and clothed in something other than his birthday suit! At times like this you ask yourself, 'Is it worthwhile?' You could be bloody-minded, but it's all a bit too hot and humid for that.

Why not forget the clothes and put one naked toddler wrapped in a towel in his car seat? There are times when confronting the toddler is just not worth the trouble.

Toddlerproofing your home

Life with a toddler can be made so much easier if you live in a suitably fortified home. Toddlerproofing becomes a necessity just after the first birthday, when the toddler is becoming extremely inquisitive and much more mobile, but still has zero sense. The aim of toddlerproofing is to give you peace of mind. Rather than constantly wondering, 'Where has he got to now? What's that noise? Why can't I find the car keys?' (although we can't always blame that last one on the toddler!), you can instead relax and enjoy the time you spend together at home.

I have seen some parents take toddlerproofing so seriously that they crawled around the house on their hands and knees, performing a troubleshooting survey from toddler level. You don't have to go to this extreme, but a few simple changes will pay huge dividends. However you do it, toddlerproofing is a lifesaver.

Safety first

When you are only knee- to waist-high, a different world of dangers opens up before you. The big people aren't named so for nothing. The front door handle, bench tops and microwave ovens are all a mile away, but down here, the electricity sockets, the cat flap and the dog are all within a hand's (and mouth's) reach.

- Think about danger from toddler level: take a look around your home and assess where the danger lies.
- Block glass doors or windows that come down to floor level with furniture; fit temporary bars across windows; and use safety glass where possible.
- Safety plugs should be fitted over power points as young children have the sort of fascination with electricity that a fly has with a zapper. It is essential to have a commercial circuit-breaker fitted to your junction box, and then at least you can rest safe in the knowledge that if the toddler does poke a knife into the toaster, he should survive to poke another day.
- Furniture and household items with sharp edges, like the coffee table, need 'buffering'. Tape can be put on the edges and corner protectors can be purchased to dull the sharp points. Items that can't be toddlerproofed are best removed altogether.

■ It is a common mistake for people who are very conscientious about storing medicines safely, to leave even more dangerous products within easy reach in the kitchen, laundry or garden shed. Common offenders such as bleach, rat poisons, weed killers and drain cleaner must be locked away out of the toddler's reach. But don't forget the everyday items such as dishwashing detergents and oven cleaner which must also be stored safely at adult only height.

All over Red Rover

Pets and toddlers generally mix well but there is no place in the same household for a child and a savage dog that bites when teased, however important his role as a guard dog may seem. Such animals should be sent back to the jungle where they belong.

Fiddly fingers

We love to display our prize possessions, and it comes as a rude shock when a little terror bursts on the scene and starts fingering the ornaments and taking the house apart. With the onset of toddler-dom, a major rethink of where we keep our valuables is called for.

Some stubborn parents adopt the attitude that 'We were here first and he will have to live here on our terms'. You can leave those tempting trinkets lying around and hope he will eventually learn not to touch them, but it is rarely worth the hassle. If you try saying, 'No!' and diverting the toddler's attention every time he goes near your Waterford crystal, generally all you will gain is a few grey hairs.

■ To prevent breakages, where possible keep fragile valuables well out of reach.
■ Sensible parents keep temptation out of the way, gradually reintroducing valuable or breakable objects several years down the track.
■ Make sure you place clear limits on what's OK to touch and what's not. Early on, nearly everything is out of bounds, but as they get older you can let them have access to more and more adult items, such as the TV.

Locks and latches

If you have an inquisitive, fast-moving toddler, childproofing is not just advisable, it is a necessity. You cannot be expected to fortify the entire home like a suburban Fort Knox but a few modifications are well worth the effort. Locks on cupboards and latches on doors keeps the toddler out and your stuff in.

■ Some cupboards and drawers need to be latched and out of bounds, while others can be open to play in and explore. So if you're worried your mother-in-law's teaspoon collection will be flushed down the toilet – put a latch on the cutlery drawer.

■ Cupboards containing pots and pans are safer and always popular with toddlers, while those holding your best china need to be safeguarded with inch-thick reinforced steel and Enigma-code locks.

■ If you have good furniture in a room with a snow-white carpet, it is surely best to declare this a toddler-free zone.

■ An inexpensive way to prevent little fingers getting into cupboards and drawers is to buy one of those rolls of wide, super-sticky tradesman's tape. A short length stuck across a drawer or cupboard dissuades all but the most determined toddler, yet it can be easily peeled back for adult access. As the stickiness wears out, new pieces can be cut and applied. One roll should be enough, as the aim is that by the time you get to the end, your toddler's sense will have arrived.

Get creative

Never a week goes by without a brilliant mother telling me of a toddlerproofing technique she has invented. Other parents seem apathetic and helpless, as they sit there and tell me, 'It is impossible to lock the door' or, 'It is impossible to keep the gate shut' or, 'It is impossible to stop a 2 year old drawing on the walls'.

This is ridiculous. Astronauts can be blasted from the Earth to fly for weeks through space before landing back where they started so it seems unbelievable that in this super-scientific world, an intelligent adult cannot devise some method to prevent a 2-year-old child from opening a door. We do not need the high technology of computers, space suits and rocket fuel; a latch, a piece of tape, or a length of string can all produce dramatic results.

Immobilise the fridge

The fridge is a wondrous place as far as the toddler is concerned, full of shiny, cold bottles and bright, plastic containers. Meddlesome fridge openers (but never shutters!) and their trusty pet sidekicks are the source of many a parent's frustration. 'How do I keep him from taking the lemonade from the fridge, or snacking on dad's rum and raisin chocolate?' parents ask me. When it comes to most toddlers, the easiest answer is not to keep it there.

- Little people can be kept out of the refrigerator with remarkably simple techniques. You can purchase velcro straps that keep the doors firmly shut, and can't be manipulated by little fingers. Some rope or a length of tradesman's tape may be equally effective.

Make-up and markers

Many toddlers have wonderful artistic talents, particularly when it comes to finger painting on walls, the floor or furniture. While we want to encourage budding da Vincis, repainting interiors can be costly and siblings might not be so washable.

- Lipstick, nail polish, make-up creams and the contents of mum's handbag need to be well guarded. Besides embarrassing mum by strewing the contents for public display, a toddler can produce amazing art works with all the pretty colours in her make-up bag.
- Indelible markers should be kept well out of reach. Any pen with ink that is not easily and instantly washable must be kept under the tightest security.
- When your interiors are next up for repainting, don't just consider your colour scheme, make sure you ask for paint that is 'toddler-strength': hard-wearing and washable. Stain-resistant carpets and floor coverings that can be mopped or wiped clean are other sound investments.
- If the worst happens, don't despair: technology has come a long way and there are now ways to remove even the most stubborn toddler graffiti.

Tidying up toys

Some children seem to be born tidy, while others are quite oblivious to the disaster area they inhabit. The former are easily trained to be neat, the latter will pose a problem, but there are a few simple ideas to make life easier:

- Have sensible expectations. Cleanliness and tidiness are possible but not usual in the under-3s.
- Restrict the number of toys on offer. Little children don't need an entire warehouse full of playthings. Put some away, then

rotate and reintroduce them. This will bring new interest in forgotten toys.

■ Avoid any product which comes apart into 20 pieces. If you don't, you will write off weeks of your life, looking for the lost bits.

■ Have a big plastic crate or cardboard box for toys and establish a habit of encouraging the toddler to replace toys at the end of play. Toddlers love to help and tidying toys can be turned into a game. Remember to reward their efforts with appreciation.

■ If teaching tidiness is not successful, use a technique I developed (born of frustration) with my own children. Purchase a plastic garden rake and put it to use in your lounge room, toddler's bedroom or wherever toys are littering the ground. A quick sweep allows you to clear a room in seconds, then with a burst of the vacuum it will look good as new. I must admit that I was finally sabotaged when my boys developed an interest in glass marbles. These slipped through the rake and later hit the innards of the Hoover like shrapnel!

Fortify the compound

If you have one of those quiet, angelic, predictable children or are surrounded by acres of gently rolling parkland sweeping majestically to the horizon, fortifying the perimetre of your home will all seem a bit unnecessary. But for most of you, it is essential. Coping with an active toddler is always easier if you have a secure garden. You can never relax unless there are fences and gates to prevent escape onto the road. They need the space to roam, but you need peace of mind. Of course, whenever your toddler is playing outdoors, it is essential that an adult supervises his activity or whereabouts. Particular vigilance must be paid around water or near cars, driveways or roads.

■ Where minimum security protection is required, some parents find chicken wire is an effective form of fencing. It does not create a compound as escape-proof as Colditz, but it is an affordable option. It won't win you first place in the annual garden competition, but needs must.

■ Where fencing is inadequate and roads are nearby, all doors leading from the house must be immobilised. The best methods are a high-level latches, security chains or deadlocks.

- Not only the perimeter fences of your property need to be secure, any access gates need to be fastened so that the toddler can't get out.
- Swimming pools need to be surrounded by regulation fencing and have childproof safety gates shut at all times.

Heart-stopping home truths

It is a sad but true fact that there has been an alarming increase in recent years in the number of toddlers injured in the driveway of their home, having been run over by the family car. The culprits are often large (four-wheel drive) vehicles with limited visibility of toddler-sized objects behind them.

When you get behind the wheel of a car, don't make a move until you are absolutely certain that there isn't a child in the way.

Reining in absconders

Toddlers need to be supervised closely as they have no road sense. Fortunately, most do not like to be separated from their parents and tend to stay close by. Some have no such worries, bolt at the first sign of open space and get lost with monotonous regularity. Here we go again in the supermarket as they announce, 'Will the mother of the 2 year old in the bright yellow Bob-the-Builder T-shirt please collect him immediately'.

This period of attempting to abscond is generally quite short-lived, and there are ways to escort the toddler in the big wide world safely. Handcuffs and a police escort aren't necessary but you do need to keep on your toes.

- Though I dislike the use of reins, there are some instances when they are literally lifesavers. Reins may raise some eyebrows with your friends whose perfect children stay clamped beside them every moment. They are welcome to their opinion but, for me, reins are preferable to exhausted parents worrying themselves and the local constabulary into nervous breakdowns every time they venture out.
- Parents can use a short length of rope with a boy scout

knot tied around the waist or one of those lightweight, telephone-like cords.

■ If your child pulls like a Melbourne Cup mount at the starting gate, a full heavy-duty harness will be necessary.

The playpen

The playpen seems a marvellous invention for keeping active children out of mischief. Although sound in theory, it rarely works in practice, because extremely active children need space and protest if corralled.

That doesn't mean the playpen is obsolete. Some parents tell me that they haven't relegated it to the garage or the attic, but put it to their own use. Inside the playpen they place a comfortable chair, climb in, then sit back and read a book while the toddler romps around the house.

Another unexpected use for the playpen is to put the DVD player, not the toddler, inside. It now acts as a palisade to protect your property.

When the going gets tough

Despite the best advice in the world, there comes a point when some children's behaviour becomes unbearable. This usually happens on those wet, windy days when your palace feels oppressively small. The whingeing starts and it seems to reverberate around the walls and ceilings, going right through your head and jangling your nerves. At this point discipline becomes difficult and I believe it's best to cut one's losses and run.

Take the children and head for the wide open spaces. Noisy children never seem quite so loud when their efforts are muffled by the great outdoors, and the movement of the stroller is usually very soothing to the active toddler. It's worth getting wet just for the peace of mind, so even if it's raining, don your raincoat and pram cover and get out there.

Take it easy

As a much-maligned Australian prime minister once said, 'Life wasn't meant to be easy'. But life is what you make it, and life with a toddler doesn't have to be that difficult. A little imagination and initiative can go a long way and simple toddlerproofing makes a world of difference. Without it, parents need eyes in the back of their heads. But once our home is secure we can relax.

It's insight, not eyesight that we really need. Once again, you'll see the power of having sensible expectations and not getting caught up in no-win situations. You're not a parent just for this four-year toddler term, you're in for the long haul. Take 'making your life easy' as your platform and stick to it!

12

Sleep problems solved

Sleep deprivation, as any experienced torturer will avow, is a sure method of breaking your spirit, determination and ability to think clearly. The mother who says 'He's not getting enough sleep', is in fact talking in code. What she really means is: 'Forget my toddler, *I'm* a walking zombie'.

The night-time antics are really only half the story; it is the aftershock the next day that causes the real harm. That's when a tired mum with a befuddled brain has to struggle valiantly to manage an irritable and unreasonable toddler.

Believe it or not, some parents and toddlers have no sleep problems at all. Lucky them, I hear you say. But for the rest of you who can't remember the last time you had a good night's sleep, help is only a few pages away. Using my easy techniques, you'll find that there is a light at the end of the tunnel. A good night's sleep will return to your household, and you can again enjoy the magic of toddlerdom.

The importance of a good night's sleep

I used to think that it was only parents who feel the effect of sleepless nights but I couldn't have been more wrong. After years of working with toddlers and their families, I now know the shock waves are far more wide-reaching. They impact on the mother, father, other children in the family, neighbours and, most of all, on the child himself.

The toddler

Living with a toddler who doesn't get enough sleep is an uphill battle. They are much more difficult to manage and this is one reason we take sleep problems so seriously.

There is no question that the child who sleeps all night becomes more settled and happier by day than the child who has sleep problems.

All the toddler trademarks that make them difficult to live with at the best of times are exaggerated in the sleep-deprived toddler. They are irritable and easily annoyed; their attention span, already short, is momentary; and they don't think clearly. **A typical toddler doesn't have much sense, but a toddler with no sleep is ten times worse!**

The importance of a good night's sleep in making the toddler better behaved is obvious, but there are also subtler benefits that make everybody's lives easier. One strange phenomenon that I've noticed over the years is that once the night-time sleep problem is cured, there seems to be a lengthening (or re-introduction) of the daytime nap. This is a paradox, but it suggests that more night-time sleep encourages more daytime sleep as well. It is due to the combined effect of both toddler and parent being more relaxed and calmer, thus producing a sleep-inducing environment. So few people seem to realise how the emotional stress and tension in their lives affects their wellbeing. The far-reaching benefits that come from curing toddler sleep problems are easy to justify.

The parents

Mothers who haven't had enough sleep tend to be irritable and less patient. Many get so tired that life with a toddler is seen as a penance to be endured, with little joy in the relationship. I have seen wonderful mothers in tears because they are genuinely scared they will hurt their children unless they get some sleep. Others have slipped past coping and sunk into depression.

It seems crazy that the sleepless toddler can inadvertantly be the instrument of his own downfall. Husbands and wives must have some time alone together if they are to communicate effectively and remain a strong team. If a child stays up half the night, destroying all meaningful conversation, this is almost impossible. I see husbands who spend as little time as possible in the tense atmosphere of home, working overtime not for financial gain but to escape. Others have to put up with being ousted from the marital bed to make way for a sleepless, kicking child. A sleepless toddler puts a great strain on any relationship.

Siblings

Most brothers and sisters of sleepless toddlers develop an amazing ability to snore their way through most of the night-time antics. A few are, however, sufficiently sensitive to noise and disruption to become sleep-deprived themselves. And they may cop it twice, which is most unfair: once from having their sleep disturbed and again the next day when they inevitably deal with tired, irritable parents.

Neighbours

If you live in a double-brick, detached residence set in the middle of nowhere, you can afford to ignore the neighbours. Unfortunately, most of us don't live in Ramsay Street where all is forgiven, and complaints from irate neighbours only add to parental harassment. Even worse, I have known excellent parents who have been reported to police and child welfare agencies by the do-gooders next door. It seems grossly unfair that these parents are accused of child abuse, when in fact it is the sleepless child who is abusing them.

The science of sleep

Before we look at the three main sleep problems that parents of toddlers encounter, let us start by getting the science of this straight. The first mistake that parents make is thinking that sleep is one consistent state of unconsciousness. In fact, sleep is made up of cycles. Each cycle has levels of deep, light and dream sleep punctuated with regular brief periods of waking (consciousness).

In a typical night, first we drift off to sleep, then hit the deepest plane of unconsciousness; we dream for a while, then lift to a lighter level, before coming briefly to consciousness – to stretch, turn over – then drift off again for a re-run of the cycle. The average newborn has a sleep cycle of just under 60 minutes; a toddler about 75 minutes; while we adults go about 90 minutes between awakenings. Brainwave studies (EEGs) back this up. These show a different electrical pattern for each stage of sleep.

One study of particular interest recorded children with a video camera as they slept in their own homes. Parents of the children studied believed that their little ones were sleeping soundly right through the night, but the recordings showed otherwise. It appeared that even apparently good sleepers wake a number of times to sit up, look around, play with their toys, kick off their covers, then perhaps have a quiet grizzle before slipping back to sleep.

I dream of Genie

Imagine for a moment you are 16 months of age, snug and secure in your cot. Sleeping soundly, you dream, then gradually lighten a bit, and as you come near the surface of consciousness, you stretch and grizzle. A minute later as you open your eyes, there out of the darkness a breast approaches. Not long after, feeling satisfied and comforted, you doze off again, down once more to the deep.

An hour later you come back to the surface, grizzle, open your eyes and there it is again! You have learnt that a good grizzle or grumble makes a breast appear, and now you believe in the Genie of the Lamp.

It doesn't take much for a toddler to form bad habits. Giving comfort immediately when the child stirs at night, whether breast or bottle, is one of the speediest ways to do it. A few nights of the scenario above and you have a sleep problem – and you can't wish it away.

We have to accept that all humans will wake regularly each night, but we do not have to accept that human children should disturb their parents when they do. As adults we surface regularly to hear a window rattle, notice it is still dark or that the clock says it's three in the morning. We register this, then turn over and 'Zzzzzz'; we don't kick our partner and say 'Hey, it's one minute past three. How about getting me a snack?' The same must apply to children. They can wake, grumble and make some noise but they cannot expect you to share in their nocturnal activities. What we parents do when they wake is what's important – we want to encourage them to return to sleep, rather than disturb the household.

The statistics of sleep

No two studies have ever shown exactly the same incidence of sleep problems in a population but a few figures are shown on the following page that give some insight into how other people's children behave at night.

Looking at the table, we can see that roughly a third of 1 to 4 year olds in this study woke every night and twice that many woke at least one night every week. If nothing else, results like this show us what is normal, and hopefully it is reassuring to see that you're not alone in your struggle for an unbroken night's sleep.

Another study, performed in the UK, has some interesting implications for how we deal with our wakeful toddlers. It showed that 37 per cent of 2 year olds living with their parents woke at night. By comparison, only 3.3 per cent of 2 year olds living in a residential nursery were waking. The main difference between the two groups was the lack of attention given to the second group of children. Sad as the figures are, they clearly show that the children who received attention and comfort when they woke in the night, woke more often than those who learned that no one would attend to them.

This study supports my view that the more readily available the comfort at night, the worse the sleep pattern of the child. Certainly, when the child enters a period of semi-wakefulness, he is more likely to roll over and go back to sleep if he realises from past experience that crying does not bring rapid Grade A

A profile of some sleeping habits

Problems	Percentage of age group				
	1 year	2 years	3 years	4 years	5 years
Wakes once or more every night	29	28	33	29	19
Wakes at least one night each week	57	57	66	65	61
Requires more than 30 minutes to fall asleep	26	43	61	69	66
Takes one or more 'curtain calls' before settling	14	26	42	49	50
Requests comforting object to take to bed	18	46	50	42	20
Goes to sleep with lights on	7	13	20	30	23
Has nightmares at least once every two weeks	5	9	28	39	38

attention. It is normal for children to wake briefly throughout the night but if we give them attention every time it happens, it can rapidly become a problem.

As a parent dealing with a sleepless toddler, you begin to wonder if everyone else is going through the same drama night after night. But as you can see, it is unusual to expect your little one to not wake during the night. Take heart; many have gone before you. Thousands of parents have dealt with sleep problems, major and minor, and, as you will see, it's how you respond in the wee hours of the night that makes all the difference.

What is a sleep problem?

What appears to one family to be a mammoth sleep problem may not concern the next. It's not the number of times a child wakes up at night that constitutes a problem but the effect this disturbance has on those around. So toddler wakefulness is, therefore, only really a problem if family wellbeing and happiness are compromised.

- A toddler who wakes up four or more times a night may not necessarily have the worst sleep problem. He may merely wake, cry briefly and go straight back to sleep after a reassuring pat on the back, and the parents may return to sleep within seconds.
- Another toddler may only wake once or twice in the night, but each awakening may be followed by considerable difficulties before sleep returns. By the time the parents have paced the floor and bounced the child up and down, the child may be fast asleep again but the parents are wide-awake, wound up and incapable of further sleep themselves.

Most sleep problems that toddlers have come from attention. **As you will have learnt from this book, giving toddlers your attention is vitally important, but not at three in the morning!** Children who are normally sound sleepers do wake on occasion when they are sick, teething, frightened or when home life is disrupted and of course these are not sleep problems. At times like these children need comfort and reassurance.

Green's sleep techniques

They say that necessity is the mother of invention and at the time that I developed my sleep techniques there was most certainly a need. I first became professionally interested in sleep problems in 1974 and you could now call them the specialty of the house. Back then, I could clearly see the damage that lack of sleep caused in families. My motivation for finding a solution rapidly accelerated when I scored two non-sleeping toddlers of my own!

The more I looked into the subject, the more disturbed I became at how many parents were suffering because of their little insomniacs and how hopeless most of us professionals were at offering suggestions that helped.

Back then, there were four popular ideas for treating night time wakening.

- Some suggested that you left the child to cry hysterically all night, for as long as it took until they were cured.
- Others recommended administering a strong sedative.
- 'Philosophers' believed it was a mother's duty to be up all night, every night, calming her crying child, no matter the physical or emotional cost.
- Then there was the psychodynamic view that all sleep problems were caused by separation anxiety and if parents improved their relationship with the child by day, the sleep problems would disappear.

Of these methods, the only one that worked consistently was to let the child cry for long periods. Unfortunately this also unnerved the parents; not to mention that, since the children became hysterical, it wasn't good for them either. But in the end it was this method which I modified: taking its strengths and discarding the upsetting elements, this became the foundation of my **controlled crying technique.**

When I developed the technique, it received some criticism from psychiatrists and psychologists. Many got the wrong end of the stick, believing that it would somehow harm children. Others would say 'It can't work'. When I asked them if they'd tried it, they would reply 'No, but it *can't* work, it's too simple!'

Throughout the past 30 years, many people have discovered my technique, some unaware of its origins. It has been adapted by many authors and experts and it is now a popular approach for solving sleep problems. If you're at your wits' end, this chapter just might provide the solution you've been praying for.

The theory behind controlled crying

As we have seen, humans have a sleep cycle that brings us close to waking almost every 90 minutes. All adults and most children learn to roll over and put themselves back to sleep without disturbing the household. When toddlers are comforted, fed and fussed over every time they come near the surface, the chances are that they will wake regularly to capitalise on so much good attention. When comfort is not readily available to toddlers, they generally decide it is easier to settle themselves and go back to sleep.

We also know that leaving wakeful children to cry unattended dissuades them from waking in the future. Having said this, we

Insurance pays off

The controlled crying technique is a little like a motor car insurance policy, if you will. An inclusion of an excess clause in their policy, which means they have to pay so many dollars themselves before the insurance company steps in and takes care of the remainder, discourages motorists from making trivial claims. They still have the security of a policy for major problems, but the excess makes them think twice before bothering the insurers over minor bumps and dings. As a further deterrent, the excess is often raised after the first claim.

With the controlled crying technique, the excess is five minutes of crying before attention is given. After the first claim has been made, the excess increases to seven minutes, and then nine minutes, and so on. Eventually the claimant says to himself 'I know they always pay up in the end, but it isn't worth all this effort.' The toddler learns you're not going to attend to every whimper and you won't rush in immediately. At this point, the sleep problem has been cured.

don't want to let children cry themselves to sleep as a means to solving a sleeping problem. Not only can this take three to four hours, which is cruel, but it is also certainly ineffective. After ten minutes, most children become hysterical and no longer have any idea why they are crying. They get themselves into a lather, sweat profusely, their hearts pound and they become very frightened. Fear is not a good way of teaching a child new behaviour, while few parents are insensitive enough to put up with so much upset from those they love.

Controlled crying is calculated to give the child the maximum message, while at the same time making them aware of what is going on. It refers to my method of letting children cry for a short period, before coming in to give some, but not full comfort. We then let them cry a little longer each time between visits, again giving some but not complete comfort, progressively increasing the crying time. We gradually build up the periods between attention, without letting the child become frightened and always keeping him aware of why he is crying.

Sleep problems – the main offenders

When it comes to sleep problems, there are three main strategies children use to pain their parents.

The most damaging is *middle-of-the-night wakening*, where the child cries once or many times, night after night and month after month. This can turn happy smiling parents into the 'living dead'. Then there are those who *won't settle when put down at night*. This doesn't deprive parents of sleep but it robs them of precious time alone together and slowly erodes their relationship. Lastly, there is the child who goes down all right but then in the wee small hours *wriggles his way silently into his parents' bed*. By itself this is a fairly innocent habit but as many night visitors also kick and push parents out the side, this is not much fun.

1. Repeated middle-of-the-night wakening

The night wakers I see are of two sorts: most have had a reasonable sleep pattern at some time in their lives but have now slipped from the straight and narrow; a small number have been appalling sleepers right from birth. Generally those who were good sleepers and then slipped have lost their sleep skills at a time of teething, illness or home disruption. At these times these children woke, were comforted and enjoyed the attention. They very soon realised: 'That was a bit of all right, let's keep calling for comfort!' and they continue to disturb their weary parents every night thereafter.

When children wake at night their cries are often interpreted as a sign of sickness or fear. A good rule of thumb is if the disturbed sleep has gone on for several days, it is more likely to be a bad habit, than an indication of illness. Of course you should always give the child the benefit of the doubt but if the night time wakening goes on and on, and crying continues night after night, blaming teething or sickness would stretch the limits of credibility. After all, teething continues until they turn 21!

If a child wakes once at night, gets a gentle pat or even a drink, and everybody can get straight back to sleep, then no harm is done. It is a different matter when middle-of-the-night antics drag parents out of bed over and over.

If your toddler is putting you through this scenario, let me say I know what you're going through and I can fix it. Sound simple? Well, it is. As a rule, my technique can cure almost all of those who at some stage had a reasonable sleep pattern, while the born insomniac poses a greater but not impossible challenge. All you need is resolve and a clock. The box on pp. 154–155 takes you through the Controlled Crying Technique step by step.

Points to remember

Don't attempt to use the technique during times of upset or illness. The arrival of a new baby, moving house or a family separation are all cause for disturbances in the toddler's usual sleep pattern. These sorts of situations make toddlers seek extra comfort and attention and bedtime or the middle of the night aren't excluded. Wait for things to settle down and use the sleep technique if the toddler doesn't follow suit.

Don't give in easily to grumbling or noisy crying with dry tears.

You will need to repeat this process each night until the night-time disturbances stop, which is generally only three days. With some toddlers it may take a few days longer but, once complete, you can return to peaceful, uninterrupted nights.

The controlled crying technique

- Your toddler wakes at 3 am Initially he cries gently, but this soon turns to a noisy protest.
- Leave the toddler crying for the length of time you have decided on, using these guidelines; 5 minutes is the average (10 minutes if you are tough, 2 minutes if you are delicate and 1 minute if you are very fragile). The length of time you leave the child crying depends on your tolerance and how genuinely upset they become. The aim is not to let them get hysterical or afraid.
- After the allotted time has passed, go into the toddler's room; lift, cuddle and comfort. Occasionally you can get away with patting them as they lie in their cot without picking them up, which is all the better.
- When the loud, upset crying turns to sobs and eventually sniffs, this is the signal to put him down and walk out decisively. The toddler will be taken aback that you dared to walk out. He will immediately start crying again in protest.
- Now leave him to cry 2 minutes longer than the previous

On the first night it may seem all too difficult; on the second night it may seem even worse as the toddler tests your resolve. Generally by the third night he has realised that there is a new order of business.

If after a few days it doesn't seem that you're getting anywhere, check that you're using the technique correctly. If you are, you have two choices: live with the night-time disturbances and hope that another month older will cure the problem, or combine the technique with sedation (see p. 167).

It can be helpful to get a friend to act as a 'sponsor'. As you struggle away at 2 am trying to be tough, it is a whole lot easier if you know you have to report your efforts to someone outside the combat area in the morning.

period, e.g. 7 minutes = 5 + 2 minutes (or 10 + 2 minutes, 2 + 2 minutes, 1 + 2 minutes).

- Once this time has passed, go back in to him again, lift, cuddle, talk and comfort. At the moment the crying comes under control, put him down and exit immediately.
- Once again increase the period of crying that will follow by 2 minutes. Then comfort and repeat the process, increasing the periods of the crying each time.
- Be extremely firm and continue for as long as it takes the child to stop crying and hopefully fall asleep. Once he falls asleep, get yourself back to bed and try to get some rest.
- If he wakes again, once more be completely firm. Start resolutely at the beginning again, letting him cry for the shortest amount of time and building up in increments of 2 minutes.
- Do the same tomorrow night and the night after. No matter what happens on the first night, the technique must be re-introduced the following evening to be successful.

I must stress here that as a prerequisite to any attempt at treating sleep problems, parents must be absolutely certain that they want a cure. They must be determined to see it through, and have the strength to put up with a short period of greater difficulty that usually precedes the complete cure.

This technique may seem simple but it does work. Don't be afraid of the name – when the going gets tough, this is the answer.

2. They won't go to bed at night

Over half of all toddlers will play up when it is time for bed if they know they can get away with it. Their internal clock's bedtime setting is considerably later than their parents would wish. Some are tired but still obstinately refuse to go to bed while others infuriate their parents by popping in and out of their rooms like Jack-in-the-Boxes.

Other, subtler toddlers, create a smokescreen of requests which succeed in keeping parents on the hop and gains the little one great attention. Little children who do not wish to be parted for the night from their loving parents have an immense repertoire of procrastinating techniques: 'I want a drink', 'I feel hungry', 'I want another story', 'I want to go wee-wee', 'I want you to lie beside me', 'I want a different pillow', 'I don't want a pillow at all', 'I want two pillows' and so on. This is a genuine wish to hang on to the parents' attention for as long as possible and put off having to go to sleep. While all part of the charm of these tender years, it must not be allowed to get out of hand. A little procrastination is fun but if handled badly, the situation can turn into a major case of manipulation.

One group of reluctant settlers are those who require less sleep than the textbooks tell us. These children will probably grow up to be prime ministers, leaders of industry or other irritating high-achievers. For them, no matter what we do, bedtime will not be the time we want. These toddlers need a later bedtime and when put down they must be made to stay in their room, even if not unconscious.

Finally there is the group that likes having an afternoon nap, but this recharges their batteries so thoroughly that they continue to run on full power half the night. They may need to lose their afternoon siesta, or at least have it shortened.

Refusal to retire is a much less damaging problem for parents than the antics of the middle-of-the-night waker. All this in-and-out drama is a pest but even though the parents may be irritated, at least they are not losing any sleep. Parents deserve the chance to have some time alone together, however, so their children should be expected to go to bed at a reasonable hour – a nice notion.

Some fortunate parents have the luxury of a child-free period each afternoon, followed by the same each evening. However, many of us can't have it both ways. Medical science is not sufficiently advanced to make non-sleepers take more sleep but we are in no doubt about how to put children to bed and how to keep them there. Here are the sure-fire techniques to take the spring out of your little Jack-in-the-Box.

The 'stay-put' technique

Create a good routine: Try to follow a regular routine in the lead-up to bed, then put the toddler to bed at a consistent bedtime. Where settling poses a problem, a later bedtime may be introduced on a temporary basis. Once the toddler is falling asleep every night at this later time, it is quite easy to bring bedtime forward a few minutes each night, until an acceptable time is achieved.

Calm them down: You will have little chance of a peaceful bedtime if you let the toddler get wound up and excited just before they assume the horizontal position. Don't fight, stir, run, chase or play wild games near bedtime. Olympic athletes do not finish a race and then go straight to sleep and we all need to unwind before bed. Give the toddler their bath, talk quietly with them, tuck them in, give them a cuddle and read a soothing story.

Leave decisively: Once the toddler is tucked in and story time is finished, parents must beat a hasty retreat. When it is time for them to sleep, say 'Goodnight' and leave as though you mean it. Do not rise to requests that have no purpose except procrastination, such as needing a drink, to go to the toilet, or for you to lie down with them. There must be no conflicting messages from you and no sign of weakening on your part.

If they get out of bed: If the toddler comes out of his room, you must return him at once. Be firm and don't feel guilty as you have given him your absolute best attention before bedtime. Never encourage Jack-in-the-Box behaviour. You put them back, no questions; you know you are in charge, they know where they stand.

If the toddler reappears: If despite your firmness the toddler gets out of bed again, get his other parent to put him back. This shows him that you are united in your determination for him to stay in bed.

If he returns, change tack and ignore him: After the child has risen a third time, an equally firm but different response is called for. He must be given the clear message that he is an unwelcome visitor and be completely ignored. Turn off the telly, depart to the kitchen with your partner and talk together as you do the dishes. The toddler will initially be puzzled, wondering why he is getting no attention when ten minutes ago he was the star of the show. In order to get noticed he will stage one of his finer performances. At this point don't continue ignoring him, put him straight back in his bed.

If he reappears yet again: If he emerges a fourth time, a serious challenge is being staged. You have one of two options: sit with him in his room until he falls asleep, or block all routes of escape (you can use the patent rope trick described opposite).

Sit with him until he sleeps: You can choose to sit beside the toddler's bed until they start to snooze, either as a last resort when they keep getting out of bed, or as a regular part of the bedtime routine. Sit quietly in the room either reading to yourself or just relaxing until they slip off to sleep. All you are offering is your presence, not an evening of entertainment. If they lie quietly you stay, but the moment they start questioning or climb out of bed, you must leave decisively.

Points to remember

Most bedtime problems are simply bad habits which can be avoided by creating a routine and determinedly sticking to it.

A classic case of failing to recognise when discipline has turned into a game is when parents tell me in all seriousness, 'I put my child back in bed twenty-four times last night'. You are playing with your child and only one party is appreciating it.

If you would like your toddler to be in bed at 7 pm, but he never settles before 10 pm, it is pointless trying to put him down so early. Instead, put him to bed between 9 pm and 9.30 pm, which should be late enough to give you a sporting chance of getting him off to sleep. Then use the technique above to slowly bring his bedtime forward.

If you are determined to achieve a cure for bedtime shenanigans, this can be guaranteed in under a week for at least nine out of ten toddlers. Whatever you do, have sensible expectations. This technique is not a way of making children go to sleep; it is only a means of ensuring that when you put them to bed, they stay there.

Green's patent rope trick

This is one of my better inventions, which came from the drawing board when I was trying to curb the escape-artist antics of my own two children. Before you get worried, I am not going to suggest that you tie your child to the bed, tempting though this might be on occasion. And I realise that to some, if not most, parents it's going to seem a little bit old-fashioned and a fair bit silly. But it is far better than using locks, and all that is required is a short length of strong rope. The box below details my ingenious invention.

The patent rope trick method

Take a length of rope and loop one end around the *inner* handle of the toddler's bedroom door. Attach the other end to the *outer* handle of a nearby door. Carefully adjust the rope so that when the bedroom door is pulled open, the aperture is just a little less than the diameter of the offending child's head. As all of you who have had babies know, if the head is not going to get out, nothing is. **The result is that the toddler is not locked in, they just cannot get out.**

A light should be left on in the passageway outside the bedroom, so that the child can see and hear what is going on around the house. This means that the child will not become frightened, yet at the same time he is made very aware that bed is the place he is meant to be. He may resort to crying to break your resolve but once again this ploy will fail when you use the rope trick in conjunction with the controlled crying technique.

However, before you all rush out to the nearest hardware shop, ordering up metres of rope, let me relate one cautionary and somewhat embarrassing tale. Late one evening it had become quite apparent that there was no way our active superboys were going to stay in their room, so the patent rope trick was primed and deployed.

Following this, there was a bit of gentle crying protesting dad's action, which then suddenly and dramatically increased in decibels. My wife and I knew we had to wait five minutes before we went and comforted them (it had to be true because I had read it in my book), but when we arrived we got a nasty shock.

The boys were still in their room but unfortunately I had made the rope a fraction too long and the older boy had skilfully pushed his younger brother's head into the crack in the door, where it was firmly jammed. Extraction almost needed an obstetrician with forceps.

Life is not without its troubles, even for child-care experts. Don't let this put you off, though, as this old idea of mine can work a treat!

3. The child who comes to his parents' bed each night

Most parents greatly resent intruders making a regular appearance to their bed in the small hours of the morning. Having your children in your bed each night may be a terrifically enjoyable state of affairs for those who are deep sleepers, or are lucky enough to have children who do not wriggle or kick. If everyone is happy, let them stay there until they graduate from university if you wish. In my experience, however, about 75 per cent of mothers and 95 per cent of fathers wish their bed to be a private, peaceful place.

Nocturnal wanderers tend to comprise the most active members of the child population, seemingly incapable of lying quietly in their own bed, let alone their parents'. It is almost as though they have different magnetism; while mother and father lie North/South, they are almost drawn to the East/West position, in which they can simultaneously kick one parent and poke the other.

Many mothers tolerate this intrusion but fathers, I find, are less long-suffering. The prospect of a busy day after a disturbed night's sleep will force them either to flee to the peace and comfort of the lounge room, or take up position in the child's vacated bed, probably with their legs hanging out the bottom. If you want a good method of evicting even the most determined squatter from your place of rest, see the box on the next page.

Points to remember
If all this seems too much effort, ask yourself if your little night-time visitor is really bothering you, as generally this phase won't last for long. Some parents I know put a mattress on the floor near their bed until the child grows out of the need to crawl into bed with them. This works best for older toddlers. We're not trying to create perfect toddlers and occasional visits are probably not going to cause too much trouble.

Some mothers, whether alone because their husband is away on business, or because of a marriage break-up, do not discourage their children from coming into bed with them each night as company. This is probably quite acceptable for both parties until things have settled down to normal.

A child who is sick or genuinely frightened will always have a rightful place in his parents' bed, though it is important to evict him once his health has returned.

All children are entitled to that enjoyable early morning romp in their parents' bed, just as long as the sun is up and the cock has crowed.

Crawling into the parents' bed in the middle of the night is the least sleep-depriving of the three major sleep problems of toddler-dom. However, the middle of the night is no time for playing games and it is worth being firm. The chances of a quick and permanent cure are excellent.

The intruder-proof technique

When the toddler gets into your bed: The moment the toddler crawls into your bed, he must be put back immediately in his own. On a cold night, tired parents must be strong to resist keeping the little intruder in bed, as such an action only reinforces antisocial night-time behaviour and must be discouraged. Some unwelcome little nocturnal prowlers can slip into their parents' bed with all the stealth of a cat burglar and lie there unnoticed for quite some time. If you are determined to stop this habit, I suggest putting a wedge under your bedroom door, which allows it to be opened a short distance but causes an obstruction that alerts you to the child's approach.

If the child returns: Give the child an unequivocal message, leaving him in no doubt as to what lies ahead if he is seen again. Then he is put back to bed, preferably by the parent who didn't deal with him the first time. I must admit, however, that most parents feel that this degree of civility is quite unwarranted at that time of the night! Many move straight to the next stage.

If the child returns a third time, block the exits: When the toddler is this persistent, various doors will need to be immobilised. At this point, the toddler will either realise that the game is up, or will let you know in no uncertain terms that he may be small but he can make a large amount of noise. This provides the perfect opportunity to practise the controlled crying technique.

Common questions

When talking to parents who sought my help for their toddler's sleep problems, I would often hear, 'But what about . . .' There were always a few niggling questions that needed sorting out. Here we will look at a selection of the most common.

'I have tried your controlled crying technique and it does not work.'

While this technique is simple, there are a few reasons why it may appear not to be working. When parents say controlled crying isn't working, the first thing to check is that they really want to use it. There are some parents who seek a cure to their toddler's sleep problems, but they are only interested if it involves no effort on their part. They appear to be motivated, then make innumerable excuses to ensure that any techniques fail. I must repeat that as a prerequisite to any attempt at treating sleep problems, parents must be absolutely certain they want a cure and prepared to carry out the technique.

Once this is ruled out, the most common mistake parents make is in regard to the timing of periods of crying – near enough, in this instance, is not good enough. Using the right number of minutes for each crying period is essential. Also, trying the controlled crying technique for just one night won't work – you have to resolutely dig in for at least 4 days. Don't let a difficult first night count as a failure and give up. And be aware that the situation may appear to get worse before it gets better. There is a little bit of pain involved for big rewards.

Most parents are not prepared for what these few nights will feel like and decide that sleepless nights are less painful than being tough. Nine minutes of crying from your little one can feel like hours, and it's certainly easier to be resolute at 10 pm than 3 am. But focus on the gains to get you through. When the controlled crying technique is performed properly, it is extremely rare that a cure cannot be achieved within days.

'My child wakes to grizzle, grumble and fuss but doesn't really cry.'

The controlled crying technique is only for use with those children who cry consistently to grab their parents' attention. Remember that each of us and each of our children will come to the surface repeatedly throughout the night. If they wish to grizzle and grumble at that time, that is their business and we should not interfere. Children who call out or want you to come and play at 2 am are also best ignored. Behaviour like this can be left unattended, as long as the child is neither frightened nor truly upset.

'My toddler wakes in the night, begins to cry and quickly becomes hysterical if I leave him for five minutes. Do I still use the controlled crying technique?'
Yes – but cut the periods of crying back to as little as 30 seconds. Tailor the technique to suit your toddler and yourself – you will soon discover what the right amount of time is for your unique situation.

Once a child is hysterical, being left to cry will only upset him further. Even a small amount of hysterical crying is too much in my book. When a child is genuinely upset, we treat it seriously. Give the child what he needs – comfort – and then once he is settled, start again, using very short periods of crying. Build on this and your toddler will resume a normal sleeping pattern soon enough.

'My 18 month old wakes and demands a feed. Is this necessary?'
If you are going to use the controlled crying technique, no bottles, breasts or high class comfort can be offered between dusk and dawn. Toddlers may enjoy little snacks delivered during the night but these are not necessary for their nourishment. We adults might also like our partner to get up and make us a hot drink on several occasions but we have more sense than to ask them. Drinking, nibbling and sucking may be nice for children, but they are more interested in the comfort obtained than the calories.

'What do I do? My husband works very hard by day, he needs his sleep and I cannot let our toddler cry.'
This question is less common now than when I first wrote *Toddler Taming*, when I would hear variations of this excuse almost every week. Nowadays people would be booed for implying that mothers can be up all night because what they do during the day really cannot be classified as work. Husbands were very generous as they shared at the time of conception and it seems only fair to

me that this sharing and caring attitude should continue. The controlled crying technique usually brings success within four nights and any husband genuinely interested in his family's psychological wellbeing should be helping, not hindering.

'We live with my in-laws and they refuse to let our toddler cry.'
There is no easy solution to this predicament; you are powerless in such a situation. If they are truly interested in their grandchild's welfare yet continue to obstruct your attempts to get a sound night's sleep, maybe granny and grandpa should offer to do the night shift. Better yet, give them this chapter to read!

'Our toddler shares a room with his sister and if we try your crying technique, they will both be awake all night.'
I can assure you that if you are really keen on finding a cure, then a shared room, although inconvenient, is not an impossible hurdle. It is surprising how many siblings are able to sleep through all the crying necessary in the first few nights of using the controlled crying technique. Older children who share the crying toddler's bedroom usually have a much higher tolerance for nocturnal noise than their parents! The technique can usually be used without causing any great disturbance to the other room occupants.

If this is not possible, a temporary sleeping arrangement must be organised and the other child moved to a different bedroom. If another room is not available, sleeping on the sofa or a mattress on the floor of the parents' bedroom won't hurt. The comparative quiet of the lounge room is often enough, but a trip to granny's for the week may be necessary.

Having isolated the offending party, you are now able to perform my technique without fear of interruption and within a week, two sleep-loving children can be reunited at night. All you need is one week of absolute firmness, during which most families are capable of rearranging themselves for the sake of ultimate peace.

'My toddler cries at night and if I go in immediately and insert a dummy, there is instant peace. Should I use your technique instead?'
If we were being completely 'correct', the dummy would be removed, the controlled crying technique used and the problem would be finished within a few days. Having said this, it is often easier for most of us to insert the dummy. If you are reasonably

rested and happy, then that is good enough. We don't need to bring our children up exactly by the book.

'What age should my toddler be before I try the controlled crying technique?'

Back in 1974 I only used this method on children 18 months of age and older. By 1980, I found that 10-month-old babies could be treated and in the 2000s I know that my technique is being used at the age of 6 months.

In the 1990s we ran a research project in which 140 children were treated by the controlled crying technique over a 12-month period. The results showed that over the age of 2 years, 100 per cent of our group were cured, usually within three days; between 1 and 2 years, 93 per cent were cured, usually within a week. With those children 6 months of age to 1 year, 80 per cent improved, though it often took as much as three weeks and the technique occasionally had to be combined with sedation.

There is no question that you can use the technique from 6 months of age, but you will have a much more difficult time at the younger end of the spectrum. I prefer to leave it until the child is 1 year to 18 months old, if possible. By this age, you will find that the results are miraculous and a few nights of discomfort will yield to peaceful nights of slumber.

'Is this technique effective with 3½ and 4 year olds?'

Yes, it is often so effective it seems like a latter day miracle. Children over the age of 3 are a joy to work with. Over half of those I saw were cured as they left my office without ever 'a shot being fired'. Once I had told the parents exactly what to do, I would then explain it again, this time in the child's hearing. Children at this age are compulsive stickybeaks and though they appeared somewhat bored as they played or looked out the window, they were taking it all in. When they left, they knew the score and that their parents were committed to seeing it through. When the parents rang me the next morning, most of them were amazed at what had happened. 'Dr Green, you won't believe it, he never woke last night!' Something simple yet powerful had transpired – the child knew exactly where he stood and could sense that his parents were going to see this through. The big people were in charge, and the game was up.

'Are you sure your technique does not cause some psychological damage to children?'

There are many things we have to do in paediatrics which cause considerable upset to the children in our care. We frighten them with X-rays, examinations, immunisations and hospital investigations. Then there is the pain and trauma of life-saving surgery. Whatever we do must always be a considered balance of the benefits versus any emotional upset.

I don't believe that my controlled crying technique causes upset to children but if it does, surely the amount is minimal. Balanced against this, there is no doubt that sleep deprivation can do immense harm to parents, who in turn bring stress and emotional harm to their children. I am convinced that the benefits of my technique when used correctly greatly outweigh any theoretical objections.

A quick word on sedation

Now before you get upset at the use of drugs in children, let me say straight out that I only advocate *short-term* use of sedatives for troublesome sleep problems in both adults and children. I believe they cause no harm as long they are used with sense and as a *last resort* when an unbroken night's sleep is vital for survival.

Over the years I have seen children who have never in their life slept more than 90 minutes at a time, a few times in a 24-hour period. In these exhausted families, sedation not only brings immediate relief but gives them strength to embark upon a more permanent cure using more effective methods.

Three situations in which I think the use of sedatives is justified are:

■ in conjunction with my controlled crying technique;
■ as a safety valve to use in times of crisis, when sleep is imperative to maintain sanity; and
■ to sedate the severely disabled child who is extremely irritable by day and is awake crying all night.

Prescribed in conjunction with the controlled crying technique, we can use a low dose of sedative to break a stalemate. In the middle of the night, the child is tired and all the crying has made him even more tired. Often it seems to take little more than the smell of the uncorked medicine bottle to send them to sleep. Sedation is only given after one full hour of using the controlled crying technique. With sedation you are guaranteed to get your sleep in a short while and the child still receives a very firm and consistent message before finally dropping off.

The secret with sedation is to give the right dose at the right time. Whether used in conjunction with controlled crying or as a last-ditch sanity saver, success lies in when the dose is administered. It is unrealistic to expect that a sedative given at 6 pm will miraculously ensure sleep right through until next morning. Instead, I recommend giving the drug, in its correct dose for the child's body weight, on the first occasion that he wakes in the night – for example, 11 pm. Given at this later time, the effect will extend to protect those golden hours between midnight and dawn, which is what we're really after. If the right dose is given at the right time, there will be few failures.

Beware that sedatives are not without their problems. Some children become quite hungover the next morning, while a minority may demonstrate some paradoxical effects, for example, becoming hyperactive and unreasonable. Some parents' first experience with using sedatives for their toddler is on a long-haul flight, such as Sydney to London – and they find that the toddler is higher than the aeroplane! However, judicious use of sedatives in combination with controlled crying can give us respite when nothing else can.

Sedation is rarely needed for more than three or four nights. My main concern with sedatives is that some practitioners prescribe them for long periods with no attempt to introduce a sleep programme. This application does not provide a long-term cure.

Sleep tight

We spend one-third of our lives in bed and we deserve to emerge well-rested, refreshed and recuperated. Instead, many parents have a very broken relationship with their pillow and night-time is a living nightmare. The lack of sleep caused by little insomniacs has repercussions far greater than most imagine. The damage is done not only to the exhausted parents but to the tired-out toddler as well.

Getting your toddler to sleep doesn't need to be a long-running battle. You now have the techniques to turn tormented hours into nights of peaceful slumber. Soon, you'll be looking forward to bedtime!

13

A–Z of other sleep-related problems

Toddlers have a multitude of tricks to keep us from a sound night's sleep. Inventive toddlers find new and creative ways to bring a bit of colour and excitement to our lives, just often enough to stop us sleeping on the job. The sleep-related antics in this chapter might make entertaining stories, but in the middle of the night, there's not much humour to be found.

Thankfully, there isn't a problem for every letter of the alphabet, and with some time-tested solutions, you can rest assured that by the end of the chapter, you will be able to focus on the letter all parents love the most . . . 'Zzzzzz'.

The afternoon napper

Children in the first two years of life enjoy their daytime nap – and not only the children, I might add. Mother looks forward to this time with equal glee. Unfortunately, this peaceful event disappears somewhere between the ages of 2 and 4, and every parent mourns its passing. In the final days before the changeover, parents are in a dilemma. If the child does not get an afternoon nap, he is unbearably irritable in the late afternoon but he goes to bed early and sleeps soundly. If he does sleep in the afternoon, peace is enjoyed but it is paid for when the revitalised child romps round the house until all hours of the night.

Solution: There is, I'm sorry to say, no easy answer to this problem. Parents simply have to make a choice. I favour sacrificing the already waning afternoon nap, believing a good night-sleeping pattern to be more important. To achieve this, the toddler needs to be entertained. Mums and dads may go round the bend with daily reruns of Bananas in Pyjamas, but an over-ripe brain is surely a small price to pay for a reasonable bedtime.

The cot escaper

Some children never consider climbing out of their cots at all and would probably remain there happily until school age whereas others have developed strong mountaineering skills long before they reach their first birthday. They lie quietly in their cots for months, planning their escape route down to the final detail.

From the time of the first escape attempt, parents are usually terrified that the toddler will fall and hurt himself. The initial descent usually ends in a bump, as he finds the climb up considerably easier to control than the journey down the other side.

Solution: Once the alpinist begins, parents have to decide whether to leave the side of the cot down or put the toddler in a bed, both of which allow easy escape and will probably lead to night-time excursions to base camp in mum and dad's room. If they leave him in the cot, it should be situated against two walls and away from windows with a soft floor-covering under the exposed side. In my experience most young children who have a tumble from their cots usually have the sense to postpone further attempts until they have become sufficiently mature to guarantee a safe landing.

Parents often ask at what age the toddler should be moved from a cot to a proper bed. This often happens precipitantly when a new baby arrives, but on other occasions it is a well-planned move. If the child has a good sleeping pattern, little harm will come from the change. The trouble comes with the child who sleeps poorly in his cot and parents misguidedly think that the move to a bed will help. All this does is transfer the bad sleeper from one mattress to another with no attendant benefit. I am all in favour of toddlers remaining in their cots at least until well into their second year. There seem to be few advantages in an early release programme.

The early riser

Some children love to sleep late while others are up and on the go from the first chirp of the dawn chorus. They want to get up, move, be fed, and share the full beauty of the sunrise with their parents. Once again, this tends to be the prerogative of those over-active members of the toddler population. Just as some adults are 'morning people' or 'night owls', your toddler may have a preference for the wee hours of the night or the morning.

Solution: In theory, a later bedtime should cure the habit, but I find that the only effect is to turn a happy early riser into a tired, irritable early riser. And cutting out the daytime sleep just leaves them hard to live with in the late afternoon.

Some toddlers may snooze through to a more reasonable hour if you install heavy curtains in their room. One approach which sounds sensible but rarely works is to ensure that the room and cot are filled with quiet toys, which will let them entertain themselves and play in the early morning.

When the early morning habit becomes a major hassle, the controlled crying technique can be extremely effective, but it often leaves you in the ridiculous situation of soothing a child off to sleep just in time to wake the rest of the family up for the day's activities. In reality it is easier for the adults to change their sleeping pattern, going to bed earlier and waking in harmony with their youngster. I fear that with early risers the most I can offer is sympathy, not a cure.

Fears

Luckily at this age, children have very few fears that will interfere with your attempts to settle them at night. The main fear that raises its head at bedtime is separation anxiety. Even the most secure children feel this uncertainty, but it will be more pronounced in toddlers that are feeling tension in their homes. Parents can unwittingly transmit the stress and turmoil of their lives onto the toddler. And in homes where there has been a split or divorce, the fear that one of their parents may disappear is all too real for the anxious child. Parting company from their parents at night must be coped with if both parents and child are to get any sleep.

Fear of separation can be disguised by the toddler as other fears. 'I'm afraid of the dark', 'There are monsters under the bed', are used at this age as a way to keep mum or dad from leaving. Just as a child who doesn't want to go to bed will use the excuse of another drink or bedtime story to procrastinate, so too can fears of beasts and monsters be interpreted as ways to keep their parents' company a little longer.

Usually these are ploys to keep you close, but we have to give the toddler the benefit of the doubt. Genuine fear of the dark is more common among older toddlers and generally not a problem for the young toddler.

Solution: When a child starts to cry at night, many parents worry that he is frightened. But when they wake once or more every night that's not fear, it's a bad habit. Most toddlers would call for their mum or dad every ten minutes if they thought it would get them the attention they crave. This repeated wakening requires the controlled crying technique, going very gently to reestablish a good sleep pattern.

Separation anxiety is something that toddlers gradually grow out of. To help with this stage, it is quite a good idea to use comfort items, such as a favourite teddy bear, a security blanket, or the don't-want-to-use-but-might-have-to dummy. A dull, low-wattage light is a small investment that will relieve a great deal of worry for those toddlers who do genuinely fear the dark. Sitting in their room until they fall asleep is another way to ease their journey to the Land of Nod.

The light sleeper

Most young children, once asleep, are dead to the world and would not wake even if set down in the middle of the 1812 Overture, cannon and all. Some, however, are uncommonly sensitive to sound, which leaves the parents tiptoeing round the house at night, frightened to run a tap or flush a toilet.

Solution: Problems with light sleepers are easily overcome. Simply place an ordinary household radio beside the child's bed. On the first night, turn the radio on with such a low volume that the sound is barely audible to all but a passing bat. Gradually increase the volume by tiny increments each night, over a period of two weeks; but always keeping the sound at a low level. The aim is to make a bit of background noise, not drown out all other sounds. At the end of this time, most children have become well and truly desensitised. From there on, they should sleep through garbage collections, car horns, the football final on television and the odd cannon.

What station should my child listen to, I hear you ask. Assess his interest. Budding merchant bankers should be tuned to the station that gives the best stock market reports, punk rockers in the making will be happy with a rock station, and a possible candidate for the clergy is probably happiest listening to hymns. Of course, I am joking; it really doesn't matter. In fact, some parents tune the radio slightly off-station, thus producing a crackle of constant, gentle 'white' noise.

The lost dummy

Some young toddlers can only survive those wakeful periods at night with their mouth firmly plugged by a dummy. If it becomes disconnected, help is summoned by loud wailing and gnashing of teeth, and the cries will only subside once the missing object is reinserted. Many parents get sick and tired of this constant midnight drama.

Solution: One way some parents deal with this is to tie a short tape onto the dummy and clip it to the child's night clothes. Unfortunately young children seem to be unable to make contact with the tape and, even if they can, find it well nigh impossible to reel it in and plug their mouths.

The only reliable cure for repeated wakening as the result of a lost dummy is to get rid of the annoying thing completely. Certainly this may lead to several difficult nights but in the long term, it is well worth the momentary inconvenience. Instead of focusing on the dummy, focus on the crying and use the controlled crying technique. Some dummy disposal suggestions are mentioned later in this book.

Night feeds

This is a problem that parents create for themselves. When their child wakes in the night, they soothe the crying with a breast- or bottle-feed. This establishes a bad pattern, encouraging the half-asleep child to cry out for comfort rather than turning over and going back to sleep.

There is a strong relationship between night wakening and night feeding. If night-time breastfeeding continues after the first birthday, there is a strong likelihood that this will be accompanied by multiple nocturnal wakenings. So great is the contentment from breastfeeding, that the child will demand the breast as an adjunct to sleep – comfort rather than sustenance is the object of the exercise.

Solution: Some mothers find night-time feeding is no major hassle. But if you want to continue breastfeeding and still get your sleep, a strict curfew must be imposed during the hours of darkness. Feeds should be given only by day, on going to bed and on wakening in the morning. Toddlers don't starve at night and, unlike babies, don't need regular night time feeds. For the sake of peace and quiet and an undisturbed sleep, all midnight snacks – be they from breast or bottle – should be discouraged.

Bottles and beakers give less comfort; when compared to a warm breast, there is minimal joy to be gained from sucking a cold rubber teat. But these should also be suspended during the hours of sleep if this problem is to be cured.

A basic law also decrees that 'what goes in, must come out'. The more fluid the child drinks, the greater the number of wet nappies, wet beds, discomfort and excursions to the toilet.

Nightmares

Nightmares are much more common at an older age, but they still can occur in toddlers. As the child wakes from active dream sleep, he may still be in the midst of some alarming escapade. He lets out an unmistakable frightened cry and is easily soothed by the rapid appearance of a parent. He quickly becomes aware that it was a dream, not a real event, and in some cases can even remember all the details.

Nightmares may occur quite regularly, and although there is some association with stress and anxiety, it is usually the sort of normal stress of life that we cannot change. The most loving, attentive parents will find that their child still has nightmares.

Solution: The treatment for nightmares is simple. Go quickly to the child, hold him, talk soothingly and stay until he slips back to sleep. Nightmares can be a nightmare for parents, as they're roused from a sound slumber just as they get to the exciting part of their dreams. But whatever you do, don't dismiss the child's behaviour or get angry. Nightmares are not a bad habit and every child needs to be comforted when they are frightened.

The 'magic side' of the pillow (i.e. the cold, unused side, which you tell the toddler is magic) works wonders at getting troubled, tired minds back off to sleep. This trick is particularly good for older toddlers around the age of 4, who are enthralled by magic, even if they are too young to enroll in Hogwarts School of Witchcraft and Wizardry.

The night prowler

Some children wake up in the middle of the night wanting something to eat or to explore the house. Others are determined to play in the small hours, which is fine so long as they are quiet and do not harm themselves or disturb the household.

But more often than not, the night prowler is less than circumspect. I was once brought a 3 year old who had discovered that getting up at 2 am and turning on the vacuum cleaner had quite an effect on his befuddled parents. Another 3 year old loved to play with his toy cars in the middle of the night. As he could not reach the light switches, he had to find an alternative source of illumination, which he achieved by setting up his collection in front of the freezer, then pulling open the door and playing by its cold, bright light. This would have been a quite innocent pastime, except that he was often overcome by sleep in mid-activity and would be found in the morning in company with piles of defrosted vegetables.

Solution: It is usually safest to deal with night prowlers by resorting to the patent rope trick (as described in Chapter 12), as well as making sure there are deadlocks on all the exterior doors. Placing wedges under other doors will limit the child's access to danger. Locking up the vacuum cleaner and a simple piece of tape over the freezer door were quick solutions for those two night owls.

Night terrors

Night terrors may upset the toddler but the real terror is for the parents, feeling so helpless in this bizarre circumstance. The child wakes from a deep, sound sleep in a state of utter terror. He sits up in bed, looking through glazed, staring eyes and cries profusely. His parents run to his aid and are confronted with a difficult situation, as the child seems almost paralysed and stuck in a different world that they cannot reach. In the morning, the child will have no memory of the previous night's events, although the parents will find it much harder to forget.

Solution: The parents always feel that they want to cuddle the child but the current thinking is to observe him and only intervene if he is likely to be hurt. Stay with him until he settles back to sleep. Providing gentle contact and letting him know 'I'm here, it's all right' is soothing. It won't snap him out if it, but it's all you can do. Your presence may not be recognised by the child, but your instinct to stay close is still spot on.

There may be repeated episodes but it is extremely rare that any treatment is required, other than letting time do the healing. As with nightmares, it is unlikely that there is any treatable anxiety-provoking event that causes night terrors, just life's normal stresses sorting themselves out.

The nocturnally deaf husband

This is a fascinating phenomenon, which I have studied assiduously for years. My observations show that when their child cries at night, most husbands appear to become suddenly stone deaf, and thus their wives are forced out of bed to cope with the problem. I don't believe this is, in any sense, true deafness, but rather a conveniently learned response to an unpleasant situation. My wife claims that, when our children cried at night, she found that my hearing could be toned up with the aid of a sharp kick. Certainly in these enlightened days, I believe there should be more sharing of the less pleasant parts of parenthood, and if kicking is what it takes, then that is as good a method as any!

The night owl

While a reasonable bedtime may be the case for the sleeping majority, a significant minority of toddlers won't settle to sleep at a sensible hour in a month of Sundays. The offenders are usually those difficult children who have been poor sleepers from birth. They are mostly active boys, which is surprising because one would expect them to need *more* sleep considering the massive amounts of energy they use up during the day.

Solution: There is no universal 'right' bedtime for all children. In my experience, 7.30 pm appears to be the accepted time that most toddlers should assume the horizontal. All we can do is understand that children, like adults, have different sleeping needs and be thankful that most toddlers are snoring by 8.00 pm. As for the late settlers, they need a later bedtime; and although they cannot be forced to sleep, there are at least ways of keeping them in their rooms, such as my patent rope trick. This must surely increase the chances of them inadvertently dozing off.

Sensitive neighbours

In these crowded days of apartment living, crying doesn't need to be in the 100 decibel range to upset the neighbours and tolerating a lot of crying by your sleepless toddler often just isn't feasible. Noise that normally wouldn't raise an eyebrow seems amplified in the still of the night and, as any parent knows, once you tune into the sound of crying, even the most powerful earplugs seem powerless to block it out.

Parents with children who sleep poorly are often sabotaged in their attempts to implement controlled crying by complaining neighbours. We're keen to keep the peace but at the same time, we need to solve our children's sleep problems.

Solution: I recommend the direct approach in these instances. Some parents, on returning home from my office, would go straight in to see the neighbours, telling them that the toddler was now in the hands of a specialist doctor from the Children's Hospital, who had designed a new treatment for sleepless kids.

They explained that this was quite revolutionary and the wacky doctor insisted that they let the child cry a number of times at night, but that the cure would come inside a week. On most occasions this super-scientific approach – blaming everything on the doctor – worked. So far I have had no reports of parents being set on by the neighbour's dog, or their tyres being deflated in the middle of the night.

While you may not have your own consultant paediatrician, you can still use a variation of this story to explain to your neighbours what's going on. Communicating is terribly important, but before you broach the subject of night-time wailings, you have to check your pitch. What may work with supportive, helpful neighbours may flop if you've scored the neighbours from hell. Being open is really your best choice – face it, the only other option is to avoid them.

Triple occupancy

Many newborn babies sleep in a cot close to their parents' bed, taking some of the effort out of the night-time feed. And some parents with older children also prefer, for a variety of reasons, to keep them close to their bed at night. This may be fine if the parents are sound sleepers and the child remains quiet as a mouse. But it may not be such a good idea for light-sleeping parents, who are stirred to consciousness every time the child coughs, turns over or passes wind.

Solution: As the saying goes, if you make your bed . . . For light-sleeping parents who value their rest, a little distance can be a good thing. Where possible, I believe that parents should have their bed in their room and the toddler a cot or bed in their own room, as unbroken sleep has great curative powers for the entire family. However, when life is stressful, such as if there is a split in the family, it can be comforting for both you and your toddler to be close. In such cases, a brief move to the same sleeping quarters may be just what the doctor ordered.

Zzzzzzzz

When sleepless nights turn into sleepless weeks and months, you could try herbal tonics, a glass of milk, singing lullabies or counting sheep to put an end to the misery. But the quickest way to lay your sleep problems to rest is to take the proven ideas in this chapter and put them into practice.

Now that you can ensure your toddler gets a good night's sleep every night, you can too. Well-rested toddlers and parents emit a glow that warms everyone they meet . . . with the possible exceptions of parking police and the tax office.

14

What should toddlers eat?

Food is the fuel that powers our young children. It helps them grow big and strong – and it gives them pleasure. Some children take their food extremely seriously, never lifting their eyes from the plate until they have almost scraped the pattern off it. Others dawdle, play and escape at the first opportunity, finding food a complete bore. Some are fussy and some are walking garbage bins.

When animals feed their young, it seems such an uncomplicated affair. Yet humans, even with all our nutritional advice, seem to find it extraordinarily difficult. We can choose the healthiest designer diet, put it on a plate, even get it into the toddler's mouth, but if they decide that's as far as it is going: checkmate – game over!

The toddler's legendary stubbornness is only part of the problem facing modern, well-intentioned parents. The overwhelming amount of often contradictory dietary information can be enough to have parents throwing in the tea towel before even one carrot is chopped. So before we look at techniques for making mealtimes less of a battle, we need to know what types of foods to serve up to our future sporting heroes and Pop Idols. This chapter is all about what toddlers should eat to be healthy and happy.

Start well, stay well

It is strange how life has changed. When I first wrote *Toddler Taming*, parents were obsessed with food intake and weight gain for their toddlers. They would come to me with the complaint, 'My child won't eat!', which usually meant the toddler wouldn't eat what grandma or mum and dad felt was an adequate meal: steak, two veg and gravy; or exotic flavours from the East. In fact, many of these hunger strikers were very well served by their preferred menu of sandwiches, milk, cheese and tinned spaghetti.

Now, the tables have turned and the worry with toddlers and food is not that they won't eat enough, but the exact opposite – many are eating way too much. **Our focus nowadays has to be not only on dealing with mealtime antics, but on establishing healthy eating habits and good nutrition.**

You may wonder why this is so important at the toddler's tender age. After all, they have plenty of time to learn good habits later. But science has discovered that it's never too early to be eating healthy foods – in fact, the earlier the better.

We are constantly reminded through the media that childhood obesity is on the rise, and you'd have to be living under a rock not to realise that we in the developed world have a problem. In some Western countries, over 50 per cent of children are clinically obese and the numbers are growing. In the future, these obese children may die younger than they should from obesity-related illnesses.

As parents we need to instil good habits as well as set a good example ourselves and where better to begin than at the start of toddlerdom, when we have complete control over the toddler's available diet. The right time to start looking after your health is at 2 years old, not at 50. So think of toddlerdom as the time to lay down strong foundations – your toddlers will thank you for it when they maintain their zip and sparkle all through their lives.

Blazing the trail of long-term health means following a few simple rules:

Start early: As already mentioned, it's never too early to start looking after our health. At their young age, if presented with healthy food, toddlers will take it for granted this is what food is all about. If this is all they know, this is what they will expect. Once you have started, keep up the good work.

It's a family affair: It is unrealistic to expect our young children to have a healthier lifestyle than the adults whose example they follow. If parents are overweight, under-exercised, chain-smoking blobs without a sniff of self-discipline, then the next generation hasn't got a hope. Healthy living, including a healthy diet and exercise, cannot be confined to the toddler alone. Children are little sponges, soaking up their surroundings, and learning from the example of their parents. Ultimately the whole family has to be involved, creating a health-focused way of life.

Balance: Our aim is to provide our toddlers with a balanced diet. This includes foods from all the major food groups, without over-doing it on any one type of food. This is the best way to ensure that they get all the nutrients they need to stay fit and healthy.

Variety: The best way to start toddlers along the path to a lifetime of health and vitality is to try to introduce them to as wide and varied a diet as possible. They need to be offered many different tastes and textures in the hope of broadening their food horizons. But be warned, some defiant toddlers will be immoveable in their desire for monotony.

Limit the 'bad' stuff: An important rule is to avoid establishing habits of eating highly-processed foods. Aside from frequently being the nutritional equivalent of a desert, they are generally too sweet, overly salty, or oozing with fat. There is nothing wrong with the occasional potato chip or chocolate as a special treat but when they form the lion's share of the diet, the toddler not only forms bad habits early on, he sets off down a path ending in obesity and a shortened life.

Food as fuel: We want to keep our toddlers active and on the go, and food is the fuel that keeps their little motors running. But many parents fall into the trap of using food for other purposes. For example, feeding their toddler a snack to alleviate boredom on a rainy day, or giving them a biscuit-shaped diversion when what they're really after is attention. Letting toddlers have unlimited access to food is another no-no, as self-control is not one of the toddler's greatest gifts.

Exercise: What we put into our bodies as fuel has to be burnt up through activity if we don't want it to be stored as fat. Generally, toddlers are naturally active and getting them to stop moving around is more of a problem than getting them started. However, we need to create a habit of daily exercise from a young age so that it is firmly entrenched by the time the child starts school. Exercise reaps even greater rewards when done as a family.

These seven simple rules are all you need to set a good example, encourage healthy habits and keep your toddler and the whole family bouncing through life.

What is a balanced diet?

Some nutritional extremists forget that food is for enjoyment, as well as nutrition, and turn it into an unhealthy obsession. The healthy diet of today is not one of 'don'ts', 'nevers' and 'definitely nots'. Our children are just as entitled as we are to have the odd moment of indulgence, as long as most of what they eat is healthy, nutritious food.

What we're concerned about today is balance. This means making sure that they don't eat too much of any one type or group of foods. It also means not leaving important foods out of their diets, while keeping an eye on worries such as too much fat, or too little calcium.

The nutrients contained in a balanced diet help the toddler's body grow. It gives both physical and mental strength and provides protection against illness and disease by strengthening the armour of the immune system. It ensures healthy hearts, strong bones and sharp brains.

Toddlers, like adults, need five different types of nutrients to thrive: protein, carbohydrate, fat, vitamins and minerals, as well as water and fibre.

Protein

Protein provides the building blocks for the toddler's growing body. It is used to make muscles, skin and all the internal organs, and is essential for healthy brains. Getting adequate protein means your toddler's immune system can fight the bugs he picks up at day care and provide his body with the materials to repair the bumps and scratches earned during playtime.

Protein is found in meat (beef, chicken, fish), eggs and dairy foods (milk, yoghurt, cheese); lesser quality vegetable proteins are found in legumes (beans, chickpeas, lentils), nuts, and grains. In our affluent country we tend to eat considerably more protein than we need. See the table opposite for sources of protein.

If your toddler is going to get his protein only from vegetable sources, you need to consult a dietitian to check that he is getting enough.

Carbohydrates

Carbohydrates provide the body with energy. There are two types of carbohydrates: the simple form such as glucose and sucrose (cane sugar); and the complex form known as starch, found in cereals, bread, pasta, vegetables and fruit.

The simple carbohydrates are very easy to eat, so it is easy to have too much. The body breaks down complex carbohydrates into simple sugars, releasing them more slowly into the bloodstream. Complex carbohydrates have much more bulk than the simple sugars, which means it is not so easy to over-indulge and thus become overweight.

Unfortunately, most of the carbohydrate we eat is often refined 'white stuff' – white sugar, white bread, white rice. To make fluffy white bread, wheat is stripped of fibre, and bleached white. During this process most essential vitamins are lost plus colours, flavours and preservatives are added. Then vitamins, along with some fibre, may be added back in! It seems an awful lot of effort

Sources of protein

Source	Protein
Chicken (½ breast, approximately 50 g)	14.0 g
Tinned salmon (50 g)	12.7 g
Milk (1 cup)	9.0 g
Peanut butter (1 tbs)	6.8 g
Baked beans (½ cup)	6.4 g
Boiled egg (60 g)	6.3 g
Yoghurt (small tub)	4.7 g
Cheddar cheese (1 slice)	4.5 g
Bread (1 slice)	3.0 g
Boiled rice, brown (½ cup)	2.5 g
Carrots (½ cup)	1.6 g
Apple (1 whole)	1.0 g

Toddlers need approximately 2 grams of protein per day for every kilo of body weight. So the average 12-kg 2 year old will cope quite well with milk on cereal for breakfast, baked beans on toast for lunch, some yoghurt or cheese as a snack and a bit of chicken for dinner. Failing that, he can always polish off two dozen apples!

to 'improve' something which ends up worse than what you had at the start.

The best way for your toddler to get his necessary complex carbohydrates is from vegetables, fruit and grains in the form of breads, pastas and cereals. Getting toddlers to eat fruit is generally no hassle and I find that most of them will eat whatever fruit is on offer. This is why I suspect parents who tell me their child won't eat fruit. Usually what they mean is that their child dislikes the stringy oranges and unripe apples on offer. Well, who wouldn't? Try them out with a wide variety of seasonal fruit and you'll soon discover what appeals. And if they won't eat it fresh, stewed is nearly as good.

Fresh fruit does contain simple sugars, but because it also has some complex carbohydrates and vitamins, it is a great way to give your toddler an instant energy boost. It is also jam-packed with fibre. However the same doesn't apply to juice. Because the fibre is usually filtered out of fruit juices, what is left is mainly simple sugars and they should be given in moderation, not drunk in unlimited quantities.

Vegetables are an important part of the toddler diet. One of the great catchphrases of parents is 'Eat your greens!', and many parents get upset when their children won't eat their vegetables. There is a myth that vegetables must be of the leafy green variety but peas, green beans and courgettes are also vegetables and toddlers generally enjoy them more. You may have to come up with ways to make vegies enticing. There are some good ideas in the next chapter.

Bread is as good a food now as it was in biblical times and along with pasta, cereal and rice is another great form of carbohydrate. Wholemeal bread and wholegrain cereals are best but again, not often a favourite with the toddler.

The Glycaemic Index (GI)

The Glycaemic Index was developed for use by diabetics, to assist them in eating in a way that maintains stable blood sugar levels. On it, foods are ranked on a scale from 0 to 100, based on how quickly and how high they raise blood sugar levels after being consumed. Only foods that contain carbohydrates are given a GI ranking.

The lower a food ranks on the GI, the slower it is absorbed and the less it raises blood sugar levels. Keeping blood sugar levels stable has been shown to prevent Type II diabetes and obesity.

The low GI diet has become very popular, especially with athletes and the health-conscious, and a symbol denoting foods that are good GI choices now appears on some packaging. The aim of the GI diet is to eat mainly low GI carbohydrates. When combined with sensible portion sizes, limiting saturated fats, and eating a variety of foods from all the main food groups, the GI diet is a balanced way of eating for the whole family.

Fats

People tend to think of fats as the bad guys but a certain amount of fat in our diet is essential for health. In fact, you can't live without it, but we must choose carefully which types of fats we include in our diets and how much of them we have.

Fats form part of every cell in our bodies, and they are especially important for nerve cells, our brains, and the production of many necessary hormones. Stored fat provides insulation and protects major organs like our kidneys. The body also uses stored fat as an important source of energy, providing double that of the same amount of carbohydrate or protein. Fats also provide the fat-soluble vitamins A, D, E and K.

Fats are present in meat, oils, dairy foods (milk, butter, cheese, yoghurt), nuts and seeds. There are two main types of fat: the 'bad' saturated sort mostly found in animal products, which increases LDL cholesterol, and the unsaturated type derived from vegetable sources like seeds and nuts, which produces HDL cholesterol and decreases LDL cholesterol. Unsaturated fats are referred to as mono- or polyunsaturated.

When fats are broken down in the body, they either create 'good' cholesterol (HDL), which reduces the risk of artery damage, or 'bad' cholesterol (LDL), which causes fatty deposits to build up on artery walls. High blood LDL levels greatly raise the risk of heart disease, heart attack and stroke.

Today's new breed of cardiologist believes that the time to start preventing adult heart disease is not at the age of 40 or 50 but in the early years. This is because studies have found that the earliest signs of coronary artery narrowing are commonly found in both adolescents and young adults, laying down the foundation for future trouble.

Two other types of fats that are important to consider are Essential Fatty Acids (EFAs) and Trans Fatty Acids (TFAs). EFAs are types of unsaturated fats, commonly known as omega-3 and omega-6. They are essential for healthy development of brains, eyes and form part of every cell in the body. Despite our often high-fat diets, most people are deficient in these very essential nutrients. The main sources for omega-3 is coldwater fish (such as salmon and sardines), flaxseeds and walnuts, while Omega-6 is found in seeds, nuts and their oils. These essential healthy fats are now being added to breads, milk and other foods.

TFAs are man-made fats found in refined foods that contain partially-hydrogenated oils. They are formed when oils are subjected to high temperatures and pressures in food production. TFAs are damaging to artery walls and are believed to contribute to heart disease. Nutritionists recommend that we avoid eating foods containing TFAs. Such is the concern that food labels in the US and Australia must now list the amount of TFAs a product contains.

Though reduced fat diets are important for adults and older children, young toddlers burn up so much energy with their activity and growth that a reasonable amount of fat isn't a problem. Try to use the 'good' fats, like olive oil, when cooking. Cut down on saturated fats in untrimmed meat or salamis, fatty sausages or minced meat and fried foods (especially commercially deep-fried products).

Sources of fat

Monounsaturated or polyunsaturated fats	Saturated fats
vegetable oils – olive, rapeseed, sunflower	meats (chicken, beef, lamb, pork) – high levels in fatty cuts
fish, especially tuna, salmon and sardines	commercial cakes, biscuits and pastries
nuts and seeds	take-away fried foods
some margarines	palm and coconut oil
	full-fat dairy foods, e.g. butter

We need to reduce the overall amount of fat in our diets, especially saturated fat, while making sure we get enough of the essential fats. And beware that sometimes things aren't what they seem: for example, good polyunsaturated fat sources such as margarine can contain high levels of the damaging trans fatty acids.

Vitamins

Vitamins are needed for energy, protection and healthy functioning of the body. Certain vitamins (A, C, E) are antioxidants and protect against aging. However, we don't need large amounts of vitamins – only small quantities of each are needed for health. There is a Recommended Daily Intake (RDI) for vitamins, to ensure that we get adequate amounts of these vital nutrients.

Sources of vitamins

Vit A	Liver, eggs, yellow fruits and vegetables, whole milk and whole milk products
Vit B$_1$	Whole grains, wheat germ, molasses, brown rice, meat, fish, poultry, egg yolks, chickpeas, kidney beans, soyabeans, sunflower seeds, Marmite
Vit B$_2$	Fish, pork, eggs, dairy products, almonds, chicken, wheatgerm
Vit B$_3$	Beetroot, pork, turkey, chicken, veal, oily fish, sunflower seeds, peanuts
Vit B$_5$	Egg yolks, whole grains
Vit B$_6$	Avocados, bananas, carrots, lentils, brown rice
Vit B$_9$ (folate)	Spinach, asparagus, lentils, soyabeans, root vegetables, whole grains
Vit B$_{12}$	Beef, cheese, eggs, milk and milk products
Vit C	Citrus fruits, black currants, papaya, tomatoes, strawberries, kiwi fruit, broccoli, peppers, cauliflower, peas
Vit D	Oily fish (e.g. salmon, sardines, tuna), fortified milk, egg yolks
Vit E	Cold-pressed oils, eggs, wheatgerm, sweet potatoes, leafy vegetables, sunflower seeds, nuts
Vit K	Leafy greens, broccoli, egg yolks, safflower oil, cauliflower, soyabeans

This table shows why variety is so important. If you restrict your diet to only a handful of different foods, you will miss out on essential vitamins. The foods here are listed in a general order of better to poorer sources.

Vitamins are found in fruits and vegetables, whole grains and fortified foods. Certain vitamins are also found in eggs, dairy foods, meats and fish.

There are two main types of vitamins. Water-soluble vitamins such as vitamin C, which is found in fruits and juices; and fat-soluble vitamins such as vitamin D, which is present in eggs and butter and is also manufactured by sunshine acting on our skin. Once we have the desired amount of each vitamin we need, doubling or trebling these levels does not make us twice or three times as fit, and can even be harmful.

There is a great deal of confusing advertising about vitamins. Children who do not have some major medical condition will be getting all the vitamins needed if they are fed a balanced diet of the sort suggested in this book. My understanding is that the best forms of vitamins come from natural foods, not from a pill laboratory. There are also hundreds of other protective factors in fruits and vegetables that work in conjunction with vitamins to keep us healthy, so going natural is best. Our aim is for toddlers to be eating a good variety and amount of fresh fruit and vegetables. This way they will be getting all the vitamins they need. Include lots of different colours, so that your toddler eats a 'rainbow' of fruits and vegies every day. Aim for one to two servings of fruit and two to three servings of vegetables daily.

One area of confusion is which is the best way to eat our vegetables and fruits: fresh, frozen or canned? Research has shown that frozen vegetables can contain three times the level of some vitamins as fresh produce that has slowly lost its vitamin content on the long journey from field to dinner table. Canned food may have good levels of vitamins listed on the label, as often vitamins have been added (some of the natural vitamin content is lost in the heat of the canning process). But they are also often very high in sodium, which we don't want. I prefer to eat fresh vegetables and fruit but if your toddler will only have frozen peas or tinned peaches, then that is better than none at all. The main thing we want is for toddlers to eat enough of these very important foods every day.

Minerals

Minerals are essential but, like vitamins, only required in small amounts for growth and body functions. Some minerals are needed in such tiny quantities they are called trace minerals.

Iron and calcium are the two minerals we think of most often. Iron is needed to make haemoglobin, which carries oxygen in the blood. It's found in good quantities in meat and in lesser quantities in fortified cereals, bread and some vegetables. Toddlers who do not eat enough iron can become anaemic. If your toddler eats no meat, get a dietitian to check that they are getting adequate iron in their diet from other sources. For parents who are overly concerned, their paediatrician might suggest an iron tonic to be taken by the toddler for a short while.

Calcium is necessary for a healthy body, especially strong bones and teeth and growing children need greater quantities than adults. Calcium comes mainly from dairy foods and levels may be low in a child who takes absolutely none of these in any form. Nowadays we hear a lot about brittle bones (osteoporosis) and we tend to think of this as a concern for the elderly, but the time to develop strong bones is in our youth.

Downing copious quantities of cows' milk is not to every toddler's taste. Milk and the calcium it contains also comes in the form of cheese, yoghurt and even ice cream. If the toddler prefers these varieties, that's fine. If your child is lactose-intolerant there are also other milks to try, such as sheep or goats' milk, as well as 'fake' milks like soya, almond and rice, some of which are fortified with calcium.

One mineral we need to make sure we don't get too much of is sodium. Sodium is mainly found in our diets in the form of salt. High levels of sodium increase blood pressure and the risk of stroke. Too much salt also makes us very thirsty.

Salt is something we acquire a taste for and we can become quite addicted. There is plenty of salt in everyday foods without needing to add any from the salt shaker. If you are usually heavy-handed at dinner time, wean yourself by adding a little less each day. And whatever you do, don't salt your toddler's food to your taste!

Sources of calcium	Sources of iron
Milk and milk products (cheese, yoghurt, ice cream)	Liver
Soya drinks (fortified) and tofu	Lean meat (beef, lamb, pork, chicken)
Tinned salmon and sardines (with bones)	Bran flakes and wheat bran based breakfast cereal
Almonds	Baked beans
Broccoli	Leafy green vegetables
Leafy green vegetables	Dried fruit

Water

While not really a 'nutrient', water is incredibly important. Children's bodies are 59 per cent water and their brains are 74 per cent. Only oxygen is more essential for sustaining life. Drinking adequate water prevents dehydration, flushes wastes out of our bodies, and is the best beverage for your active little toddler. Now I'm not talking about the fancy French stuff, but straight from the tap – it's cheap and easy. In this form it has even fewer calories than Diet Coke and your dentist will approve it.

It's a good idea to encourage the drinking of water at this young age. Children don't need added cordials or fruit juices; you can jazz water up with a few ice cubes! Just make sure that a cup of water is always available and they'll soon learn to help themselves when they are thirsty. It might mean a few more trips to the toilet during the day but it is a small price to pay for their health. However, be warned: don't give them too much water late in the day if you are toilet training your toddler or you will tempting Fate for a wet bed!

Most of our water is now fluoridated and despite various pronouncements, this is safe. As for other pollutants, we can protest about discolouration or too much chlorine, but the water we use is surely purer and safer than that available to 90 per cent of the world's population.

Fibre

Fibre – or 'roughage' as our grandparents used to call it – is the bulky part of fruits, vegetables and grains that we can't digest, and so passes through our systems. Fibre in foods helps us to feel full and satisfied after a meal; soluble fibre also plays an important role in maintaining healthy blood cholesterol levels. Most of us don't get enough fibre in our diet and this is true of our toddlers too. Fibre keeps our bowel movements regular and not eating enough fibre is one of the main causes of constipation.

When a child tends towards constipation, more dietary fibre needs to be introduced into the diet (also check they are getting adequate water). This roughage can be increased with selected palatable breakfast cereals, vegetables and more fibrous breads and biscuits. Processed bran is one way of increasing fibre and a popular choice with health enthusiasts – and horses. Toddlers are not without wisdom and dislike eating something that tastes like

sawdust. If you absolutely want to get bran into little children, some of the high roughage (but tasty) breakfast cereals or fibre-rich loaves are the best answer.

For most young children, however, it is better to leave bran in the stables and rely on the more enjoyable fibre that comes in fruit and vegetables. Fruit provides a most palatable and effective way of giving the sluggish bowel a push. Legumes such as beans and lentils are a terrific form of fibre – even the humble but popular baked bean is an excellent source, having exerted a regularising effect on an entire generation of cowboys who won the West.

Overall, we are looking to provide our children with the foods that will give them the biggest nutritional bang for their buck. Toddlers are always on the go and, like Formula 1 racing cars, need to be fuelled with the best quality 'petrol'.

Unlike fad diets, which can be taken with a healthy dose of scepticism, the balanced diet is all about healthy amounts of commonsense. We're not aiming for an exact science; we want to create a healthy way of eating that is achievable in everyday life. As we'll see, toddlers can be notoriously fussy eaters, and what we'd ideally like to feed them isn't always what they'll eat. But if we start with good, healthy food early on, we'll win them over to a healthy life without too much effort.

Hidden dangers

While only a small number of children – around 5 per cent – are affected by food allergies, the rising incidence and exposure in the media have made many of us more aware of the dangers of this potentially deadly condition.

'Food allergy' is the term used when the body's immune system mistakenly believes that a food is harmful and produces an immune response. This is different from a 'food intolerance', in which the reaction does not include the immune system.

Symptoms of food allergies range from hives and itchy eyes to the very serious reaction of anaphylaxis, where histamine floods the body and can lead to death. Death from a food allergy is rare in children but can happen and the most common causes of this tragedy are peanuts, tree nuts, fish and shellfish.

The most common food allergies are triggered by nuts, shellfish, milk, eggs, wheat and soyabeans. Children suffer most from milk, eggs and peanuts. Food allergies can start in infancy but many become apparent when the child is weaned and new foods are introduced into their diet. Generally, the later the onset, the less likely the child will grow out of it. Some experts believe that up to 20 per cent of children won't outgrow their food allergies and allergies to peanuts and fish usually become more severe. Allergies are to some extent genetically determined. If both parents have allergies then there is a 60 per cent chance that a tendency (not the actual allergies) will be passed on.

There is no specific treatment for food allergies except avoidance. Children with severe allergies should have an emergency action plan in place, which can be advised by their doctor. These days, all childcare centres are well aware of the dangers of food allergies and have taken measures to ban common allergy-inducing foods, such as peanuts, from their premises.

Parents of children with allergies learn to be vigilant and watch every mouthful but they can't protect their child when they aren't around. When the child visits friends or family everyone must be made aware of the seriousness of the condition; there is no room for mistakes. The great danger is that in this age of processed foods, allergy-inducing foods can be hidden in unexpected places. It only takes a tiny amount of a food to set off a reaction in someone who is allergic.

Summary: the toddler's balanced diet

- Provide them with plenty of complex carbohydrates (such as wholegrain cereal, pasta and bread) as well as fibre-rich foods (such as fruit, vegetables, legumes, grains and seeds).
- Give them moderate amounts of lean meat, fish, nut products and dairy. Younger toddlers need full fat dairy products. Once past 2 years, however, choose low-fat milk, low-fat cheese and low-fat yoghurt.
- Allow very small amounts of fried foods, sweet drinks, butter, margarine, cakes, lollies, honey and sugar.
- Make sure they drink adequate water.

Healthy foods and healthy choices

Knowing what makes up a balanced diet is the first step in deciding what your toddler should eat. The next step is a little more tricky, as it involves putting your newfound knowledge into practice. Shopping for foods that are healthy choices should be a simple affair. But the weekly supermarket ordeal now involves scouring food labels for vitamin and mineral content; wading through enticing advertising slogans; and trying to determine the origin of produce, and whether we should go organic.

Food for thought

We aim to buy and eat lots of fresh foods but the reality is not always easy. 'Fresh' fish may be 'defrosted for your convenience'. A recent television exposé in Australia showed that the apples in supermarkets can be up to a year old, kept in cold storage until they are back in season! Even when you make the healthiest choices, you can still be sabotaged.

What do we do? We can't get our food quickly carbon dated before we eat it. Perhaps the answer lies in supporting your local greengrocer, fish monger, butcher and deli. The proprietors of these establishments are more likely to know where their produce came from and what is fresh that day.

Hiding the truth

The major trap to look out for is foods that you believe are healthy but are in fact the exact opposite. The true nature of the foods we eat is sometimes hidden by added ingredients, or slick marketing. For example, as I was writing this chapter, I decided to look at the food choices I was making in my diet. For the past 15 years, my breakfast has been a bran flake and sultana cereal, with low-fat milk. Was I in for a surprise: I discovered that I have been unwittingly getting it wrong all this time. It turns out that this 'healthy' cereal is full of added sugars, doing me as much harm as a bowl of frosted, flavoured, puffed stuff.

Adding sugar is the most common way to make a healthy food unhealthy. But it's not just the foods that have been sweetened that are the problem. 'This juice has no added sugar' trumpets the label, making it seem a healthy choice. However, the truth is that the juice in question probably doesn't need any more; it already contains truckloads of sugar in its natural state.

Just because a substance is 'natural' doesn't mean that you can relax your guard and go overboard. You can rot your teeth, become fat or poison your system just as well with natural substances as with factory-produced ones. Tobacco and opium, for instance, are two very natural substances.

I've probably now confused you with everything you can and can't, should and shouldn't give your toddler to eat. Surely we don't intend that toddlers only eat carrot sticks, celery sticks and water? Healthy can sound pretty boring! **The real message is to give your toddler foods that haven't been fiddled around with too much.** These aren't only more nutritious, they're more filling and tastier too. Snacks of fatty chips or chocolate may be easy and appealing, but try to follow Eve's example, and tempt your toddler with an apple instead!

Fast food fix

Junk food is a term created by the media to describe all those fun treats like soft drinks, lollies, thick shakes, chips and fast foods. Now, I am not a killjoy who believes that anything that tastes good has to be bad for you or that strict avoidance of anything pleasurable is the only way to health and holiness. I do, however, worry that these foods have far too much fat, salt and sweetener.

Despite these concerns, I am a great believer in the therapeutic powers of fast food restaurants. It seems to me that these are some of the best places for any demoralised parent to visit. You just have to walk in the door and immediately you know that there are other children even worse-behaved than your own. For many mums and dads, the occasional 'kiddies meal' brings the realisation that they are normal. This lifts morale with probably as much effect as a year of visits to a psychiatrist – and all for under five pounds!

What makes a fat kid fat?

Early on in my dealings with children and food, I was consulted on how to get toddlers to eat. Now parents are worried about their toddlers eating too much! Babies with puppy fat are cuddly, but there comes a point when it's no longer cute.

In the press and on television, doctors worldwide have been pushing for a reduction in the alarming incidence of childhood obesity. **As a parent, you just can't let your toddler get fat.** Childhood obesity starts the toddler down a path that ends in heart disease, diabetes and many other diseases and symptoms that are preventable.

Children, like adults, become fat when they have a genetic tendency to lay down fat and then take in quantities of food greater than their body's needs. There are also periods of our lives when we lay down fat far more easily – most mothers and grand-mothers will know exactly what I'm talking about! Our bodies store fat for times of famine, when well padded people have reserves of energy to live on and supermodel types literally fade away. But in the Western world we have very little risk of famine, so what are we storing all this fat for?

For years, the experts have debated whether it is overeating or heredity that causes obesity. Every scientist and health expert is aware of the genetic link to obesity but these days they are urging us to focus on those things that are under our control and that we can change – our diet and exercise.

The obesity crisis

We are facing a global obesity epidemic. World Health Organization figures suggest that currently more than one billion adults are overweight worldwide. The crisis is also affecting children, with one in ten children classed as overweight – more than 155 million in total. Within that group, 30–45 million are classified as obese, which is 2–3 per cent of the world's children between the ages of 5 and 17. An estimated 22 million children under the age of five are also overweight.

Overweight and obesity are generally assessed using body mass index (BMI). A person's BMI is equal to their weight (in kilograms) divided by their height (in metres squared). For children, a BMI between 22–25 is considered healthy. A BMI of over 25 is defined as overweight, while a BMI over 30 is classed as obese.

Childhood obesity is increasing in countries across the globe. In the UK the prevalence of obesity in children *doubled* between 1984 and 1994.

Even more alarming is how this trend is believed to be accelerating. A recent study showed that about 20 per cent of children in the UK are now overweight and 2.5 per cent are severely overweight or obese. It is predicted that by 2020 one in five children in the UK will be obese!

These rising levels of obesity in children are thought to be due to a number of factors, including increased promotion of energy-dense foods (high in fats, saturated fats and sugar), larger portion sizes, reduced opportunities for recreational activity, increase in the use of motorised transport and the use of more technology in the home.

What we are creating is a time bomb, slowly ticking towards a future filled with devastating but preventable diseases. The direct link between obesity and conditions such as heart disease and stroke, type 2 diabetes and some cancers makes you wonder how we could even consider becoming overweight, let alone watching as our children do.

Puppy fat

A 2-year-old toddler has a very different shape from a 1-year-old baby. A baby usually has rolls of fat on their thighs, arms and abdomen, with very few muscles visible. Once the toddler gains his legs, the puppy fat disappears and the more grown-up proportions appear. He looks less like the Michelin Man and more like a miniature adult.

Babies in their first year of life gain weight at a remarkably rapid rate. This slows down dramatically after the first birthday, often grinding to a halt for some. Many parents become concerned around this time, when they observe their children becoming fussy, negative eaters. The child appears to be getting skinny from not eating enough but these parents are worried about the wrong thing – this slimming down is not only normal but desirable. The appearance of fussy eating habits is equally normal. What I worry about is the toddler who is not slimming down.

Numerous articles have been written expressing concern that fat babies become fat adults. However, studies show that there is minimal connection – what's most important is what happens after the age of 1 year. From this time, there is an increasing relationship between the growing child's weight and his future adult build. The message here is that while it may be OK for a baby to be chubby, by the time the child reaches preschool age, it is certainly not.

Over-eating

Nobody questions that the amount you eat has a significant bearing on weight and body fat. Some people think they get fat just looking at food, but as a doctor I can assure you that you actually have to eat it! **If you eat more calories than your body uses, you get fat. It doesn't matter if you're an adult or a toddler, it's the same principle – your body stores what it doesn't use.**

A great many parents set a very bad example to their children with the type and quantity of food they consume. Others use food as a substitute for providing love and attention. Some parents seem to delight in fattening up their offspring, as if they are cattle being prepared for market. To parents, fat may be beautiful but when the competitive teenage years arrive, few children give thanks for obesity. By that time it takes incredible resolve to attain a healthy figure.

Parents are responsible for ensuring their children get enough nutritious food to be healthy. They are equally responsible for not

Cookie monsters

Occasionally a concerned parent says, 'My 2 year old seems to eat nothing but chips, chocolate, chocolate biscuits and more chips. What can I do?'

Is this parent saying that Junior gets up in the morning, takes the keys to the Landcruiser, drives down to the supermarket, loads up a trolley with goodies, and then drives home and eats them?

I think the answer might be as close as the shopping dockets in mum's purse.

letting them gorge themselves through boredom or opportunity. Overeating can lead to a lifelong battle with being overweight, not to mention an increased risk of heart disease, diabetes and stroke.

Heredity

Overweight toddlers often have overweight parents. The question is whether heredity is to blame for the toddler's excess kilos or, as we know that no one can become fat without overeating, simply a case of the parents inflicting their own overeating habits on their offspring. Parents like to blame heredity alone, saying that Junior is '"big-boned", just like his father!'

No one has yet identified a single cause for obesity. A positive genetic relationship has been demonstrated between overweight parents and fatness in their children and some of the statistics are interesting:

- If neither parent is overweight, there is only a 10 per cent chance that the child will have a weight problem.
- If one parent is overweight, this increases the child's risk to 40 per cent.
- If both parents are overweight, the child's risk increases to 70 per cent.

This would appear to give all the evidence we need to show that the child's weight is predestined by heredity. However, one humorous piece of research has rather shattered this view. A group of researchers successfully showed that fat parents had fatter children. Meanwhile, another group discovered that they also tended to have fat pets! This rather threw a spanner into the works of the heredity lobby and once again we are left in some confusion. Also, children who have been adopted tend to exhibit the fatness of their adoptive parents rather than their genetic ones. So while there is a genetic influence in body type and body fatness, environmental factors appear to play an important role.

All this goes to show that, while tempting, we can't go blaming our genes for everything. So if we're serious about stopping our toddlers from becoming overweight, we can't avoid the role that unhealthy food choices and overeating play in the equation. The other important factor to consider is lack of exercise.

This generation of obese children will raise the next generation of obese adults, so it is clear that starting young is important. While we can't change their genes, we can definitely control what our toddlers eat.

A watery excuse

Many parents are convinced that their child is overweight because of a glandular problem. This may be true – but only in relation to the child's salivary glands, watering whenever he sees any food! Other than this, a connection between glands and obesity in children is extremely rare.

The importance of exercise

The reason we are getting fatter is because not only are we eating too much of the wrong types of foods, we are also doing less exercise. When I was a boy, my mum and dad didn't have a car. If we wanted to go somewhere, we had to walk or catch a bus, which involved a long walk to the nearest bus stop. Nobody we knew had a washing machine and we used almost no time-saving gadgets. Life was hard work. These days we don't pick up a broom or a rake in the garden, we use a leaf blower. You don't even have to move one buttock to change the channel on the TV. Today's easy lifestyle means people are more likely to succumb to diseases as a result of poor diet and lack of physical activity.

That's not to say that I'd like to return to the old days. Our labour-saving devices have made life easier and created more leisure time. Unfortunately for most people, this free time is sedentary to the point of immobility. If we aren't doing so much manual work, something else in the 'energy in, energy out' equation has to be adjusted. We can compensate by eating less but this idea isn't very popular with most people. The answer lies in doing more physical activity.

Get moving

Everyone knows that exercise is good for our bodies. Being physically active keeps our cardiovascular systems healthy and our

body fat levels within a healthy range. It also lowers blood pressure and reduces unhealthy cholesterol levels. Weight-bearing exercise, such as walking or running, keeps our bones strong, which is particularly important for women. And what we often forget is how important exercise is to our emotional health. Regular gentle activity reduces stress levels by using up the excess stress hormones, like adrenalin, that our bodies produce when we are feeling tense, harried or angry. You can quite literally walk off a bad mood! Research also shows that exercise is a powerful weapon against mild to moderate depression. When we get our bodies moving, we produce more of the substances that lift our moods. A daily walk has been shown to be as effective as medication for treating the symptoms of mild depression.

With most parents juggling many responsibilities and roles, the last thing you need is me telling you to do half an hour of exercise every day. By the end of the day, you probably have barely enough energy to lift the duvet and crawl into bed. But the benefits of exercise are not only physical. It gives you the mental strength to tackle whatever life with a toddler throws at you.

We would do well to follow the toddler's example – they're always moving! The toddler is constantly buzzing with energy and all they need is for mum or dad to steer that energy towards kicking a ball in the back garden or dancing around the lounge room.

Good habits start early, so from the toddler years onwards exercise, activity, and getting out and about need to become a priority. This is not a message to start training your toddler for the Olympics, merely a reminder to turn off the television more often and get moving. If the child gets more exercise, mum and dad will get more active, too, and they'll be fit enough to look after their grandchildren and great-grandchildren.

Exercise takes many forms. Jogging, cycling and swimming are what we think of, but mopping kitchen floors and washing the car do count as physical activity, provided you put a bit of elbow grease into them. For the toddler it doesn't have to be Gymboree (although this is one way to get him moving), everyday activities still count. We want to aim for a minimum of an hour of physical activity every day.

To increase physical activity:

- Get out and about as a family. Go to the park where your toddler has space to run.
- Get active with your toddler. Don't sit on the sidelines and watch – join him as he builds sandcastles at the beach, splashes in the baby pool or climbs at the playground.
- Walk to the shops and preschool. Try to limit driving to non-local trips. We know this is good for our health but it also benefits the environment.
- Let the toddler lend a hand when you do your household chores. Toddlers love to feel important and many will quite happily 'help' you sweep, dust or dig in the garden.
- Include your toddler in the exercise of your choice. Take him in a stroller when you go on your daily run, or put him in a seat on the back of your bicycle when you go for a ride.

Children and TV

There is no question that television is a wonderful technology, but I want to give a couple of warnings. While TV can be successfully used to give parents some toddler-free time and a 'mental break', it also plays a role in keeping children from being active.

Television and DVDs are an inevitable part of life in most modern homes. And they have their place if they are not abused.

Many of the popular programmes for toddlers, like the *Tweenies*, *Bob the Builder* and *Balamory* are geared towards getting the toddler moving, while being educational. Children love all the music, colour and activity of these shows, which has them joining in and jumping up and down instead of just sitting staring at the box. What we need to watch out for is television viewing taking the place of more active pursuits.

Another problem we need to be very aware of is the power of advertising. TV advertising, especially of food products, is very powerful. **Over 80 per cent of TV food ads directed at children promote poor nutritional quality foods.** I know many 3 year olds that can sing TV food ad jingles by heart. I'd rather they sang along with the *Tweenies*.

It is important to keep TV viewing to a minimum for toddlers. Set up a pattern that will follow through into their school years. When the programme is finished, it's time to stop. See television viewing as a special treat and above all, remember to turn it off!

Diet and behaviour

There is a lot of debate about whether diet can make toddler behaviour problems worse. It is claimed that artificial colourings, preservatives and even some natural foodstuffs negatively affect behaviour.

The most talked about problem is that diet causes hyperactivity, now known as Attention Deficit Hyperactivity Disorder, or ADHD. I certainly know that for a number of children with ADHD who I worked with, various foodstuffs made them more difficult to live with. However, diet was only a small part of the management of these children. Parents would focus on the hyperactivity instead of the big problem of lack of attention and lack of judgement. (Please refer to my book *Understanding ADHD* for more information on hyperactivity.)

ADHD aside, too much of certain foods can make any child's behaviour worse (cola drinks and chocolate being obvious examples). I find that generally parents know how these foods affect their toddler and either keep them out of their diet, or at least cut down on their consumption.

Some parents take the idea of limiting certain foods to the extreme. They put their toddlers on strict elimination diets, in the hope of miraculously eradicating all sinful behaviour. These parents blame bad behaviour solely on diet and focus their efforts on eliminating this or that food, making life extremely tedious. Very rarely have I found this approach to be of any benefit. They would be better served by more sensible expectations, understanding behaviour triggers and a tailor-made discipline programme.

The 'red devil'

An urban myth that has grown to legendary proportions is the hyperactivating properties of red cordial. Parents tell me that they took their usually docile toddler to a birthday party and the red cordial had her and her little friends bouncing off the walls.

Rather than blaming the liquid refreshments, I think that it's just as likely that 15 toddlers winding each other up is the reason for the madness of toddler social gatherings. If you gave them the purest spring water, the result would be just the same. Stressful as it was for mum, as far as the toddler is concerned, it was a pretty great party!

Staying alive

Staying healthy doesn't take a miracle – although loaves and fishes do play a part. But wholemeal bread and coldwater fish aren't enough; we need a balanced diet made up of a wide variety of foods that haven't been fiddled about with. It is easy to make unhealthy food seem interesting; it is very much harder to make healthy food and exercise enticing. To most people, there is nothing too sexy about an apple, and we really don't like to sweat.

Toddlerdom is the time to get your child hooked on a healthy diet. He is still too young to follow the flock to life in the drive-through lane. You can use your God-given parental powers to influence how he relates to food for the rest of his life.

The same applies to exercise. If you want to set a good

example, the main activity in your household can't be turning the key in the car ignition. Not to labour the point but obesity is such a threat that we have to start early and take it seriously by exercising not only our bodies but our healthy choices. We need to move more and move often.

At the end of the day, with the basics of a balanced diet and plenty of physical activity, your toddler and your whole family will be set on a path to long-term health and happiness.

15
Feeding without fights

Parents use up an enormous amount of energy forcing stubborn but otherwise well-nourished toddlers to eat against their will. All the parental antics are a great source of mirth to the child but, when the final score is taken at the end of the meal, not an extra pea has been eaten. Playing aeroplanes or dive bombers, singing, dancing, and threatening that they won't grow up 'big and strong like daddy' are all a complete waste of time. Just as adults don't eat bigger meals while being entertained at a theatre-restaurant, toddlers' consumption won't be improved by all this activity either.

In life, there is always an easy way and a hard way of doing things. When it comes to feeding toddlers, parents need to learn to take the easy route. What is called for is a pinch of creativity, a spoonful of patience and an ounce of cunning. Whether you are vexed by a vegie hater or stumped for snack ideas, this chapter makes one thing clear: there is no need to get into fights over food.

Cooking up a storm

Most babies in their first year of life are in no doubt about what to do with food and mealtimes are fairly straightforward. They don't mess about, generally getting the food to where it belongs with a minimum of fuss.

Toddlers, on the other hand, are a completely different ball game! A large number will have no problems at all but others show their toddler traits to the extreme. They are stubborn, wilful and, all of a sudden, food becomes one of the best ways to wind up their increasingly frustrated parents.

The root of most fights over food lies in a phenomenon that occurs in about half of all toddlers. During the natural slimming down stage that happens once the child gains his legs, they simultaneously display a dramatic change of attitude to food, becoming fussy, picky eaters. The child's weight gain has naturally slowed, stopped or even gone down, due to increased activity burning up stored 'puppy' fat. But parents put two and two together and assume that the toddler isn't getting enough nutrients. They decide it is imperative that he eats more. And so the start of many a fight over food.

If you have scored a child who is a beautiful eater, interested in anything culinary that comes his way, you will be less likely to face food dramas. These children clean their plates, burp contentedly and smile as if to say, 'I'll eat here again!' Mealtimes are a breeze.

For those of you with a picky eater, it will seem that battles are on the menu at every meal. To ensure that anguish isn't served up along with your best spag bol, there are creative and sneaky ways to make sure your toddler is getting the variety and good nourishment he needs. Once you have mastered these, he'll be tucking in quicker than you can say Jamie Oliver!

Force-feeding is never the answer. With the classic toddler negative streak always just around the corner, as with most toddler activities, forcing them to eat is nothing but unproductive.

Choking on food

Toddlers are still learning to eat solid food and don't have the back teeth needed to chew and grind lumps of food properly. Food swallowed in large pieces can 'go down the wrong way', lodging in their windpipe (trachea) and blocking air from entering their lungs.

Avoiding the danger:
- Do not give foods that can break off into hard pieces, such as nuts, popcorn, hard lollies, corn chips or uncooked fruit and vegetables (eg raw carrot, celery or apple pieces). Grate or steam raw fruit and vegetables. Mash peas and the like.
- Take pips and seeds out of fruit.
- Remove all bones from fish and the skin from fish, meat and sausages. Cut meat into small pieces.
- Always stay with young children and supervise them while they are eating.
- Don't allow children to run, play, laugh or cry while eating. Ensure they sit comfortably and quietly for meals and snacks.
- Never force a child to eat, as this may cause them to choke.

If a young child starts choking on food:
- Check if the child is breathing, coughing or crying. If the child is still breathing and coughing, encourage him to remain calm but to continue to cough, to help dislodge the food.
- Do not pat or hit the child on the back in an attempt to dislodge the food, as this can cause it to lodge more firmly in the windpipe and make the child stop breathing. Do not apply the Heimlich manoeuvre or squeeze the child's stomach, as this is no longer considered safe and may cause further choking.
- Stay with the child and watch to see if breathing improves.
- If the child is not breathing easily within a few minutes, phone 999 for an ambulance.

If the child is not breathing:
- Try to dislodge the piece of food by placing the child face down across your lap so that their head is lower than their chest.
- Give four sharps blows on the back just between the shoulder blades with the heel of your hand to dislodge the food.
- Check again for signs of breathing.
- **If the child is still not breathing, urgently call 999 for an ambulance.** The operator will talk you through the correct first aid procedure until help arrives.

Something to chew on

During the toddler years, children have to master a whole range of new techniques and culinary experiences. There are great variations in how they adapt and for parents it can be difficult to know what's normal, as normal is all over the place. Here is a general guideline of the milestones they'll pass in the next few years:

- At 9 months, food goes down with relative ease, and the chewing pattern is becoming well-established. Even so, the first teeth are just tiny ornaments that do little damage to the food as it hurries past.
- From 6 to 12 months, children learn to hold their own bottle and then transition to cups with built in spouts.
- By 1 year, the child eats a diet similar to that of the rest of the family and the teeth are used more for chewing. Toddlers start to want foods they can get their teeth into.
- After 18 months of age, most children will suck the end of a straw rather than chew it as before.
- At 3 years old the toddler learns to cut soft foods with a knife – the safe, ineffective plastic kind that are offered these days with airline meals. The next step is attempts at buttering their own bread, which will follow soon after.
- By 4½ the child should be able to use a knife and fork after a fashion, and – believe it or not – it is just before this age, that Chinese children generally learn to use chopsticks!

Feeding problems: the main offenders

A quick survey of any group of parents will reveal major differences in the feeding habits and preferences of their offspring. On closer inspection, we uncover a few main offenders. You'll instantly recognise if you have one of these usual suspects in your midst by the telltale clues at mealtimes.

He doesn't eat enough

On occasion, I would be confronted by parents who were insistent that their toddler wasn't eating enough: 'Dr Green, he hardly eats a bite'. I would look up and there would stand an infant heavy weight, about as puny and malnourished as King Kong. You cannot get this build from swallowing air. At least a few calories must have slipped down along the way.

Most children who seem to eat too little are in fact getting a very adequate and healthy diet, if only we realised it. The inconspicuous calories are 'hidden' in all the milk, snacks, and half-finished main meals they consume. **If you are worried, note down all the food eaten by your toddler throughout the day.** When this is added up you will be surprised at just how much goodness goes down the big tube.

Like adults, children have different food requirements. They eat like birds: some like sparrows, others like vultures. There is no correct amount of food for all children to consume in a day. Food intake and growth are not the only indicators of good health; energy levels are also important. If my car only used half the manufacturer's recommended amount of petrol to cover a given number of kilometres, I would not complain; I would be grateful that I had an efficient machine that was obviously tuned to perfection.

Fed up

It is a very special occasion and you are booked to eat at the best restaurant in town. Out comes the food, immaculate with cordon bleu sauces flowing off the meat. Your mouth is watering at the very smell.

Then up marches the head waiter, looks you in the eye and with a stern voice says, 'Just one thing, madam. You will not be leaving the table until you've eaten every bite. What's more there will be no dessert until your plate is completely clear.'

Then the chef appears, takes out a carving knife and fork and proceeds to cut up your meat into little pieces and mashes it in with the vegetables. Loading up a forkful, he aims for your mouth . . .

If you clamped your mouth shut and flatly refused the offered bite, no-one would blame you. The same applies to your toddler – trust that he knows when he has had enough.

He won't eat his vegetables

Modern nutritional science has proved something that we all know anyway: vegetables are very good for us. They contain not only fibre, complex carbohydrates, vitamins and minerals, but also many protective factors, like antioxidants, that prevent chronic diseases in adulthood. Unfortunately vegetables also turn out to be children's least favourite food. And let's face it, many adults don't find them particularly mouth-watering either.

Some toddlers love their vegies, but with others, it's as though they were born to dislike them, no matter what you do. If your little one is one of these, adopt an open-minded, go-with-the-flow attitude. If he refuses to eat Brussels sprouts, he may be happy with green beans or peas. Experiment with the full spectrum of

A new spin on vegetables

- Offer a wide range of different vegetables; don't just stick with carrots and peas.
- The sweeter vegies like carrots, corn and sweet potato are more popular with children and can be a good place to start.
- Just because you don't like a particular vegetable, doesn't mean your toddler won't. Give everything a try.
- Serve a variety of vegies at each mealtime – it only takes a little more effort for a greater chance of success.
- Choose dishes that include vegetables as part of the recipe.
- Hide chopped up or grated vegetables in toddler temptations such as rissoles or bolognaise sauce.
- Cut steamed vegies into fun shapes.
- For convenience, use frozen vegetables. There is now a wide variety available.
- Avoid adding the instant flavour enhancers of butter or salt in order to make vegetables more appealing.
- Make homemade, healthier versions of high-fat treats. For example, instead of deep-fried chips, serve baked potato wedges.

vegies, and try to introduce small amounts, different tastes and lots of variety from the earliest days.

If all this is a non-event, don't despair. Just make sure that your toddler is getting his nutrients from other sources – fruit can provide vitamins and minerals, and whole grain cereals and beans provide fibre. This doesn't let the toddler off the hook completely; you have to keep offering small amounts of vegetables at meal-times, without any force. Persistence without pressure is the key to success, so good luck!

He won't eat any meat

Parents often tell me, 'My toddler won't eat any meat'. 'What does he eat then?' I innocently ask. 'Oh, just a little chicken, rissoles and bolognaise sauce.' We should remember that not all meat comes as a thick slice of cow or sheep. There are other animals and presentations, one of which may tempt the tastebuds of your toddler. And we have to realise that once it hits the stomach, it is irrelevant whether the meat was lamb, pork or beef or whether it was minced or carved. The body is more impressed by nutrients than the species it consumed.

Meat provides protein and iron, so when the toddler has declared a total embargo on meat, you need to get creative and find other options. Eggs are an excellent source of first-class protein. And if all else fails, dairy products like cheese, milk and yoghurt do the trick.

Good sources of protein

- Chicken, beef, lamb, pork
- Fish
- Eggs
- Milk, cheese and yoghurt
- Legumes, grains, nuts and seeds
- Soya products (e.g. tofu)

If your children are vegetarian, consult a dietitian, who will recommend meat alternatives to make sure your toddler is getting all the protein he needs. Beans, lentils and nut products (for

example, smooth peanut butter), when used wisely, can keep vegetarian children healthy. But parents tell me that those toddlers
who refuse to eat meat can be equally militant when it comes to
these alternatives.

He won't drink any milk

Dairy products provide by far the most important source of
calcium to the growing child. Most toddlers love their milk, but a
few just haven't got the message that it's good for them. Thankfully, there are other ways to get three serves of calcium in – it
doesn't have to be liquid white stuff. Cheese is the great stand-by
and is one of the more universally popular toddler foods. In fact,
some years ago we surveyed parents and found that cheese and
chocolate were equal favourites behind the number one food,
ice cream.

If cheese doesn't suit them, there are other popular products
such as yoghurt, dairy desserts, milk-based ice creams and
flavoured milks. But beware that while these contain milk,
most are also high in sugar. If your toddler is firm that milk is
only for baby cows, calcium-fortified soya milks are now readily
available.

There are a few children who have a true milk allergy and in
these cases their paediatrician will suggest alternative sources of
calcium. If you wish, you could always try spinach and sesame
seeds. They would be sprouting out your toddler's ears before
he got even the calcium of half a glass of milk, but oh what a
feeling!

Cream of the crop

A toddler relies heavily on the full cream dairy products
that would cause spasms in the adult heart watcher. At this
young age (under 2 years) they need all those fats to fire
up their furnace and to keep them going. After that they
can join the queue for low fat alternatives like the rest
of us.

He's hooked on bottles and baby food

The milkaholic brings joy to dairy producers, as he lives and thrives on milk, each day consuming litre upon litre, leaving no room for solid food.

If after 8 months of age the child's diet is still milk and bland, untextured baby foods, it may be extremely difficult to change him over to a proper mixed diet. Obviously prevention is better than cure, so parents must be encouraged to provide a variety of textured solids after 6 months, avoiding milk as the sole source of nourishment.

For those toddlers who *are* hooked on bottles, the best solution is to cut down dramatically on their milk intake. Some experts are extremely tough on these toddlers and exclude all milk immediately, substituting other, less calorific fluids (water is the perfect choice) until the child gives in and starts eating a reasonable diet. I prefer a gentler approach, which in the end achieves exactly the same results. The milk intake should be reduced by about half and other fluids and a variety of interesting nibbly things should be introduced at the same time. This is usually all that is required to remedy the problem, but if it does not work immediately, then the milk can be gradually reduced even further. Like all such procedures, the parent must not weaken midway.

For children who won't eat solids and only take mushy foods, we need to slowly introduce them to chewy things and lumpy bits. Firstly, halve their milk intake so that it cannot be used as a substitute food. Then, the secret lies in slowly adding texture to each meal. Begin by making their food almost liquid consistency using a blender or liquidiser. Whirr away until you have achieved the preferred slushy texture. Then each day depress the button for a shorter time, leaving the odd chunk swimming in the mix. After a couple of weeks, you can leave food in its recognisable pieces, like mum and dad's.

A choc-coated cure

Parents say to me their toddler won't chew anything and the slightest lump causes him to gag. And yet I have watched in amazement as somehow he exerts an incredible hidden chewing ability when a piece of chocolate is popped into his mouth. It seems the gag's on us!

Down the hatch

In this age of 'speedy this' and 'instant that', there is one type of toddler that stands out like a tortoise at a rabbit convention. Compared to everything around him, the dawdler seems to move in slow motion. His slowness while dining is in direct contrast to his parents' galloping heart rates. Every mealtime he sits and fiddles quite happily with his food as mum and dad silently fume. Any attempt to gee him up just makes him go slower and slower. For the tired parent, who at the end of a long day just wants to get the show on the road, it's enough to make them close the kitchen for good!

If your toddler dawdles over his food, the first solution is to leave him to it without an audience. This may be enough to get dinner down the hatch instead of pushed around the plate. If after a while he's still constructing rather than eating, lift him down from the table and put the uneaten food in the fridge. He will get the very clear message that food is not a game. If perchance he wants it an hour later, you can whip the plate from the fridge and as quick as you can say microwave, everyone is happy.

The point is to not get stressed. Whether the toddler wants to spend five minutes or thirty-five minutes over dinner, it's his call.

At the other end of the spectrum we have the drive-through toddler, who never sits down to eat and is always on the go. He's in training to be a corporate high-flyer, who has a phone in one hand, a sandwich in the other and makes a million on the stock market all before the last bite hits his tummy!

Feeding the militantly independent child

From their first birthday, some children are hell-bent on feeding themselves without any outside assistance. Unfortunately the most independent children are also usually the most impatient – a sure recipe for trouble. The amount of food that escapes in all directions as they dig in is only matched by their determination to do it 'all by myself'.

By 15 months, these children are keen to hold a spoon, although few can keep it level between plate and mouth – the contents usually slip off as their arm tries to negotiate the bend. It helps to give them a spoon large enough to allow them to load the food with some accuracy, a spade being the number one choice for a select few. To further help the impatient and hungry child determined to have a go at feeding himself, you can try giving him one spoon while feeding him with another.

To cope with inevitable spillage on the long journey from plate to mouth, a 'pelican' bib – one of those strong plastic bibs with a large catchment area at the bottom – is recommended. As the drop-out food is caught in the bib, it can be quickly recycled, cutting down on mess and wastage. The toddler can amuse himself scooping out bits that didn't make it to their target. And remember, if children want to feed themselves with their fingers, that's fine (if very messy).

Don't force-feed

Toddlers have none of our funny adult ideas about food. When they are hungry, they want to eat. When they are not hungry, they don't. The biggest mistake that most parents make is trying to force-feed their obstinate toddler. Whether toddler or adult, no-one is going to swallow food that they don't want. If you attempt to force a toddler to eat, they will quickly show you who is really in charge of what goes into their mouths. They may only be aged 2, but in this case they are infinitely more sensible than the grown ups.

We don't want to fuel the problem with futile efforts that can quickly escalate into angry, messy food fights. Parents think that they have to show who is boss and that the big people will win at all costs. All this does is create feeding problems where there weren't any in the first place.

What the toddler really needs is gentle encouragement. **Remember, no child has ever starved to death through stubbornness.** If you are really concerned that your child isn't eating enough, keep track of every bite he consumes in a day. Your attention has to be on what *has* been eaten, not what has been left on the toddler's plate, face or clothing. Make sure your expectations are realistic – if the toddler is getting enough of the important nutrients he needs in a day, there is no sense in trying to force down extra.

Many mums take it personally when the toddler refuses a meal, setting the stage for a determined clash of wills. 'You're going to eat this dinner. You will learn to eat up!' says mum, hands on hips and a look like thunder on her face. The toddler clamps his lips together, a steely glint in his eye showing quite clearly he's thinking, 'You and who's army?' If food is being refused, check that what you are giving him is toddler friendly, then get on with your day.

Hunger strikers

I once told a group of parents that no toddler had ever starved to death through stubbornness. Almost before the words had left my lips a mum at the back was on her feet complaining.

'Dr Green, you're wrong. My child once refused to eat for 12 hours and if I hadn't forced him he would certainly have starved.'

'Do you know how long it takes the average hunger striker to die?' I asked. 'About 68 days.'

'Do you mean that at the Sydney Children's Hospital you recommend only feeding children every 68 days?' she exploded.

With this, the dietician sitting beside me could no longer contain himself. 'If you are really worried in the future, how about giving Dr Green a call on the morning of the twentieth day?' I think she got the message.

Toddler tastes

Toddlers can be notoriously fussy eaters. Just because we decide they are going to have a balanced, healthy diet, doesn't mean they will oblige. Children start life with only one type of food and the only variety they get is drinking from the left or right breast. In the 80 plus years of their lives, there is great room for improvement on this narrow selection. But with hundreds of foods to discover over the next few years, they will go at their own pace. There will be foods that we introduce that are an instant hit and others that are a flop, for no apparent reason. A food they eat happily one day might be rejected the next. It can be frustrating for parents.

Some children are accepting, adventurous and willing to try anything. Others are more cautious and perfectly happy with monotony. Some get hooked on certain foods, and even parents are guilty of falling into food ruts. When it comes to toddler tastes, they're going to go their own way, so acceptance is the key.

Tastes of their own

Toddlers have a right to their own tastes. Parents often feel that toddler foods lack flavour or have an unpleasant texture but that is none of our business. Let's face it, adults have some pretty odd tastes of their own, such as oysters, anchovies, chillies and smelly cheese.

Parents who themselves dislike liver, beetroot and brains will never give these to their child. In fact the toddler may be quite happy with these foods, but parental hang-ups don't give them a chance to decide if they like them.

We may think that the toddler's preferences are bland or boring and be tempted to add salt or sugar, but toddler taste is very different from mum or dad's adult palate. They'll probably live longer than our 'flavoursome' generation! We mustn't pollute them to our tastes.

The spice of life

Some children take to new food like a duck to water; others are much more stuck in their ways. For this group the daily diet is: Weetabix, Weetabix, Marmite sandwich, Weetabix, another Marmite sandwich, then goodnight! This would never be a hit on the a la carte menu at the Ritz but some toddlers love it today, tomorrow and forever.

While we should aim for variety in the toddler's diet, it is pointless fighting about it. I've looked after many toddlers and I know that no matter what you or I say, they'll only eat what they want. The only winning way is to introduce small amounts of new foods every few days, until they are no longer a novelty. Use your parental gift of guile and eventually they will have a varied diet. Remember that persistence, not pressure, is the way to go.

Too much of a bad thing

As I have said earlier, a healthy diet does include occasional moments of indulgence. There is nothing wrong with the odd square of chocolate, as long as we don't go overboard. As adults, we are supposed to have conquered the sin of gluttony and overcome our desire to finish off the block of Dairy Milk. So we sometimes forget that toddlers are not little adults, and expect them to have adult-like control. However, one of the toddler's trademarks is impulsiveness and lack of self-control. Adults can have difficulties knowing when to stop, but the toddler relies solely on mum or dad to put the brakes on for him.

Problem-free feeding

Because parents spend so much time worrying about the amount, type, balance, source, colour, shape, cooking style, entertainment value and – of course – the healthiness of every morsel they give their little ones, they may forget one of the most important things about food: it should be pleasurable.

I think we have to rid ourselves of some of our rigid and old-fashioned ideas about feeding toddlers. **Within reason, try to give them what they want, where they want it, and when they are hungry.** Of course this doesn't mean junking the healthy way of doing things. It means being more flexible and seeing food from the toddler's point of view. They are going to have to learn adult eating habits sooner or later, but for now it is important to get them enjoying the process of eating.

Make food fun

When serving fine food to adults, a chef prides himself not only on the taste but also on the presentation. The different textures and the variety of colours on the plate all add up to create an enjoyable dining experience.

In order to grab your toddler's attention and interest, it helps to take a leaf out of the chef's recipe book. We need to get creative to make mealtimes more appealing.

- Engage the toddler's senses: their sight, smell, taste and touch. Vary texture and colour of meals wherever possible. Include something chewy, crunchy, creamy textured or slippery. Take a colourful approach to mealtimes and include a vibrant array of bright green beans, rosy red strawberries, rich purple grapes or brilliant orange carrots.
- Garnishes can be used as 'baits' to reel the toddler in. A little grated cheese on top of veggies, or a dollop of yoghurt on fruit arouses the toddler's curiosity and tempts him with the unexpected.
- Make boring everyday food fun. Cut toast into triangles or other shapes with cookie cutters, use unusual shaped pasta. Homemade biscuits can be baked in animal shapes.
- Try offering the toddler a selection of small 'courses' rather than one huge meal: an entrée followed by a main course then dessert. In the same way that aeroplane food always seems more interesting because it is apportioned into little trays, novelty can work wonders on the toddler's attention and appetite. Just remember, portions need to be toddler sized, not adult sized.

- Vary the venue. Move lunch to the balcony or the garden for a picnic, where the toddler can drink milk through a straw and eat little sandwiches out of a lunch box.
- When it comes to snacks, use the adult idea of finger food, like at a cocktail party. Offer a few cubes of cheese, some pieces of fruit or dainty little sandwiches.
- Embrace the power of the unexpected. 'Hide' a piece of chocolate in a healthy dessert to make it more exciting for the toddler.
- Get the toddler involved, as at this age they love to help. It makes them feel grown up and develops a healthy interest in food. When preparing a meal, give the toddler safe tasks to do, or let him make his own version of adult food, for example, when baking biscuits, give him some dough to roll into his own shapes.

Labour-saving food preparation

I'm sure that at some time or other you've slaved over a hot stove for hours preparing a delicacy for your child, only to find he takes one look at it and turns his nose up in disgust. At moments like these you feel your blood boil and wonder why you bother at all. To save your sanity, may I recommend a bit of labour-saving cooking instead.

We are lucky to have at our fingertips technology that is a dream come true for busy parents. Microwave ovens make cooking and reheating food a snap. Quick-cooking methods such as stir frying means we no longer have to spend hours getting dinner ready. There are a host of kitchen gadgets, from food processors to steamers, that take the drama out of preparing meals, and mean we have more time for the important things, like spending time with our toddlers.

The time-honoured idea of cooking in larger batches and freezing leftovers is still the best way to save time in the kitchen. When mealtime comes, all you have to do is look in the freezer and decide on the menu, defrost it, and there you have an instant, but home-made meal. Pairing a reheated main with some fresh vegetables and a quick, healthy dessert is all you need to feed the family well. This idea is especially helpful when feeding a toddler as you fight to stay ahead of his changing whims. If the toddler demands chicken stew for dinner, you can reply, 'We have that as a special today, served with green beans and peas.'

You can cook up a variety of dishes ahead of time and your toddler's next meal can be prepared as quickly as it takes an ice-cube to melt. If it is then refused, it can be placed in the refrigerator (not the freezer) with a serene 'See if I care!'

Nibbling can be nutritious

A number of parents believe that the only way for their toddlers to eat is to have three square meals a day, with perhaps a snack thrown in. But it is not just sheep that like to nibble away all day; whole flocks of toddlers also prefer to graze. Children thrive well on this type of regime as long as we ensure that the pasture they nibble is of good quality. Rigid fixed mealtimes are more appropriate to top restaurants than to the toddler. We want to encourage the main meal habit but when this is obviously failing, cut your losses and let them eat when they are hungry.

Even toddlers who eat breakfast, lunch and dinner need refuelling between meals to keep their engines humming. A small, healthy snack is all that is needed. The ideal snacks for the busy toddler are 'finger foods': cubes of cheese, slices of fruit and sliced, cooked vegetables are all easy to handle and portable. There are also the classics of bananas and cold sausages – anything that you can both eat and poke the dog with has got to impress the average toddler.

Sandwiches, too, make an easy, healthy snack. All that you need is a bit of imagination with the fillings. We've come a long

Snack menu for toddlers on-the-go

- Fruit, cut into bite-sized pieces
- Cheese sticks
- Sliced, cooked vegetables
- Dried fruit
- Milk
- Sliced cold meats
- Child-sized yoghurts
- Smoothies made with fresh fruit

way since honey, peanut butter and Marmite were the only choices to spread on bread. Brain-building tinned salmon or tuna, chopped egg, and cheese and tomato are nutritious fillings. Baked beans or spreads like hummous are also good choices. Salad vegies such as lettuce provide some crunch.

As you will gather, I am a great believer in between-meal snacks and I think they should be treated with as much enthusiasm as the main meals they accompany.

Problem-free meals

Mealtimes should be a time to come together, relax, enjoy good food and company. I admit to having old-fashioned views of mealtimes being a way for the family to connect and communicate. My wife and I ate breakfast together with our boys almost every day when they were growing up, and I continue this ritual as often as possible to this day. I got this habit from my parents, who did the same with my brother and me.

This picture of domestic bliss is but a fantasy for many parents today. So often meals, especially for mums, are rushed, harried affairs, eaten on the run. Or they are consumed sitting exhausted in front of the TV at the end of the day. These are obviously not good examples to be setting for our toddlers.

Feeding toddlers – especially the younger toddler – can be a challenge that frustrates even the most even-tempered parent. Once you have mastered the tricks for getting a healthy variety of food onto their plates, it's time to make the act of dining easier. The box below details how to achieve problem-free meals.

The *Toddler Taming* technique for problem-free meals

1. Be smart and be organised. Have everything ready before you sit the toddler down – the food cooked, the drinking cup filled up, the toddler's seat set up, a bib handy as well as a cloth for wiping up spills.
2. Make sure you won't be interrupted. Switch off the TV, let the phone calls go to voice mail and focus on the toddler and the meal ahead.
3. Seat the toddler comfortably. You can use a high chair, a booster seat or a toddler-sized chair and table. Choose an option that will anchor the toddler in place long enough to have a chance at getting the food down. At the same time get a comfy chair for yourself, and try to make sure that you don't have to be an acrobat to reach his mouth.
4. Serve simple, fuss-free meals, food that the toddler will enjoy. Bear in mind the toddler's tastes and whims when cooking. Build up a repertoire of dishes that are always a success, then throw in a few new ones from time to time to spice things up.
5. Gently encourage the child to eat, *never* force him.
6. If the toddler prefers picking foods up with his hands rather than using spoons or other eating utensils, let him go for it! It is the delivery of the food to where we want it that counts. Manners can wait for finishing school.
7. Let the toddler eat at his own pace. Toddlers also have creative ideas about the order of meals, so if your child decides to return to the main course after having polished off his dessert, that's fine.

8. If the child is dawdling over his food, leave him to dawdle without an audience. Turn your attention to something else for a short while and come back to him later.

9. Don't get angry if he won't eat up. It is the child's right to eat or not to eat his food as he wishes. Put untouched plates in the fridge and bring out later on request to try again.

10. If a child flat out refuses to eat a meal, don't allow him to top up on milk, sweet treats and the like. Toddlers quickly learn that if they refuse the nutritious food, they are 'rewarded' with foods they would rather have on the menu.

11. Once it is obvious that the child is not going to eat any more, wipe his hands and face clean and allow him to get down from the table. Don't make him sit until his plate is cleared.

12. Above all, remember that mealtimes are not only for nourishment, they are for enjoyment.

16

Toilet training

Despite various opinions to the contrary, children become toilet trained when they, and only they, are ready. No child can be trained until the appropriate nerve pathways have sufficiently matured, a process that is completely outside the influence of even the most brilliant childcare expert, doctor or parent. Once sufficiently mature, toilet training is controlled by the child's desire to comply or his determination to defy, which, in turn, is dependent on his temperament, as well as the skill and cunning of the trainer.

As a stage that all toddlers and their parents pass through, toilet training can appear to be complicated, frustrating and never-ending. Some parents push their child in an attempt to advance him through this part of development. Others hesitate, uncertain how to begin and whether they have the strength to see it through. But with a basic understanding of the processes involved, a few rules to follow and a sensible attitude, you and your toddler can flow through toilet training with ease. This chapter has everything you need to know to take the pain out of training.

Gone potty

At the beginning of the twentieth century children were toilet trained much earlier than today, with the process starting in some cases at the unbelievable age of 3 months; there are many reports of children being completely trained by their first birthday. However, there was a lot to be said for promoting early training in those days of cloth nappies, harsh soaps and washing by hand in galvanised tubs.

That era was also a time when people had a great obsession with bodily functions and the clockwork regularity of bowel movements. It was vigorously drummed into new mothers that if a baby was started off on the right path in his earliest months, he would be spared the horrors of constipation in later life. All of this set up the idea that you can toilet train children from an early age.

Although we are now 100 years on, the myth of early toilet training still lures and ultimately confuses many parents. When we look more closely at this practice, we see that back then, as now, people were being fooled by a subtle distinction – the small but all important difference between toilet training and toilet timing.

Toilet timing vs. toilet training

If a parent decides to start toilet training early, it is easy for them to make the universal mistake of thinking that the very different activities of toilet timing and toilet training are identical.

Toilet timing: Babies, from their earliest days, tend to empty their bowels or bladders when their stomachs are full after a feed. This is a completely reflex action, being no more clever or voluntary than the response when a doctor hits you with a patella hammer and your leg jerks. If a child is put on the potty after a meal there is a sporting chance that something will 'pop out'. This display is most interesting but only a reflex, and nothing to get excited about.

Toilet training: As the child approaches 18 months, the reflex appears to weaken and voluntary control begins to take over. This is completely different to the pot luck attempts of toilet timing. An older toddler uses his brain to decide whether he wishes to go to the toilet and then makes a deliberate attempt to oblige. This is true toilet training, where the child uses a voluntary action and is in full control.

During the first 1½ years of life there is no proper bowel or bladder control, just the toilet timing reflex. Parents often start training too early, motivated by the illusion this reflex provides. In this age of washing machines, Napisan and disposable nappies, there is less need to have our toddlers dry at the earliest age possible. Some parents are convinced there is a link between early toileting success and intelligence in their child, based on the innocent bragging and competition of play group. Early training is no more a sign of intelligence than early development of teeth. As far as I am aware intelligence comes from the brain, an organ somewhat distant from the bladder.

No child is toilet trained at the age of 1 year, and any children who give this appearance are just demonstrating a particularly strong toilet timing reflex. The effect may reduce the load on an overworked washing machine, but this is a temporary lull. Copious loads of laundry will reappear as soon as the child begins to exert voluntary control. I can't stress enough not to start too early as this invariably leads to unnecessary problems.

Toileting: normal development

Even though every child is different, there are some basic stages of development that they all pass through. The process of voluntary control that the toddler needs to acquire in order to become toilet trained develops over time, and there is no way to hurry it along.

When it comes to toilet training your toddler it helps to know what lies ahead so that you don't have unreasonable expectations for the toddler or yourself. Most toilet training difficulties today are caused by unrealistic expectations and misleading advice. Below are the stages that children go through on the road from nappies to toilets.

■ Around the age of 18 months, the toddler begins to realise when he is wet or dirty.
■ In the months that follow this dawning awareness, the child

makes another discovery – he becomes aware of his toileting needs before the event rather than after.

- Between 18 months and 2 years of age, there is a great breakthrough – bladder training. There is however one unfortunate flaw: although a warning is sounded, the child's alarm system is only adjusted to tell of the impending puddle 5 seconds before it arrives.
- By the age of 2, the amount of warning has increased and the toddler can start to notch up a few successes. At about this time bowel control will also become established, though occasionally in some children it occurs before bladder control.
- By the age of 2½ years, more than two-thirds of children will be dry most of the time. The majority can take themselves to the toilet and handle their pants without too many mistakes.
- Even after the age of 2½, when most children are bladder and bowel trained, the whole procedure is still surrounded by a great sense of urgency – the child needing to go 'now' rather than when it suits the parents.
- From 2½ years night-time wetting also starts to come under control. The toddler makes it through some nights dry, with interspersed periods of dampness.
- By 3½, the toddler will make his first attempts to wipe his own bottom, although it will take a further year before the operation is at all reliable. At this point, toilet training can be declared complete.

In toilet-training development, there is a great variation from child to child. There is a strong relationship with family history, and parents with late bladder training, especially at night, frequently find that their children are endowed with similar characteristics. Girls tend to become trained slightly earlier than boys, possibly because of their slightly advanced development, different anatomy or, perhaps they have a more compliant personality at this age.

The fundamental rules of toilet training

While gaining control over their bladders and bowels is a very natural process that can't be hurried you can help your toddler along by sticking to a few simple rules. Success will be hard won until you embrace these four truths:

Rule 1: A child must know the difference between the feeling of wet and dry before he can be bladder trained. You are wasting your breath trying to convince a youngster that he should have done his wee wee in the toilet when he is quite oblivious to the fact that he has just done it in his pants. Understanding the feeling of wet and dry is where it all starts. It is pointless to consider serious toilet training until the child knows at least this.

Rule 2: A child must first learn to sit on the toilet before he can learn to open his bowels on that toilet. Sitting on the toilet or potty is the first step to performing, as the child has to learn the association between this activity and toileting. Seagulls may be able to do it as they fly over Sydney Harbour, but little humans need to be firmly in place if they are going to hit the target.

Rule 3: A child must be able to produce some dry nappies at night before you can expect a dry bed. If the toddler's nappies have been consistently wet every night, it stands to reason that if you remove them, the bed will become wet every night too. Before beginning night training, the sign to look out for is dry nappies.

Rule 4: Relaxed little children find toileting easiest. Forcing little children causes tension and tension causes little humans to clamp closed all bodily openings. Don't hurry, don't force – things will go quicker if you go slower.

These are my basic rules for toilet training children. Remember that the child alone has the ultimate power to go where and when he wishes. There is no point in rushing the child.

Bladder training

Of the three phases of toilet training – bladder, bowel and night training – most parents start with this one.

You can commence a bladder-training programme some time around 18 months of age, when little children start to realise when they are wet. They don't like the feeling, and you can spot this new sensation by the funny walks or fidgetiness of the toddler with a wet nappy. By the age of 2 years, the toddler develops a sense of urgency and a little warning is given before he needs to go.

The bladder-training plan has a dual pronged approach. Firstly, to introduce the new activity of sitting on the potty and make it rewarding. Secondly, to make a connection between the toddler's newfound awareness of the urge to empty his bladder and sitting on the potty. Over the next few months we want to develop a habit, where the child will eventually take himself to the toilet when he needs to go.

The bladder-training plan

- The first step is to purchase a potty and get the toddler used to sitting. We are trying to build an association between the urge to go and sitting.
- Swap daytime nappies for training pants. These pull ups are a cross between nappies and underpants, providing protection from leaks while giving the toddler training in using underwear.
- Every time you see the warning signs, dash to the potty, yank down the training pants and deposit the toddler. During the day, try to catch the toddler before he wets himself.
- Encourage the toddler to sit regularly on the potty or toilet each day. Here we harness the power of toilet timing to our advantage. Sitting before or after mealtimes is a good routine to establish, and also before leaving the house or coming in again. Sitting together as a duo when mum or dad goes to the toilet is another way to encourage the activity.
- When the toddler is sitting on the potty, drop subtle hints of encouragement. Be patient, because the day will come when they surprise you and themselves.
- If something happens, reward the toddler with praise. The reward provides the reinforcement he needs while learning this new skill. If the toddler does nothing but sit there happily, reward his effort and good behaviour. If you keep this up consistently in a matter of days or weeks you will have a reliably trained toddler.
- If you are getting nowhere, stop and try again when the toddler is a month older. Don't force: time and maturity can make all the difference.

Points to remember

Check the toddler is old enough to start training by making sure they know the difference between wet and dry – before 15 months, they are generally unaware. As we've already discussed, 18 months is really the earliest age to consider commencing bladder training. Two years is an even more realistic age to begin, and if you wait until 2½ years, you will find it all slides into place. The older the toddler is, the fewer headaches for their parents.

Most toddlers will be enthusiastic and keen to oblige but a few with a negative streak will use toilet training as an excuse to exercise some power. Remember, forcing is a complete waste of time. If the toddler rebels by refusing to sit, don't reward this behaviour with attention. Pull up the training pants, put clothes back in place and get on with life.

Training pants are of great benefit given the precarious state of toddler urgency. If your best Berber can cope, you can try progressing straight to regular underpants but you may have to take advantage of carpet cleaning specials.

A few children are very comfortable in their nappies, and see no need to advance to this next stage of toileting. For these children, a change to underpants is on the cards. As the frigid winds whistle up from Antarctica, the chill factor of wet undies increases in the nether regions, bringing icy feelings to sensitive bits. This jolting move out of their comfort zone is usually enough to speed up the training.

If you are frustrated that your toddler is getting nowhere, remember that there aren't any children refusing to use the toilet by the time they are at school. It may seem to you that this stage is taking forever, but we are generally talking about a few months of everyone's lives.

Common questions

'My toddler won't sit on the potty or toilet. Do you have any tricks?'
As this is the place to start in bladder training, a toddler who refuses to sit presents a small obstacle to success. There are a few tricks that you can try, depending on your toddler's reason for refusal, which I discuss later in this chapter.

'My toddler is 3 years old and is still not toilet trained. What should I do?'
This is one of the most common questions from parents of children this age. These parents often feel that they are the only ones in the country who cannot toilet train their toddler. 'What have I done wrong?' they cry. The truth is they have done nothing wrong and thousands of other parents are in exactly the same boat.

Perhaps the child is just not ready. Even though the average toddler is ready by this age, the nice thing about toddlers is they aren't average. If you resort to pushing, then there will only be a clash of wills. In cases like these we have to remember our goal of a well-trained child, instead of focusing on the problem. The best thing you can do is back off, suspend all attempts to train and regroup. Put all failures and any fights behind you. Once calm has been restored you then have to start again from scratch, focusing just on sitting, without any pressure on a result. Gently and cunningly build up a happy, positive sitting habit.

Bowel training

The principles of bowel training the toddler are the same as bladder training. The main one is that the child has to be comfortable sitting before anything can happen. And like with bladder training, we are trying to get the child to associate the urge to go with sitting on the toilet.

Generally, I suggest beginning bowel training around the age of 2, when voluntary control starts to be established. Though there are many different ways of bowel training a toddler, in my experience there is only one way that is really effective, as long as it is not started too early and not pushed too hard. I call this the 'sit and wait' method. It is really just a large chunk of good, old-fashioned commonsense.

The 'sit and wait' bowel training plan

1. Get the toddler to sit happily and regularly on the potty or toilet.

- At this point we aren't even trying for a deposit, we just want to increase the interest in sitting. The mood should be positive and encouraging. If you have already been bladder training, this step should be easy.

- Aim for three sits a day, preferably after meals, when the stomach is full. Twice a day may be enough for some children. The toilet timing reflex means that the bowels are stimulated to empty, although by the age of 2 this has weakened. However it still has a little power and it helps to harness what you can.

- The secret to success is to make this activity fun. 'How about sitting on the potty? I'll read you a story. "Once upon a time there was a girl called Goldilocks who went into the woods."' Maybe at this age the toddler doesn't understand the finer points of bears and porridge, but he certainly understands being the centre of attention.

- To encourage more of the desired behaviour – sitting – you have to reward the toddler when it happens. Keep the toddler glued in place with attention while he is sitting, and praise his efforts. When it is obvious he has had enough, let him get on with life.

- Don't make a fuss of any refusal to sit; this will only reinforce unwanted behaviour.

2. Gradually increase the length of time that the child sits.

- The length of sitting depends on the child. Some active toddlers find it almost impossible to sit for two minutes, while others are content to remain in an almost meditative state for most of the day.

- Keep the toddler's attention focused for longer by diverting his attention with activities such as singing, counting or reading. Remember, toddlers have very short attention spans. Keep a special book or activity game in the bathroom just for use when sitting on the toilet or potty.
- Know when to call it quits. If there has been no sign of action after a few minutes, then there is little point in prolonging the process.

3. **Once the sitting habit is firmly established, it's time for business.**

- Engage in a little amateur psychology. The aim is to get the child's brain to focus on bowels and bowel motions, when there are so many other things for a toddler to pay attention to.
- Drop gentle hints to get him thinking positive thoughts about a bit of action. 'Big 2-year-old boys do poos in the potty. If you do, we could give all the nappies away and get grown up underpants, and Grandma will be so proud.'
- When the big event does happen, make a fuss. Bring out the marching band you have stashed away for just such occasions, and let off some fireworks. At this age soft rewards of fuss, attention and praise work wonders. Call dad at work so your toddler can tell him the earth-shattering news. This may seem a bit over the top but it works.
- If you are getting nowhere, wait a few weeks and try again. Sometimes all that is needed is for the toddler to become a month older.

Points to remember

It may take time before you hit the jackpot. Don't force the child or put pressure on him to perform. If you establish a regular sitting routine, remain relaxed, and encourage his efforts, eventually something has to drop into the bowl.

Never suggest anxiety, frustration or impatience on your part. If two minutes after leaving the potty empty they dirty their pants, this must be dealt with calmly, saying nothing more than 'Next time you may do a poo on the potty – I would be so proud'. Remember, you can only encourage them to sit, they have the ultimate control over what happens and they know this.

Make sure you have each step going smoothly before moving on. For example, if the toddler stalls in step 1 of the programme, wait for him to catch up. Don't hurry him along to the next step.

Relapses are very rare except in times of diarrhoea, constipation or sickness. Times like these are not the right times to stick to a plan. Let the child get well again before returning to the training.

Like so much in this book, bowel training will not work unless the parents are fully committed and prepared to persevere with the technique. If you don't feel strong enough to see it through at present, then wait a while.

Common questions
'Are there any reasons why I shouldn't begin bowel training my toddler?'

There are some situations where beginning a training plan is not the wisest idea. Parents often want to get training out of the way before the arrival of a new baby or before undertaking an overseas trip, but remember that the toddler's body is not governed by these outside timetables. Also, if the home is in turmoil, with visitors, illness or family tension, you will have more success if you postpone training until the dust settles.

'How often should my toddler open his bowels?'

Parents' concern over what goes in the feeding end of their child is rivalled only by their obsession as to what comes out at the other. They need reassurance that, though it is best for bowels to open every day, this does not always happen. An eminent doctor once claimed that the normal toddler's bowel habit was between five times a day and once every five days. This may be a rather extreme view, but it is probably quite sensible. Whatever is a regular pattern for your child is what's important. If you are concerned, see your doctor who will determine if all is normal.

'My toddler only opens his bowels once a week. Does he need a laxative to help him along?'

Bowel patterns can be regulated by diet, through fibre content, the hydrating effects of adequate water intake, fruit consumption and even eating various spices. If you feel the need to give your child something to help move his bowels, check that he is getting enough water during the day and try increasing his dietary fibre. Always check with your doctor before giving your child a laxative.

'Should I worry if my child is constipated?'

Some children are born with a 'sluggish' bowel and always tend to be constipated. Others become constipated as a result of bad toilet habits; still others have problems that started following a feverish illness. Constipation can lead to a vicious circle in which the more constipated the child becomes, the more difficult it is to pass a motion, and the more reluctant the child is to try. If the constipation is associated with a small tear in the anal margin, the resultant pain may cause a major problem of withholding.

As there can be a medical reason behind constipation, it is worth discussing it with your doctor. As mentioned above, diet plays a big part and making small changes such as offering the toddler more fruit can loosen things up.

Caught in time

There are a couple of other bowel-training methods that deserve a mention. At some time or other, many a mum has had a go at this first one. Basically, the parents do nothing until they hear a grunt, and see that strange look which appears at times like these on the toddler's face. This is accompanied by an ominous silence, an odd posture and finally a characteristic smell. At the grunt, the child is rushed to the potty or toilet in anticipation of the big event.

This may be easy in theory but it often fails in practice. Firstly, the parent needs all the speed of an Olympic sprinter to reach the toilet on time and the dexterity of Houdini to untangle the obstructing clothing. Then, if all goes smoothly there is a sporting chance that he will announce he has changed his mind. It is not a bad method to try, as it is based on identifying the urge to go. But I suggest it be used only as a back-up to the more reliable 'sit and wait' method.

A slightly more bizarre method of bowel training is one I describe as 'the broody hen'. When the child dirties his pants, he is immediately taken to the potty instead of being changed. Here, his offering is placed in the sacred chamber, and the child is made to sit above it like a hen incubating a newly laid egg. This is a form of conditioning, getting the child to associate bowel motions with the toilet.

I know many parents who swear by this method however I find it a bit weird. But it takes all kinds and if this works for some, then far be it for me to criticise.

A message to dad

A mother once told me how she toilet-trained her son. Her husband worked at the North Head Sewerage Plant in Sydney where the sewage is treated and collected before being pumped out to sea, so she would say to the boy: 'John, sit on the toilet and do something – pass a message down the pipe to dad.'

Night training

Wet beds – this phenomenon goes with the territory of having children, but even knowing it is so common offers little comfort to parents. Night training conjures images of stumbling through dark corridors at 3 am, dragging damp, semi-conscious toddlers from their soggy beds; finding clean sheets and pyjamas and putting mounds of wet linen in the wash. Nocturnal enuresis (the name doctors use for bed wetting) is something most parents will thankfully only have to contend with for a short time, but there are the unlucky few who score a toddler that seems destined to squelch indefinitely.

We can talk about the average toddler attaining night-time dryness at about 33 months, but you will find that your toddler won't be aware of this statistic. Even if he was, he'd be unimpressed, as this last stage of toilet training will be completed to his own schedule. This is one reason parents find night training so frustrating, as there is a great range of when the toddler is ready to go through the night dry. In fact, in Australia, it is between 18 months and 8 years! Rarely does it occur early enough for the parent.

Before you begin night training your toddler, you must have daytime toilet training (bladder and bowel) squarely under control.

This means the child will no longer be in nappies during the day, instead using training pants. The signal for the right time to start is when you find that a number of night nappies make it unannointed through the hours of darkness. Attempts can be made before this but it tends to be a long uphill battle.

The night-training plan

Plan A

- Once you notice nappies that have made it through the night dry, acknowledge them to let the toddler know they have done something clever: 'You were dry all night, well done!' That sort of praise gets the toddler thinking in the right direction.

- Switch the toddler to pull up training pants at night. Let him know that he is a big boy and doesn't need nappies at night any more. The idea that they are grown up can speed up this process, and for some children this may be all they need to produce dry nights from now on.

- Build on any success and reward any dry night with praise. This reinforces the dry message and provides momentum.

- If you find a few wet nights sprinkled in among the arid, take them in your stride: 'That's a pity but we'll see how you go tomorrow'. Remember, Rome wasn't plumbed in a day and we certainly don't want to discourage the toddler's best efforts.

■ If Plan A isn't producing results, go to Plan B.

Plan B

■ Continue using the steps in Plan A – keep the training pants on, notice and reward the occasional dry night and don't punish or blame the toddler for any wet nights. Don't rush or pressure the toddler.

■ Take the child to the toilet during the night until he learns to hold on until morning. The easiest time to do this is before you go to bed yourself. Continue until mainly dry nights are achieved and you think it's safe, then go back to Plan A.

■ Some toddlers seem to stick with watery nights with no end in sight. Don't despair; go to Plan C.

Plan C

■ Stop all attempts to night train the toddler and go back to nappies at night time. Resume training in a month's time, which can make all the difference.

■ Keep an eye out for a number of dry nappies in a row which is the key to commencing training again.

Points to remember

Waking the child in the night can work well as long as he doesn't become too distressed. Some children find being woken startling, and the last thing you want to do is introduce an element of fear to the training programme. If this is the case, you will have to stick to Plan A, but it may take a little longer.

If you're game, you can decide to skip the training pants and go straight to underpants, in which case your washing machine will get a great workout. Waterproof mattress protectors are a must if you choose to go this route.

Some parents believe that restricting the fluids you offer the toddler in the early evening will do much to reduce night time wetting. From my simple way of thinking, it seems that what goes in must eventually come out and if it doesn't go in it is less likely to leak out.

Remember that all toddlers are different and that for some night training will take longer than others. Don't discourage yourself by making comparisons with other children at play group, day care or preschool. Your toddler will get the hang of it in time.

Common questions
'Is there a family link to bed wetting?'
Delay in bladder training at night seems to have an extremely strong genetic relationship. Some studies show almost 70 per cent of wetters have a parent who had, or sibling who has, a similar problem. For more statistics, see the box on p. 247.

'Is there a difference between night training boys and girls?'
Bed wetting is more common in boys while I find that day-time wetting in the older child is almost completely confined to girls. But the ways to manage either is the same for both boy and girl toddlers.

'My toddler was night trained, then he started wetting the bed again. What could be wrong?'
Some doctors get very worked up when they hear of a dry child who regresses to becoming a wetter again. They believe that this secondary enuresis is caused by infections, or emotional trauma. Certainly infections can cause a relapse but other unmistakable symptoms such as urgency or pain are usually very much in evidence if this is the reason.

As for emotional trauma, it may well be a triggering factor in some cases but in most of the children I see, I doubt whether even Sherlock Holmes could find the real trigger for the relapse. When the cause is unclear and the situation doesn't resolve itself within a short time, you can go back to the training plan again, which should be enough to put things back on track. However if you are genuinely concerned you need to consult your doctor.

'When is my toddler too old for nappies?'
Whether dry or wet there comes an age when nappies have to go. This is some time about 4 years of age, but it depends on how the child copes with wet nappies and how you handle wet beds.

'My friend used a reward chart when night training her toddler. Will this help me?'

When 4 years old, out of nappies and still untrained, some suggest star reward charts to encourage toddlers to 'think dry'. But in my experience, soundly sleeping children have little interest in star gazing. Star charts are more use for astrologers than night wetters. They are, however, useful to keep track of how many wet and dry nights the toddler is having, so you can see if you are making progress.

'My doctor says that we should try one of the drugs that reduce night wetting. Are these effective?'

If at 5 years bed wetting is still a real problem there are prescription drugs available to help you out as a last resort. Imipramine and desmopressin are two of the drugs given but success only lasts as long as the prescription. They are not a cure but can be of some benefit. These are temporary measures, and it is best to discuss them with your paediatrician.

'I've heard there is an electronic gadget that can cure bed wetting. Is this true and where can I get one?'

Bed wetting can be cured using an electronic bedwetting alarm. This gadget has two electrodes, kept apart by a thin dry sheet, which is placed in the child's bed. When the bed gets wet the sheet shorts out and bells start to ring. No-one seems sure why this works but in children 6 years and over, more than two-thirds will be dry within a month of use. Your doctor, local pharmacist or community health clinic should all be able to assist you in acquiring one.

'Is it better to night train in the warmer months?'

When possible try not to begin training in a cold snap, or the dead of winter. When a warm child lies in a warm bed, he sweats and loses fluid. When a cold child lies in a cold bed, there is little reason to sweat and the fluid may choose another route for escape. Generally it is more difficult in cold weather, and you may even find that it brings a relapse in the already trained child. However, if the toddler is ready to night train, you can still go ahead and ignore the seasons.

The bottom line

- The average young Australian will be night trained at 33 months.
- The normal young Australian will become night trained somewhere between 18 months and 8 years. Note this is a large range.
- One in ten of all 5 year olds still wet the bed at night. That is three in every nursery class at school. From this age, if left untreated, 15 per cent are cured each year until it is relatively rare in teenagers.
- If one parent was not night trained before the age of 6 years, there is a 40 per cent chance their children will follow suit.
- If both parents were not night trained before the age of 6 years, there is a 70 per cent chance their children will follow suit. (Children, please choose your parents carefully!)

The reluctant sitter

It is all very well for me to tell you that all toilet training begins with forming a sitting habit, but there are some toddlers who flatly refuse to sit on a potty or a toilet. It is very difficult to deal with children who scream and protest if you so much as take them near a toilet, then wriggle off in seconds. This scenario can quickly degenerate into the parents forcing, pushing and punishing the toddler, and the tension level in the home can run extremely high.

The refusal to sit may be due to a number of causes: pure stubbornness; too busy doing toddler things to spare the time; fear of toilets; or the pain of trying to move constipated bowels. Most of these reluctant sitters become willing when there is calm and their parents approach them in a confident and convincing way. How you approach and cure your toddler's refusal to sit depends on the reason, but each are easily solved.

The on-the-go toddler: For the toddler whose social activities leave little time for such prosaic endeavours as sitting on the toilet, a little cunning is called for. The clear message the on-the-go toddler sends is: 'Not now mum, I've got a mess to create, then the *Tweenies* to watch'. But even Donald Trump has time for toilet breaks and your toddler needs to learn to take pit stops.

The trick with the on-the-go toddler is to snag his attention before he can focus on more interesting activities. You will need to be creative in finding diversions that work for the time required to remove the necessary clothes and seat him on the potty or toilet. Remember that we aren't looking to keep him in place for hours. To begin with, mere seconds of sitting in the right place counts as a victory. Build up the time and have a supply of new distractions and enticements on hand to keep the ball rolling. If he leaves his seat prematurely, there should be no fights, but the attention must simply stop.

The fearful toddler: It can be the flushing, the water in the bowl, the claustrophobic feeling of the smallest room in the house – for whatever reason, some children are fearful of the toileting experience.

In the case of the fearful toddler one needs to resort to a little desensitisation. This starts with using a potty rather than training using a toilet as to many toddlers they are strange, scary items. To make the process more toddler-friendly, place the potty in front of the television, and get the child to practice sitting with training pants in place. From here there is a gradual move to no pants, then no television and the potty relocated to the bathroom.

Once the toddler is using the toilet, it is best if a parent stays near by. They can gradually move a little farther away each time, until eventually the child learns to 'fly solo'.

The stubborn toddler: Stubborn children will establish a good sitting pattern if rewarded with praise and attention when they comply. In the older child (over 4 years), I use a star reward system which is very effective, or I negotiate a simple, no-fuss agreement such as, 'You go and sit and I will have a milkshake waiting for you when you come out'. This smacks of bribery but it achieves the desired effect without threats or reprimands and soon enough the toddler won't need enticements to sit.

The constipated toddler: If the child has been constipated and possibly also has a small tear in the anal area, there may be great

All in good time

Some children will engage in quite extraordinary parent-manipulating toilet rituals. A stubborn little 3-year-old girl I saw had it down to a fine art. She had been bladder trained long before but when it came to bowel motions the fun really started. When such a motion seemed imminent she summoned her mum. A warm, freshly laundered nappy had to be brought and carefully pinned in place. The little dictator then gestured the family to assemble at the dining table. She sat in her chosen chair, her favourite doll seated on her right-hand and mum on her left. Then her favourite book was opened at a special page and placed in front of her. Then, when all was exactly to her liking, she gave a great heave and peace was restored for another day.

The cure for all this drama followed a rather bumpy course. As a first shot I got all her nappies donated to a newborn baby down the road. Our little lady's response was swift. She entered a stage of concrete constipation. A dose of laxative was administered which worked like a dream, the trouble was that the resultant movement was in her pants. At this point mum and I wondered if dirty pants were really any sort of improvement on the ritual. But we were pursuing greater goals and persevered, and with a great deal of guile and gentleness a good sitting habit was started and in three weeks we had achieved a complete cure.

reluctance to sit on the potty or toilet. Even if he has healed a long time before, the fear can remain. In the case of the constipated toddler, once the constipation has been resolved, you must focus on reestablishing a sitting routine without any concern for what may or may not drop out. Any tension or expectation will be transmitted to the toddler and these do not encourage the opening of bodily orifices.

It is wise to seek a medical opinion, particularly if this is not the first constipated episode. Laxatives and faecal softening agents are useful, as well as a little lubricating gel for the tail end which can be purchased from the chemist.

These approaches will work with both the child who has never been trained and the one who has regressed. The aim is to make the experience of sitting easy and enjoyable so the toddler has a positive association that can be built on through the toilet-training process.

Toilet-training troubles

While you really can't go wrong if you relax and focus on making the toilet-training process positive and rewarding, there are moments that cause stress for many parents, particularly if they are determined to get it right. Below are some of the common toilet-training troubles.

Potty or toilet?

A decision that every parent faces is whether to train their toddler on a potty or a toilet. There is no right or wrong choice, as each has its pros and cons. Frankly, I'm more interested in getting bums on seats than whether the seat in question is plastic or porcelain.

Most parents start toilet training their child using a potty. Over the years the humble potty has been modified until it is the perfect throne for toddler backsides. A potty is reliable, convenient, and has the great advantage of being portable. It can be taken with

you on family outings or trips to visit the rellies. It can be moved from room to room to accommodate the toddler's desire for 'location, location, location' while learning to sit.

There are, however, a number of independent little toddlers who are bored with being children and who wish to use the toilet like grown-ups. If this is the case with your toddler, there are a few things to keep in mind to make your loo toddler-friendly.

One modification I recommend is placing a step under the toilet for the toddler's feet. Sitting perched high on the toilet with legs waving in mid air is not the physiologically ideal posture for moving one's bowels. This also makes it easier for the child to climb up, and gives support for his legs when bearing down. The second modification is to place a child's toilet seat inside the adult one, providing more stability for little bottoms and dispelling any well-founded fears of falling into the bowl. Whatever you do, don't flush when they are still sitting, or they will think they are about to blast off and join the astronauts in space.

Eventually, all children will progress to the toilet and leave the potty behind. If at present your toddler can't get up there without falling off or falling in, a potty is probably a wiser way to go.

The toilet of doom

Chain flush toilets are pretty obsolete now but I remember in one old hospital in Belfast where I worked, there were vintage toilets in the children's wards. These antiquated devices gave one adventurous toddler a most terrifying experience. After successfully using the toilet, he climbed on to the seat and just managed to grasp the dangling chain before losing his balance. The toilet started to flush, and still holding on tight, he hung like Indiana Jones over the raging whirlpool below. Eventually, as his strength ebbed, he fell, becoming wet to the knees. His toilet training was delayed by at least six months.

The right thing in the wrong place

Some children gain control of their bowels but then insist on displaying the fact in various places around the house and garden.

This can cause anxiety and even anger in parents, as they try to interpret these small messages. Is this deliberately anti-social behaviour? Is the toddler expressing how they feel about their parents? While this reaction is obviously far fetched, something must be done.

Parents wonder if they should completely ignore this behaviour in the hope the toddler will soon confine his activity to the potty. After all, we are told to ignore behaviour that we don't want. But I believe the best way is to show the child what we want them to do, without making a great fuss. Quietly mention to the child that this is not welcome, and give great rewards when the right thing is done in the right place. Remember that at this age, toddlers have so many things that they have to learn. This behaviour is just an example of where a little fine tuning is needed. Be thankful that all the equipment is working – it really is quite incredible that they have come so far with bowel training in the first place!

Boys: should they sit or stand?

There is always some debate over whether little boys should learn to wee standing or sitting. I believe that it honestly doesn't matter one way or the other. What you may find is that if you opt for standing, bladder training will come fractionally faster due to the rewards of hearing so much tinkling water and also being in charge of one's own equipment.

There are, however, several drawbacks to training a toddler standing up. At this age toddlers are prone to what I call the 'Fireman Syndrome' – they are hellishly inaccurate and spray water all over the place. In addition, some get so carried away with this new skill that it's almost impossible to ever get them to sit. So while you have promoted bladder training, you may have delayed the bowel habit.

In the first edition of *Toddler Taming* my only cure for inaccuracy was to remove any carpets from the bathroom, after which you had to call in the plumber to insert a big drain; then all that was required was to hose the scene down with great regularity.

With the input of some parents' creative genius, I have developed a better, and dare I say more level-headed, way. Tear up some bits of paper and roll them into little balls. Drop these into the toilet pan and there before your very eyes floats the entire

The party pooper

I remember a birthday party my boys attended as toddlers, on a hot summer's day in Sydney. Semi-clothed children chased each other around the large veranda of the host's house, disappearing inside occasionally as relaxed parents chatted amiably.

This idyllic scene was shattered by the discovery one parent made on the way inside to fetch a drink. There on the rug in front of the sofa lay a little brown present. At first all the parents gathered around to inspect the gift. Then slowly they began backing away, shaking their heads, and convincingly stating that, 'It couldn't have been *my* child!' As the party broke up I was reminded of the tale of Cinderella and wondered if we could resort to a princely approach to figure out the identity of the party pooper!

Navy fleet, just waiting to be scuttled by the truer-aiming toddler's target practice. A variation of this method uses ping pong balls in place of paper – I'll leave you to decide the hygienic and environmental impacts of each.

Toddler urgency and reliability

When you are out and about with a toddler, you learn very quickly that when he says 'Wee wee, now,' he means *now* – and not in 5 minutes. Parents are forced to throw modesty to the wind, aiming the child towards the gutter or helping him water the flower arrangement outside the town hall.

Urgency is a fact of life for toddlers. After all, it is quite a big ask to go from free flowing one day to having sluice gates in place the next. The reality is you can't expect the toddler to be reliable in the early days. Small patches of dampness appear, particularly when the child is excited or engrossed in play. Major and minor accidents will happen for at least a year from the time they gain bladder and bowel control.

Car travel is particularly difficult, with frequent stops being required, usually in places where it is impossible to pull over. You quickly learn not to go too far from home without a spare change of clothes and some Wet Ones. And taking advantage of every opportunity to use toilets is not a bad idea either.

Flushed with success

As the poet said, 'They also serve who only stand and wait'. Although Milton wasn't talking about toilet training, his words do sum up one of the cornerstones of toilet-training success. Patience is the key and forcing or attempting to rush the toddler will get you nowhere. Most of this miraculous process will unfold before our eyes in the toddler's own time.

The main mistake parents make is starting too early. If you just wait a little longer and watch out for the signs that the toddler is ready, it will all go more smoothly.

17

Nasty habits in nice children

In those dreamy days before you had a toddler, I doubt you ever saw yourself reading a chapter like this and recognising your child. But now you are better acquainted with the inventive antics of the average toddler, you have probably discovered that even the nicest of nice children can display some of the nastiest of nasty habits. Let's look at some of the most common concerns:

- Biting • Finger up the nose • Whingeing
- Interrupting adults • Playing with privates
- Stealing • Using bad language • Refusing to buckle up • Absconding • Teeth grinding
- Head banging • Breath holding
- Vomiting • Smearing

Biting

Of all the toddler nasty habits, this is the one that I have fielded the most questions about during my career as a paediatrician. Parents and playgroup leaders alike all need to know how to curb the chomping habits of the average toddler.

In my experience, biting is found mostly in the 1 to 2½ year age group. In the toddler it is not a premeditated, spiteful act, just a symptom of this age of little sense. Little biters don't get up with the lark and hatch a plot to get into playgroup early, hide behind the door and ambush Freddie Smith when he enters, sinking teeth into his arm like a demented piranha. It's more a case of Freddie happens to be passing and your little angel is a bit overexcited and not thinking. A bite is an impulse – it just seems like a good idea at the time.

Many babies in the first year of life suddenly sink their teeth into whoever is carrying them, unaware of the pain they may cause. If put down on the floor immediately, it does not take the average baby long to work out that, if he wants the pleasure of a cuddle, he shouldn't indulge in cannibalism.

With the toddler, it is usually a piece of brother or sister that finds itself wedged between the closing teeth and as this is a sort of family feast, it is much easier to discipline, as you own both the biter and the bitee. When it is a neighbour's child that has been nibbled, however, the parents may expect you to instigate some sort of major retribution. If justice is not seen to be done, friends may ban their children from your house and it can lead to feuds more vicious than that of the Montagues and Capulets.

Biting can be quite prevalent at playgroup, partly because of all the available prey, combined with an excitable, busy atmosphere. Rather than greeting one of their little friends with outstretched arms, the toddler approaches with a wide open mouth. Embarrassed parents tell me their toddler has become unaffectionately known as Jaws.

What to do
How you react to a bite will depend on the circumstances.

- If the toddler just gives a minor nip in times of excitement, a gentle warning is all that is needed. Say, 'Don't bite; that hurts'. Without making a big deal, they will sense your displeasure.

- Divert the toddler's attention to something else. There is no need for mouth guards, just keep a close eye out for follow-up attacks.

- If a stronger message is needed, ignore the biter and give attention to the bitee. This works equally well whether the victim is a sibling or a play friend.

- If the biting is repeated, premeditated or major and a stern warning has been ignored, then use Time Out.

- Try to limit the toddler's socialising to the length of his attention span. Toddlers are more likely to strike when they are tired, bored or irritable.

- When your toddler bites another at playgroup, you are in the full public view, without Time Out to fall back on and whatever you do, half the audience will criticise. Often the best you can do is to watch carefully, warn firmly, divert when an impending attack is anticipated and then, if a bite occurs, ignore the biter and give the best toys and attention to the injured party. This may sound rather wishy-washy but when outside the home, your hands are tied.

- I have known children who would really benefit from playgroup being unable to attend due to a groundswell of reaction to Junior's habit of sinking his pearly whites into other children. In this position, don't deny the child the important

A tooth for a tooth

Some parents view the warning and diverting technique as pathetically weak. They believe the answer is to give a short sharp smack to register the limits of acceptable behaviour. For other parents there is only one answer – if their child bites, they bite him back. This is the eye for an eye and a tooth for a tooth approach that was probably pretty modern 2000 years ago. It comes from the same school of thought as washing out mouths for using bad language and rubbing noses into wet beds. I am convinced that there are better ways of doing things now.

activity of playgroup. Find some allies among the other parents, and be especially vigilant when your toddler attends, intervening and diverting at the slightest hint of a nibble.

Don't despair: remember that biting is only a habit of the first 2½ years and be reassured that they will not be going round biting others as adults, unless they become heavyweight boxing champions.

Finger up the nose

Little noses are to little fingers as burrows are to bunnies – a comfortable place to explore when there is nothing better to do. When the toddler is bored, his mind slips and along with it a finger, sliding ever upward and inward.

On a lecture tour in the United States once it seemed that every time I talked on air some parent asked about fingers up noses. Such was the concern, you might have thought this habit to be exclusive to North American nostrils, but it isn't; this is a universal toddler pastime.

Though most toddler fingers find toddler noses at times of tiredness or boredom, occasionally an older child with an easily baited parent will do it just to annoy. A little finger parks in a small nostril – dad explodes. Finger up again – dad explodes again. What great entertainment for the toddler! Soon this little arm is going up and down like a fiddler's elbow.

What to do
- With toddlers, the solution is to divert them and keep those little hands and minds fully occupied.
- If you are truly offended, you and any other adults can go to another room – out of sight is, after all, out of mind.
- When this habit is made into a game to get a rise out of you, let the toddler know you aren't prepared to play. Stop rewarding the toddler with an outburst, which only gives him attention and reinforces the behaviour.

I believe we should not be too tough with our youngsters; after all we adults have some not dissimilar habits ourselves. The next time you stop at a red traffic light, take a look at the car beside you. You can see where one hand is, but you have no idea what is happening with the other. That's why rock stars have tinted glass in their limousines.

Whingeing

Whingeing is one of the most parent-destroying activities that any child can indulge in. Naturally we expect children who are tired, sick or teething to whinge but there still remains a great band of healthy, well-rested children who continue to devastate their parents. As practised by some children, this habit is equal in potency to the Chinese water torture. In my experience, boys generally take the prize for overactivity and really bad behaviour but when it comes to whingeing, the fairer sex usually gets the gold medal every time.

The trouble with whingeing is that we can unintentionally make it into a much repeated behaviour by the way we react. The 4 year old is not allowed out to play because it is raining. He complains and whinges. This gets particularly painful after ten minutes so you give in, in order to preserve your sanity. Now you have blown it. You have set a precedent that a definite 'No' can be turned to an equally definite 'Yes' if the toddler whinges long enough. This is not a wise way to run things.

What to do
- Skilful parents can divert lesser whingers back to the straight and narrow by noticing something around the house or setting off on some interesting activity. This strategy works best in the not-very-determined, low grade whinger.
- If diversion does not work, the child must be ignored. Mortal man has only a limited ability to actually ignore whingeing, so *pretending* to ignore it is probably the best we can hope for. It gives an equally strong message to the child.
- When the parents can no longer ignore the irritation, or the situation gets way out of hand, this is the moment to employ the Time Out technique.
- A clever, failsafe way of dealing with unrelenting whingeing is to sweep up the offending party and head for the great

outdoors. Most children suspend hostilities as soon as they escape from the restrictions of the home battleground, and with the minority who continue, the whingeing never seems so bad when competing with bird song and noisy motor vehicles.

Interrupting adults

One of the greatest sources of irritation with small children is their constant interrupting when adults are talking. In some houses it is almost impossible for parents to communicate with each other when there is an awake toddler around.

Toddlers don't think like adults and they can't see a problem with their irritating interrupting habits. Due to his short attention span, the toddler knows that if he does not say his piece immediately it will be forgotten and lost forever. And his self-centred world view makes him think that his wise sayings are of earth-shattering importance and that everyone must immediately shut up and listen. Not to mention, he does not like others stealing his much enjoyed position centre stage.

Toddlers' habits of interrupting are highlighted when visitors call and want to talk at length to the parents. The child interferes so much that tempers are lost or the visit becomes a complete waste of time. They may also refuse to let their parents talk on the phone, by either making so much noise that reasoned conversation is rendered impossible, or creating such havoc in the house that the call has to be abandoned.

What to do

To some extent every toddler will interrupt, so this is pretty normal behaviour.

- Visitors who are real friends will realise that the toddler needs a lot of attention, and if they are not sharp enough to see this, their absence is probably not a great loss anyway.
- Be prepared for disjointed conversation. Share your attention between your guests and your toddler.
- It is best to reserve long telephone calls for the evening, when the toddler is in bed.

Switched on

Several years ago I looked after a young disabled boy whose favourite trick was to wait for the phone to ring and then set off at high speed round the house, turning on every possible electrical appliance he could before the call was terminated. By the time his mother got off the phone, the house was buzzing with the noise of vacuum cleaners, food mixers and hair dryers, while lights blazed in every room, and the electricity meter raced round and round like a Grand Prix car.

- Create a stash of special toys or DVDs that are only used when you are in need of some uninterrupted time so they don't lose their novelty value for the toddler. This can be especially useful if working from home.
- Cordless phones are almost essential for today's parents.

The constant interruption of conversations will resolve itself by the end of toddlerdom, by which time the child will have a better short-term memory, be less impulsive, and will have learnt to wait his turn.

Playing with privates

Most toddlers play with their genitals at some time or other. It is normal toddler behaviour, and it has no true sexual overtones. They may touch, rub, rock or move their legs, for no other reason than they enjoy it.

Historically, so much fuss has been made over children masturbating that even the most broad-minded parents still have a twinge of concern when they see their children doing it. Tales of how it would send you mad or deaf, or both, still ring in their ears. It was even claimed in Victorian times that it sent you blind. This of course is utter rubbish, but even if it were true most of our children would opt to do it a little and wear glasses.

What to do

Playing with their 'privates' occurs in both boys and girls. It usually starts in the second year when the nappy region is unveiled and a new area of discovery is made available.

■ The treatment is to completely ignore what is, after all, a perfectly innocent habit. These days, parents are encouraged to relax and not let their own hang-ups get in the way.

■ Diversion is a good tactic if the fiddling is wearing on your nerves or the child is overdoing it a bit. Don't make a big deal, just encourage another activity.

■ I emphasise that at toddler age this behaviour has no sexual connotations and it almost exclusively happens when they are bored, tired or tense.

■ If the child has his hands down his pants at an inappropriate time or place, say when he is standing in church, or when the grandparents are visiting, don't make a big fuss. Gently divert the offending hand or interest the child in something more sociable. Ignoring, diversion and keeping them active is the answer – not humiliation or punishment.

Sometime later in the preschool years, children discover that little boys and little girls are not identical. This leads to a certain amount of innocent interest which is a quite normal and natural stage of development. This needs to be viewed with a broad mind and a relatively blind eye.

Concerns of sexual abuse

The statistics vary from study to study but, at the most conservative estimates, 1 in 10 adult women and 1 in 20 adult men have suffered sexual abuse in childhood. The extent of this varies from an incident of touching to major repeated sexual activity.

In sexual abuse, power is inappropriately misused. Children are made to feel guilty for what is being done to them and the older child may be frightened to speak out. The most insidious part of sexual abuse is that the perpetrator is usually a trusted adult or adolescent who is well known to the child. They may be a relative, family friend, step-parent or even biological parent.

It can be extremely difficult to diagnose sexual abuse, but any hint of this ill-treatment must be taken seriously.

- In its most clear-cut presentation, abuse shows as obvious physical damage or there are unmistakable signs.
- More commonly, the only sign is a change in behaviour. The child may withdraw into themselves, become angry, or display inappropriately explicit sexual behaviour.
- When an astute parent sees any of these changes, they may pick up clues of the assault, but often the school-age child feels so guilty, confused and scared they maintain a code of silence.
- One of the saddest aspects of abuse is that the child can no longer trust the adults who are supposed to protect them. The sad part for me is that statistically I will have probably diagnosed only a small proportion of the children in my care who have been abused.

The main message for parents is to gradually educate, but not terrify, children about the possibility of abuse, stranger danger and the importance of saying no. A 2 year old will not understand much of this at first, but by school age the message must have been received loud and clear.

Stealing

To a child under 5 years of age there is no such crime as stealing. This is because whatever is lying about is seen by the toddler as having no owner – surely all these interesting things are there for his entertainment! However, adults are obsessed with who owns what, and they spend thousands of pounds guarding, insuring and locking away all their treasures. Many take offence when toddlers misappropriate items that clearly don't belong to them.

What to do
Although toddlers may collect items with all the zeal of a bower bird, this is not done with any malicious intent.

- Remember toddlers simply lack sense. Pretty objects like coins, pens or other treasures are just nice to hold, often forgotten in a pocket as a result.
- All that is required, therefore, is a gentle reminder, when objects are taken, that they should really be left alone. Nothing more needs to be said.
- When out visiting, a slightly firmer line is required, more for the benefit of the person whose house you are visiting than as a genuine reprimand to the toddler. A quick frisk before you depart will reveal any goods that were about to make the journey home with you.

There is no need to get heavy – this is not the time for police detectives, fingerprinting or searching for caches of stolen goods. Soon enough the toddler will learn the adult values of what is mine and what is yours.

Using bad language

Toddlers are great mimics and they love learning new words, which means that repeating bad language is almost inevitable. But unlike royalty, who only use rude words in private, the toddler seems to delight in hearing words in private and repeating them in public.

Generally, however, bad language is not a major problem in toddlers. Much of the obscene language they know is learnt at

Copy cats (and dogs)

A mother once told me the following story. Their family's garden was her husband's pride and joy; the problem was that the dog from next door kept digging it up. One day the father finally snapped. Nearly bursting with rage, he called the dog a 'bloody mongrel', not noticing their toddler was nearby, all ears. Later, while walking to the supermarket the family passed a beautifully coiffured poodle. The toddler pointed to the poodle and announced to all and sundry, 'Bloody mongrel!'

preschool, and then regurgitated parrot-fashion elsewhere. Indeed, parents like to believe that all bad language is from school, but some must come from a source nearer to home. Just remember that the next time you spill your coffee on your freshly laundered shirt, or express your opinion of someone else's bad driving!

When new, undesirable words come from the toddler, the chances are that he does not know what they mean but is aware of the interesting effect they have on adults. Of the few adjectives at the toddler's disposal, 'pooey' is one that annoys parents and delights the toddler. Bottoms and bodily functions make fascinating topics of conversation, and most toddlers have an extraordinary interest in 'lavatory' talk. This is probably because in the toddler's world of limited experience, these are subjects that they can talk about with real authority.

What to do
Undesirable language can be gently moulded out of the vocabulary.

- When the toddler says a rude word, don't make a big deal of it. A major confrontation will lead to nothing but trouble and will probably only suffice to implant the behaviour even more firmly. If you throw a tantrum every time, it gives him a potent weapon to stir up the household whenever life begins to look a bit boring.
- Quietly say, 'I don't want to hear that'. With no reward, eventually he will stop using it.

- In handling this problem, some degree of selective deafness will be necessary.

- The bodily function fascination usually disappears of its own accord well before the age of five.

Our children start out as wonderful, clean slates, and then these vulgar utterances creep in. We can't live in a bubble; all we can do is let our toddlers know what we will and won't accept.

Refusing to buckle up

Every parent knows that when we are going out in the car, we should put children into a car seat and not drive off unless they are firmly buckled in. This, however, can be easier said than done, as there are some children who figure out how to undo their seat belt and refuse to stay in their seat.

A child roaming around in the car is obviously very dangerous. If there is an accident the child may be injured or even killed. Not to mention, if the police pull you over, you will be fined heavily. They won't be impressed when you tell them, 'I can't make my 2 year old stay in his seat'.

What to do
This is one of those nasty habits that has to be dealt with firmly and decisively, for the safety of all involved.

- If your child gets out of his seat, immediately pull over to the side of the road and stop the car. Buckle him back in and once he is secured, you can drive off.
- As soon as you are moving again, get the toddler's attention focused on something other than his seat belt. Divert him by singing along with a cassette or spotting all the red cars on the road. Like many bad behaviours, the trigger for undoing his belt might be boredom or the need for attention.
- If the toddler frees himself again, pull over once more. Look your child in the eye and speak firmly: 'This car will not move unless you have your belt done up. I'm not going to let you undo it again'. Usually with this firm attitude, the toddler will settle down and let you continue to your destination.

- Remain calm, be persistent and don't allow the situation to escalate out of control. Every parent will have a different level of tolerance, and the amount of warnings you give will depend on that.

- At some point, when you have given sufficient warnings and are obviously going nowhere, you may choose to throw away political correctness for the sake of safety and give a smack. This shows the limits of the behaviour that will be tolerated. Some parents feel that this is the only solution to a dangerous situation.

Realistically, with some children you may have to limit them to short trips, or engage the help of a passenger in the back seat to keep the toddler buckled in. Above all, focus on getting where you are going safely. Averting danger is essential.

Absconding

Any toddler worth his salt, and who has read up on his child psychology, will realise that he is meant to be clingy and loathe being separated from his parents. A small percentage, however, seem ignorant of this fact, and they are forever running off and getting lost.

Absconders are a real trial to their parents, who are forced to take part in high speed pursuits down the main street, and play hide-and-seek in the supermarket. Then there is the interminable wait for the voice to come over the loudspeaker informing them that the escapee has been corralled and is awaiting pick-up.

I can joke but of course there is an element of danger associated with these little escapees' antics. Thoughts of toddlers tangling with traffic, flights of stairs, escalators and lifts, or strangers can cause parents' hearts to race for good reason.

What to do
Luckily most absconders' craving for the great open spaces is short-lived.

- If your child is an absconder, make sure you toddler-proof your home, using the tips in Chapter 11 and the Appendix. Child-proof locks, secure perimeter fencing and sturdy gates limit the toddler's breaks for freedom.

- Take a few cues from Paddington Bear and ensure the toddler carries some form of identification when you are outside your home. While there are fancy new gadgets that can accurately pinpoint your toddler's whereabouts from space, one clever mum used a very low-tech idea. After many frantic searches for her active little boy, she wrote her name and mobile phone number on his hand whenever they were out and about.
- In less than ideal security situations, you may need to improvise. In my office at the hospital, there was no lock on the door, and quick toddlers could make a break for it before I was even out of my chair. I soon resolved the problem by placing a sandbag in front of the closed door. This provided just enough resistance to guarantee that I could catch up before the toddler was out and racing down the corridor. Temporary hurdles such as these are good for when you are visiting friends or relatives.
- Fitting reins is sometimes the only solution for the extremely adventurous. I recommended toddler reins for many children including two who had the curious habit of jumping on passing buses. The first did it as a form of attention-seeking but was always extracted before the bus started off. The second child managed to get as far as the terminus, his mother following in hot pursuit in a taxi.

Curbing the habit of these active toddlers is never easy. My best advice is that parents remain fit and vigilant at all times.

Lost and found

One mother told me how, while shopping in a department store, her toddler wandered off and became lost. Panicking and unable to find him, Mum contacted the store security team. The police were called and a frantic search was quickly mounted.

It later turned out that the little adventurer had gone up the escalator to the next floor. There he had discovered the bed department, and decided to try out a few beds. When he was found, he was fast asleep, snuggled up on a King-size deluxe Posturepedic.

Teeth grinding

The noise of grinding teeth sends a shiver down any parent's spine. In the old days, it was thought to indicate that the child had worms or was suffering from a form of lunacy. These days we know that it is only a harmless, if highly irritating, habit.

Grinding the teeth during sleep is a common, normal occurrence. A small number of normal toddlers grind their teeth noisily by day but, in my experience, this is almost exclusively the behaviour of a child with a major disability.

What to do
- Parents worry that teeth grinding is due to stress or anxiety in the toddler. This is unlikely; it seems that toddlers just do this. There is little that can be, or needs to be done to lessen the amount of nerve-shattering noise.
- Another concern is that the toddler will wear down his teeth. Before the permanent teeth come in around the age of 6, they can't do much damage.
- In very extreme cases dentists have been known to intervene, but this is rare. If you are truly concerned, a visit to the dentist will alleviate your worries.
- Relief for the school-age child and your nerves may come through investing in a mouth guard. This prevents wearing

down molars, which is the concern with the older child's prolonged grinding at permanent teeth.

Head banging

When some senseless young toddlers do not get their own way, they may fall to the floor and bang their heads. They rarely hurt themselves and if they do, it is certainly not intentional. They are usually careful to seek out the surface with the greatest noise potential and the lowest pain-inflicting factor.

Head banging is a habit which can occur for one of two reasons. Usually it is part of a tantrum in the senseless 1 to 2 year old, though it may be a form of innocent entertainment in the child of a slightly older age.

Head banging tantrums are short lived, as the child soon develops sufficient sense to realise that self-inflicted pain is a poor way of punishing others. It is as silly as a robber who enters the bank and says, 'Hand over the money or I will poke myself in the eye'.

Some children head bang when bored or tired. This is usually the speciality of active children who enjoy rocking and gentle head banging, particularly in the cot. They do it because it is enjoyable and sends them to sleep as reliably as counting sheep, a form of innocent entertainment that gives as much pleasure as thumb sucking. Though it may be soothing for the child, the rhythmic thump is far from soothing for the adults of the house.

Parents fear that a bit of head banging will damage their child's brain but when you look at football players and boxers, you realise that even the most persistent toddler's efforts are pretty trivial by comparison. Other parents believe that this is a sure sign of disability or mental disturbance, but if the child is normal in every other way, head banging is not a sign of significance.

What to do
■ If your toddler is head banging as part of a tantrum, approach it as you would any other tantrum. Act unimpressed, underplay this display of frustration and don't change your stand.
■ Try diverting the toddler's attention elsewhere.
■ If diverting doesn't work, just let them go for it. Toddlers may

have little sense but they are not stupid – remember, head banging is very self-limiting.

■ If the toddler is head banging in his cot, unfortunately, there is not much else you can do about it other than padding the edge of the cot. In extreme cases, put a pillow under each cot leg to deaden the transmission of sound.

Before the age of 2, children lack sense, which causes them to do all manner of things that adults would never consider. The small window of time in which head banging is seen will shut quickly.

Breath holding

Breath holding is among the most alarming of all toddler behaviours. Luckily the vast majority of toddlers never indulge in this scary habit in their lives.

Breath holding comes in two forms, the more common cyanotic (blue) type and the rarer pallid (faint) type. With the cyanotic attack, the child voluntarily holds his breath to the point of passing out; it is a kind of super-tantrum used to stir up anyone preventing the child from getting his own way. Although less common, the pallid form is associated with a painful experience. For example, the child sustains a minor hurt and passes out rapidly in a form of fainting fit.

1. The cyanotic (blue) attack

Let me say straightaway that breath holding attacks terrify parents but generally do not harm the child who performs them. These attacks most commonly occur from 18 months to 4 years, although they may occasionally be seen before the first birthday in the really negative child. This is not a new behaviour pattern brought about by the hectic life-style of the twenty-first century. Hippocrates described something very similar happening among the terrible toddlers of ancient Greece.

What usually happens is that the child is thwarted in the midst of some action that is vitally important to him and, reviewing his repertoire of reactions, he decides that breath holding will be a more effective reprisal than one of his lesser tantrums. He then gives about three long cries, the last going all the way until his lungs are completely empty of air. The audience waits in anticipation for the next breath but the ensuing silence is deafening; no breath is heard. Over the next 15 seconds the child voluntarily holds his breath, which inevitably leads to him going blue in the face and passing out. Once unconscious the child loses voluntary control of his breathing; the body immediately switches over to 'automatic pilot' and breathing restarts, with full consciousness returning about 15 seconds later. Very rarely the episode may end in a minor short convulsion, leaving the parents even more upset.

What to do

- Although the treatment is extremely easy for a doctor to prescribe, I realise it is very difficult for a parent to administer. If breath holding is to be stopped it must be viewed in the same light as a tantrum or any other challenging behaviour. It must simply be totally ignored, as making a fuss about it will only ensure that it is repeated.
- Firstly the parents must be quite certain that this is a breath holding attack and not some completely different medical problem which they are misinterpreting.
- Once sure of this, the techniques of diversion and ignoring must be used. Diversionary tactics will usually fail, so when the child stops breathing, he must be left to his own devices.
- Difficult as it is to do, parents should watch carefully while the child is briefly unconscious but the moment consciousness begins to return, they must move away immediately.
- Once conscious, he will open his eyes and look around for the appreciative audience, but he has wasted his time because they have just walked out.
- Some experts suggest splashing cold water on the child's face as he starts to hold his breath. This may be effective, but it will only work if done in the first seconds of voluntary breath holding. After that it is pointless and even dangerous once unconsciousness has occurred.

I have no illusions that this is an easy treatment but I know that firmness and ignoring the child, although hard, are the only effective methods of curing this behaviour. After the child reaches the age of 4, breath holding becomes extremely rare.

2. The pallid (faint) attack

This is not the true breath holding attack, as it is more like a simple fainting spell than a form of attention-seeking tantrum. Children who have pallid attacks seem to be particularly sensitive to pain or fear, either of which may trigger off an attack. (They are generally thought to become the sort of adults who faint at the thought of a hypodermic needle or the sight of blood.)

A 2 year old may be walking under a table when he hits his head hard on the edge. In the pallid attack, he would not cry out or hold his breath but will simply go limp and fall to the ground. His heart rate drops dramatically, and he looks very pale. This is the child's equivalent of an adult faint, and recovery is usually quite quick.

What to do

This is labelled a behaviour problem, but it isn't. It is closer to an adult faint, so treatment is roughly the same:

- Ensure that the child is lying flat on their back or side, and check that their breathing is unhindered. Once horizontal, normal blood flow returns to the brain. If the child is lying flat nothing else needs to be done and nature will remedy the situation. You can elevate his feet slightly until he comes around.
- Once recovered, a consultation with your child's paediatrician is a good idea to rule out other causes of the faint. Though most of the time this is just the response of a sensitive child to pain, it's better to be safe.

In my experience, these pallid attacks are extremely rare. I have only seen a handful of cases in all my years as a paediatrician.

Vomiting

In some children, parents find that profuse crying or coughing can result in a return of the child's last meal. They seem to have 'weak stomachs' and be very easily upset. This vomiting can cause problems when parents try to instigate discipline programmes, but find themselves sabotaged at the crucial point. I am told by anxious parents, 'Dr Green, I can't use your controlled crying technique on Jimmy, because it makes him vomit.' Time Out can be equally sabotaged by the toddler who gets so worked up, he throws up.

What to do

The solution is not to abandon effective discipline techniques, but to modify them to avoid the vomiting.

- Firstly, it is a good idea to rule out any other reason the child may be vomiting.
- When using the controlled crying technique to resolve sleep problems, periods of crying must be kept short. Timing is the key and with these toddlers, you have to tailor the technique to suit. The toddler may be left to cry, but as soon as this changes from gentle to upset, you must intervene quickly if disaster is to be averted.
- The same approach is used for the child who vomits when you put him in Time Out. Cut down the time in Time Out – keep it short.
- If the child does vomit, you have to be calm and not make a fuss. Quickly change the child, sponge off using cool water,

Double trouble

I once worked with a brilliant mother and her 2-year-old twins. These little girls were unbelievably militant and unfortunately they could also vomit with the greatest of ease. One had quite severe asthma which required inhaled medicines and the other went hysterical when put down to bed. When either of these young madams was pushed to these activities, they didn't argue, they just threw up.

Fortunately, their mum was way ahead of them. When it was time for medicine, she handed one girl a bucket and then produced the pump. With the other, the bucket appeared at bedtime, after which stories were read, kisses and cuddles were given, but it was made obvious that vomiting was not going to be tolerated. Within two days, this awful problem, which would have floored many of us, was past history.

then return him immediately to his cot or the Time Out room. This must all be done in a matter-of-fact way, without anger, emotion or any good quality attention. The toddler will quickly get the message that this course of action is not worth the effort.

- A very small percentage of children take this resistance to extremes, and can vomit on demand for the sole purpose of manipulating and punishing their parents. For these few, you have to be tough.

I must emphasise that it is extremely unusual to be faced with this problem but by modifying the techniques, you will be back on track in no time.

Smearing

The unpleasant habit of smearing is seen in toddlers aged about 18 months. It is usually restricted to the early morning – the damage is done when the toddler wakes before the rest of the household. He is bored and has a dirty nappy, so to wile away the hours he engages in some 'finger painting' on the walls or himself.

This habit is rarely talked about, as it makes even those of us with cast-iron stomachs queasy.

What to do
This behaviour shocks and disgusts parents, so we use two methods to cope with the problem.

- First, we change the toddler's nappy the moment he wakes in the morning. If he is not left to his own devices, he can't perform the dastardly deed.
- If you find there is still a problem, the child must be prevented from getting his hands near the nappy area. This is achieved by dressing him in firmly fastened garments. If the right style is used only the infant Houdini would be able to get his hand into mischief, and even then he couldn't extract it loaded!

Luckily, smearing in normal toddlers tends to be a very short-lived problem, a two- or three-week period that quickly passes.

All in good time

As you can see, even the nicest children can develop some nasty habits. But rest assured that most of these problems pass with maturity. Most in fact are over by the third birthday.

You may even look back on these innocent days and smile at the silliness of it all. For once past toddlerdom, your child will collect all manner of obnoxious grown up habits – far less endearing than those in this chapter.

18

Fears, comforters and security

Everybody has their fears, and toddlers are no exception. Whether real or perceived, all that really matters is that our toddlers' fears shouldn't be dismissed or ridiculed. Facing fears is all part of growing up but luckily the toddler has mum and dad's support to help him along.

Parents are never quite sure what is normal for well-adjusted offspring. Some toddler fears may seem quite 'off the beam', and some children's comfort habits may seem distinctly strange.

Most fears at this age are temporary problems that evaporate with the passage of time, but in the meantime, we have to look at ways to make scary situations as stress-free as possible. In this chapter we look at some common toddler fears, as well as security and various methods of comfort.

Different fears for different years

Children are born fear-free, which is a good thing – if they knew all that is required in order to be birthed into the world, they may very well choose to stay in the confines of the womb. But this fearless existence doesn't last for too long. As they get older, a number of objects and activities cause trepidation, whether through experience or the result of an overactive imagination.

- At birth, babies are immune to the fears that beset the rest of us. When you think what the inside of a modern neonatal nursery looks like, with all that space-age gadgetry, this is a convenient arrangement. Instead of fear, babies have a startle reflex, brought on by sudden movements and noise. For example, when a tray accidentally crashes to the floor of the nursery ward, the whole gang will leap in unison.

- Somewhere around the seventh month, the first real fear emerges. Known as separation anxiety, the baby suddenly becomes inseparably attached to his main caretaker, usually his mother. From this time onwards, any attempts to separate him from his caregiver may cause distress and floods of tears. Children at this age are often described as 'clingy'.

- At 1 year, separation is still a major problem, and the child will also often react badly to unexpected loud noises, such as doorbells, vacuum cleaners or food mixers. Strange people, strange objects and sudden movements can also cause distress, and send him rushing to mum or dad for a cuddle.

- By the age of 2, the fear of separation becomes slightly less intense and more predictable than in the 1 year old. Loud bangs still cause upsets, as will the unexpected screech of brakes, ambulance sirens or the violent barking of dogs.

- Between 2 and 4 years, the tight attachment to mum or dad weakens further but a whole new package of fears starts to emerge, animals and the dark featuring prominently. The fear of animals hits its peak around the age of 3; fear of the dark usually peaks nearer the fifth birthday.

- Between 4 and 6 years, children's imaginations are particularly fertile, and great uneasiness is generated as a result of hearing stories or watching television. They easily conjure up visions of monsters and travellers from outer space. Fear of the dark is worsened by visits from ghosts, bogeymen, and things that go bump in the night.

- At the age of 6, a few children add the worry of being injured, and some may even start to fear death. However, they do not have the adult understanding of either of these possibilities.
- By the age of 12, the child has been lumbered with the burden of most common adult fears, which to some extent he will carry with him for the rest of his life.

Specific toddler fears

Whether we like it or not, fear has always been a major part of life, both for adults and children, and nothing I can say is going to make it go away. What we can only hope to do is find ways of dealing with the situations or objects that commonly make toddlers frightened.

All young children have one overwhelming fear in common: the fear of being separated from their parents. While other fears come and go, whether of the child's own making or sometimes transferred from the parent's own anxieties, a toddler's fear of separation is something all parents have to deal with.

Separation

As we've already seen, the fear of separation is common to all children from the age of about 7 months. It is at its most intense in the early years, and it wanes slowly by school age. Just how slowly it ebbs varies greatly from child to child. Temperament plays a part – for the shy toddler it takes longer to acclimatise to being separated from his parents, while for the naturally outgoing type, this stage may pass in the blink of an eye.

Fear of separation shows itself in the child who suddenly cries and carries on when parted from his mother. In the beginning, the child resents being handled by anyone except mum, but this eases to allow all the other members of the family, and even close friends, in on the act. When playing, he is never far from mum, and if playing outside or in another room, he reappears every few minutes to reassure himself of mum's presence.

Dealing with fear of separation is not a matter of curing the child or getting rid of the fear, as this is something the child grows out of in his own time. It is more about understanding and managing those situations where separation is necessary. The most common time the problem arises is leaving the toddler with a babysitter during this period. Most parents need babysitters at one time or another so that they can maintain some outside life. The second greatest hurdle is leaving the child at preschool, or at day care in the case of working parents.

What to do

- Many parents are forced, for a variety of good reasons, to leave their child with a babysitter whether they like it or not. To ease the ordeal for the toddler, choose the babysitter carefully. The ideal first-time babysitter is a grandparent, other relative or close friend. The toddler will sense that this person can be trusted, which will relieve a little of his anxiety.
- When left with a babysitter, the child should be accompanied by his preferred security items, and he should never be left in a great rush. Give him a little time to acclimatise, after which you should leave decisively.
- Don't dawdle and draw out the process and don't weaken if he cries when you are halfway out the door.
- Profuse tears may be shed on departure and again at pick-up time. Between these times there is usually relative happiness, which can be confirmed by a quick phone call.
- A few children seem immensely unhappy when left in the care of a babysitter and never really settle. If this happens, the parents must ask themselves if separation is really necessary and if it might not be kinder to wait several more months before trying again.
- By the age of 3, preschool is usually the toddler's first major separation. He must know what is going to happen to him when he is left, and he should be gently introduced to his new surroundings before being abandoned.
- Once the parents have made up their mind to leave the child and go, then go they must, without lurking in the bushes to spy on the child.
- Parents are never sure, when they bring their child for the first time, whether it is best to stay with him for an hour or so, or leave immediately. This advice is probably best left to the

individual preschool director, who has a great deal of experience with making this transition go smoothly.

■ Occasionally the child will not settle happily, and where this is the case, there is little point in forcing him to go on. Better to wait 3–6 months and then try again. Non-attendance for this short time will not cause him to miss out in the warm-up heats for the academic rat race.

I believe that toddlers were designed to remain close to their families for a number of years and rushing a child out into our far from perfect world seems rather unkind and unnecessary to my old-fashioned sentiments.

All God's children

A concerned mother asked me for advice on a problem that was worrying her. For 6 months she had attended church each Sunday morning, placing her toddler in the church crèche, where he cried inconsolably throughout the entire separation. What could be done to make the child less unhappy? I explained that I was certain that an understanding God would probably much prefer to see a happy child than a pew occupied in His church.

Baths

Most babies like water and enjoy splashing in their baths. After all, they have spent the first 9 months of their lives submerged in water. But for unknown reasons, after their first year some take a strong dislike to this activity and the very word 'bath' or the noise of a running tap will set them to arching their backs, crying and complaining bitterly.

Fears of the bath are generally short lived and, if handled with gentle desensitisation, they are quickly overcome.

What to do

■ To prevent bath refusal, it is important to avoid frightening the young child with such things as spluttering taps, gurgling plug holes and slippery baths.

■ For the toddler who absolutely refuses to bathe, a good start is to stand him in an empty basin in a warm place and sponge him with warm water.

- After a few days of doing this, some water may be put in the basin and, when he is braver, he can be sponged in a bath with a maximum depth of water of 2–3 centimetres.
- Next, encourage him to sit down and start increasing the water level until you have a child who baths in the right place, at the right time, and with the right attitude.
- Bathtime can become one of the best playtimes of the day, and this should be actively encouraged. Fill the bath with toy boats, submarines, rubber duckies and discarded detergent bottles, which double as excellent water squirters.
- A bubble bath is a sneaky way to encourage happy aquatic toddlers. All children love bubbles, and they have the added benefit of disguising the few centimetres of water underneath. Be generous to begin with, then cut back on the suds as the fear subsides.

Genuine fear of the bath should not be confused with the theatrical antics of a manipulating, attention-seeking toddler, who, out of principle, refuses to bathe when told.

Absentminded routine

A 3½-year-old girl I saw greatly upset her mother with her power play in the evenings. She wouldn't bathe unless the water was turned on by her dad, and she had to be carried to the bathroom and undressed by him as well. This was so entrenched that when dad was out, the child refused to take a bath. Her mum soon gave up trying, as she found it wasn't worth the fight.

This situation was cured in a rapid, though slightly devious, manner. Dad continued his role, running the bath, undressing his daughter and putting her in the water, but one minor adjustment was made to the routine. 'Absentmindedly', he consistently forgot to turn on the hot tap when he was running the bath with the consequence that the water had an Arctic chill – the balance of power was immediately redressed and mum's care at bathtime was once again in equal demand.

Gorillas in the midst

An irate mother complained to me that her 3-year-old daughter had lost all her previously excellent toilet training skills as the result of the girl's father.

Browsing through a shop one day he came upon a poster of a gorilla climbing out of a toilet bowl. So impressed was he with this piece of visual art that he brought it home and stuck it up on the back of the toilet door. Well, the little girl walked in, sat on the toilet, the door swung shut and, after seeing this horrific vision, absolutely refused (not surprisingly) to sit there ever again.

Toilets

Some children are afraid to sit on the toilet, which obviously makes toilet training well nigh impossible. This fear may arise from a number of causes – maybe the association with a severe pain when passing a particularly hard motion; or fear of being sucked into the toilet when it is flushed and being washed out to sea. Some children are frightened of the extractor fan in bathrooms that start automatically when the light is switched on. In such a confined space, these may sound like a jumbo jet about to take off. Other children refuse to sit on the toilet purely out of attention-seeking, toddler stubbornness.

With children who will not sit on the toilet for whatever reason, we once again must introduce gentle desensitisation.

What to do

- The most resistant should start sitting on a potty with their nappy still on. There should be no forcing but lots of rewards given.

- From here progress to sitting without the nappy; sitting on the potty beside the toilet with mum close by; sitting on the toilet with mum close by; sitting with mum outside giving encouragement; and finally going solo while mum rustles up some interesting treat in the kitchen.

- More ideas on dealing with reluctant sitters can be found in Chapter 16: Toilet Training.

These ideas may all seem rather cumbersome and excessive but often you will find that some of these steps can be bypassed. The important message is that forcing children will not get you anywhere. As far as I'm concerned there is no need to rush, so take the easy road.

Things that go bump in the night

In daylight hours, you will find that some toddlers are frightened of a great variety of noises, even such common ones as household appliances. Vacuum cleaners, screeching car tyres or food processors can all give the toddler a fright.

But when the sun sets and darkness appears, the older toddler's vivid imagination can conjure up visions of robbers, monsters and other assorted bogeymen, lurking in hidden places. In the dark, noises can seem magnified and feed the toddler's already fertile imagination.

Fear of the dark usually hits its peak somewhere between 4 and 5 years, and then largely disappears by the child's seventh birthday.

Once upon a time . . .

Can we blame all these childhood fears on the 'junk viewing diet' that we feed our children on television? Actually, the element of fear in childhood upbringing is as old as childhood itself.

Children listen to stories told to them by their parents, grannies or friends or read books full of varying degrees of mayhem, terror and violence. Hansel and Gretel get lost in a big, black forest and are almost eaten by a witch. Snow White was poisoned by the wicked queen. The Pied Piper took all the town's children hostage and never returned them to their parents. And what about those three mice who, as well as suffering severe visual disability, had their tails severed from their bodies?

Children have been terrified at night-time for centuries, long before John Logie Baird's invention became so popular.

What to do

- For fear of the dark, a low wattage night-light will usually do the trick. These globes make little contribution to the Greenhouse Effect, but have a huge impact on bedtime routines. If the child wakes in the night, he won't be frightened by the blackness, and there will be no dark corners for monsters to hide in.
- Fear of ghosts, monsters and bogeymen can be handled with a quick search and banishment with the toddler while the lights are on. 'Magic spray' (a cheap water spray container) applied to ghostly curtains does wonders as you search out monsters together.
- Sitting quietly with the toddler for a few minutes until he falls asleep may be all that is needed. Remember to provide a comforting presence, but don't get drawn into requests for drinks, another story or assorted excuses. Some 'fears' are really calls for attention in disguise – we need to give the toddler the benefit of the doubt, but that doesn't mean we were born yesterday.

We have to make sure that toddlers aren't frightened at night time, even if it means playing ghost buster. If they sleep well they wake refreshed and full of beans, ready to get on with the day.

Dogs

It is common for the under-4s to fear animals, especially dogs. Most commonly the child who fears dogs will sight the offending beast, stiffen, then hold on tight to his mother as he cries uncontrollably.

Naturally, we don't want to encourage the toddler to poke passing German shepherds or pat every surly mongrel in the street, but equally we don't want them running in terror from a ball of fluff that doesn't even reach their knees. We want our toddlers to have a sensible respect and affection for our four-legged friends.

What to do

- If your child reacts with fear around dogs, you may find that even if you do nothing, he will grow out of it.
- To help overcome the fear, talk quietly to the child about 'nice

dogs', friendly ones who like children. Introduce him to some of the gentler of the species. Be confident, talk openly about the animals and try to get a toe in the door with some distant dog contact.

■ For easy introductions, try the securely caged puppies at the pet store. Start by looking through the glass, then see if the shop assistant will let the toddler have a pat.

Some therapists I know introduce stuffed dogs into their treatment, but I feel that once you go to those lengths you're only a hair's breadth away from turning serious therapy into a sketch worthy of Monty Python.

Doctors

As a paediatrician, I have learnt the hard way that busy days surrounded by anxious, crying, unco-operative children are extremely stressful. We enjoy working with children, otherwise we wouldn't be doing it, but it is important for our own sanity, as well as the happiness of the children we serve, that doctors' surgeries are made as friendly and non-threatening as possible.

Some parents are amazingly skilful at stirring up children the minute they enter the doctor's office. Nervous mothers twitter in the child's ear like a bird warning of impending danger. Combined with being told not to touch anything, or even talk in some cases,

it is not surprising that some children are a mess before the doctor has even said 'Hello'.

As mentioned, most babies up to the age of 6 months don't mind being separated from their mum, so it is easy for a doctor to lift them up and examine them on a couch. From about 7 months until preschool age, however, this separation is a problem, and we have to use a few tactics to ensure a quick, stress-free visit.

What to do

- A good doctor will try to put the child at ease, introducing him or herself in a way that shows they are a human being and not an ogre. Thereafter, examinations should be quick and confident, accompanied by quiet, reassuring talk.
- Utterances such as 'the doctor is not going to hurt you' are counter-productive, since the thought of getting hurt had probably never even crossed the child's mind until you mentioned it.
- Children should be allowed to sit quietly on mum's knee so the doctor can make the initial examination.
- The doctor should engage the child's eyes, communicating gently with him and watching carefully for those early signs of distress that appear seconds before the first tear is shed.
- Painful and uncomfortable procedures, such as throat examinations, should be left until the end of the visit, followed by a quick cuddle.
- Neither parents nor doctors should insist on things like painful blood tests unless they are of indisputable diagnostic and therapeutic value.

A visit to the doctor should not be a fearful experience for either child or parent. Doctors are really very nice people, as long as they keep their scalpels, syringes and tongue depressors to themselves!

Hospitals

In the not too distant past, hospitals were places of dread, run purely for the business of curing the sick and without much interest in protecting the emotional wellbeing of the patient. This was particularly horrifying for children who had to go into hospital. Thankfully we've come a long way, and making patients comfortable and easing the experience is now the order of the day.

Hospitalisation may be upsetting for toddlers, but it is often even more upsetting for the parents, watching helplessly. There are a few tricks that make this nerve-wracking experience more bearable.

What to do

- If you get some warning that your child may have to be admitted to hospital, it is important to prepare him, discussing what is going to happen. Edit what you say to suit the child's age and level of understanding. Try and mention the 'positives' – food served in a fun way or rooms full of children to play with. Reassure the toddler that mum or dad will be there. For the older toddler, you could try medical pretend play with dolls and teddies, as suggested by some psychologists.
- If possible, take him to visit the ward before admission. Some hospitals allow this to make the experience less scary for the child.
- Make sure that when he does go in he has his favourite cuddly toys and comforters with him.
- Open visiting hours allow parents to spend as much time as possible with the toddler, and in most cases some form of bed is available for mum or dad if they want to stay overnight.
- 'Day' surgery is encouraged now, so that the child can go home to the care of his parents as soon as possible.
- If the child requires surgery, when he goes to the anaesthetic room, he is accompanied by his teddy bear and his mother or father, and he will find both parent and bear waiting for him in the recovery ward after the operation.
- In a good children's hospital, any child from birth upward is afforded the same, or an even greater, standard of postoperative pain relief than we might expect for ourselves.

Good guys

As an example of how the atmosphere of most children's hospitals has changed, groups of preschoolers visit the wards at the Children's Hospital, Westmead. On these excursions they have a ball, realising that it was really quite a fun place run by 'good guys'!

■ If you point out your local hospital when you pass it on your daily travels, and talk about what goes on inside, your toddler will realise from an early age that it isn't some dreaded institution; it is a place where sick people go to get better.

Much of the fear our children have of hospitals is fed by anxious parents, desperately wanting their child to be well and at home where they belong. Luckily, these days hospital visits are as short, pain-free and supportive as possible.

From an adult perspective, toddler fears may seem very unscary indeed. But we were all toddlers once, and we have all been afraid of something. Dealing with toddler fears and insecurities is a very real part of toddlerdom, one which we have to approach with understanding and comfort. Talking about your toddler's fears and providing security will do much to diminish the power they have over your little one.

Comforters and security

Little children love their comfort objects – the cuddly bears and security blankets they carry around with them, their dummies and their thumbs. I think these are one of the really cute things about toddlers. Psychiatrists call them 'transition objects': items that give children a feeling of security. At the day care centre, granny's, or even in hospital, even though mum and dad may not be there with them, the child still has a familiar and beloved object to hold on to.

We spend an awful lot of time trying to rid toddlers of their comfort objects. But adults have many worse ways of dealing with stressful situations – we relieve our tensions by chewing gum or our fingernails, smoking cigarettes, or drinking cup after cup of coffee. Toddler comforters are a great deal less harmful to health, and so far there hasn't been any evidence suggesting negative effects of teddy bears.

Thumb sucking

Despite Sigmund Freud's inevitable emphasis on the sexual connotations of sucking one's thumb, modern thinkers believe that thumbs are sucked because it seems a good thing to do at the time.

Thumb sucking is not a sign of a scarred psyche or emotional insecurity. Little children do it for only one reason: they enjoy it. If there were not some comfort and satisfaction in sucking the thumb, I doubt whether children would bother. It seems a most natural thing to do, with ultrasound pictures showing babies in the womb happily sucking away. Most experts believe that there is no harm in the habit.

By the age of 3½, most children have spontaneously removed their thumbs from their mouths, although some studies suggest that up to 2 per cent still have this habit in their early teens.

Children certainly seem to suck their thumbs more when they are either tired, bored, frustrated or tense, and it is a good way of getting to sleep, particularly for those children who have not yet attained the mathematical skill to count sheep. In times of stress, and particularly when a new baby arrives, many toddlers regress to this old habit.

One of the main worries with thumb sucking is that it can cause teeth to become displaced and stick out. This is of particular concern to today's parents who seek the perfect alignment of a Colgate commercial, yet know that getting wired up with an orthodontist comes mighty expensive. Certainly before the age of 6, thumb sucking does not damage permanent teeth and after that, it takes more than just a few minutes of thumb-in-mouth at bedtime to cause harm.

What to do

- For a child's emotional wellbeing, there is much to be said for leaving nature to cure this habit rather than engaging in tugs-of-war with firmly lodged thumbs.
- Below the age of 4 years I believe that sucking should be totally ignored. After this, hands can be subtly diverted and bodies can be busied into something more productive. This is the best way to slowly modify the behaviour.
- Notice when the child goes for a period of time without sucking his thumb, and reward him with praise, 'You didn't suck your thumb today, what a grown-up boy you are!'
- Whatever happens, thumb sucking must never become the cause of a fight or the child will continue it, just to annoy.
- If you are worried about the effect thumb sucking will have on your toddler's teeth, discuss it with your dentist.

Thumbs up for Eskimos

Thumb sucking is a worldwide phenomenon, although some writers claim it is less frequent in some races; apparently little Eskimos hardly ever do it at all, but I presume this is a practical move on their part, keeping their hands in mittens to prevent their digits falling off through frostbite.

Dummies and pacifiers

Despite the fact that many people have an inbuilt dislike of these plastic or rubber devices, no-one has ever found any evidence to indicate that they really do any harm. There are claims that they are unhygienic, but so for that matter are the 10 dirty digits that would be inserted in the mouth if the dummy was not there.

My objection to them is more on aesthetic grounds than medical ones. I dislike the way a dummy can make an intelligent child appear dull, delayed and a dribbler. However, there is no doubt that when a child is stressed or having trouble sleeping, they are helped by a dummy. Unfortunately while dummies undoubtedly precipitate sleep, they also have a habit of precipitating wakefulness when they become disengaged in the early hours of the morning.

All in all, I think their pluses out number their minuses and happier kids and parents make for happier homes. However, if dummy use does concern you, there are ways to kick the habit.

What to do

- There are no long-term side effects from sucking these comforters, so before you decide to wrestle it away from your toddler, ask yourself if you really need to do anything at all.
- When the time comes to discard the dummy, it is usually best to be brave, throw it away, and then brace yourself for the repercussions. There will inevitably be some hours, or even some days, of trouble but the dummy will soon be forgotten. Going cold turkey is really for those parents who like their lives to include a bit of drama.
- Those who do not have the courage to discard it so abruptly may try a gradual withdrawal by 'accidentally' damaging the dummy with a pair of kitchen scissors. By deviously creating a slow leak, you will reduce the appeal of the offending item.
- After 3½, the child may well be reasoned with and the dummy given up after some hard bargaining.

Many parents who are determined never to resort to these pacifiers relent when confronted with an extremely irritable, difficult child. In these situations, they live up to their name.

Teddies, cuddlies and security blankets

Most youngsters have some object that they seek out and cuddle up to when tired or upset. This can be some exotic imported stuffed animal, mum's own battered but much-loved teddy, a sheepskin rug or even a rapidly disintegrating bit of old fabric.

Whatever the 'real world' value of the object, in the eyes of the child it is priceless. As I noted earlier, these items are often referred to as 'transition objects'. They give security, continuity and comfort to a child when the environment and those in it are changing. It is his link with his home base; without it he feels a stranger in a strange world.

As the child becomes more and more attached to his comfort item, greater is the distress when it falls apart or is mislaid. To the

toddler, this is a disaster of major proportions, not unlike a death in the family.

What to do

- Security blankets of the type favoured by Charlie Brown's friend Linus get progressively grubbier and grubbier, until eventually they simply must be washed. This needs to be planned with all the precision of a military operation to ensure that they are in and out of the washing machine and returned dry to the owner with the minimum of time wasted.

- For those with an attachment to a teddy bear or other soft toy, when their dirty friend is in need of a wash, it can be a very trying time. The child watches the window of the machine and/or drier, glued like a soap opera addict.

- Surprisingly, despite great attachment, a bit of high-powered salesmanship from an enthusiastic parent may steer a toddler towards another, reserve comforter if the need arises.

- When a blanket is wearing out, it may be wise to remove a part of it to keep in cold storage until the fateful day when the original is in irretrievable tatters.

- Even without this foresight, a minute, disintegrating patch of material may be reincarnated if clever mum sews it onto the corner of some new material. This is rather like the horticultural grafting of roses and, when properly achieved, ensures years of blossoming comfort.

A touching twist

Parents can spend big bucks on a top-of-the-line soft toy, but find that what interests their child the most is the maker's tag. Some children twist this round a finger as they settle to sleep, while others love to rub the silky label against their skin. The ultimate comfort experience is to clutch a teddy, suck a bottle and twiddle a tag, all in unison.

Other children are touchers – as they drift off to sleep, they fiddle with their mother's hair, or rhythmically stroke a patch of skin. At least, unlike tags, these won't wear out!

■ Due to toddlers' inseparable relationships with their teddies, parents have been known to drive halfway around the city to retrieve lost bears. If possible, I recommend careful labelling to give them a half a chance of finding their way back home.

Comforters and transition objects are normal, natural and healthy. They promote and provide security. Like Christopher Robin and his trusty bear, Winnie-the-Pooh, the young child armed with his blanket can accomplish many a daring feat that would never have been possible alone.

Pretend friends

After the second birthday, little children start to develop a vivid imagination. By late toddlerdom, this has become so intense that sometimes there is a blur between real and make believe. Between the ages of 4 and 6 are the peak years for pretend friends.

Some preschoolers are greatly comforted as they discuss the meaning of life and the universe with an imaginary mate. Others are befriended by strange animals. Whatever the choice of pal, this stage will generally pass before they get to primary school.

What to do

■ Savour this highly imaginative and creative time.

■ You may at times have to point out the line between reality

A game of bridge

Some children even talk to inanimate objects. The daughter of one of my friends used to talk to the Sydney Harbour Bridge. Soon her dad joined in the game, both conversing with this structure every time they crossed.

One day, they were driving with his mother-in-law in the car. As dad talked knowledgeably to the bridge, grandma asked the girl, 'Who is your father talking to?' 'Beats me if I know,' was her reply.

and fantasy. If an imaginary friend is blamed for misbehaviour that is clearly the toddler's, make sure the child knows you are not fooled.

Fear not!

Children's fears are very real to them, and whether the fears seem rational or not, parents need to approach them with understanding and patience. We are there to give comfort, not belittle their beliefs.

The biggest fear for most children is the fear of separation from their parents, which is a major stage of toddlerdom. Like most fears at this age, fear of separation is temporary and will disappear as the child gets older.

To cope with their fears and life in general, toddlers will recruit a number of comforting objects. These generally consist of thumbs, dummies, teddy bears and security blankets. I am all for more comfort and security; life is tough enough without those things that cushion the knocks. There is no need to wean toddlers off the fluffy things they drag around with them – they are part of the magic of this age, which make toddlers a little more special.

19

Day care, playgroup and preschool

When our grandparents were toddlers, they spent their early impressionable years in the care of mum, dad and their extended family. They learned all they needed to know at the knees of their elders, until they were old enough to go to school.

Whether we like it or not, the world we live in now is a very different place. There has been a shift away from family-based supervision and education of toddlers. While some parents still choose this stay-at-home approach, others use one of various types of childcare now available outside the home. In this chapter we will look at the two main types of childcare, day care and preschool, as well as the important role of playgroup.

A clash of ideals

As increasing numbers of our little ones are looked after by carers other than family members, there are those who still proclaim that it is only parents who should be looking after their own children. While this attitude grabs headlines, providing fuel for talkback radio and current affairs shows, is it realistic?

We live in a modern world and with it comes some harsh realities. Over recent decades there has been an increase in the number of families in which both parents work; the extended family is breaking down and there are more single parents. For many parents, having either mum or dad staying at home with the kids while the other goes to work, or leaving children in the care of grandma (who may also be working), just isn't a viable option. The choice, it seems, isn't really a choice at all.

There are many reasons why parents choose for their children to attend childcare facilities. For parents who need to work, sending their child to day care is a foregone conclusion. Having enough money to survive is a strong motivator and I am sure all parents would agree that the most expensive period of your life is the time when you raise children. Paying the mortgage or simply wanting a few creature comforts instead of just getting by can mean that both mum and dad need to work.

Equally important for some parents in making the decision to use childcare is the need to pursue a career. While a few parents have the enviable flexibility to combine work and home life without either suffering, they are the exception rather than the rule.

Even less talked about are the surprising number of parents who just aren't cut out to be full-time parents. We assume that all parents want to be with their children all the time. However, a proportion recognise that they need time to themselves. These parents use childcare to provide themselves with some space so that when they are with their children, they can give them their best.

A tiny minority of parents are blessed with no financial constraints. They choose to put their child into day care a number of days per week because of the benefits they feel it offers the child – the structure, early education and socialisation.

The use of childcare for young children raises heated debates. One thing everyone agrees on is the need for more quality places

– even politicians reluctantly admit that there are severe shortages. In an ideal world, all families that want or need it would have access to high quality, affordable childcare with skilled, professional carers. Until that time perhaps we should focus more on supporting parents than criticising their choices.

Catch 22

When people say that someone should stay at home to look after the children, what is most often implied is, 'Mum, you should be at home – isn't that your job?'

Modern mothers have an incredibly difficult choice to make. They have to balance the needs of their children, financial pressures, their own career aspirations and society's expectations. All this is made even harder by other people's opinions. No matter how pro-equality they are, mothers can still be made to feel guilty about leaving their children to go to work; that if they don't stay at home, they are a 'bad mother'.

In a perfect world, mothers would get paid for the very important task of raising the next generation. All women are entitled to a minimum of 26 weeks' maternity leave and some even receive a certain amount of paid leave, usually a percentage of their full salary. However, if they do decide to take further time out to raise their children, it can be difficult to return to the workforce. Once they return, often the cost of childcare may wipe out any income they bring in. Which leaves most mothers in a Catch 22.

The benefits of childcare

Childcare used to be somewhere children had fun and played while mum and dad were off doing whatever it is that grown ups do all day. Nowadays it is so much more. The best centres provide more than just a babysitting service – they give children a broad, interactive foundation in early learning that attends to the needs of their growing minds and bodies.

Modern childcare centres make sure that the activities and tasks that children are involved in stimulate their learning. Larger centres and preschools will have educational plans and goals for the children in their care. You may even find that the lady next door, who looks after a few children in her home (family day care), is in on the act, spending time on both fun and learning.

One of the most important benefits of childcare is socialisation. Through mixing with a group, the toddler learns to get on with other children and adults. Some forms of childcare can provide resources that the parents can't, both fun and academic, such as a library of books, a playground with a sandpit and climbing equipment, art and craft tools, costumes for dress ups, and musical instruments.

Who really pays?

Surely looking after children is one of the most important jobs in the world, and yet it is so undervalued. Childcare workers are chronically underpaid, centres are underfunded and the impact of all this is overlooked. If our children are the future and we don't give them the best now, ultimately we all pay the price. I think we have lost the plot.

Day care

Long day care is centre-based childcare, offered on a full-time or part-time basis. Day care centres are run by private operators, local councils, non-profit organisations and community organisations such as churches. Day care is also provided by some employers.

Day care is available for children from 6 weeks of age, although it is more common for children to start attending around 9 months or 1 year, when mum returns to the workforce. The centres are generally open longer hours, allowing working parents some flexibility in the busy schedule of dropping off and picking up their littlies before and after work.

There has been a steady increase in day care attendance in Australia in the last 15 years. According to one study, between June 1993 and June 2002, long day care numbers rose from 11.8 per cent to 25.1 per cent, almost doubling attendance. By comparison, in that same period there was only a very slight increase of roughly 2 per cent of 4 year olds attending preschool. The increase in day care numbers is mainly due to more mothers returning to the workforce.

The current shortage of day care places in Australia is a major problem. A recent survey showed that over 188,000 children needed more hours of care, but more than one-third of these were unable to receive it because centres were booked out. This is troubling as with demand ever growing, the problem will only increase.

Choosing day care

We want the best for our children and perhaps nowhere is this more important than when deciding who looks after them when we aren't around. Choosing the best day care for your child is a fairly straightforward affair. The greatest hurdle is the distinct lack of available places in many areas, with parents forced to register their child many months before the child is due to start attending. In some suburbs in major cities, parents must list their child before birth in order to secure a place.

Thankfully, for many parents the difficult choices are limited to how often the child will attend and the convenience of the day care facility's location. Once they have decided on whether the child will attend full-time, part-time or on an occasional basis, parents can then decide whether to use long day care or family day care. Most parents choose a centre or carer close to home, often one attended by the children of friends.

The first step in finding out about your local childcare facilities is through your local authority. Also, talk to other parents in your area.

When deciding on a facility, consider its location and the surroundings. The best centres are not necessarily the flashiest, with the latest décor. They are the ones that are welcoming and feel friendly from the moment you enter, putting yourself and the toddler at ease.

Next consider the warmth of the staff. You will quickly sense if they are friendly, caring and attentive. The ratio of staff to children should be high, guaranteeing more individual attention for each child. Assess the staff turnover rate by checking how long the current staff have been there. This is especially important as children need to form attachments and have a feeling of stability. It also shows you how organised and well-run the facility is, as happy staff tend to stick around longer in this demanding industry.

You can choose the best day care available for your toddler but it doesn't guarantee an easy transition. Some toddlers are very unhappy at being left and will vocally let everyone know. They just prefer the company of mum or dad to anyone else. This can add to the already considerable stress that the milestone of care outside the home involves.

Day care is a very personal choice and there are no absolute rights and wrongs to your selection. At the end of the day, if your child and you are happy, then that is all that matters.

Preschools

Preschools take children from about 3 years old until school enrolment; in Australia and the UK children generally start preschool around the age of 4. Preschool attendance is not compulsory but it is very popular with parents and a child's attendance is almost seen as being the norm. Most long day care centres also offer a preschool programme.

The best way to describe the activities of preschool is 'learning how to learn', and they are designed to help the child get ready for school. These include sitting, settling, listening and sticking to a particular task. Many children find this immensely difficult at first but trained teachers know how to hold a child's waning interest and encourage him, bringing some structure and gentle discipline into the child's life. Preschool teachers aim to build on the child's natural curiosity, developing an enthusiasm for learning, as well as encouraging the child to both make and be a friend.

An important part of preschool is socialisation. Children mix, learn to share, to take turns and to respect other people's property and wishes. They get to know other children and at the same time, they start to experience a little independence from mum and dad.

Language also develops in leaps and bounds. Speech accelerates, as all those busy little beings chatter among themselves. I think that preschools provide some of the best speech therapy available in the world. In fact, if a child I saw was slow to develop speech, the first thing I would suggest was enrolling him in preschool, as this always seemed to speed things along.

Currently there is great debate about whether preschools should provide a formal curriculum for children. Those in the formal camp argue that children at this age are learning so fast, we should take advantage of their 'sponge-like' minds and use preschools to speed their development. They believe that firm guidelines need to be set for what children should be learning inside their walls.

Those on the opposing side believe that children learn most of what they need to know at this age through play and from the adults in their lives – namely through watching and being involved with everyday activities. Good preschools provide these for the toddler with lots of stimulation through games, reading and imaginative play.

I have to wonder what toddlers would miss out on if preschool learning became too formal. What types of fun would be sacrificed to teach a second language or intensive literacy and numeracy skills? While I am a strong believer in the importance of early learning, children are only children for a very short time.

Some benefits of preschool

Preschool is a time for children to enjoy and develop a wide spectrum of skills needed for school and life.

- Preschool provides an opportunity for gentle separation in a child who has previously been close day and night to his parents.
- The child is not the only one who benefits from preschool. At last mum will have some time to herself to 'recharge her batteries'.
- If there is a younger child in the family, he will now receive some valuable one-to-one care, which he deserves without the competition from an older sibling.
- If you have scored a difficult child, preschool can provide much needed relief for yourself and activity for the youngster.

- Not only does preschool prepare the toddler for the separation of going to school, it also prepares the mother for her feelings when she views the 'empty nest' after the child has flown.
- Generally, preschool brings a maturity and better understanding of sharing, mixing and living at peace with one's fellow man (though possibly not brothers and sisters).

Taking a tumble

A TV news story I saw recently grabbed my attention. It reported that irate parents were suing a childcare centre because while playing in the playground, their toddler had fallen and injured herself, breaking a collarbone. Over the next few days, on the heels of this story, came further complaints from other parents – illnesses that were diagnosed too late, bumps and cuts and bruises sustained by active little children at play.

I am not for a minute suggesting that it is OK for children to be injured or sick. But I have to wonder if some of the parents' anger is actually misdirected guilt? Do they in fact blame themselves, feeling they are wrong for putting their child into day care? Why are they reacting so strongly to something that could just as easily have happened at home?

If we're going to let children tumble and play, eventually in even the safest playground – or family home – someone will be hurt, because accidents happen. In fact, having worked in a hospital all my life, I can tell you that the vast majority of children's injuries are sustained at home when mum and dad are around.

Starting preschool

The right time to start preschool will depend on a number of different factors: if the child is ready; if there is a place available; if the parents can afford it; and if the parents are ready.

Children are all different and some will be ready to start preschool at 3 years, others not until they are 4. We are looking for the child's emotional readiness, and if you are unsure about your toddler, see how he compares to his friends of the same age. If you are really uncertain, and your child is at the younger end of toddlerdom, it is generally safer to wait a little longer. The preschool director is the best person to consult when making this decision.

Places at preschool can be scarce and to avoid missing out, early registration is more than just a good idea, it is essential. Put your child's name on a waiting list well in advance. Waiting lists are called that because you have to wait, so don't expect to go on the list today and have a place tomorrow.

For most parents, the cost of preschool puts a strain on the family budget even with government incentives and tax benefits. It is sad that children might miss out on something so important for this reason.

Parents can sometimes be reluctant to enrol their toddler as they feel he is learning well enough at home. But being a member of the preschool group is a large part of preparing for school classes. Preschool class sizes are smaller and much more individual than a school class, and help to lessen the rude shock of 30 other boys and girls clamouring for attention. This is thankfully not a scene found in the average lounge room.

The major hurdle to starting preschool is usually separation. There is a great variation in each child's ability to separate. Those who are militantly independent will cut loose from mum at the preschool gate, leaving her to follow as they zero in on the main action. Most will be more tentative, becoming more clingy and cautious for the first week or so. Then there are a few for whom the start of preschool will be very stressful. For this last group, the advice of the preschool director is essential to making the transition less daunting. Whatever sort of child you have, separation will be smoothest if you prepare in advance for the first day.

What to do

- In the months before, mentally prepare the toddler. Talk about preschool and explain what will happen, 'After Christmas, you'll be going to little school with your friends'. Walk past and even go inside for a visit.
- Get the toddler used to his new gear, for example the backpack, lunch box, etc.
- Make sure you are familiar with the preschool's requirements and policies. (For example, name tapes on clothing, whether a

favourite toy is welcome, the type of food you may send, sunscreen, hats, and so on.)

- On starting day, set out in good time. Don't rush and try not to transmit any uneasiness to the toddler. If we big people get tense, it is likely the little ones will follow suit. It has to be a bit stressful for them: remember how you felt the last time you changed jobs or came cold into a party to face 30 complete strangers?

- Be sensible with clothes you dress the toddler in. Take care to avoid high fashion designs with stiff belts or many buttons that take on the style of a straightjacket when toilet urgency is at its peak.

- The food you send should be simple, nutritious and easy to eat and should follow the preschool's guidelines on healthy eating and allergies. Don't be tempted to compensate for your guilt about leaving your child at preschool by giving out chocolate or other payoffs. Make sure that it is clear which packet is for little lunch and which is for big lunch. Food should be packed in an easily opened lunch box with the child's name clearly marked. (Don't triple wrap items in some film that seals in freshness but renders it childproof.)

- When entering the centre, go in with purpose. Hang up the toddler's bag and take him on a tour of the premises. Alternately, pull up a small chair and help the toddler to find a toy to occupy himself with.

- The toilets should be one of the stops on your tour, as these will be much used in the months that follow. Many little people find the lack of privacy and so much collective flush a bit mind boggling at first but will get used to it.

- On the subject of toilets, don't worry if there are a few accidents. The preschool staff will have been there many times before; they know that recently trained toddlers are prone to leak in times of stress. Pack a spare pair of pants in the toddler's bag and leave the staff to do the worrying.

- Don't rush your departure on the first day. Sit and play with your child and give him time to settle. If you are a working mum, arrange some cover for that day so that you don't need to race off. When it is time to go, be sure the centre has your contact number, say goodbye and then leave decisively.

- Like General MacArthur, tell the toddler, 'I will return', and like the General, keep your promise. Explain, 'John, you will play, have lunch, a little snooze, more playing and then I will be back'. Don't use transparent untruths like 'I am just going out to move the car'. Even a 3 year old knows it's a mighty poor car that takes 5 hours to move!

■ If in doubt about settling your toddler and leaving, be guided by the staff. After you've left, if you are worried about your child during the day, ring the preschool – they are used to it!

■ Most children will settle well, though for a few it sometimes becomes necessary to postpone preschool for a few months. Some will settle well but after a couple of weeks will start to drag their feet as the novelty wears off. This is rarely more than a minor hiccup.

■ At home, be prepared for a tireder toddler whose behaviour, in some instances, may worsen as a result. Beds that were dry may become wet again but this is usually only for a few nights.

When to graduate from preschool

Ideally, no matter what the child's age, we wait until they are emotionally ready to graduate preschool and start school. School enrolment is usually not compulsory until the age of 5 years and young children vary greatly in their social and emotional maturity. Some are ripe for an early start, but others need more months to develop.

But for some modern parents, life is lived at such a pace there is no time to savour the present. From the moment of birth they push their children on the fast track to independence. If the local law allows their child to start school education at 4 years and 7 months, then that's when they will begin, and not a day later.

Unfortunately other parents have no choice but to graduate their child as early as possible as, for them, school provides the only affordable form of childcare.

If your child is eligible to start school young, look carefully at their social readiness. Discuss the coming year with their preschool teacher. They know how your child compares with the others who are also preparing for school. If the teacher says no, take their opinion seriously. As long as your finances will support it, take the safe option and hold back. A late start will never do harm, but starting too soon can cause problems that have long-term repercussions.

Playgroups

I am a great believer in and supporter of playgroups. In fact, I was a patron of Playgroups Australia for many years. Although younger children do attend, playgroups are mainly designed for children aged 1 to 3 years – the peak of toddlerdom – and are all about fun and interaction. Young children come along with their mothers to play and attempt to mix with each other. Although they are too young to play *with* other children at this age, they play happily alongside and generally enjoy their company. However as this is the peak age for biting, kicking, pushing and not sharing, some parents are surprised at the strange ways children have of showing their enjoyment.

At playgroup, toddlers get their sticky hands on a multitude of new toys and are also directed in some simple structured play. While all this is going on, mums can chat, socialise and most importantly, keep a close eye on the proceedings. So the toddler experiences a little bit of independence, yet is never far from mum, and receives lots of encouragement and attention.

Playgroup has advantages for both children and parents. By attending playgroup isolated mums avoid becoming entombed in their own homes. They hear the sorts of problems other mothers are experiencing, and realise they are normal and not alone. Playgroup used to be the sole domain of mums, but these days a handful of fathers can also be seen at the sidelines. Playgroups are great places to compare notes and pool resources with one's fellow toddler tamers.

Taking care of toddlers

If I were writing this book as a work of fiction, I could create ideal situations; mums and dads that only had to work part-time, at jobs with good salaries, leaving them with plenty of energy to spend enjoying their toddlers. Children would spend some days being looked after by mum, some by dad and a few in good, affordable quality childcare for the benefits this provides. This scene of course is not just regular fiction, it is pure fantasy.

Back to reality and we have to make the best of what we've got. If we do place our children in the care of others, even part of the time, we have to ensure two things. Firstly that the care they are receiving is warm, reliable, consistent and of a high quality. And secondly that when we are with them, we give our toddlers our best love and attention. Not out of a misplaced sense of guilt but because we know how important it is to them.

There is no doubt that these early years are important. Whether at home or in childcare, toddlers are constantly learning through play and interaction with adults and other children. In the next chapter we'll look at early learning and how to make the most of these formative years.

20
Early learning

Babies start learning from the moment they take their first breath, and by the time children reach the active toddler years, their learning has jumped into high gear. Children learn more in the first four years of their lives than they will in all the rest of their years combined. The toddler spends every moment exploring this strange, complicated world we live in and many learning milestones are passed at this age such as first steps, first words, the first refused meal and first tantrums.

One of the greatest gifts we can give our children is education and the topic of early learning causes great debate among experts and parents alike. All children have a thirst for knowledge and there is no doubt that these early years are vitally important, providing a solid platform for the future. So when it comes to early learning, what is involved at toddler age? How structured should the learning be? How much is too much and how do we strike a balance? In this chapter we will look at various aspects of early learning and help you to figure out what's best for your child.

Live and learn

When we think of early learning, the image that most often comes to mind is the pushy parent, cramming the child's every waking moment with lessons, flash cards and activities, desperately trying produce the next Einstein. But it is possible to take early learning seriously without adopting this no-holds-barred approach. I believe that the most natural, easiest and enjoyable way that toddlers learn is through living.

The apprentice

Toddlers learn so much just from watching their parents, mimicking their actions and being actively involved in the world around them. The toddler is like an apprentice to the big people in his life and they teach him through involving him in their daily tasks. Tagging along as mum or dad does the household chores and being a 'little helper' is the equivalent to the toddler of lessons in a classroom. The value of watching, listening, copying and just being around mum and dad can never be underestimated. While all this goes on, he feels very important and loved, and he develops a great interest in life.

Learning through living involves time, providing lots of Grade A attention, and making sure the toddler feels he is noticed and

A depressing fact

There are many occasions when it is almost impossible for children to learn from mum and dad. If parents are too busy or if they are single parents overwhelmed with too many responsibilities, the child won't receive the face-to-face time they require. Depressed parents don't have the emotional energy to give a child high-quality attention and, for children from split families, shuffling between two homes can be confusing if one parent provides a stimulating environment and the other doesn't. By acknowledging how vital our role is as educators to our children, we can ensure that we don't short-change them at this critical time in their lives.

important. A major component of how we learn is through reward, and the best reward for the toddler is the warmth and admiration from a happy and proud parent. This, along with the toddler's own feelings of accomplishment, provides all the reinforcement needed to cement new experiences in his brain.

This apprenticeship is the main way that toddlers learn and so the greatest educators our children will ever meet in their lives are their parents. From them the toddler learns not only the basic skills for life but also the beginnings of language, and about forming relationships and values. With this hands-on approach, the child learns more than just information; he learns how to put it into practice.

This process is very natural and everything you need is at your fingertips: you don't require any special tools. It is an active process, where every moment can be used as a learning opportunity. Of course it only works if you engage with the toddler, taking on the role of master/teacher to your little apprentice.

A life full of lessons

We associate the qualities of excitement, wonder and spontaneity with toddlers for good reason. They are rarely bored as there is always something to explore. So plain, everyday activities expand the toddler's experience and teach him something new. Opportunities for this are easy to find; something as simple as a walk around the block can provide learning moments. For example, on the way down the street to the post box, the toddler spies a leaf on the ground. When he picks it up, instead of telling him to 'Put it down, it's dirty', or that you are in a hurry, you say, 'That's a leaf. It comes from a tree, like the one in our garden. Trees are where birdies have their homes, where they go to rest. When the wind blows, leaves fall out of the tree – can you feel the wind?'

There are hundreds of daily examples. A lift going up or down; pressing the button for the lights at the pedestrian crossing; watching a plane soar through the sky – all these and other everyday moments can be used to teach the toddler new words, explain the workings of the world and keep him entertained and interested.

Obviously this is easiest for stay-at-home parents but working parents can make the most of any time they spend together with their toddler. When you come home from work in the evenings, there are activities that need to be done that can be turned from a chore into an enjoyable, educational experience. Instead of bath time being a rushed affair, take a few minutes longer and turn it into a fun-filled playtime where the toddler learns about ducks, boats, counting or letters.

However easy this type of early learning is, parents, despite the best of intentions, sometimes manage to take all the fun out of it. To use the earlier leaf example, the toddler does not need a lecture about photosynthesis, the greenhouse effect and fossil fuels – it is enough that he now knows that leaves come from trees. We need to keep extremely reasonable expectations and remember that toddlers are toddlers. They have limited patience, attention spans and understanding and we have to adjust our expectations accordingly. And we have to be realistic about our own needs too – we can't stop every time the toddler discovers something new or we'd never get anything done. Time-wise and energy-wise it is impractical to make every minute of every day a lesson.

Doing it in style

Believe it or not, there are three main ways in which we learn – visual (sight), auditory (hearing) and kinesthetic (touch) – and every person has a preferred style. While toddlers are all highly kinesthetic, each will develop a preference for learning in one of these ways over the others as they grow. At this young age it is hard to tell what their natural style is and parents can unknowingly focus on teaching their child in the style they prefer themselves.

As your child progresses through his schooling, I think it can be useful to recognise his main learning style, as it will make learning easier and more enjoyable.

Valuable beginnings

These days we realise that it isn't enough to know a lot or have a high IQ. To be happy and successful we need what is called EQ or Emotional Intelligence.

Toddlers learn much of their EQ as if through osmosis. What is termed 'social–emotional learning' – learning about feelings, values and relationships – isn't so much taught as observed and absorbed. By watching how mum, dad and other adults relate, the seeds are planted for the way the toddler himself relates to others, which will become important in later years when he starts to form personal relationships of his own. Adults in his life also teach the toddler how to communicate, how to build strong connections and where he fits into the world. The best way to increase social-emotional learning is to include discussions of the toddler's feelings in everyday situations. Helping them to identify and name sadness, happiness, anger, frustration, excitement, love and many other feelings is the first step in mastering their emotions and forming close relationships.

From his parents, the toddler learns about values. Sharing, not wasting, looking after possessions, being helpful and caring for people are just a few examples of the sorts of values that parents try to teach their children from an early age, through their words and their actions.

We can't change the temperament our toddlers are born with, but we can provide them with the skills they need to make the most of what they've got.

Playing the game

Though it all seems like fun, play is the way that the young of all species learn important skills for life. Lion cubs, for example, stalk, chase, pounce, grab and bite their siblings at play. In their harmless games, they are learning how to hunt and defend themselves, sharpening skills and practising for the real game of life.

Young humans are no different. Toddlers spend much of their day at play and this is by no means wasted time. Some parents think that children should be learning instead of playing, however they are one and the same. Play is perhaps the most important activity in children's lives.

We don't have to teach children how to play; it comes naturally. Physical play includes activities such as running, dancing and chasing. Toddler favourites such as hammering, pouring, scooping, throwing, splashing and creating a mess all fit in this category. In imaginative play, children use make-believe to become a tiger, a fairy or Bob the Builder. Creative play is activities such as painting, modelling with Play Doh, drawing and gluing. Mental play involves words, numbers and shapes. Singing songs, rhyming, counting and matching objects are some of the ways that toddlers fire up their brains while having fun.

The parents' role in toddler play is obvious. Not only do we provide the toys and other objects that make playtime fun *and* educational, we are usually the first choice for a playmate. Toddlers are happier with someone to play with and there is no doubt that they will learn more playing with mum or dad than playing alone.

In the early toddler years, children are generally not interested in playing *with* other children. Instead they 'parallel play' next to each other, doing their own thing as their playmates play alongside. By the age of 3 they will play together, showing the earliest forms of socialisation. Later on, once their speech and listening skills are developed and they can communicate better, they begin to play cooperatively. In the preschool years, play helps toddlers to learn to take turns to share and to pay attention to instructions. Playing also teaches them to stick to a task until completion and to solve problems.

Techno toddlers

Emphasising the educational component of playtime has become very popular and these days it is easy for parents to take advantage of all that technology has to offer their little ones. There are computer-based learning programs available for children as young as 3 years old, and books, DVDs and toys created as learning aids for children from a few months of age.

As parents, we can build the basic skills of reading, counting and recognising shapes and colours with a few well-chosen, clever toys. However, that doesn't mean that the good, old-fashioned games like building blocks should be forgotten. We need to find a balance between education and fun.

Let's get physical

Toddlers are naturally active and seem to be perpetually on the go. How parents channel this active streak is an important part of early learning and development. Physical play builds co-ordination, gross and fine motor skills, balance and fitness. One of the most important lessons that a toddler learns from an active lifestyle is good habits for the future. A large part of being healthy for life is exercising and being active every day and we need to encourage the toddler's innate inclination to move.

It's up to parents to set a good example. If mum and dad are active then the toddler will be influenced without realising it. Activity for the toddler doesn't mean laps around the oval or

In the swim

One activity that most toddlers enjoy is swimming. It is a great all-round activity, not only for obvious safety reasons but because it provides exercise and fun. Some children are born water babies, others are less amphibious, but learning to swim is a good goal for all toddlers.

Children's swimming classes can be very popular. They take children from the age of 9 months although it isn't until the age of 2 that the first real attempts at swimming are shown. The aim of swimming classes is to get children used to the water and slowly build up the skills necessary to swim properly. Floating, splashing, kicking and putting their face in the water are all part of the fun. A form of 'dog paddle' swimming develops somewhere between the third and sixth birthdays, depending on the child's determination and the practice he gets.

Learning to swim stops children being afraid of the water and reduces the risk of accidental drowning. In Australia each year 28 children under the age of 5 die as a result of drowning accidents, often in their backyard pool. Under the age of 5 it is dangerous for children to be around water and they must be supervised by an adult at all times. Even past this age, they *must* always be closely watched when in or near water.

sessions at the gym. Everyday activities provide all the exercise he needs. He builds up his muscles on the arduous walk up to the park, sitting on swings, ascending the climbing frame and the sprint to chase some unfortunate pigeon foolish enough to land within a hundred metres of this active little bird scarer. The average toddler will keep going for hours as long as he has someone to play with.

There are some programmes for toddlers, such as playgroup and Gymboree, that provide a more structured form of activity. But a play date with his little toddler friends is just as exciting and a great way to get physical, so if you aren't a fan of the organised activities, there is no excuse to ignore this important part of his early learning.

Language development

Toddlerdom brings the major milestones of walking and toilet training but the most far-reaching and exciting of all is the development of language. Our use of language is what makes us different from every other species on the planet and in terms of a child's development, it is the one with the greatest impact. Parents are always asking what the most important characteristic is they should be looking for in their child's development and my answer is 'Language, language, language'.

We now know that children gain knowledge of language, reading and writing long before they start school. Babies from their earliest days react to the sound of their mother's voice and, although we may not realise it, children from as young as 6 months are collecting words – building a dictionary in their heads well before they can even speak.

Language is the use of words, spoken, written and comprehended, and literacy is how we use language in everyday life. It is not just reading and writing, it is speaking, listening and understanding what others say. The better your use of language, the more literate you are; the more literate you are, the further you can get on in the world. There is no point in being clever if you can't show people that you are – this is one more reason that having good language skills is so important.

So what assists language development for toddlers? Being surrounded by language, both spoken and written, is the key. Birds

This is your life

Just by talking about daily activities the toddler learns not only about the world around him but also about language. During the average day all kinds of adventures take place in a toddler's life and he will want to verbalise his experiences to anyone who will listen. On the way to the shops he will want to talk about the cars, the dogs or anything else of interest that passes. Once home, he will help to put away the groceries, accompanied by non-stop chatter. He listens to mum and dad, copies their sayings and asks innumerable questions. Day by day his verbal abilities increase, and so does his interest in life.

may tweet without learning from mama bird but little toddlers need their parents to nurture language. Parents teach toddlers by talking to them, repeating words and asking questions. Chatting to the toddler through the day gives him a host of words to learn and collect. The more they are exposed to words and encouraged to use them, the better their language skills will be.

All toddlers gain language at a different pace but to most parents' surprise and delight, the development of language, once begun, is swift. At 1 year of age, the toddler will begin with simple words such as 'da da' or 'ma ma' and the ubiquitous 'no'. By 18 months he will have a vocabulary of up to 20 words, and will repeat others that he doesn't yet understand. At 2 years, his range will have increased to around 50 words and he will understand many more. By 2½ he will use more than 200 words, increasing his vocabulary by a staggering 400 per cent in just six short months! When we compare that to the average adult, who past school age is lucky to gain 20 new words a year, we have to marvel at the linguistic ability of the toddler.

Reading

Reading is such an essential part of adult life that we forget there was a time when the words on this page would have seemed to us a meaningless jumble of squiggles and lines. While the skill of reading is generally acquired at school, in toddlerdom there are important steps parents can take to lay the foundation for future reading success.

At the toddler age, children don't read as such, because they aren't developmentally able. In any case, it is just about impossible to teach active young toddlers to read, as their interests lie more in the areas of running, playing, helping mum or dad, and just enjoying the fun life of being a toddler.

Some children may be taught with flash cards to recognise 'sight words' at the age of 2. When the appropriate response is given, the child is immediately rewarded. This is a skill that greatly excites most parents, who are convinced that their child is a little genius. In fact, this skill can be imparted to any child who is prepared to settle and concentrate and has a good photographic memory for differences in patterns. Pigeons and chimpanzees have been taught to recognise shapes using very similar techniques.

Teaching a child to recognise words is not the same as teaching a child to 'read'. To read properly, recognising patterns is only the beginning. The real skill is in being able to look at a word, sound out its letters, apply a multitude of rules, short cuts and exclusions, and then come up with the right pronunciation. Once this skill has been mastered, words never seen before can be read with ease. Coupled with good comprehension, this is the real adult reading skill. Unfortunately, the human brain is not sufficiently mature to handle all this computation before the developmental age of 6, and it is then that we see which children are destined to be the good or the average readers. But toddlers do engage in pre-reading tasks and we need to encourage them as much as possible.

Reading is an essential part of literacy and is based on language comprehension and pattern recognition. And because language and speech are tied so closely to reading ability, focusing on language is really the first step. Parents have to set the stage, not by trying to get the toddler to read but by encouraging an interest in books and other printed materials and those activities that make reading easier and fun.

Early reading does not have to take a formal approach. To be successful you simply need to expose the child to books and stories from a very early age and make sure these interactions are positive. Many parents ask when they should start reading to their children. The answer is that it is never too early. At first children

No lifetime guarantee

There is an argument that a child's reading ability at school age all comes down to how involved the parents were in the formative years. And while it is certainly better for parents to read to their children as a foundation for reading skills and literacy, their concerted efforts do not always guarantee a good reader as the outcome.

While most children grow to become comfortable readers, a small percentage will find it challenging throughout their lives. For the 5 per cent of children with dyslexia, reading is a lifetime struggle, no matter how much effort they or their parents put in. And I believe that a further 5 per cent of children have 'relative dyslexia', meaning that reading will never be a joy.

will probably only fiddle with the pages and look at the pictures, but soon they will start recognising images. Under the age of 9 months they certainly won't appreciate the intricacies of plot or characterisation but reading to them will build closeness and communication, which is never a bad thing. And, as parents soon discover, children are happy to have their favourite books read to them again and again.

These days, life is made easy for parents with a wide range of child-friendly books on the market, filled with simple shapes and colours, easy to follow story lines and tactile pages that engage the child. In my childhood, books of nursery rhymes had few pictures and a real highlight was a pop-up story book. Today we have books for toddlers that are waterproof to read in the bath – even books with computer chips in the pages which read themselves to the toddler! But it doesn't have to be an expensive exercise. You can take advantage of your local library, swap books with friends who have children the same age as your toddler, look out for garage sales and junk shop bargains or even make little books from cuttings out of magazines.

Good reading ability is tied closely to academic success and I believe that in later years being able to read well boosts a child's self-esteem. Even discounting the possible financial and social gains that come from good reading skills, this is enough reason for most parents to recognise its importance and help their child to become a good reader.

Thinking outside the box

Over the years many a young child has been asked by his proud parents to stand up and count to 100 for me. The child sounds very impressive until asked a simple question: 'If you pass a field in which there are two cows and open the gate and let one out, how many cows would now be in the field?' – Silence! While rote learning (learning by memory) does play a part in learning, parents can mistake their child's ability to learn something by heart for true intelligence.

Rote learning is of no benefit in answering real-life problems unless you can think laterally. By 'lateral thinking' I refer to the ability to be given one piece of information and use it to generalise for other situations. Lateral thinking is important in becoming a creative, intelligent person. A child can have an astonishing photographic memory but sadly this is no compensation for the multitude of real-life skills he does not possess.

Parents can encourage lateral thinking by including games and activities that make the child explore options and think outside the box. Improvisation and imaginative play are ways to produce an extremely inventive brain which is often lost in the 'spoon-fed'

Safe and hound

Jake is a dog I know, a mad Rhodesian ridgeback that has no lateral thinking ability – that is, if he thinks at all! A few years back poor Jake ran out onto the road and was hit by a bus. He was badly hurt but thankfully recovered. Recently I asked his owner: 'Is Jake now more sensible on the road?' The answer was that he was terrified of the spot where the bus hit him but was just as mad on every other road. Jake is a classic rote learner: he doesn't use his hard-earned knowledge to generalise.

child. A cardboard box becomes a garage for toy cars; later it is a rocket base from which the cardboard innards of a toilet roll blast off into space. One moment the dining chairs are all lined up and money is being collected and counted by the toddler conductor; within minutes he is piloting an amazingly noisy jumbo jet down the middle of the lounge room.

By playing in this way the toddler begins to draw comparisons, act out possible scenarios and solve problems. Ultimately it will make them better thinkers. Our aim in life must be to teach children the basic skills of learning, then encourage and enthuse them to work from there.

Spotting gifts

As we go about providing a fun, well-rounded early learning environment for our toddlers, we can stumble across surprising gifts or talents. For example, we may have in our midst a budding Tiger Woods, discovered after spotting his remarkable hand–eye coordination while playing in the garden.

Parents are generally the ones that spot these gifts and they will most easily recognise those talents they possess in some quantity themselves. Whether it is the result of genetics, or the child's exposure to his parent's preferences, we often see patterns of talent in families. It seems a sporting hero is more likely to have a child equally gifted with athletic prowess. The same applies to musicians, artists, race car drivers. A family of actors or even doctors is a common phenomenon.

Even in these early years we can shine a spotlight on the gifts and talents that the toddler possesses and recognise and encourage activities that the toddler naturally excels at. Everybody needs to feel that they are good at something and encouraging talents builds a child's self-esteem. There is nothing wrong with encouraging these gifts, as long as we don't put undue pressure on the toddler. The focus has to be on nurturing these remarkable talents and holding reasonable expectations of our children – never forcing.

So how much is too much? When does encouraging go too far? The surest sign is if you are more excited about the activity than the toddler is. If the toddler is no longer enjoying himself it is time to back off and allow events to unfold in a more relaxed, natural way.

High hopes for high IQs

All parents naturally believe that their child is brilliant, but the law of averages suggests that this can't be the case. For the less than 1 per cent of children who truly are geniuses, how do we spot their exceptional abilities at toddler age?

If you have scored one of these brilliant children, you will probably know quite early. One of the first signs will be the child's language skills. These children will not only speak early and well, but will have exceptional comprehension. They will also have great lateral thinking ability and be able to see how things fit together in a way that is unexpected at this age. And the genius toddler is likely to have advanced early reading ability, with an extraordinary interest in the written word at preschool age. All this will be combined with an uncommon ability to focus and pay attention when needed, enabling them to stick to tasks and complete them. As you can see, this isn't the description of your average toddler!

Giving them a push

Whether we like it or not, the world is a very competitive place. It seems that everyone is constantly trying to get ahead – a better job, a newer car, a nicer place to live. And while right now school days may seem eons away, many parents are already thinking of their child's academic future.

One of the strongest arenas of competition is the fight for places at tertiary institutions such as universities and colleges. The benefits of a tertiary education are indisputable. Gaining a tertiary qualification opens doors, allowing greater choice in careers. It generally guarantees a better salary and enables you to meet people with similar interests. There are many parents who believe that by pushing an academic education from a very early age, we can help our children achieve the top grades they need to be academically successful.

There is no doubt that in life lots of practice and exposure create a better outcome. This applies to any field, from sport to music to academic learning. Parents with 'Ivy League' aspirations for their children spur them on to ever higher levels of scholastic achievement and keep them focused on that Harvard MBA. But at what cost? The downside to these children's amazing grades is the lack of scope and breadth in their young lives. Fun activities are sacrificed so the focus can be placed on exams.

In a large group of children, some are destined to do well academically, some will be average and some will sit at the bottom of the class. Not everyone can be in the top ten; someone has to be number 11.

So the question is: is all the pushing worth it? Are there perhaps more important things in life?

Who are we trying to help?

Unfortunately, the efforts of some parents in encouraging their children can escalate to unhealthy extremes, and such a fo cus on academic goals may blind them to the many different ways children can excel in life. For some parents this approach is gradual and unintentional but for others, producing a brilliant child is a crutch to prop up their own crumbling egos.

The pushy parent arranges for extra home tutoring in the hope of widening the gap between their child and his peers even further; they withdraw him from activities that involve mixing with children of inferior abilities; he is given little exposure to anything that might loosely be termed 'fun'. The result? An incredibly intelligent child who is socially and physically backward; an interesting showpiece but a boring nerd.

In their obsessive crusade to produce a 'superchild' these parents leave other casualties in their wake. Sadly, any other children in the family who are 'only normal', are often to a large extent ignored in the process.

Little sponges

As any parent quickly realises, toddlers are like little sponges, soaking up the details of their environment with seemingly little effort. Early learning has an impact on the child's future academic success but even more importantly, it produces well-rounded, happy, interested children.

If we as parents include our children in our daily activities, stimulate them with play and then boost their learning with some well chosen toys, books and activities, they will receive the best education a child of this age can hope for.

21
Sibling rivalry

Sibling rivalry refers to the competitive streak which makes children squabble, fight and then accuse their parents of favouritism. You can't have sibling rivalry without a sibling and the trouble really starts as our little families expand.

I don't want to annoy my readers by saying this, but toddlers and animals have a lot in common. Like all young members of the animal kingdom, they love to taunt and fight. In the grand design of life this serves a purpose. It builds up their bodily reflexes and muscles, making them safer and better able to cope in the big, wide world. The downside is it drives their parents mad.

The only surefire way to avoid sibling rivalry is to have only one child. However, I am certainly not suggesting abstinence or contraception as reliable means to end this problem. I think there are much better ways to deal with our children's fighting, as we'll see in this chapter.

Double trouble

When the Green family had just one toddler, I thought I knew all about children's behaviour. When we had two, I realised how little

I really knew. A duet of toddlers can devise ways to get into mischief well beyond the imagination of any adult or child alone. The creative genius of such young people is always astonishing. **Two toddlers are never difficult when separated by a distance of at least a kilometre; it is when they come together that they set each other off.**

How you approach your toddler's rivalry depends very much on their age. The very young are keen to protect their pitch from interfering intruders. They behave badly when their toys are touched by brothers, sisters or visitors and they hate anyone monopolising their mum's attention.

Sibling rivalry is probably at its worst in older toddlers and beyond: the 4- to 10-year-old bracket. Older toddlers have a different but equally effective style – they bicker, bait and complain of inequality. Children at this age also have a very odd way of showing their affection. They can't bear to be apart from their sibling but when they are together, they squabble and compete. A 3-year-old toddler is taken to the park with Dad, to separate him from his 4-year-old sister and the fight that just ended in tears. But all the time at the park, he can't wait to see his sister again and wants to know where she is. Meanwhile, at the supermarket with Mum, big sis is pining for her brother. This deep affection lasts for five minutes once they're reunited in the lounge room . . . until the hugs turn to fighting and the cycle starts all over again!

Perhaps the greatest problem our children have is that they are too much like the grown-ups they live with. If you come to think of it, adults are remarkably competitive and jealous beings. Most humans seem to have a strong drive to get more and do better than their peers, even if a few people get trampled along the way. If adults start wars and take advantage of their fellow man, then we can hardly complain about a toddler having a few skirmishes and shows of strength.

Fairly equal

If you are going to survive at the front line of childcare, you have to be a realist. We all know that each of our children must be treated with equal love, limits and discipline. We also know that this admirable goal is out of touch with reality. Our expectations may be equal, but the children we raise are not. True equality, it seems, is only to be found in Fairyland.

I feel that there is little true equality in our adult world. He who is strongest and shouts loudest gets the most. Parents of twins quickly realise this: the difficult, noisy twin hijacks an unfair slice of the action, while the docile one misses out. When parents are faced with two children with dramatically different temperaments, fairness is impossible and it is necessary to adjust their parenting to suit each child. Trying to get all children to behave exactly the same way is foolhardy and futile.

Your time and attention may not be divided fairly but your love can still be transmitted with complete equality.

Fighting

Fighting between our young is one of those universal but irritating parts of family life. While some children are so serene you wonder if they are training for the Peace Corps, others could start a fight in an empty room.

Over the years I have talked to hundreds of parents trying to discover an effective peacekeeping plan. The following method may help to secure an uneasy truce between your combatants:

- *Ignore it:* Turn a deaf ear and a blind eye to as much bickering as you can.
- *Divert their attention:* When siblings start to spar, divert their attention to something more innocent and interesting.
- *Lose the audience:* Fighters like an audience and few fights take place without one. Bundle brawling children into another room or banish them out the back door. Can you imagine Ali or Tyson holding the World Title in their back room, watched only by the cleaning lady and her dog? It seems to me that if there is not an interested audience most fights will fizzle out. When our children squabble it is best to either move away from the ringside, or move the ringside away from us.
- *Hold back:* Don't rush in like the United Nations at the first hint of trouble. Children have to find their own means of resolution. The main mistake we parents make is to get drawn into our children's battles. If they know that you will always

intervene, you may still be intervening when they are twenty. And if the moment they start you rush in like the anti-terrorist squad, gas grenades and guns at the ready, soon they will act up just to see you in full action.

■ *Ditch the interrogation:* It would take a team of detectives to discover who started a fight between siblings. Don't hold an enquiry into who fired the first shot as, at the height of any conflict, it is peace not recrimination that is needed. Don't waste your time. (Although in my opinion, as in other walks of life, it is usually the one who protests the loudest who is most guilty.)

■ *Take decisive action:* When you do intervene, it must be decisive, without debate and with 100 per cent firmness. If you are eventually forced to become involved, do so properly. Don't enter the feud yourself. Pull rank, say, 'That's it!' and leave them in no doubt that you are not going to take sides or tolerate any more.

■ *Use Time Out:* When all else fails, separate the squabblers with a brief period of Time Out in different rooms. It doesn't matter who's the 'good guy' and who's the 'bad guy' – both children have to be relocated and defused.

Always the victim

It becomes a different matter when one child is being unfairly and continually victimised. We call this bullying, and it can take place in the home just as it does in the playground. We often see this victimisation in blended families, where two single parents have formed a relationship and brought their unwilling children into the mix.

In the case of bullying, it is beyond the ability of most parents to sort through the maze of complicated feelings and recriminations while trying to remain impartial. It helps to seek the advice of a child psychologist who can intervene to stop the situation from developing further. Bullying must be dealt with as soon as it is recognised, to lessen any potential damage to relationships and the child's self-esteem.

Taunting

At the end of toddlerdom our children master the school-age skill of taunting. The most skilled taunters will always appear innocent, and this is often the best way to spot them! A trail of trouble seems to follow in their wake. Their brother's homework book mysteriously falls to the floor. The TV channel changes in the closing minutes of the movie. While your back is turned, little sisters are poked, tripped or insulted.

Boredom brings out the worst in a taunter as they pace around like a hungry lion on the lookout for a Christian. At moments like this it is best to keep them occupied. The trick is to divert their attention as they position themselves for the pounce.

As I've said before, try to keep out of children's squabbles. If you do intervene, lay down the law quite firmly. There is no place for debating and democracy – if they are unhappy with your decision, let them take their case to the Human Rights Commission.

Oh, baby!

The way our families seem to happen, there is usually a gap of about 1½ to 2½ years between our first and second child. Now you don't need a degree in psychology to know that this timing spells trouble. The unsuspecting baby is going to drop in on the self-centred toddler at the peak of his privileged, 'I'm in charge' reign.

I used to think that toddlers didn't get upset until the new baby arrived. But in fact, parents tell me toddlers start to act differently when mum is pregnant, even before they have been told to expect a new brother or sister. It seems the toddler feels the vibes in the air even though they don't know exactly what is happening.

Pause for a moment to see it from a 2 year old's view; he thinks he's the most important person around. He likes having his mum and dad's undivided attention and he doesn't understand the meaning of the word 'share'. And anyway, no-one asked his permission before bringing that thing into the house. He thinks it should be sent back immediately to the hospital with directions to put it back where it came from!

Making the right introductions

Most toddlers will accept their baby brother or sister without the slightest hiccup. In my experience, most mums and dads handle this period of adjustment very well and there are usually few problems. But we can help to get things off to a good start by making the right introductions.

Before and after the birth

■ While pregnant, talk to the toddler about the advent of a new brother or sister. Use language that he will understand. You can always mention the impending appearance of all those dirty nappies – toddlers can relate to this, as they are world experts on bodily functions.

■ Make the toddler feel involved in the preparations. For example, he can help to choose a toy for his new brother or sister. As toddlers love to feel important, involving him makes him feel grown up.

■ When mum is in hospital, leave the toddler with someone he knows well, where he will feel secure, for example grandma or a close friend.

■ These days toddlers are encouraged to visit their mothers and the new baby in the maternity ward. It should be a fun time with lots of attention paid to the toddler and a few presents on hand to make him feel special.

■ Before visitors come to see the baby, prime them to first fuss over and notice the toddler. After all, toddlers see themselves as the main attraction.

At home

■ From the first days at home, encourage the toddler to carefully get to know his baby brother or sister. Guide him in stroking a soft cheek or touching tiny fingers and toes. Explain that when the baby cries she has a wet nappy or is hungry.

■ While mums are highly protective of their newborn infants, this must never be allowed to drive a wedge between the toddler and baby. If the toddler is scolded for going near the baby, who then receives attention and comfort, it is the surest way to sow the seeds of a magnificent sibling rivalry.

■ That said, it is important to protect the new baby without overdoing it. Remember that the toddler's explorations are innocent and even putting fingers near the baby's eyes isn't done with any malicious intent. The toddler also sees the wonder of a new baby and is just trying to get close. After all, sibling closeness has to start somewhere!

■ The toddler should be allowed to cuddle and play with the new arrival, just as long as he is gentle. Obviously, he shouldn't be allowed to pick up or carry the infant.

■ Once the baby is a few months old and the toddler has a little more experience, he can be allowed some more independent contact with his little sibling. Parents should stand a short distance away and out of the corner of one eye watch that the baby is OK. Meanwhile they must try to act nonchalant, which of course is easier said than done.

■ Despite the demands of caring for an infant, don't neglect to give the toddler attention. This can be achieved by what I refer to as 'sidestream attention'. As you feed the baby, make the toddler feel like he's involved: talk to him or read him a story. If you don't he will hijack your attention, often by disappearing somewhere you can't see, which leaves you poised for the sounds of breakage as you imagine what may be demolished.

A poke in the eye

With the arrival of the new baby, the toddler has been provided with the most potent weapon he has ever held in his armory. When life becomes boring, all that the toddler needs to do is walk a few paces and poke the baby. The result is quite dramatic. He quickly discovers how sensitive his mother has become.

The *pièce de résistance* is usually reserved for very special occasions: those times the toddler is in need of attention or is perhaps just having a bad day. A dirty digit is poked within a few centimetres of the baby's eye, which is usually quite close enough to guarantee an emotional eruption from one's mother. As a way to get attention, this scores ten out of ten!

■ A few toddlers will accept their new sibling initially, but when the baby is around 6 months old, there is a backlash. At first the new baby was seen as an interesting animated doll, but when the 'doll' sits up and starts to do other clever things that gain lots of attention, a sibling becomes a great threat to the balance of power. Suddenly there is real competition. The solution is to focus on the toddler's gains and achievements and make sure that he hasn't been forgotten in the excitement of the baby's development. The balance has to be shifted back to both children.

Baby talk

Even with a smooth introduction, the toddler's behaviour may change with the arrival of a brother or sister. Your toddler may seem to regress when the new baby arrives home, and start to behave like a baby himself. Some toddlers want to be picked up and carried all the time and revert to talking baby-talk. They want mum or dad to feed them their meals, demand a bottle or even want to be on mum's breast again.

'Why is he doing all this?' ask frustrated parents. Well, he's just following the baby's example. All this is working really well for the baby, who is getting most of the attention, so the toddler thinks, 'Anything you can do, I can do better!' When you look at it like this, it's easier to understand why they do it.

But if parents have been strong enough to get rid of other attention-seeking behaviour, there is no reason to surrender to toddler strongarm tactics now. The solution is to fall back on what we already know works – encouraging the behaviour we want to see and ignoring the behaviour we don't want. Don't indulge the toddler in his babylike ways. Instead, focus on all the clever toddler behaviours he shows. Do more activities together that show how much more grown up the toddler is than his little brother or sister, like reading, playing with puzzles or blocks, throwing a ball around in the garden or doing chores together.

As with any change in the status quo, children who have been toilet trained may start to wet their pants or beds again. This is usually a temporary change and can be remedied by following my techniques in the Toilet Training chapter.

The 'only child'

Many parents worry about raising an 'only child'; that is, one without any brothers or sisters. The big concern seems to be whether an only child is disadvantaged. But the way I see it, both being an 'only child' and having siblings has its advantages and disadvantages.

On a positive note, only children get more of their parents' time, attention and energy, as these don't have to be shared with other children in the family. Their parents are less likely to be stressed by the demands of parenting just one youngster, which hopefully translates to a happier, more peaceful home. Only children also don't have to share toys or bedrooms with a sibling and their parents only have to feed and clothe one child, which is never as difficult as providing for a whole tribe. Their parents can also put more focus on learning, so they may get more and better education.

On the other hand, there is a greater risk of these children being lonely and they miss out on playing with brothers or sisters. They may spend more time in adult company and so can be expected to have rather more adult attitudes. They risk being spoilt, particularly if their parents have waited a long time to have a child. Lack of siblings means some only children feel out of place in the company of other children and so they may find it harder to settle down when they get to preschool. And they may miss out on rough and tumble games if they are the child of older parents, who don't have the zip to keep up with an active toddler lifestyle.

Having siblings of course also has its pluses and minuses. As one of many, a child has company growing up and always has someone to play with. He learns to cope with other children better, which makes the transition to preschool easier. Younger siblings seem to pick up language quicker as they strive to match big brother or sister. Siblings do, however, have to share their parents' time, attention and energy. And finally, from the parents' point of view, there is more noise, more mess and they need to be more organised. To top it off, as we've seen in this chapter, sibling rivalry is pretty much guaranteed!

When you add it all up, I don't think there is any great disadvantage in being an only child and parents shouldn't worry if that is the way things are. These days there is a trend toward having children later in life, which means there will be more only children. Playgroup, the children next door or other children in their family, such as cousins, can provide the socialisation they would otherwise miss out on without a brother or sister on hand. In the end, what really matters is the health and happiness of our children, whether we have one or five.

It's part of the territory

Sibling rivalry is an unpleasant and unfortunate fact of life. Unlike some toddler behaviours discussed in this book, children only seem to get better at it as they get older. No amount of reasoning with children will make them stop. 'Will you quit fighting?' and 'Don't you love your sister?' fed up parents beseech their little ones. But, as far as the toddler is concerned, love doesn't rule out biting, pulling, shoving or yelling at their beloved sibling. It is all about territory and children understand this even if parents don't.

As parents we have to learn to keep our cool, overlook the squabbling and focus on the benefits having brothers or sisters brings to the toddler. I think the joy of a larger family is worth the small amount of pain.

22
Working parents: making it work

Since I first wrote this book more than 20 years ago, this chapter has become essential reading for the average toddler tamer. More mums and dads are working parents today than ever before, and though the numbers have increased, the difficulty and guilt this causes many parents hasn't eased at all.

While I wish the percentages of working parents could be lower I believe in being realistic. What we really need is a way to make it all work. Toddlerdom passes so quickly, and once it has gone we cannot ask for a re-run. Working parents are extra time-poor but have the same need to play an active part in their toddler's life as stay-at-home parents. In this chapter, rather than enter the debate about whether or not mums and dads should be working, I want to look at some ways to make life easier as a working parent.

A working life

As many of you know all too well, life as a working parent is a juggling act. Trying to balance the demands of a job while raising a toddler calls for superhuman feats of time management, organisation, flexibility and patience. At the end of a long day at the office, working parents must find hidden reserves of energy and attention for the toddler. The situation is even more difficult for working single parents. With little backup and the same child-rearing responsibilities, they are really stretched to the limit. The pressure never lets up and there never seem to be enough hours in the day to get it all done.

Today, 51 per cent of Australian mothers of under-5s are in paid work. Of these, a proportion are working part-time or flexible hours, but no matter the number of hours involved, being a working parent means time away from your children. Of course, I'm not suggesting that stay-at-home parents aren't also working parents. Having young children around is exhausting and being put through the wringer all day, every day, is draining work. By the end of toddlerdom, stay-at-home parents can resemble pale shadows of their former selves.

A novel concept

Working mothers are often expected to do two full-time jobs, only one of which receives pay or thanks. All husbands are generous to a fault. They give with absolute equality at the time of conception but, unfortunately, for many that's where all giving seems to end. For some fathers, you might well ask: 'Is there life after conception?' It's time for some true equality. If fathers can have a night out with the boys or go off to soccer training, mothers should be able to go off to the gym or for dinner with the girls.

Guilt

Guilt saps parental confidence which then has a flow-on effect to all areas of their lives. The main reason working parents feel guilty is because they believe they are short-changing their children. Even worse, some worry that they may be damaging their child by not being around more of the time.

Many studies have been done on the effects on children of having working parents. In a study at the University of Massachusetts, published in 1998, Elizabeth Harvey evaluated and compared the language development, academic achievement, self-esteem and behaviour problems of the children of working and stay-at-home mothers. She found no statistically significant differences.

Despite results such as these, it doesn't stop the pointing fingers and blaming of working parents, particularly working mothers, for their children's difficulties. A quote from the internationally respected writings of Sir Michael Rutter, a psychiatrist in the UK who studies developmental psychology, might ease the minds of some: 'Although frequently blamed for their children's troubles it is now apparent that working mothers have children with no more problems than the children of women who remain at home. This has now been shown in a wide range of studies using different measures of children's behaviours'.

If parents, particularly mothers, who either wanted to work or were obliged to work could just get on with it and stop feeling guilty, their lives could be much easier. Feeling guilty helps neither yourself nor your children, so it is time to get rid of the guilt.

Guilt busting

Guilt is mainly the result of other people's opinions of our choices. The guilt caused by pondering whether we are doing a good job as a parent is par for the course. But I find that working parents have a particular set of guilt-inducing worries.

The primary worry is that because their child is spending a significant amount of time in day care, he is losing out on love and one-to-one attention. But these days, good quality day care services recognise the importance of attention in children's development. They are designed to give the young children all the attention they need, focusing on the individual requirements of each child. And they have loving, caring staff to make the children feel safe and secure. If the parents work the child doesn't miss out; he gets all the attention and love that he needs during the day and another dose at home from his parents.

A secondary concern is that if the parents stayed at home to look after their child, the toddler would be receiving the very best care that only mum or dad can provide, and that day care is only ever 'second rate'. Of course, no-one would suggest that anyone else can look after your child better than you can yourself. But the best way to alleviate your fears is to do your research and be confident in your choice of childcare. Also, be as involved as much as possible. What really matters to the children of working parents is that they get your best whenever you *are* at home.

We are all quite capable of making ourselves feel guilty without family members, friends or even complete strangers getting in on the act. Drowning out any 'helpful suggestions' is essential in order to maintain your peace of mind. People will always have opinions – it's important to remember that it's *your* child, *your* life and *your* choices.

Childcare and working parents

One of the toughest decisions that working parents have to make is who will look after their children while they are out bread-winning. There are three main options: using family or friends; enrolling the child in professional day care; or sharing the role between themselves and their partner.

Most parents will use a combination of these. Those lucky enough to have family support usually grab it. Leaving the toddler with a responsible family member is cheap and effective childcare. This is a win–win situation, as family are often keen to spend more time with the next generation. With some grandparents, it is not so much a question of leaving the toddler with them, it's getting him back again! In the absence of family, parents may choose friends or neighbours they can trust.

Many working parents arrange for day care through accredited centres or through their local authority. For more information on day care choices, see Chapter 19.

These days, more parents are sharing the childcare responsibility between themselves. For example, my dentist drills away three days a week and minds the children on the other days while his wife works. Obviously not everyone is lucky enough to have this sort of flexibility but it is ideal if it can be arranged.

No matter which option you choose, you have to feel secure in the knowledge that your child is being cared for in a way that is second-best only to how you care for him yourself. Then, knowing your child is happy and safe, you can have the confidence to focus on your work.

In sickness and in health

After their first year of living in the relative isolation of home, our children have little immunity to all the bugs that cause colds, coughs and fevers. When they start attending day care they are at their most vulnerable and they seem to catch everything that is going around.

Childcare centres are not designed to cope with unwell toddlers and sick children place a great strain on parents. Most parents are forced to take time off work to care for a sick child. Using their own sick leave to be at home with their unwell offspring usually means that parents are forced to soldier on when they are sick themselves. Some companies grant parental leave but others aren't so generous, and taking time off without pay eats into already tight budgets. Even if you call on grandma or aunty as nurse it's not easy: children really want to be around mum or dad when they are unwell, as they provide comfort and security.

The first few colds or flus can be tough, but bouts of sickness decrease as the child gets older and develops immunity. For better or worse, there is a light at the end of the tunnel.

Quality not quantity

It is clear to me that it is not the number of hours parents spend away from home that make the difference to the toddler. What does make the difference is how the time is spent when they are at home. **In parenting it is not only the amount of time, but how we use that time, that matters.**

The quality of the child's day care arrangements only goes so far. The other half of the equation is the quality of the parent–child relationship. However good day care is, I believe it is only acceptable if accompanied by good parental care at home.

Short-changed Charlie

Charlie was a 2-year-old boy whose mother brought him to me because of a sleep problem. No matter what she tried, he wouldn't settle at night. Charlie wouldn't go to bed and shouted, complained and cried at the mere suggestion. If mum did manage to get him horizontal, he was up and into her room in the night. His mother was a working single parent and rapidly coming to the end of her rope. With a demanding full-time job, she just wasn't coping with toddler-induced sleep deprivation.

For a number of weeks I worked with Charlie using controlled crying and various other techniques. We even tried a short course of sedation but as the days passed we appeared to be going backward. It seemed the more I tried to help, the unhappier Charlie got.

Preparing for failure, I stepped back and took another look at Charlie's problem. It turned out the answer was right in front of our eyes. Charlie was dropped off at day care at 8 o'clock every morning and came home at 6 pm. Charlie didn't have a sleep problem, he just wanted to be close to his mum! His mother would rush through dinner and bath time, racing towards five minutes of story time before bed. Charlie knew he was being shortchanged.

The solution to Charlie's 'sleep problem' was simple. We made his bedtime later so that mum could spend more time with him in the evening, sitting and reading to him or watching TV together. He didn't need a lot of entertainment, he just wanted them to do things together. Soon Charlie would go to bed at night with no problem at all.

At the end of a long day away from his parents at day care or preschool, what a toddler wants most is the closeness and attention of mum and dad. He wants to share with them the excitement and adventures of his day. The work-tired parent may have little spare energy to talk and play with the toddler. Even the best of parents, whether working or not, can only give so much, but we have to remember that the toddler has his needs too.

Some parents expect their children to entertain themselves so they can relax after a hard day at work. But the toddler doesn't want to be put in front of the TV or put straight to bed. As we've seen in earlier chapters, toddlers thrive on attention and are very good at demanding it. If you won't give it to them voluntarily, they will take it by force.

Sharing the load

It seems only fair that if children are conceived together, then their care should continue together. In the twenty-first century, there can be no place for a sleeping partner in a two-wage family. **When two tired parents with an excited child get home each evening there must be a fair division of labour.** The most efficient way to manage this is for one parent to spend time with the toddler while the other is engaged in the drudgery of everyday chores. For example:

- Dad gives toddler his bath while mum organises dinner.
- Mum plays with junior while dad puts a load of washing in the machine.
- One parent reads their child a story while the other makes his lunch to take to preschool the next day.

This is by far the fairest way for the toddler as he doesn't get pushed to the sidelines to watch the main action. But shopping, cooking and housework must not be allowed to consume all of one parent's time. Both parents need precious time together with their child. Some chores, however, can be a source of fun and learning and shared with the toddler rather than excluding him. Toddlers love to help and the banalities of fetching the mail, putting away groceries or sorting the washing are much more interesting to the toddler than they are to grown ups.

Family planning

So many activities in life are easier with a plan and the jam-packed schedule of working parents with a toddler is no exception. Here are a few suggestions for making life as a working parent easier:

■ Get into a routine. It keeps all the family members in the loop and, if everyone knows what is going on, you save on time and screw ups. For example, the family knows that on Wednesday dad picks up the kids from school while mum works late. A whiteboard or a weekly planner recording the family's movements is the simplest method and reduces the risk of forgotten appointments, double bookings and running out of time.

■ Make daily tasks and chores as simple as possible and take time-efficient short cuts wherever you can. For example, internet banking and shopping can cut hours of time wasted in queues – time better spent with your toddler.

■ Spend a few minutes every evening preparing what you can for the next day. Lay out the toddler's clothes, make his lunch and put his lunch box in the fridge. Place his backpack by the front door ready to go the next morning. This avoids the chaos of stressed-out mornings and allows the family to spend some quality time together over breakfast. And you will deliver the toddler to day care physically and emotionally topped up.

■ The pick up from day care can be a frantic race from work to get to the centre on time. Arriving in this state you transmit to the toddler your frustration and frazzled nerves. If this will be a regular occurrence, arrange for a friend to be on call to relieve the pressure.

■ Share aftercare with other working mums or dads that you know well. Inform the toddler's day care of the arrangements for safety. At least one day per week you will gain precious afternoon time which you can use to do activities and chores that are better done without the toddler in tow. For example, going to the gym.

■ Have a list of people you can call when you get in a jam or in times of emergency. Most preschools and day care centres request such a list, too. Car breakdowns, migraine headaches or last-minute work deadlines can wreak havoc on the most organised schedule. Have different friends or family members 'on standby' to provide last minute assistance. Also, find a local doctor for your toddler close to home and day care.

- Make the most of weekends. Divide up the tasks at hand: one parent can shop, clean or take the toddler to the pool or park, while the other irons and prepares for the week to come.
- Make sure you have sensible expectations. Cleanliness, hygiene and relative tidiness are desirable but obsessive house pride is out.
- The meals you prepare don't need to be too exotic or time-consuming; all that matters is they are nutritious, tasty and easy to prepare. For those with big freezers and an organised brain, there is much to be said for weekend cooking and freezing binges.
- Take a break from being chef. Arrange a weekly visit to a local restaurant that is toddler-friendly, or order take out food. It can be worth the splurge on the budget for the luxury of sitting down with the family as diner rather than chef.
- Make sure you spend time together as a family. Choose some activities that you all enjoy and block out time in your busy schedules to fit them in.

Planning isn't very exciting but life with a toddler is exciting enough. Of course we can't anticipate every moment to come and we all get thrown the odd curve ball. As John Lennon so eloquently put it, 'Life is what happens to you while you're busy making other plans'. But a little planning can go a long way to ensuring that you have plenty of time to spend doing fun activities with your toddler.

Making the most of it

There is no doubt about it, it's tough being a working parent. We have to juggle the demands of a job and a family life and there always seems to be another task demanding our time and attention. Working parents also have to face the guilt that comes with leaving their children in the care of others while they go to work. Working mothers in particular can feel burdened by opinion that they should stay home to look after their children in these early years.

In my opinion, as long as working parents ensure that the time they do spend with their toddler is quality time, then they have nothing to feel guilty about. Of course, day care arrangements must be of a high standard so that you can rest assured that the toddler is not missing out. And the workload at home must be shared by both parents otherwise one of you will crack under the pressure. With some planning and care, however, you can make the most of it.

23

Flying solo: single-parent families

Today's statistics show that more than a quarter of our children can expect to be part of a single-parent family before the end of their school years. In my more philosophical moments I despair over us human beings. We can split atoms, explore space and create computers but we can't seem to chose a compatible partner and live with them in peace. It seems that as science races ahead, human relations lag far behind. My main message in this chapter is simple: no matter what, we cannot allow our children to suffer as a result of our choices. All parents, single or otherwise, have to do what's best for their children.

A single life

Whether the result of separation, divorce, the death of a partner or – for some parents – simply the way it has always been, these days single parent families are a fact of life.

Each single-parent situation comes with its own special set of challenges. We can analyse and talk about the many causes and reasons for being a single parent, but the result is the same: no matter how they got there, single parents find themselves facing daily challenges ranging from loneliness and isolation to increased responsibility and a reduced social life.

The way that single parents deal with these challenges has a direct and profound impact on their children. When it comes to raising a toddler, who is too young to understand the vagaries of adult life, single parents need to be especially careful to ensure that their child doesn't become an innocent victim of circumstance.

Going it alone

As a single parent you often tread a very lonely road. But it is important to remember that your feelings and emotions affect the toddler: if you try to go it alone, it will only make it all much harder.

Isolation is a worrying pitfall for stay-at-home single parents. You can easily become housebound when you spend all your time looking after your toddler. Building a strong support network around yourself will not only ensure you avoid becoming isolated but it should help to ease the loneliness that comes from limited adult company.

What to do

- Family, friends and other parents you meet through parent groups, playgroups or day care, as well as child and family health nurses, are all good sources of support and are ready to help if you reach out a hand. For goodness sake, take whatever help is on offer.
- Getting out of the house and spending time with other adults is not just a good idea, it's essential. It will help to remind you that there is a world outside your front door and release you from your cocoon of potties, high chairs and toddler messiness.
- It can be easy to slide from isolation into something more dangerous. If you become emotionally flat, lack drive or enthusiasm, or have sleep and appetite problems, it's time to

seek professional help. These can all be signs of depression. Hiding how you feel and pretending you are OK won't fool anyone, least of all the toddler, who will feel that things aren't right even if he doesn't understand.

Wait a second

Lonely, isolated people may crave adult companionship, but they are also emotionally most vulnerable. It can be all too easy to be drawn into a relationship only to discover further down the track that it is not what you expected. Even worse, some of these relationships are truly damaging. For example, many women who escape from one abusive partner, find themselves with another not long after.

Statistics show that more than 50 per cent of divorced parents with young children will have remarried within three years. Unfortunately, more than 50 per cent of these second marriages will not survive beyond five years. This may be hard for the parents, but stop and think how disastrous it is for the children involved.

A place called home

At times when life is falling apart, we need to hang onto familiar places, people and routines. Like birds, we all need a nest to provide shelter and comfort. Not having this safe place to call home adds to the stresses already faced by single parents. The challenge of creating a warm, safe home for your children is closely linked to your financial state. Nowhere do we see this more clearly than when single parents are struggling to make ends meet.

What to do

■ After a divorce, separation or the loss of a partner, if possible try to stay in your home, where the toddler has the security of the spaces he knows and feels comfortable in. It is an important way to ease the transition and both you and the toddler will do better emotionally.

- Keep in mind how the toddler will react if you have to move homes. He needs consistency, and settling into a new location will take time. Moving can stir up behaviour problems so mums and dads have to be even more sensitive to the needs of the child. Disturbed sleep, lapses in toilet training and tantrums are all ways the toddler sends the message that he is unhappy with the new environment.

- It's important to maintain a stable base but this can be especially difficult for single parents who rent. Continually moving from place to place upsets the toddler as each time he has to regroup and deal with all the uncertainty. Moving often also upsets necessary routines such as day care, preschool or visits to family members who no longer live just around the corner.

- Moving back in with your parents can be a temporary solution that kills two birds with one stone – not only do you get a place to call home for a while, you also get physical and emotional support and the toddler gets to spend time with his grandparents. However, while moving back home is fine in theory, in practice it is often less than rosy. For many single parents this creates new stresses.

Money, money, money ...

How often have you heard that 'as long as you've got love, you don't need money', but in real life you can't get very far without it. For single parents, money or the lack of it is an ever-present source of worry. In the case of divorce or separation, the change to the solo state can bring a drastic drop in standard of living, particularly for those who previously relied on a combined salary. Often one parent has a lot less income than the other and it isn't fair that it's usually the one who looks after the kids.

Raising a child on a single wage is never easy. Some parents who sought me out could barely afford the bus fare to bring their children to appointments at the hospital. It is an unfortunate fact that a large number of single parents fight to stay above the poverty line.

What to do

- Relying on government assistance can be a constant struggle to make ends meet. Make sure that you are receiving every scrap of government assistance that you are entitled to.

- Working single parent have to juggle everyday living expenses with the often exorbitant costs of day care. By the time you factor in childcare costs, a job has to pay well to be worth pursuing. To reduce the cost of childcare, if possible ask grandparents and other family to help with care or share childcare with another working parent who you know and trust. And then there is the occasional good fortune of an employer who offers crèche services as part of the package – almost the ultimate luxury!

- Make sure that you do all you can to ensure you are receiving what you and your child are entitled to. If you think you're getting a raw deal, there are free legal aid services that can assist you.

- The toddler doesn't understand money or the financial difficulties you face. However, whenever there is stress around, no matter the cause, the toddler certainly feels it. While there is no solution for this, shield your child as best you can from your concerns.

Reduced social life

Single parents are in a social straightjacket: coping alone with the demands of a toddler leaves little free time. It is extremely difficult to get out to meet other adults when tied to the home with small children, no babysitter and a limited budget. Being single can be particularly difficult if all your friends are couples. It often feels as if life is designed for couples and that you stand out from the crowd. At parties you are a 'third wheel' and invites can be few and far between.

Not to mention that when you spend all your time with a toddler, you begin to think like one. The desire for adult conversation and perspective on life can make your lack of social life especially frustrating.

What to do

- After a separation or divorce, it is never easy to get back into the social set you knew before. When friends have divided loyalties and don't know who to support, it's easiest for them to talk to neither party. They'd much rather sit on the fence than upset anyone. As time goes on you very quickly discover your real friends – you don't need an army, just one or two who will stick by you.

■ Some married couples may feel uneasy with a single in their midst. They keep their distance as though being single is contagious or poses a threat to the stability of their own relationship. Fortunately there are many singles groups and single-parent organisations that can provide opportunities for mixing and mingling (such as Parents Without Partners). If you don't like the idea of a group, befriend other parents at your toddler's playgroup, or check out your local church.

■ Toddlers can be very territorial of your time and attention. They don't want anyone coming between you and them, thank you very much. This can result in even the simplest of outings with a friend turning into an ownership dispute. Don't let these battles turn you into a hermit – life is too short so get out there!

The buck stops here

Being a single parent can feel like you're walking a tightrope without a safety net. Unlike two-parent families, there is often no-one else to count on. If you are the sole person responsible for looking after your child, you can't afford to get sick, lose your job or not be there because there is no-one to take your place.

What to do

■ Have a backup plan in place in case you get sick, or just run out of hours in the day. Arrange for friends, family or neighbours to be available to help out when the unexpected happens, such as if you need to pick up your toddler from preschool but your train is running late.

■ There is a host of responsibilities that you must deal with when you are on your own: finances, decision making, household chores. Consider asking a financially-savvy retiree to look over your finances to prevent any unnecessary screw ups. Teenagers are always looking for pocket money so ask a responsible one in your neighbourhood to look after the toddler while you, for example, take a quick trip to the gym.

■ To make life even harder, you have to be both mum and dad when it comes to disciplining your toddler. There is no-one to back you up when you're ready to tear your hair out. The key for single parents is to be absolutely consistent. On the bright side, however, you may not have to negotiate rules with the other parent, so it's your way or the highway.

Low self-worth

Parenting is tough, full of moments when you're sure you've got it all wrong and you'll never get through. It's very easy to feel that you're a second-rate parent. When your self-esteem has been knocked about by single life and all its challenges, it's even easier to think that you're a second-rate person. Low self-esteem and low self-worth are underrated and frequently unacknowledged as major challenges of being a single parent.

What to do

■ In the case of separation or divorce, often one parent will make the other feel that they're to blame. This can make them feel even guiltier than they already are. But in a busy life as single parent to a toddler there's simply no time for guilt or blame.

■ After a split it can take a long time to feel worthwhile again. One single mother I know is only just now starting to feel good about herself, *ten years* after divorcing the husband who treated her so badly. While I can see that she is a wonderful person and a good mother, she still feels like a failure. Don't wait ten years – surround yourself with family and friends who are positive and see your worth.

■ There is a stigma attached to being a stay-at-home parent. When asked 'What do you do?', I often hear these parents reply, 'Well, I *used* to be a . . .' As a *single* stay-at-home parent, you can feel that you're getting a double dose of judgement from the rest of the world. Remember that looking after children is one of the most important jobs there is. There is nothing to feel guilty about if you choose to focus on your children instead of a career.

■ However, returning to work can be one way to pump up deflated self-esteem. By using your skills and talents outside the home, you remind yourself that you have a lot to offer.

I understand and recognise the hardships of being a single parent. It is easy to be dragged down by any one of these difficulties, let alone a combination, which is what most single parents face every day. But every one of these can have a devastating impact on the toddler and our priority has to be the wellbeing of our children. So always stop, put yourself in the toddler's shoes, and ensure that any decisions you make support both your needs *and* the toddler's.

Separation and divorce

No matter how unhappy life was before a separation or divorce, most parents find the final split emotionally shattering. Although there may be an initial feeling of relief, the year that follows the separation will be one of confusion, regrets, doubts about self-worth, sadness and anger. There may even be uncertainty about whether the current situation is any improvement on the one left behind.

It may be tough for us adults but at least we had a say in the course our lives have taken. Don't forget the children who had no choice in the decision to split up the family. A toddler may be too young to understand what's going on if you separate or divorce, but they will be rocked by the aftershocks that follow nonetheless.

A toddler's security comes from routine, close contact with family members and the attention of loved ones. To minimise the inevitable upheaval, focus on keeping things as much the same as usual. We need to make the transition to single parent family life as stress free as possible for our toddlers.

Fractured families

At the wedding celebration there were guests on the bride's side and guests on the groom's side. At the divorce, the relatives still have to take a side. But young children don't understand the dynamics of a break-up; they have no interest in branding people as good guys or bad guys. They rely on relatives from both sides of their family to let them know they're loved.

You may have divorced your partner, but there is no need to divorce their family as well. Legislation now guarantees grandparents contact in Australia, but until recently I would meet grandparents who had completely lost touch with the grandchildren they love. One grandmother told me that, after her son's separation, she had cared for his children every day for three years. But when a new partner arrived on the scene all access to the grandkids was blocked and the only time she saw them was a glimpse as the school bus passed. Life for the children of divorced parents is hard enough already; they don't need to be caught up in silly games.

When a close network of family and friends is maintained, separation is so much smoother for both adults and children. An on-side grandparent provides sanctuary and comfort that children need when their family splits apart. Any relatives who are prepared to keep out of the politics and give support should have open access to the children. An amicable settlement involves being amicable to all friends and relatives who genuinely wish to help. Whatever you do, don't divorce everybody!

Tug of law

Janet is a grandma who, as a single mother, had raised her daughter, Gail, with little help from her ex. So when her daughter's marriage in turn hit a rocky patch, Janet pulled out all the stops to do what was best for her grandchildren.

Life really hit rock bottom when Gail's husband did a runner, left his wife and children and decided to move back in with his parents. He'd had enough of being a husband and father; he decided it didn't suit him anymore. But while the husband disappeared from the scene, Janet certainly didn't. She and her daughter grew even closer and with their strong bond were able to provide the little ones with security and comfort.

Six months later, the husband reappeared. The closeness between Janet, Gail and the children irritated him and brought out a nasty jealousy. Giving no thought to how his children felt, he decreed that Janet was to have nothing more to do with them. He gave his wife an ultimatum 'It's me or grandma!' Despite the fact that his actions had destroyed the family, he believed he had a right to call the shots. Gail was in a difficult position – she had to choose between saving her dodgy marriage or sparing her mother's feelings. She sided with the husband . . .

Janet was devastated. After being so close to the children, she couldn't even give them a hug. In Australia by rights Janet should have contact with her grandchildren and the law says she can. But the law doesn't always help the good guys and Janet doesn't want to worsen matters by enforcing her rights. While there is no doubt that the husband is a loser, the real losers here are the children.

Residence and contact

I may have an over-simplistic view of the law but I see little point in parents fighting over residence or contact. Many fathers get upset, feeling that the mother will automatically be granted residence, but these days this is not always the case. Successfully negotiating residence is often a huge hurdle to peaceful separation.

After being called as a reluctant witness in a number of disputes, my feeling is that the infrequent successes never justified the huge emotional and financial costs to the children and parents. Contact arrangements are another cause of pain. In the interest of the child, it's best if they are as open and considerate as possible.

Contact visits can be used by an irresponsible ex to gain entry and disrupt the happiness of your home. They may deliberately not arrive when expected, act in an inflammatory way when they do finally turn up and be vague about the time of return. Mothers tell children that their dad is unreliable while dads may fill the kids' heads with equally spiteful comments about mum. Children can end up dreading the tension of the weekly visits as they become an event to be endured, not enjoyed.

Whether you like it or not, contact visits are going to happen. You have the option to either let it get to you or take it like a Swami, with a divine aura of acceptance. If you let yourself get worked up, it will only stir up the children. The only thing you can do is rise above any childish behaviour yourself.

I'm not suggesting that this is easy. Of course it hurts when your children are with your ex and their new friend. Of course it hurts when you don't have a penny to spare and they live in relative affluence. Of course it hurts if you wash, feed and care for your children all week while your ex comes and goes, taking all the rewards with none of the responsibility. But unfortunately that's life. Nobody says it's fair, that's just the rotten way it is.

There are times when issues of residence and contact can get really ugly. We hear dreadful stories about children being hurt or even killed by violent parents trying to come to terms with separation. If the situation you or someone you know is in becomes dangerous, remember there are people ready to help. Telephone counselling helplines, community service organisations, and even the police if the need arises, are available and must be used. The safety of our children comes first.

Battlegrounds at home

Many thousands of children throughout the world live in the midst of war and conflict. But you don't have to live in downtown Baghdad to be in the middle of a war zone. The most dangerous battles occur where it hurts most – in our own homes.

The break-up of relationships is only a small part of the problem. A great many toddlers continue to live unhappily with parents who are physically together but emotionally a million miles apart. Many thousands of parents bicker, nitpick, hold grudges and escalate events. They set out to cause stress rather than choosing to make their home a happy and peaceful place.

Many parents are shameless in the way they abuse each other. Then they recruit their innocent children to become pawns in their battles. These unwilling conscripts are used to cause pain to the other parent. Dad says to the toddler: 'You're too old for a dummy, take it out!' Mum counters with: 'Don't worry, darling, would you like the pink dummy or the blue one?' Dad says: 'It's black!', Mum says: 'It's white!' If one parent doles out the discipline, the other contradicts, just for spite. You can imagine how confused and bruised the little ones become.

These guerilla tactics, used both during marriage and through the break-up period, can keep tension and bitterness running high for years. I don't see this as a right of any parent. It is a form of legalised child abuse which should never occur in any country that genuinely believes in the welfare of its children.

Doing it right

In the case of separation and divorce, it is not the breakdown of a marriage that does the damage. Rather, it is all the hostility and associated aggravation that upsets our children. You may be angry at your ex but they should still be treated with respect. They are, after all, the mother or father of your children. When two parents are committed to separating in a responsible and amicable way, it results in a totally different situation from the angry aftermath of a bitter break.

Thank God for sensible parents. **Not only are amicable settlements possible between divorcing partners but thankfully they are also common.** In these cases, parents split in a way that causes the least amount of upset to their children.

In these families there will be no sabotage, no point scoring or trying to win affection away from the other party. Discipline remains consistent, residence is not an issue or is shared, property is divided fairly and contact is looked forward to and enjoyed.

How to split successfully

- With your ex, commit to doing all you can to make the split amicable. If you could ask the toddler, they would tell you that this is what matters most.

- Make as few changes as possible. Children like consistency, so try to keep the toddler's routine, preferably with the primary carer remaining in the family home.

- Explain what is happening, in a way that is appropriate for the child's age. While a toddler cannot be expected to fully comprehend the meaning of the separation, careful explanation is still important. This should be done using simple, reassuring language that they will understand. If not, little ones may feel that they are somehow responsible for sending one of their parents away, perhaps blaming their own naughtiness.

- Children need to know they still have two parents and that both love them. They must realise that although their parents no longer live together, both will continue to care for them.

- Children need to know where they will live and where the non-resident parent will live. This gives them a picture to store in their minds and assures them that their dad or mum has not departed from the face of the earth.

- Contact should be kept as flexible as possible, with both parties committed to making it go smoothly. Children need to know when they will see the non-custodial parent. Contact must be encouraged and made easy. Make it enjoyable, never a time of tension.

- Keep close to grandparents, any extended family and friends who can provide support. You may divorce your partner, but your children do not want to divorce their grandparents. Don't cut this vital link as this helps the toddler feel safe.

- Don't spy on or slander the other parent. Toddlers have no idea or interest in the rights and wrongs of the situation and they have no understanding of why they now have only one parent around. You may feel that their father is obnoxious and unreasonable, for example, but they don't care. They only want to see him, because they still love dad even if you don't. And you can't prevent your child being cared for by your ex's new partner, so there's no point raising your blood pressure about it.

Unlike children who go through spiteful, nasty divorces and separations and bear the long-term emotional scars to prove it, children of peaceful settlements usually come through their parents' split relatively unscathed.

The main priority is always the emotional wellbeing of our children. Never underestimate the detrimental effect of stress and hostility on them. Parents may feel angry, but that's their problem, not the child's. The best single-parent situations for our children are those in which the parents remain friends even though they don't want to live together. In this climate, the children have two caring parents who can work closely to create a secure present and future.

Shattered by accident

The tragic death of a mum or dad, particularly if they have young children, seems much worse than even the ugliest separation or divorce. But the surprising reality is that these grief-stricken families often fare better than many other single-parent families. Statistics show that the young child whose parent is killed in an accident tends to emerge emotionally many times sounder than the child of a bitter, long-running divorce.

Even though life is suddenly shattered, there is a funeral and in the ensuing years the events fade and the family starts to heal. Family, friends and the community as a whole tend to rally around with support. In this situation there is no bickering over property, contact or residence. The wounds are deep but they are allowed to heal without unnecessary interference. The bitter truth is we humans have the ability to do much more harm to our children by our unthinking actions than through life's unavoidable tragedies.

New relationships

New relationships, though exciting, are tricky at the best of times. Trying to blend two lives and adjust to each other's habits is challenging enough without throwing children into the equation. So combining the single parent of a toddler with a new relationship produces an uneasy mix. For many single parents, just when they've decided it's time to re-enter the Land of the Grown-ups, their toddler troubles seem to start.

See it from the child's point of view. After having 'lost' one parent, they have resumed a sense of security and stability by staking out mum or dad as their territory. They sure as heck aren't going to lose another parent and they perceive any change as a challenge to the status quo. So start slowly. At first it is best to keep any dates outside the home, as it takes time for children to adjust to someone they see as an intruder on their turf. And when leaving the toddler, use grandparents or other family members as babysitters so the toddler feels secure.

After a while, introductions need to be made. Be prepared for the probability that the toddler may not embrace this new person with as much openness as you have. It's very easy to interpret your toddler's downright unfriendly behaviour towards your new partner as pure nastiness. But it's simply the toddler's way of letting you know 'I don't want this person coming between us!' Whatever else, don't be punitive when they stand up for their 'rights'. They're feeling threatened and need understanding, not punishment. And then we get to the subject of beds . . . many toddlers will have squirreled themselves into mum or dad's bed and any suggestion of eviction warrants a monumental protest. Nevertheless there comes a time when they have to return to their own bed. You can use the techniques in the sleep chapters in this book to evict the toddler without too much fuss. After all, parents have rights, too!

In new relationships, stepchildren may arrive as a sort of package deal. This adds problems of personality clashes, territorial claims and divided loyalties to the mix. Again, the secret is to move slowly. What's needed is time, time and more time. But be realistic: you may never achieve the peaceful, blended family that you dream of. We can't expect to automatically become the Brady Bunch.

Behaviour problems are normal

With separation or divorce, life as we know it has changed and you don't have to be Freud to realise that it is upsetting for the toddler. Since the peak time for marriage break-ups coincides with the stage of having young children, preschoolers represent the main age group of children involved. Each child expresses his hurt in different ways, but it is usually during the first 12 months after the break-up that toddler behaviour is at its worst.

Insecurity hits with a bang. The child has lost one parent so they don't want to let the remaining parent out of sight. Even at home they need to keep you close. The toddler may watch a video in another room while mum is busy in the kitchen, but he will return seconds later to check she's still there. Outside the home the toddler will cling like a limpet, reluctant to move far away even to play. At day care or preschool he will protest loudly when left and won't settle through the day. The best way to deal with insecurity is with lots of touch and reassurance when you are around. Make sure the toddler knows he is safe and loved. If you have to leave your child, let the carer know the situation – don't pretend that everything is OK and just rush out the door.

Regression of skills Before the split, there were many new skills that the toddler was mastering. For example, toilet training was underway and was on the verge of being reliable. Now the toddler is prone to leaks and you can't believe that everything's going backwards. Relax: it's not a disaster and it won't be permanent. They learnt it all once and they'll learn it again once the dust has settled.

Sleep It's hardly surprising if the toddler – or the parent – isn't sleeping too well. The toddler may wake often through the night demanding comfort and needing reassurance that you're still there. Many will slip into the parent's bed. The fact is they'll probably settle once they know you're still around, although this doesn't help the sleep-deprived parent.

Behaviour often takes a turn for the worse. The toddler may be angry at a situation they don't understand and they take this out on those nearest to them. They feel the sadness, confusion and tension in the air but are not at an age to verbally express how they feel. Instead they'll create trouble and act out. For parents in an emotionally weak state and feeling flat, it seems much worse than it is. The upset toddler and the wits' end parent escalate each other, and soon you have war. We tend to forget that our little ones are also upset and it's very easy to get heavy. Tread gently. The toddler needs more cuddles and closeness than 'No!', 'Don't!' and 'Stop!'.

Withdrawing One of the lovely things about toddlers is they're so alive and full of curiosity. With a split, the older toddler may show their hurt by retreating into their shell. Before losing a parent, they were active and energetic. Now it seems they've lost their spark and their battery is flat. This behaviour is probably very worrying, as the toddler can seem depressed but they don't need an emotional jump-start. Some space and lots of time will have them running smoothly again.

A singular success

It is a fact of life that many relationships will fall apart and many children will feel the repercussions. But there are ways we can protect our children from the worst of it. By splitting amicably, keeping family close, not allowing the challenges of single parenting to affect the toddler and by starting new relationships carefully, we do the best we can to look out for our children's wellbeing.

Life for the single parent is not easy, with many upsets and injustices in their path no matter what they do. However, it is not whether they are part of a single-parent or a two-parent family that affects children. The roller-coaster ride of stress, tension and emotional upheaval caused by bickering parents is far more damaging. What matters most is having a family life that is stable, secure, happy and calm.

24

Thank goodness for grandparents

Grandmas and grandpas are our most valuable natural resources. Unfortunately, like many other non-renewable resources, they are often under-utilised or taken for granted. Over the past 50 years, as a result of what we call 'progress', the tight-knit families of yesteryear have slowly unravelled. Some families are separated by great distances but others just lose contact and drift apart. Even in the same city, family members live in relative isolation, rarely crossing paths in their busy lives.

With this great move forward, the biggest losers are our children, who miss out on contact with the older generation. I write here in praise of grandparents and their great value to us and our children.

Older and wiser

Historically, in families that lived together, the younger members would call upon the experience of the older ones for advice. The elders were seen as wise and were consequently respected. Everyone knew they had the answers to life's tough questions.

However, these days parents either lack easy access to that wisdom or disdain it and choose to go it alone. Many young parents view the older generation as 'past it' and out of touch. I think this is a strange attitude when, even now, many of the world's most powerful countries are ruled by grandfathers or grandmothers!

Life is lived at a more realistic pace as we get older, and it is viewed with a mature, 'been there, done that' attitude. Most older people have lived through wars, lean times and all manner of hardships. As a result, these grandparents are able to see what is really important: family, relationships and closeness, and they value these irreplaceable elements in life.

Gently does it

Even though they are at opposite ends of the spectrum, somehow the mix of always-on-the-go toddlers and slow-moving grandparents seems to work. Children who won't sit still are often quietened, as if by hypnotism, when in grandma's care. Grandfathers may not be able to engage in rough and tumbles, but they are streets ahead in other areas. The toddler will sit and listen to all manner of stories, viewing grandpa as the world's greatest wit and raconteur.

Grandparents have learnt that life is precious and full of wonder. They delight in pointing out the early dew or a hovering butterfly as they lead their grandchild on exciting safaris around the garden or the neighbourhood. There is so much of interest to see when joined by someone who is as excited by the little details as they are and has the time to share it.

When it comes to discipline, you will find that grandparents are generally softer than parents and they often take the toddler's side. With years of wisdom, they are often less obsessive about rules and what is necessary.

Help is at hand

I believe there is no better form of temporary child care than that provided by grandparents. They really are the next best thing to the child's parents – not least because genes and years of brain-washing by grandma have ensured that one parent is really an extension of herself. Grandparents can provide a much-needed extra pair of hands in times of stress and there are tremendous benefits for all involved if the assistance they offer is accepted and appreciated.

Grandparents can help by:

- Providing regular day care when parents are at work.
- Babysitting of an evening so parents can go to the movies or out for dinner.
- Caring for the toddler if the child or parent is sick.
- Organising a regular day for minding the toddler every week so parents can recharge their batteries.
- Offering to look after the grandchildren for the weekend, giving mum and dad time to themselves for a mini-break.
- Joining the family on holiday to share the child care load.

In all these efforts, grandparents not only provide valuable child care for the toddler but also get to be a part of the action at this exciting time of their grandchild's life. The more time they spend together, the stronger the special bond between grandparent and grandchild grows. In an ideal world parents would have four grandparents to choose from, as well as countless aunts, uncles and cousins. But if you find yourself like many modern parents do without the support of grandparents, older neighbours can stand in as foster grandparents.

Common ground

As you can see, I am a great believer in the benefits of grand-parents being actively involved in their grandchildren's lives. However, there is one common complaint from parents that is the main cause of friction: when it is thought the grandparents are interfering and criticising.

When it comes to raising children, it seems everyone is an expert. Even those who have never had anything to do with children think they have the answers. Within a family, interfering is usually done out of love. I'm not going to mention mother-in-law jokes but I must point out the subtle but important difference between giving advice and interfering. Grandparents interfere because they find it hard to sit back and watch their own children making the same mistakes they made themselves. This 'helpful advice' is generally greeted by the parents with either a deaf ear (the wisest approach) or resentment. Fights can occur over trivial matters wasting the energy of everyone involved and upsetting the delicate balance of family harmony. Squabbles are surely a waste of time and it is not wise to let egos and ruffled feathers get in the way of family closeness.

For the sake of peace ground rules need to be set down in regard to the care of the toddler. Both the parents and the grandparents have to have an understanding of what is expected and accept that the other has rights.

- **When the child is in the care of the parents, then the parents are in charge of the show.** Although advice may be given by grandparents, it does not have to be accepted by the parents.
- **When the child is being looked after by the grandparents, then they are in charge.** They should not be forced to adhere to the parents' rules but do what works best for them.

Basically, whoever is looking after the toddler is calling the shots at that time. However, there has to be some sensible understanding from both sides and neither can be allowed to undermine the other's authority. It isn't always rosy and there are times when parents may have to draw the line. Grandparents who stubbornly insist that theirs is the only way to do things may have to be reminded of who is actually in charge of the toddler's wellbeing. And if they continue to stir up trouble, they will be the ones that are sacrificed. Grandparents have to know when to butt out and there can be no ganging up with their child and taking sides against their sons- or daughters-in-law.

The blame game

Some parents tell me there is no point in disciplining their toddler as whenever they go to Grandma's, she lets them do whatever they like. However, while toddlers may be very small, they are also very clever in learning what the rules are. As long as the rules are clear, they can cope easily with each generation's eccentricities and adapt according to what's asked of them. Laying the blame for their offspring's misbehaviour on grandparents is a tempting but weak excuse used by parents to avoid effective discipline. It is the parents who are the majority shareholders and they are the ones who really determine a toddler's behaviour. The responsibility lies fairly and squarely at their doorstep.

Great-ful for grandparents

Both children and parents have much to learn from the older generation, who these days are more likely to be 'with it' than 'past it'. They have so much to offer us and our children – time, love, energy, advice and commonsense solutions.

I'm not naïve enough to suggest that all grandparents are interested in being closely involved with their grandchild. Come to think of it, some have had little enough time for their own children and, having screwed them up, should not be afforded the privilege of doing the same to the next generation. But for those grandmas and grandpas who dote on their grandchildren we need to do everything in our power to support and encourage these special relationships.

25

Children who are hard to love

We all know that because they are our own flesh and blood we will automatically love our children, faults and all. But the truth is that some children can make themselves extremely hard to love. As infants, these children cry inconsolably and demand every kilojoule of their parents' energy so by toddlerdom the parents are worn out.

Those who have only experienced an easy angel have no idea how the parents of difficult children feel. Their idea of hard-to-handle behaviour is a gentle breeze compared to the category five cyclone that is the difficult child.

The parents of difficult children not only feel misunderstood and alone in the world of 'normally' behaved children, they also battle guilt as they try to find ways to struggle through the tough days. Telling these parents that 'it will all be OK' just doesn't cut it. They need a hearty dose of understanding and some ideas that work. We can't change a child's temperament but I can offer some techniques to help you cope.

The constant crier

While looking at difficult toddlers, we can't escape the fact that their trying ways probably began long before toddlerdom. For many, the clues to their future behaviour were there when they were babies.

Quite a number of babies cry and are hard to console but some seem to be constant criers. The crying can start right from birth, or be turned on for tired parents once they arrive home from the hospital. Though a few of these irritable infants have some medical cause, most cry for no apparent reason.

Doctors often attribute this irritability to colic. The symptoms are reasonably consistent, generally starting in the first two weeks of life and usually over by the fourth month. These babies are unsettled after most feeds but they are at their worst in the late afternoon and evening. They suck a bit, then look unhappy, stiffen and cry. We lift and burp them, and provide comfort but nothing really seems to help. Though the cause of colic is uncertain, the result is well known to anybody who has been there. Confident loving parents soon become confused and stressed.

What to do
In dealing with these fussy, irritable criers we use some good old-fashioned ideas that have been tried and tested over the generations:

- Try to find the most comforting posture for the baby; for example, lying over an arm, a shoulder, or on a pillow.
- Soothe with gentle movement: carry the baby while walking slowly or place him in a pram and wheel over a slightly uneven bump in the carpet. Take the baby for a walk during the day. Or at night, try a drive around the block in the car.
- Have the baby with you as you sit in a warm bath.

- If you reach the limits of your patience, put the baby down safely, get outside the room momentarily and phone a family member or friend for help.
- Seek support from your midwife, doctor or paediatrician, regarding medication to help ease colic.

In some babies, the constant crying continues right through their first 12 months. Constant criers can also be demanding infants.

The demanding infant

Though most of the early criers soon settle, some go on to be irritable right through to toddlerdom. These infants are amazingly demanding; they need to be entertained every waking minute. It really hurts when your friend's child is so placid and self-contented, yet you can't move a metre without your child carrying on. Some parents accept this as inevitable, give attention constantly and remain close and happy. Others become resentful, complain and try to change the unchangeable. It's at this point they may fall out of love.

What to do
- Keep the child close to you. Use a sling, a backpack, or sit them beside you as you work.
- Jumpers and walkers, when used with care, can keep these demanding infants entertained even if they haven't found their own feet yet.
- When friends visit, entertain the child on your knee while you entertain your guests.
- Try to get grandparents, friends and family to provide some respite.
- A short time in day care may be a lifesaver. This is not a luxury – it can be a necessity!

We can give quality attention which stops most crying or we can resent and end up at loggerheads. At this age, giving is the best course. Most of these demanding infants become much easier once they become mobile toddlers.

Irritable twins

A mother I looked after had the most difficult irritable twins. They cried all through the first year of life, rarely slept and at about 18 months they were still dissatisfied. Everything was wrong: when they were up they wanted down, when they were down they wanted up and when they were being fed they didn't want food.

When I asked her how she was coping, the mother told me, 'Recently I went to the dentist for root canal therapy. It was wonderful having an hour to myself'.

The out-of-step toddler

We expect little children to be busy, exuberant and into mischief, but some parents get a child who is right over the top. We could call them Super Toddlers, as all the normal toddler characteristics are amped up. These children put immense strain on their parents. When shopping they run off, protest or stage a tremendous tantrum. At family get-togethers, they upset, damage, grizzle or explode. Parents can't understand why their friends with other small children have such a normal life, while they have become isolated and exhausted.

The two behaviours that cause most trouble are extreme overactivity and zero frustration tolerance.

The **overactive child** hits like a tornado. From the moment they can walk they are into everything and, unless entertained every minute, they create havoc. These pacy children run, touch, fiddle, break – and when they see open space, they're off.

The **intolerant child** is less active, but more difficult. They tend to be irritable, rarely satisfied and the smallest trigger sets off an unbelievable bang. They want up on your knee, then they want down; they want out, they want in. Nothing is ever right and unless things happen immediately they blow up. They intrude, demand, object and brainwash their parents. Keeping the peace with these children is like juggling gelignite.

I certainly understand just how difficult these children can be but we have to remember that even they have their lovable moments.

What to do

Volatile toddlers are best handled by anticipating, diverting and steering around trouble.

- Ensure that the child's development is normal. Do they hear? Can they speak well? Are they clever? If there are any doubts see your doctor or clinic sister.
- Fortify the home and make it toddler-proof using the tips in Chapter 11, Making life easier for yourself.
- Restrict visits and social life to secure situations with friends who understand.
- When tantrums are extreme, it is safer to separate than snap. Use Time Out so both toddler and parents get some space to cool off.
- Get out to the wide open spaces whenever possible, to use up all that excess energy.
- Accept any help or respite offered by friends and family.
- Get the toddler's name on the preschool waiting list. When that time comes you will be glad of the break.

I see many excellent parents with out-of-step toddlers who are 100 per cent certain they will never consider another pregnancy. They become angry and resentful, and for them time is spent enduring, rather than enjoying, their children. I know it is difficult, but try and see the lighter side if you can. When things seem bleak, we really have to rely on the funny moments to give us the strength to go on and buoy our confidence.

Love actually

Describing children as 'hard to love' may seem harsh, but for a few parents that is the grim reality. People can assume that the antisocial behaviour of these children is the result of bad parenting, which only makes life more difficult for the embattled, exhausted parents. But it seems that these children are born to test our patience and our assumptions.

Having accepted that it is their temperament, which we can't change, that is the real cause of their difficulty we have to set about avoiding conflict at all costs and focusing on the better moments. Don't become disheartened by those parents whose children are little angels. While their behaviour may be over the top, difficult children are actually just as lovable.

26

Attention Deficit Hyperactivity Disorder (ADHD)

CLASS OF 2006

It is unusual for a child to be diagnosed with Attention Deficit Hyperactivity Disorder (ADHD) before school age but it does happen. Complaints about these children commonly include low frustration tolerance, lack of sense, demanding behaviour, generally dissatisfied, busy, noisy, and launching unthinking attacks on other children. 'Sounds exactly like my child', I hear you say.

Many parents think their child is hyperactive when in fact they just have a normal, very active child. Parents also think that ADHD is just about hyperactivity. However ADHD is actually a mix of a number of troublesome behaviours which may include hyperactivity. It is the degree and the combination of these behaviours which causes the problem. ADHD causes clever children to under-function intellectually and under-behave for the quality of parenting they receive.

ADHD in children: an overview

ADHD affects at least 2 per cent of the school-age population, and some quote figures as high as 5 per cent. Boys are more commonly affected than girls. The first behaviours of ADHD are usually apparent before 3 years of age, but few of these children require treatment before they start school. ADHD is a chronic condition and it is now believed that approximately 60 per cent of those affected will take some of their symptoms with them into adulthood.

Until relatively recent times, professionals blamed the parents' lack of attachment or unhealthy relationships for causing ADHD behaviours. Others said that ADHD was due to additives in food. Now we know that neither of these is the cause, although the standard of parenting and some food substances may influence already existing ADHD. Two things are certain: firstly, ADHD is strongly hereditary. The majority of children who present with ADHD will have a parent or close relative who has experienced many of the same difficulties. And, secondly, it is a biological condition. The behaviour and learning problems of ADHD are caused by a subtle difference in the fine-tuning of the brain. This mostly affects those parts of the brain which control reflective thought and put the brakes on ill-considered behaviour (the frontal lobes and their close connections).

ADHD in the under-fives

Some of us enter parenthood with the expectation that our preschoolers will be obedient, self-entertaining and behave like little adults, but anyone who has experienced a toddler knows that there isn't a hope. But with these well-rooted misconceptions, it can be hard to determine whether a suspicion of ADHD is real, or a parent's misunderstanding of a normal, high spirited youngster.

Also there is such an extreme of behaviour which is accepted as normal in the preschooler, it is hard to know where the 'terrible twos' end and ADHD begins.

While there are good academic ways of diagnosing ADHD, they can be time-consuming and expensive. I have come to believe that an equally reliable measure comes from experienced eyes and ears observing the child's behaviour and listening to what the parents say.

In simple terms, ADHD should be considered when a certain package of behaviours causes a child to be significantly 'out of step' with others of the same development, age and equal quality of parenting. The diagnosis of ADHD will only be considered when the out-of-step behaviours are causing difficulty. A child can be active, impulsive and explosive, but if everyone is happy there is no need to consider a diagnosis or treatment. As I have come to say: 'A behaviour is only a problem when it causes a problem'.

At this young age diagnosis also involves excluding ADHD look-a-likes. We frequently see young children diagnosed as ADHD when in fact their restlessness, low frustration tolerance and lack of sense are due to intellectual disability. Of course ADHD and delayed development can coexist, but in these cases the child must be 'out of step' with the extreme that is accepted at that developmental age.

How parents cope

With a difficult ADHD child of any age, the parents must find a way to cope with the challenging behaviour that they are faced with every day. After years of working with these frazzled parents, I find that they generally seem to adopt one of three approaches:

- They try to drive the bad behaviour out of the child and force him to comply.
- They become overwhelmed, feel like failures and lose direction.
- They accept their child's temperamental differences, make allowances, adjust their expectations and discipline to suit the child.

Most parents at some time try the firm, confronting approach, but fortunately back off when it fails. Some get stuck in the middle ground, being overwhelmed and unable to move ahead. It seems that those who are successful in managing ADHD eventually discover the third approach, then get on with life.

Waging war

In the USA it is said that 60 per cent of ADHD children will become oppositional and defiant, with 20 per cent showing the severe, almost amoral behaviours of conduct disorder. At the hospital where I worked, the figures for these problems were much lower.

It may be a simplistic view, but I believe these conditions are exacerbated – if not in part caused – by the forceful, confronting approach some parents take when dealing with an ADHD child. When parents decide they are going to 'make' their child conform and behave, a conflict of Middle Eastern proportions often results. At the end of the day the peacekeepers may be in place, but hateful relationships and lifelong distrust remain.

Turning around discipline

Parents of extremely difficult young children can't understand why the behaviour techniques that work so well for their friends are so ineffective with their children. They feel criticised by onlookers, friends and family. There seem to be no easy answers and they wonder what happened to the joy of parenting.

When the simple behavioural techniques are not working, it's time to reevaluate each of the available methods. Parents have to identify those techniques that bring them success, even if it is only 80 per cent of the time. They have to acknowledge those that work in rare instances. And most importantly, they have to recognise those that never work with their child; that are a complete waste of time – and dump them.

Some parents find it hard to let go of methods which, in their child, are clearly not working. 'Are you telling me we should stop correcting his bad table manners?' they ask. 'Is this working?' I respond. 'No, it makes things worse.'

I'm not advocating letting the child get away with everything. Rather, that if the technique you are trying is not getting you anywhere, backing off is essential to finding the best sort of discipline for the ADHD child. Parents need to accept that the ADHD child is different, and make special allowances as a result.

In my experience, success comes from trying the following techniques and discovering which work:

- Rewarding the 'almost good' behaviour.
- Focusing on the positive – looking at what the child does, rather than what he doesn't.
- Anticipating problems before they hit and steering around the unimportant.
- Using clear, convincing communication.
- Harnessing the power of diversion and Time Out.
- Getting outside to the wide open spaces and keeping young children moving.

It is so easy to become negative, and focus on all the discipline that doesn't work. But with trial and error, you will find those things that work for your child. The important thing is to start somewhere.

As with all discipline, parents with misguided determination can very quickly and unintentionally make the situation worse. In the case of an ADHD child, this escalates an already volatile household. Nitpicking and over-use of the word 'No', getting bogged down in the unimportant, confronting, debating, shouting and withholding privileges all take the home further away from peace.

In the challenging child, smacking is especially ineffective, escalating and dangerous. Parents smack to 'make' their child conform. He defies, they smack harder; he resists, and things get out of control. The rigid discipline of your parents' generation has no place here. The general rule with the ADHD child is to use an olive branch.

Medication can be a miracle

Many paediatricians and parents are uncomfortable with the use of drugs to control behaviour. This seems especially true in the case of young children. However, it is my experience that ADHD medication can provide the miracle that parents have been looking for.

There are a number of medications used for ADHD, but the two most commonly used are the stimulants Methylphenidate and Dexamphetamine. Over the past 15 years, these stimulants, with their quick action and clearly documented effects, have been shown to be safe and successful, even in 3 and 4 year olds.

Drugs are *only* used when the problem is *severe*. In our clinic, medication was only trialled at the parents' request and with their informed consent. And, after an initial 3-week trial, no drug was continued unless the parents, with feedback from the preschool, were certain of the benefits and freedom from unwanted side effects.

We have now realised that with drugs we can first reach, then teach. Because the child's behaviour is more even, our behavioural techniques are much more effective. Using medication allows parents to communicate with their ADHD children more easily, helping to build closer relationships.

A happy ending

I once worked with an explosive ADHD 3 year old and his defeated mum. I asked if his behaviour was as difficult for everyone, to which she replied, 'Even our German shepherd guard dog is frightened of him!' After redirecting discipline, adopting survival psychology and a successful trial of medication she returned for review. When asked 'What's different?', she was quite clear: 'Now I love him'. You can't ask for more than that!

Survival psychology

Unfortunately, nothing is going to completely change a difficult child's temperament. And as a result, over the years I moved from proposing complicated structured behavioural programmes which, if we are truthful, rarely work, to regrouping and promoting the art of 'survival psychology'.

Survival psychology is based on being realistic and accepting that no matter how much we would like things to be different, this is the way things are. We need to become committed to a few firm rules. Firstly, we have to steer around strife. Then we have to plan ahead, not allowing for opportunities where things can get out of control. And lastly, we have to recognise when it is time to quit while we are ahead.

- If lengthy time in the supermarket is a nightmare, avoid it; instead use late-night shopping or bundle the child in the trolley and use the 'smash and grab' approach.
- If gatherings with friends and family cause embarrassment, drop in for a high quality half-hour and leave before the bomb explodes.
- If travel is a torment, stay near home.
- If the child is a runner, fortify the compound to limit breaks for freedom.
- If ornaments get broken, lock them away. If the DVD is being reprogrammed, put it in a playpen.
- If you are feeling trapped and have no space, put on a favourite DVD to give a short period of peace.

It's not the way it should be, but using survival psychology makes life for parents who live with a demanding, difficult young child feel not only bearable, but easier. Our aim is peaceful co-existence and a child who is still close to their parents at the age of 18.

Let's get real

ADHD is a real, biological condition that is seen in children even at preschool age. Children who present with ADHD behaviour at this young age will probably continue to be a challenge to their parents for many years to come. While it is so much easier to do nothing and wait until school age, if it is not taken seriously in these very early times, the emotional fallout can create wounds that never heal.

Parents of ADHD children have to accept their child's differences, make allowances, then get on with being the best parent they can be. I encourage parents to use survival psychology and focus on those discipline techniques that work.

For more detailed information on ADHD in children, see *Understanding ADHD* by Dr Christopher Green and Dr Kit Chee.

27

The disabled child: behaviour and discipline

This chapter is not designed to be an in-depth guide to dealing with a disabled child as, due to the extensive range of disabilities, that would require a complete book. Rather, I will focus only on the most common problems.

In my work over the years with children with disabilities I found that the best forms of behaviour techniques to use with disabled children are the same as with any toddler. We focus on rewarding and praising the behaviour we want to see, and ignore undesirable behaviour, or at least pretend to ignore it.

As a general principle, the child is treated appropriately for his developmental age, no matter what the actual age may be.

However, even using this approach, discipline can be difficult, due to these children's lack of sense and concentration.

Discipline

Parents may want to discipline their disabled child, however, the success rate is less than spectacular. It is common that behaviour techniques are not seen through with determination, because parents find it hard to be strict with a child who has physical or intellectual problems. Playing the role of the tough guy makes many parents feel guilty. While all the books advise them to be as unbending as possible, their hearts tell them not to be so hard.

The main problem with many such children is they have bodies that are strong and advanced in physical skills. Meanwhile the brains that control all this power lack insight, sense and sometimes the ability to learn easily from experience. Keeping this in mind, it is often best to lower our sights and aim first for a percentage improvement rather than a miracle. This is not defeatism, merely realism. **Any small improvement will bring benefits to overwhelmed parents.**

In my work with children, I found a number of conditions would make it much more difficult to discipline them.

Epilepsy: Children who have poorly controlled epilepsy are often more irritable and difficult than average. Their problems are worse just before a seizure and in the days that follow it. Some of the medications they are prescribed, although giving perfect control to the seizures, can make the child virtually impossible to live with and actually worsen behaviour.

Expressive speech problems: In my experience, children with major expressive speech problems suffer a great deal of pain. They show this by getting very frustrated and behaving badly.

Brain trauma: Children who were developing normally but then suffer a head injury or an illness such as meningitis can develop many of the worst features of the hyperactive child. They may be of normal intelligence but so disabled by restlessness, poor concentration and negligible sense that their parents are driven to distraction.

Autism: Autistic children tend to have obsessive, repetitive behaviours and, hard as we may try, these can be very difficult to overcome. We concentrate more these days on diverting these immovable problems to more socially acceptable activities. For example, the child who flaps his hands may be diverted to clapping, and the child who repeatedly flicks the light switch can be diverted to a torch.

All the discipline techniques explored in this book can be attempted and adapted for disabled children. The foundations of effective discipline, of using clear communication, being consistent, setting routines and maintaining a positive attitude are a good place to start when disciplining any child. We then give the child lots of Grade A attention and stay focused on the behaviours we want to see. Once we have accepted our limited abilities to change the situation, we stop wasting time attempting the impossible. We can channel our full energies into those areas where we have the most to gain and we can focus on what really matters – enjoying our children.

Dealing with specific problems

Such is the variety and degree of disabilities that there is no universal remedy for behaviour and management problems. However there are simple ways to approach common problems associated with sleeping, feeding and toilet training the disabled child. There are also some means to address behaviours that are more pronounced in these children.

Sleep problems

Sleep problems are a common issue in disabled children, but seeing through techniques such as controlled crying can be challenging for their parents, who seem especially reluctant to let them cry. That said, the technique can be applied and in many cases will prove successful if the parents are resolute.

In some severely disabled children, I have had no success with anything other than sedation. If the parents are to survive the day, they cannot afford to be up all night with a crying child. The secret with sedation is to give the drug not at 6 pm, just before bedtime, but when the child wakes up later in the night. This at least gives the parents some chance of gaining those golden hours of sleep between midnight and dawn.

Feeding difficulties

Feeding of disabled children can take ages. Some parents tell me they spend up to two hours each mealtime, leaving little time in the day for anything else. I suggest that you experiment to find what works best for you and your child. For example, a child who drinks his milk painfully slowly from a bottle may be given it from a spoon or cup. For a child who has difficulty with solids or lumpy food, different textures can be created. There are also ways a therapist can help to desensitise the child's mouth, making swallowing easier.

Toilet training

Toilet training disabled children can be problematic, so I readily suggest using the alternate technique of toilet timing. Shortly after the child has been given food or drink, sit them on the toilet. There is a 70 per cent chance they will hit the jackpot.

Some children, such as those with cerebral palsy, may get quite constipated. In these cases, it is a good idea to introduce a simple laxative or a 'depth charge' of extra fruit in the diet, to ease the situation. And of course remember that a common cause of constipation is not drinking enough water, so keep the child topped up with fluid throughout the day.

Irritability

This is quite a common behaviour problem parents have to deal with in disabled children. Some intellectually disabled or cerebral palsy children in particular are extremely irritable. To soothe them, we use movement. There are many other techniques that therapists use and recommend. If irritability is extreme, sometimes we have to use medication, which would be prescribed by a paediatrician.

Lack of sense

In the older disabled child, all my greatest failures have been with those who have the major problem of having 'little sense'. Day after day, year after year, the same behaviour occurs despite my best advice. The problem is that these children do not learn from their experiences. Their poor parents try their best but as nothing helps, they soon begin to feel quite impotent. Unfortunately, some professionals don't understand that a child may have the severe disability of 'lack of sense'. They place all the lack of success on the parents, making their lives even harder.

A reason for respite

With a really difficult child, it is often necessary to provide care away from home for one or two half-days each week. This is so the exhausted parents have time to recharge their batteries. In really desperate situations, I encourage the use of temporary respite care for the child. Arranging this keeps the parents on the rails and also allows time for the other children of the family.

Facing the pain, facing reality

In my work I found that even the strongest parent of a disabled child has considerable inner sadness. They are under a great deal of stress, which often they attempt to hide.

Following the realisation that they have a disabled child, the parent may go through a form of grief reaction. This is not unlike the feelings experienced after the death of a loved one. When they first hear the news, there is a period where they feel stunned and disbelieving. This soon progresses to a painful stage where they try to come to terms with the situation. This may take months, years or even a lifetime.

During this time, the parents feel the need to protect themselves from harsh reality and let only a little of the realisation sink in each day. Denial, anger and activity are all methods they use to survive.

Denial: The parents may refuse to accept the degree of the problem and shop around from doctor to doctor in the hope of hearing better news. I often found, after compassionately inform-ing parents of their child's situation, a colleague some weeks later would tell me that the parents said I 'didn't tell them anything'. I understand this reaction is a form of denial – the reality hurts too much.

Anger: Anger is often misinterpreted in this case, when it is merely a way of trying to release excess tension. It is a strange defence that we all use in times of immense stress. It seems that displacing a bit of our anger onto those around us makes us feel better. What we are really doing is trying to get rid of our sense of frustration and lack of control.

Activity: Activity is a defence that we all engage in to some degree. Sitting immobile and worrying only makes the problems seem even larger. The parents may take up a good cause, take on full-time employment, or work day and night for their disabled child. The activity will probably make them very tired, but it does help them to feel better.

It is not clever for anyone to try to break through these defences. If the shutters are torn down and the full light of the problem hits the parents, they may be precipitated into that state of immobility and isolation called depression.

These reactions are all normal and healthy. I believe that with time, talk, and good practical help, most parents get through this need to defend themselves. They still feel the hurt, but they can look past it to plan constructively for the future.

A helping hand

Once the reactions I have mentioned above are understood, it is easier to offer help and understanding to the parents of disabled children. Family, friends and even members of the local community need to rally round and lend support.

With denial, do not force the issue. Equally, you must not be afraid to talk gently and openly about what has happened. Pretending that the disability doesn't exist fools no one and only serves to upset the parents.

Anger is quite natural and may land on even the closest of friends. The anger is not really aimed at the person; it is more a sign of the parents' tension and upset at their lot in life. Friends could even view it as a privilege that some of the anger more correctly levelled at the Almighty is landing on their humble shoulders instead.

Activity is far preferable to the lack of enthusiasm that it generally replaces. Never criticise the parent who wishes to work or strive for some noble cause. They may well need this, and to suddenly remove it is like pulling the rug out from under them.

Those parents who have become isolated require a great deal of understanding. They need encouragement to get out and socialise, as well as practical help with child minding. Most valuable of all, they need your listening and non-condemning ear.

Always remember how stressed the parents are and how you can help by sticking by them. They may not say it in so many words but they need their friends. They will be grateful – if not openly, then certainly in their hearts. It takes time to heal.

28

Common toddler illnesses

It seems that hardly a day goes by without some toddlers suffering from some ailment, be it tonsillitis, an ear infection or a cold. Getting infections is a natural part of growing up. While these illnesses are quite common, they cause many parents a great deal of stress. This chapter is a guide to dealing with common toddler illnesses and conditions, as well as those like meningococcal, that inspire fear and concern.

Here we cover:

- asthma • bow legs and other problems • bronchitis
- the common cold • croup • ear problems
- fever • fever fits (febrile convulsions)
- meningococcal infection • tonsillitis
- vomiting and diarrhoea.

Asthma

What is it? Asthma is a condition that causes spasm of the middle-sized airways in the lungs. We quite often see a pattern of asthma in a family, as there is a genetic link. The symptoms are shortness of breath, coughing and wheezing. Its hallmark is a musical wheeze that comes from the depths of the lungs, mostly when breathing out. Asthma is often triggered by viral respiratory infections, and it can also be allergy-related.

Asthma affects about 30 per cent of all children. Parents would tell me their child had a dry cough, which was worse in the middle of the night. In my experience, this is asthma. In the case of asthmatic children, inhaled substances can irritate the airways and trigger attacks. One of the most common irritants is cigarette smoke from adults smoking around children. As a doctor (and a non-smoker), I get angry when babies, toddlers – or in fact anyone – has to put up with the passive smoke of others.

Many parents are distressed when their child is diagnosed with asthma. They worry their child will have to miss days at school and also that it will stop the child from enjoying sport. However, most asthmatic children can live a completely normal, unrestricted life.

Treatment: It is very important that your doctor gives you and your child a step-by-step asthma action plan for intervention. These plans let you both know how to deal with mild attacks as well as how to pull out all the stops when a severe attack hits. Your child has to learn to recognise the symptoms of an attack and what to do once one has started. Treatment during an attack involves medicines to open up the air passages, such as Ventolin. These medicines are inhaled either with an inhaler (or 'puffer') or more usually via a spacer, a small device into which the puffer is inserted to maximise the amount of medication reaching the lungs. These products are extremely safe and highly effective when used properly.

Prevention is better than cure, and the aim is to prevent attacks. Regular use of an inhaled steroid such as Flixotide is often prescribed to achieve this.

Always remember that although most asthma is easily controlled, it can be life-threatening. In the case of a severe attack, contact emergency help immediately.

Bow legs, knock knees, flat feet

What is it? When the child first walks, his untried feet can be seen pointing in all manner of interesting directions, although they generally right themselves within months. At around the age of 1½, you may notice that the child's legs are bowed and he is walking around in his nappy with the posture of a saddle-sore cowboy. Then, at about 2½, the legs will straighten, although this adjustment may be overdone and the child will then suffer from knock knees. Happily, by the age of 5, most children's legs are relatively straight and the feet point straight ahead.

Treatment: In the majority of minor leg and foot problems, no treatment is needed. Some children continue walking with their toes turned slightly inwards and, if mild, this is of no great concern. In fact, one specialist colleague of mine has a theory that these children may make the best footballers, being able to change direction and weave faster than anyone else on the field. There has to be some compensation for having feet that point in two different directions simultaneously!

All babies and toddlers have flat feet. It often takes until the age of 6 for the ligaments of the feet to tighten up and produce a proper arch. This may never happen in some children where there is a family history of flat feet. Some parents believe that the child should walk around without shoes to strengthen his ligaments; others believe that orthotics/insoles in the shoes produce better arches. Nowadays, more and more orthopaedic doctors are moving towards the 'no treatment' approach.

Once again these are general observations. If the bends or postures cause any concern, see your local doctor and ask if a specialist opinion is needed.

Bronchitis

What is it? An old-fashioned name for bronchitis is a 'chest cold'. It's a viral infection that often starts with the sneezing, coughing and running nose of a cold and ends up on the chest. Despite a lot of coughing, the child with bronchitis should still be relatively happy and show few signs of illness, though some children will have a fever and shortness of breath.

Treatment: Because it is caused by a virus, bronchitis will not respond to antibiotics. As for treating a cold, use paracetamol preparations if the child seems uncomfortable or whingey. Keep in mind that if the coughing is associated with wheezing and shortness of breath, the cause could be asthma. In my experience, asthma is often misdiagnosed as bronchitis. Bronchitis is very common and generally not something to worry about. However, occasionally some children do get very sick with bronchitis and may develop pneumonia. These children need to be reviewed by a doctor who will prescribe antibiotics.

Even though these days most children are immunised, bronchitis may also be the first symptom of approaching measles in some children even before the very first spot has appeared.

The common cold

What is it? 'Cold' is the everyday name for an upper respiratory tract infection (URTI). The common cold is *very* common indeed, and the symptoms include sneezing, coughing, runny noses and sore throats. A runny nose is the most common presentation, and though most books say that URTIs don't cause aches and fever, these can appear at the start. Some children seem to get the full complement of symptoms while others just have a nose that runs like Niagara Falls. The simple cold seems like such a small problem, yet in the middle of the night, when the toddler is crying and can't sleep, there is nothing simple about it!

The toddler's worst year for infections, and especially URTIs, is when he first goes to day care or preschool. There he is coughed over by hoardes of virus-splattering classmates. Eventually he acquires some immunity, and the number of illnesses gradually decreases. Average toddlers will get up to nine colds each year, which works out to about one every eight weeks. Just when you thought it was safe, another starts.

Colds are spread by people with whom the toddler comes into contact; they do not come from getting wet or playing out in the cold – those are just myths. Despite years of trying to prevent colds with vitamins and other alternative treatments such as echinacea, there is still nothing that is scientifically proven to help.

Treatment: Colds are caused by a number of viruses so they don't respond to treatment with antibiotics, which only work on bacterial infections. They usually cure themselves within four or five days of appearance. There is no specific treatment, although paracetamol preparations may make the child feel more comfortable. Parents who have a cold feel 'fuzzy', old and 'achy', and we can guess that toddlers feel the same way!

Croup

What is it? Croup is usually caused by a virus and is a narrowing of the airway just below the child's voice box (larynx). The child with croup makes a characteristic and often frightening 'crowing' noise when breathing in. This is accompanied by a cough not unlike the sound of a sea lion barking at his trainer for a herring.

Treatment: In its mild form, croup's bark is much worse than its bite and doesn't require much treatment. My grandma was in no doubt of what to do – she used the old-fashioned remedy of an inhalation, using a bowl of hot water and a towel to make a tent over the child's head. (Australian parents sometimes put a few drops of eucalyptus oil in the water.) Grandma's technique does work, however I worry about mixing toddlers and bowls of hot water, as well as the dangers of scalding steam. So I think the technique of sitting the child in a steamy bathroom is safer. You can also purchase or rent electric vaporisers that may assist the child to sleep better at night.

Children who do not settle with reassurance, especially those with increasing shortness of breath, need to go to the hospital. A small minority of children can become seriously ill very suddenly. Call an ambulance if you are on your own or very worried.

Ear problems

Hearing loss
What is it? Hearing is just so important for a child's speech development and understanding. If you can't hear, you find it very difficult to learn and to communicate. A baby with normal

hearing is comforted by his mother's voice and changes his crying rhythm to match her speech pattern. At 6 months, he will turn his head towards the direction of quiet sounds from objects he cannot see. Just before 1 year, there is much tuneful babble in some strange, unintelligible language, which is soon followed by repeating appropriate words. If the theme tune of the *Tweenies* is playing, a child with normal hearing will turn toward the music. At this stage we know there is no gross hearing problem.

Treatment: Nowadays, children's hearing is checked when they are still babies. This means any hearing loss is diagnosed early. If the child does not respond to quiet, unexpected noises, if his speech development is slow, or if there is the slightest doubt in the parents' minds, the child's hearing should be tested. See also Glue ear.

The ear

The human ear has an external and an internal part. The internal part is the ear canal, which leads from the outside to the eardrum. The area behind the eardrum is called the middle ear. This is a small chamber filled with air, containing a number of delicate little bones that transmit soundwaves from the eardrum via the auditory nerve to the brain. There is a narrow tube (Eustachian tube) connecting the middle ear to the back of the nose. This tube helps to equalise pressure in the middle ear, which most of us know from 'popping' our ears when travelling in an aeroplane.

For the middle ear to transmit sound efficiently it needs to be filled with air, which gives it resonance, rather like some musical instruments. If it fills with fluid, the tone and hearing volume is diminished in much the same way as filling a drum with sand would affect its musical quality.

Otitis media (middle ear infection)

What is it? Following a cold, a swim, or diving into a pool, bacteria may enter the middle ear via the Eustachian tube and an infection can then develop. On examination, the eardrum looks 'angry' and red. Parents know their child has a middle ear infection when the child becomes sick, irritable, has ear pain and sometimes partial hearing loss. Unfortunately, children don't always know what's wrong; they just know they're unhappy. Your toddler can't tell you which bit is sore though some toddlers will pull at the ear that is infected, giving you a clue.

Treatment: As the infection is usually caused by bacteria, antibiotics are usually given, along with a gentle painkiller, such as a children's paracetamol preparation. However, recent research suggests that ear infections may recover just as well if antibiotics are not given at all. Nature will cure this condition either by reopening the tube to the nose and releasing the infection or through a perforation in the eardrum. While we would rather that the eardrum not perforate, if it does, it usually heals easily by itself.

Glue ear

What is it? Fluid may remain in the middle ear after a bout of otitis media, or collect in association with a cold without infection. This fluid is trapped and thickens, causing 'glue ear', which deadens the hearing in a chronic manner. This is most commonly seen in early school-age children. In toddlers, parents notice that their child seems to be deaf, or is ignoring what's said to them. This sign can be difficult to detect, as toddlers are well-known for ignoring what you say anyway! If in doubt, get your toddler's hearing checked.

Treatment: Pain is usually not a problem with glue ear. It is often cured by time or nature. Sometimes it will require a simple operation, in which plastic tubes (grommets) are placed in the eardrum to let the fluid escape. The tubes drop out after a number of months, which is usually all the treatment that is required.

I recommend steering a middle road. A proper hearing test should be conducted. If there is evidence of hearing loss, surgery can then be contemplated. It's preferable to wait at least six weeks before surgery, since nature has an obliging way of fixing things itself.

Fever

What is it? When the body has an infection, whether it is a common cold or something more serious, its temperature will rise in response. This defence mechanism of trying to 'cook' the invader to death is one way the body uses to rid itself of illness. Some illnesses, such as measles, can cause extremely high fevers while others, which may in fact be more serious, have quite low fever levels. The presence of a fever is merely an indication that the child is sick; the height of temperature is not an accurate measure of the severity of the illness.

Most fevers in children are caused by self-curing viral infections and simply run their course. But a fever may also be the only sign, especially at first, of a severe infection such as pneumonia, urinary infection or meningitis.

A high temperature will upset the already unhappy child and make him feel even more miserable. His parents will start to worry since they know that some children with fevers are also prone to fits. For both these reasons, young children with temperatures tend to be treated more aggressively than their adult counterparts.

Treatment: A feverish child must be dressed sensibly, *not* wrapped up in extra vests and woollens and put to bed heaped up with blankets. If very uncomfortable or miserable, he can be given one of the children's paracetamol preparations. Children usually find this liquid pleasant to take, and it has few side effects. Reducing the fever with paracetamol won't shorten the duration of the illness but will make the child more comfortable. It is generally not recommended to give aspirin to children as international studies have shown that it can cause serious liver and brain damage at this age.

Plunging the feverish child into a bath filled with water straight from the Arctic is counterproductive. When the sizzling body splashes down into the icy water, the skin reacts by diverting blood deeper inside. As a result, little heat is lost by the child, despite the unpleasant experience. Being stripped and sat in front of a gale force fan is another bad idea. This will only cause the child to shiver and thus, paradoxically, generate more body heat. If you feel the need to do something, you can sponge the child over gently with tepid, rather than cold, water.

Of course, if the child's fever persists or rises higher and the child looks unwell, take him to a doctor or hospital.

Fever fits (febrile convulsions)

What is it? In some children, the developing brain seems particularly sensitive to temperature rise. This causes them to throw a fit if they have a high fever. These fits are most common between the ages of 6 months and 3 years, and rarely happen after the age of 5 years. They are not uncommon: 4 per cent of children in this age group will have a fit, usually a febrile convulsion.

For parents it is an alarming experience, and they can be forgiven for fearing that their small child is about to die. The fit can come on very quickly. Many children are only slightly unwell beforehand and give no warning at all. The child will suddenly go stiff, the eyes roll back, and breathing becomes laboured. They will then start shaking or twitching, before relaxing to lie dazed and confused. After this they become sleepy, and having slept, will appear fully recovered. Luckily most of these fits last for less than five minutes, although to the watching parent it can seem like an eternity.

Treatment: If a child has a high fever, the cooling measures discussed in the Fever entry should prevent most febrile convulsions. If the child does have a fit, he should be placed gently on his side to prevent choking. Difficult as it may be, try not to panic. The short fever fit does not damage the child, only his parents' nerves. Stay with him rather than run off for help. Don't force spoons or other objects into his mouth. The apparently difficult breathing is not due to a blockage in his throat but rather a tightening of his respiratory muscles.

If your child has a febrile convulsion, particularly the first one, make sure you see your doctor. They will provide you with a care plan for when your child has a high fever. A child who has a simple febrile convulsion does not have epilepsy, and these fits will not continue throughout his life. After one febrile episode, however, the child is more likely to have another before he grows out of the convulsion-prone age group. Occasionally a fever fit may be an indication of an underlying severe infection, such as meningitis. For this reason, it is advisable to see your doctor.

If a febrile convulsion does not end within five minutes, you must contact your doctor immediately or call emergency 999.

Meningococcal infection

What is it? Meningococcus is one of the most feared infections of the moment. It can come on rapidly and without warning and, if not immediately treated, the results can be devastating. Despite its ferocity, this bacteria is one of the easiest to kill, responding to even the simplest antibiotics. If you get to it in time, it is easy to treat. Media publicity, though aiming to increase awareness, has led to much greater fear of this disease than it deserves.

Children with meningococcal infection often start with fever then develop fine, dark red spots (1–2 mm wide) on their skin which don't disappear with pressure (a finger pressed on the skin for a few seconds). In a more advanced infection, the child may develop what appears to be severe bruising.

The meningococcus bacteria is commonly carried by many people without any symptoms. Why it infects some people and misses the majority is unknown. It is spread through droplets from the nose or throat of affected people and through close, face-to-face contact. If infected, the bacteria causes sudden septicaemia (bloodstream infection) or meningitis (an infection of the tissues that cover the brain). Most children I have treated have both the septicaemia and the meningitis. Septicaemia is suspected if the child has a bruised-looking rash that increases every minute, and is extremely sick. Meningitis usually accompanies these symptoms, causing headache and a stiff neck.

Treatment: The main treatment for this condition is antibiotics that must be administered intravenously at a hospital. I can't emphasise enough that if you have an extremely sick child with any of these symptoms, they must be rushed to hospital immediately. Even a doctor can easily be caught out, seeing a vaguely sick child in the morning, giving reassurance, and sending them home. But some hours later the infection becomes all-consuming and the child crashes into a downward spiral.

If any child looks sick and is deteriorating fast, this is the most urgent of urgent emergencies. The only way to prevent death and disability in meningococcal infection is a quick diagnosis, immediately followed by that first dose of life-saving antibiotic.

A vaccination exists for specific forms of meningococcal infection. In Australia, immunisation of all children at 12 months of age is recommended (and is available free of charge). However, if any child shows signs of the disease, even if they have been immunised, they must receive urgent medical attention.

Tonsillitis

What is it? The tonsils are two lumps of lymphoid tissue situated on either side at the back of the throat. They act as the first line of defence against invading infections. Tonsils are very small in newborns, gradually growing larger and reaching their peak size somewhere around the age of 7 years. Tonsillitis is not the sore throat found at the beginning of a cold – we often see red throats in children. It is the specific infection of the tonsillar tissues and their associated glands at the angle of the jaw. The tonsils are not just red but 'angry' looking, with flecks of pus. Tonsillitis is usually caused by viruses in younger children, less than 4 years old, and by bacteria in older children.

Large does not mean unhealthy, and some children have large tonsils with no problem. Only rarely does this cause feeding difficulties. Very occasionally a paediatrician sees a child whose very large tonsils are causing obstruction to the breathing during sleep (sleep apnoea). The child may be tired and irritable during the day, due to lack of normal night-time sleep.

Treatment: The main treatment for bacterial tonsillitis is antibiotics and this is usually effective. In the old days, tonsils were whipped out at the drop of a scalpel, being regarded universally as useless appendages. Nowadays, removal of the tonsils is relatively rare, and the operation is not performed unless there are some major reasons for doing so. The decision for surgical removal is not dependent on the size of the tonsils. The main reason for removing tonsils these days is to prevent airway obstruction during sleep. However, persistent severe infections may sometimes be the reason for a tonsillectomy. This is a decision usually made by a paediatrician or ear, nose and throat (ENT) specialist.

Vomiting and diarrhoea

What is it? Vomiting and diarrhoea are both extremely common in the toddler. When they are present together this often means an infection of the gut (gastroenteritis, commonly known as 'gastro'). If vomiting occurs alone, it is more likely due to an infection in the body, possibly a cold, flu or occasionally some more serious problem. Diarrhoea may also occur on its own.

The main worry with vomiting and diarrhoea is that if left unchecked they can lead to dehydration, which particularly in children is a great concern. However, if the child is not too unwell, the following tips will help you to manage it.

Treatment: The correct treatment for vomiting and diarrhoea is to give **small** amounts of **clear** fluids **frequently**. If vomiting and diarrhoea are caused by gastroenteritis, it is almost always of viral origin and will not be helped by antibiotics. Children with acute gut infections need fluids, not solids. If too much water and salt are lost from the body, dehydration can occur rapidly, especially with young children.

Small amounts of fluid means no more than one whisky measure at a time (i.e. ¼ cup or 75 ml). Although this may seem very little fluid, you can in fact administer 1.5 litres a day in this fashion quite effortlessly. When a young child nags for fluids and the parents give in to his requests on demand, it can result in further vomiting. Parents don't like seeing their child 'suffer', but sometimes you need to be cruel to be kind!

Clear means fluids you can see through when you hold them up to the light: water, diluted lemonade or preferably an oral electrolyte solution from your local pharmacy (such as Gastrolyte™). It does *not* mean milk, soup, or solids. As every mother knows, it is very much more unpleasant to clean up second-hand milk than diluted lemonade. Lemonade may be convenient, but unfortunately it contains far too much sugar and is too concentrated for a child with gastroenteritis. If you do give your sick child lemonade, it is important to dilute it with water, one part lemonade to three parts water.

I strongly recommend using an oral electrolyte solution from a pharmacy, as these are designed to replace all the essential electrolytes lost through vomiting and diarrhoea. Some parents find it easier to present this solution as an ice block. Please don't use sports drinks, which are designed for running athletes, not children with running bowels!

Life being as it is, unfortunately parents often find themselves dealing with a sick child in the middle of the night when it is difficult to get to a pharmacy. The World Health Organization (WHO) recommends an oral rehydrating solution that can be used for any child, anywhere in the world. It is important to measure the ingredients carefully, as using too much salt or sugar will cause further problems, not cure them:

1 litre cooled boiled water

6 level teaspoons sugar

½ teaspoon salt

Mix ingredients together in a large jug and keep in the fridge until required.

Frequently means each quarter- or half-hour throughout the day and night. Even when vomiting continues, keep offering the child sips of fluid. A simple way to ensure you maintain the frequency is to set a cooking timer to ring every 15 minutes. Using a timer can also be a game that lets the toddler know when his allotted fluid time arrives.

While most of what is discussed here is to do with vomiting, the same principles apply to treating diarrhoea. If clear fluids are given, the bowel has little to discharge and the diarrhoea will quickly stop. In the days that follow diarrhoea, some parents worry that their child is constipated due to lack of bowel movements. However, the bowel is quite empty and has nothing more to get rid of, so no treatment is needed.

Be aware that some children with gastroenteritis require more treatment than frequent oral fluids. If the vomiting and diarrhoea are very severe, or if the child is becoming lethargic, exhausted or sunken-eyed, take him to a hospital without delay.

Clearly unclear

You'd be amazed by the stream of odd cures I've been confronted with by parents of vomiting toddlers.

'What's the problem?' I would ask.

'He vomits everything up, doctor.'

'What are you giving him?'

'Oh, not much. A glass of milk with an egg and a little added custard just to keep his strength up.'

After all that, the parents would be genuinely surprised when the child throws it all back up at them!

Medicines: how to give them

Doctors have no difficulty in writing prescriptions for children. The problem comes when it is time to force the strange substance down the toddler's throat. I am all for using the purest and most modern preparation but if the latest 'no sugar, no preservatives, no artificial colouring' product tastes like cat's wee, I feel that someone has missed the point.

- If an unpleasant-tasting medicine has been prescribed for your toddler, ask your doctor for a more palatable alternative.
- For the child who is a militant drug refuser, request preparations that require fewer doses a day to be taken. With antibiotics, this is particularly useful, as often two-dose-a-day drugs can supplant the more usual four-dose-a-day types.
- Most drugs can be given in liquid form to toddlers, preferably slipped into the mouth on a spoon and chased down by a favourite drink.
- For the reluctant child, sometimes a plastic syringe is a more effective way to administer liquid medicines. Even if the toddler won't fully open their mouth, the medicine can be squirted through a small crack. (Watch out for the fine spray that can blow around the room once the medicine has hit the child's tongue!)
- Tablets and capsules are not normally prescribed for toddlers because of the dangers of choking. If you do have to give your toddler a tablet, as prescribed by their doctor, ask your chemist if it can be crushed and placed in a little ice-cream.

Hospital visits

Having a toddler in hospital is bad news. However, these days when it is necessary for a child to be admitted, the trauma for both child and parents is eased in the following ways:

Shorter hospital stays: If the toddler needs a surgical procedure then 'day surgery', in which the child is operated on during the day and sent back home that evening, is often possible. This cuts down on the amount of time the toddler spends away from home.

Parents are kept close: If the child needs to stay overnight, parents are encouraged to stay with them, sleeping on a reclining chair or bed next to their child. When the child needs surgery, parents accompany them as they receive the anaesthetic and are there to greet them when they wake up in recovery. This stops children from being frightened.

Pain medication: In the old days, they used to say that little children didn't feel pain the way adults did. Nowadays, thankfully this view is seen for the rubbish that it is, and doctors will provide sick children with pain relievers in the same way they do for adults. Even the tiniest newborn undergoing surgery will be given pain relieving medication with the same attention that adults are afforded. Sick toddlers get the same care, as we don't like to see children suffer.

Our main aim is to not frighten children who are already sick and in pain. We realise that recovery is speediest when they feel safe and are surrounded by family, especially mum and dad.

Bed rest for toddlers

For sick children at home, the old-fashioned idea of bed rest is no longer seen as a necessity. In modern hospitals even children who have undergone major surgery will be seen up and about the next day. If a sick child at home feels well enough to want to be up, good for him. If he leaves his bed to lie on a rug and watch a video, that's just as good. If he feels so miserable that all he wants is the peace and comfort of bed, he'll let you know. Whatever he chooses, a sick child must be given the benefit of the doubt and allowed to rest and heal in the way that suits him best.

Toddler development worries

Books on childcare usually list a multitude of developmental milestones for the child to attain at any given age. These involve his gross motor skills, fine motor skills, hearing, vision, communication skills, social and play skills. After working for many years in a developmental assessment unit, my only aim here is to point out those general patterns that suggest success, and those which cause concern.

Communication

By far the most valuable skills are those in the area of communication. At 6 months, the child who communicates vigorously with his eyes, takes in everything in his environment, and 'doesn't miss a move' has a good start to life. In the second year, the child with good, appropriate, non-repetitive speech (usually just single words) is doing well.

However, some children are late to speak. In these cases, the first thing to ask yourself is, can the child hear? Have a proper hearing test performed by an audiologist. If your toddler's hearing is normal, and development and understanding are fine, then you shouldn't worry too much about late speech.

If the child has no speech, good comprehension is what we look for. The child should be able to point with accuracy to objects in pictures and books or to things in his environment. Comprehension shows that the child's intellect is hidden, but is there.

Subtle signs of intelligence

We can learn much about a child's intelligence by watching him play. Look for constructive qualities, where he uses the toys provided in an intelligent way. For example, the sandpit and toy cars become a Formula 1 racetrack. Look also for imagination and pretend play, such as flying around the room like Superman. These show that the toddler has 'got the goods', and it is unlikely he has any major problem.

Going for broke

Walking, running and climbing tend to be of most interest to the parents when they are seeking signs of their child's intelligence. However, early walking bears little relationship to advanced intelligence and is much more likely to be an inherited family trait. Children who walk early often have a mother who was an early walker.

As proof of the lack of connection between good gross motor skills and intelligence, I cite the case of the greyhound – it is probably one of the most advanced animals as far as gross motor skills go. But any dog that spends its entire life chasing after a stuffed hare without suspecting it is being fooled is, to my mind at least, not very intelligent.

Developmental concerns

With young children, these are the points that concern me in regard to their development. I worry when a child has little interest in his surroundings; if he walks around in a purposeless manner; if he is slow to respond to sound. I worry when there is little understanding of simple messages and only parrot-like repetitive speech. I worry when there is apparently little understanding; for example, the child may flick through a book in an obsessive manner, without displaying any interest or recognition of what is inside it. I worry when a toddler does not talk to me with his voice and does not communicate with his face or eyes either. I worry when the child has no pretend or constructive play and is stuck at the stage of throwing and banging toys together or running around aimlessly.

If you are at all concerned about your toddler's development, you *must* see your paediatrician. Many books are available on the developmental assessment of young children. (See also Appendix I, Meaningful Milestones.)

The sick child: when to worry

When teaching junior doctors I always impressed upon them that their greatest skill lies not in knowing hundreds of rare medical facts but in being able to reliably spot 'the sick child'. It is essentially a 'gut feeling' combined with years of experience.

However, I believe that you don't have to be a doctor to know if your child is sick. We can get a very clear idea from looking at the child's eyes and observing his alertness.

These are some signs that are medical emergencies and you *must* seek medical assistance for immediately:

- The child is dull-eyed, distant and confused.
- The child is pale, sweaty and looks anxious.
- The child has sunken eyes, a lack of elasticity in his skin, a dry mouth, and is passing little urine. This can be indicative of severe dehydration.
- The child has a stiff neck, which is painful to move or bend. This can indicate meningitis.
- The child is panting, over-breathing or has deep, rattling breathing. This can indicate a serious lung condition.

- The child has a fever and a rash that develops rapidly, with or without bruised-looking blotches that increase rapidly. This is a sign of meningococcal infection.

On the other hand, a sick child who appears alert, has bright eyes, and takes a lively and keen interest when you walk into the room, generally lets us know that things aren't quite an emergency.

In my experience, if mum is worried, I worry. If mum *and* grandma are worried, I worry a lot!

Now that you've tamed your toddler, a new challenge awaits ...

- An A to Z of children's behaviours
- Positive discipline and how to put it into practice
- Starting school and developing school skills
- Confident children: beating shyness and making friends
- How to have healthy and active children now – and prevent problems later
- Sole parenting, step families and other family issues
- Talking about sex and death
- TV and the internet

APPENDIX I
Meaningful milestones

Note: There is a wide range of normal development, each child having relative strengths and weaknesses in the profile of abilities presented. If one or two items are delayed it is generally of little significance. If many items are delayed, and there is a lack of comprehension, disinterest in the environment and an absence of quality play, then an expert professional opinion should be sought.

Here is a guide to the general pattern of development at different ages.

At 1 year

- Walks reliably holding onto furniture.
- Some may be walking alone (average age 13 months – range of normal between 9 months and 18 months).
- Picks up small objects between the tip of the thumb and the forefinger.
- Understands the word 'No!' and at this age usually obeys it.
- Knows name and will usually turn when it is used.
- Babbles in a tuneful, foreign-sounding language.
- Understands 'Give it to Mummy', but only if accompanied by gesture.
- Says 'Da da' and sometimes one or two other words with meaning.
- Uses a drinking cup with some assistance.
- Can hold a spoon but unable to load it at the plate and navigate without spillage to the mouth.
- Putting toys and other objects in the mouth is now on the wane.
- Waves 'Bye bye' and enjoys 'Peek-a-boo' games.
- Understands the permanence of objects. If a toy is hidden as they watch, they immediately know where it is.

CONCERNS Be concerned when:
- No tuneful babble is produced.
- Hearing seems to be a problem.
- No interest is taken in the environment.
- Not yet standing upright beside furniture.
- Not using the finger/thumb grip.
- A child does not 'feel right' in any way or is significantly different to a brother or sister at that age.

At 18 months
- Walks reliably without any support.
- Squats down to pick up a toy.
- Pushes wheeled toys around the floor.
- Loves to put objects in and out of containers.
- Delicate pincer grip allows picking up of crumbs and other small objects.
- Holds a pencil like a dagger and scribbles without purpose.
- Talks tunefully to self in own language.

- Uses between six and 20 appropriate words. (Note: 'appropriate' does not include repeats of what mother has just said.)
- Most start to show preference for one hand.
- Points to shoes, hair, nose, feet, on request.
- Responds to a simple one-part verbal command.
- Points to objects in a picture book, e.g. dog.
- Holds a spoon securely and is reasonably reliable in feeding.
- Manages a feeding cup unaided.
- No longer mouths toys.
- Piles three blocks on top of each other.
- Starts to show discomfort when wet or dirty.
- Starts to go upstairs holding on tight.
- Fluctuates between being very clingy and resisting attention.
- Not the age of reason. Do not know what they want but know they want it immediately.

At 2 years

- Walks well. Runs reliably.
- Walks upstairs placing both feet on each step, holding lightly to a rail. Almost able to come down again upright.
- Enjoys ride on toys, pushing them along.
- Walks backward while dragging a wheeled toy on the end of a string.
- Attempts to kick a ball.
- Piles six blocks on top of each other.
- Removes a wrapper from a lolly.
- Holds a pencil almost correctly.
- Scribbles in a circular manner.
- Can imitate a vertical line.
- Enjoys looking at picture books.
- Turns one page at a time.
- Can usually point out 'Which boy is happy?'
- Hand dominance is established in most.
- Over 50 words in vocabulary and many more understood.
- Puts two and occasionally three words together.
- Refers to self by name.
- Joins in nursery rhymes and songs.
- Delivers simple messages, 'Daddy, come'.
- Chews food well.
- Spoon feeding a success.
- Usually dry by day.
- Usually tells when wants to go to the toilet.
- Imitates mother doing household duties.
- Will help tidy away toys.
- Real help with dressing.
- Demands mum's attention constantly.
- Plays beside, but not directly with, other children.
- Clingy – plays in another room, but checks every couple of minutes to

ensure mother is still there.
- Rebellious when does not get own way.
- Possessive of toys and attention.
- Not a time for sharing and seeing another's point of view!

CONCERNS Be concerned when:
- There is minimal or no speech. (In this case, check hearing, comprehension and other areas of development.)
- Toys are still being mouthed.
- Toys are being thrown in an unthinking way.
- Play is always repetitive – e.g. spinning wheels and banging blocks.
- Interest in environment is not being shown. Should be a real 'stickybeak' at this age.
- There is a lack of 'body language'.
- There is unusual irritability.

At 2¹/₂ years
- Uses 200 or more words.
- Uses pronouns, 'I', 'Me', 'You'.
- Holds pen with a reasonable adult-type grip and imitates a circle and horizontal line.
- Builds a tower of seven blocks.
- Pulls pants down for toileting but usually unable to get them back up.
- Knows full name.
- May stutter in eagerness to get information out.
- Plays alongside in parallel to other children.
- Little idea of sharing playthings or adults' attention.
- Won't wait, expects everything immediately.

At 3 years
- Walks upstairs using alternate feet on each step and comes down using both feet per step.
- Jumps off bottom step with two feet together.
- Runs around obstacles with speed and accuracy.
- Pedals tricycle.
- Can walk on tip toe.
- Can catch a ball with arms outstretched.
- Threads large beads on a shoelace.
- Copies a circle and imitates a cross.
- Matches three primary colours, but still confuses blue and green.
- Cuts with scissors.
- Speech intelligible even to a stranger.
- Uses most plurals correctly.
- Will volunteer full name and sex.
- Still talks to self at length at play.
- Able to describe an event that has happened, simply but reliably.
- Questions start: 'Why?', 'Why?', 'Why?'.

- Listens eagerly to stories and likes a favourite one repeated and then repeated once more.
- Recites several nursery rhymes.
- Rote counts to ten.
- Counts to ten, but only understands practical counting of two or three items.
- Washes hands but needs supervision to dry.
- Can dress self except for buttons, tight tops and shoes.
- Likes to help adult with home activities.
- Behaviour is less impatient and self centered.
- Able to wait for a short time before getting what wants.
- Understands sharing toys, lollies and attention.
- Plays directly with other children.
- Vivid imagination, loves pretend play.
- Separates reasonably well from mother, but this varies greatly.

CONCERNS   Be concerned when:
- There is an inability to communicate easily through appropriate speech.
- Body language is poor.
- Repetitive play shows little imagination, or richness.
- Behaviour is still like the senseless, sparky and unsharing 18-month-old.

At 4 years
- Walks and probably runs up and down stairs without holding on.
- Throws and catches well; starts to bounce a ball.
- Piles blocks, two to the side and one on top, to copy a bridge.
- Holds a pen like an adult.
- Draws a person with trunk, head, legs and usually arms and fingers.
- Draws a reasonable likeness of a house.
- Names four primary colours.
- Grammar and speech construction is usually correct.
- A few sounds still mispronounced and immature.
- Can describe an occurrence in an accurate and logical way.
- Can state address and age.
- Questioning is at its height. Constantly asks 'Why?', 'When?', 'How?'.
- Listens intently to stories.
- Tells stories, often confusing fact with fiction.
- May have imaginary friends.
- Understands yesterday, today, tomorrow; i.e. past and future.
- Rote counts to 20 and understands meaningful counting up to five objects.
- Enjoys jokes and plays on words.
- Eats with skill and cuts with a knife.
- Rarely uses a knife and fork before age 4.
- Washes and dries own hands.
- Brushes teeth with supervision.
- Blows nose reliably.

- Wipes bottom after toileting.
- Can fully dress and undress except for inaccessible buttons, bows and shoelaces. (Shoelaces are rarely tied before the age of 5 and since the advent of Velcro, for many children it is much later.)
- Plays well with other children.
- Now argues with words rather than blows.
- Verbal impertinence and bickering are developing fast.
- Understands taking turns, sharing and simple rules.
- Starts to believe in justice and everyone keeping to the rules.
- Many like to be the king pin, 'bossy-boots'.
- Shows concern for younger siblings, playmates in distress.
- Usually separates well from mother.

Reference: *Children's Developmental Progress*, Mary Sheridan (N.F.E.R. Publishing Co., UK).

APPENDIX II
Miscellaneous facts

- At the age of 2 years most toddlers have attained half their adult height.
- From birth till 2½ years every parent can expect to change between 7,000 and 8,000 dirty nappies.
- A toddler requires 2½ times more food to power each kilogram of body weight as would a mature 20-year-old. This explains why toddlers eat so much to keep their furnaces fired up.
- The average children of today will have witnessed at least 18,000 murders on television by the time they have left school.
- A toddler cannot comprehend the permanence of marriage break-up or death. To them both are reversible states.
- Religion has little meaning for toddlers, who follow without question the beliefs and example of those closest to them. Independent inner faith is first found in late adolescence.
- Home is a very dangerous place. Domestic violence is much more common than street violence.
- About 33 per cent of Australian men and 29 per cent of Australian women smoke. The number of young men smokers is reducing at present, the figure for young women smokers is increasing. Passive smoking is not without its problems. Adults can escape this, but our children are not so fortunate. They have to inhale whatever we put in their environment for 18 years until they are in a position to be able to make up their own minds on whether they wish to smoke or not.
- There is no necessity for routine worming of the average Australian family. Worms are incorrectly believed to cause abdominal pain, pallor and malnutrition. When worms are seen in the motions, or children have an itchy bottom, particularly at night, treatment is needed.
- Sun in excess is extremely damaging to skin, making young adults look prematurely old and wrinkled. Worse than that, there is a strong correlation between UV exposure (especially intermittent) and all types of skin cancer. Now is the time to be sensible in sunshine. Hats, high factor sun screens and covering up are needed from the earliest years.

APPENDIX III
Immunisation

Diptheria, haemophilus influenza type B (Hib), hepatitis B, measles, polio, tetanus and whooping cough are unpleasant illnesses that can kill. Nowadays there is no need for this to happen if we take the trouble to have our children vaccinated.

Before vaccines were available, many thousands of children died from infectious diseases. Babies continue to die from diseases such as whooping cough because community vaccination levels are still too low. This means that very young babies can be infected before they can be vaccinated themselves. Other vaccine-preventable diseases will return, in large numbers, if vaccination rates are not kept up.

All vaccines recommended are safe and effective, though they occasionally have side effects. These are usually no more than a minor inconvenience. Vaccine-related permanent harm or death is very rare, and thousands of times less likely than death from the actual diseases themselves.

Please note: the information in this section is for educational purposes only. For specific information relating to your child, please consult your doctor or health professional.

Chicken pox (varicella-zoster)
Chicken pox is an ugly, itchy rash with little fever or feeling of general illness. This viral complaint takes about two weeks to incubate. It starts with a crop of itchy, raised red spots, usually on the trunk. There are often little spots inside the mouth. The spots enlarge, fill with fluid and form vesicles (blisters), which eventually burst and are covered by scabs.

The child with chicken pox may look awful and feel intensely itchy but he will have only a low fever and feel relatively well in himself. The old-fashioned pink Calamine lotion (available from chemists and supermarkets) is probably as good as anything to ease the itching.

A vaccine for varicella is now available.

Diphtheria
These nasty bacteria set up a focus of infection in the throat, which sometimes causes a sudden obstruction to breathing that can be fatal. The infection also releases poisons that can cause paralysis or heart failure. Luckily diphtheria has become very rare since immunisation has been widely available.

Diphtheria vaccine is given by injection, as part of a combined vaccine for tetanus, pertussis, polio and Hib, known as DTap/IPV/Hib. It is well tried and very safe. Doses are given at 2, 3 and 4 months of age and again at around 4 years, with a booster administered between the ages of 13–18.

German measles (rubella)

Not as unpleasant or dangerous as ordinary measles, rubella is usually a minor illness. The exception is that when a pregnant woman contracts rubella, the unborn baby is likely to suffer serious, permanent heart, brain or liver disease as well as deafness. The only way to prevent this serious problem is for all children to be immunised against rubella, via the triple vaccine known as MMR (measles, mumps, rubella). The vaccine is given at around 13 months and again at around 4 years.

Haemophilus influenza type B (Hib)

Hib is a bacteria and, despite its name, has nothing to do with the 'flu' – which is a short name for viral influenza.

Before use of the DTap/IPV/Hib vaccine, Hib infection was widespread in the community, most children becoming immune from mild infection. However, Hib was the most common cause of bacterial meningitis, and caused many other serious, often life-threatening infections. Hib will again become a major cause of disease if all infants are not vaccinated.

Hib vaccination is given by injection in three doses at 2, 3 and 4 months of age.

Hepatitis B (Hep B)

Hep B is a viral infection which causes inflammation of the liver. It is very infectious, very common and can also be fatal. Most commonly passed through blood contact, open sores and wounds, the sharing of needles between infected drug addicts, or even normal sexual activity can transmit this infection. It can also be passed from an infected mother to her baby, usually at the time of birth.

However, there is a reliable vaccine against this disease and babies born to an infected mother should be given hepatitis B immunoglobulin (HBIG) within 12 hours of birth.

Measles

This is just about the most infective of childhood illnesses. Without vaccination almost everyone will catch it. Measles is a viral infection and is more than a rash – it causes children to be very sick, have a high fever, a nasty cough, sore eyes and feel very sorry for themselves. In Third World countries, where nutrition is poor, it is a much feared illness. Children who contract measles in this country often become extremely sick, and occasionally there are long-term serious complications.

Babies are born with high antibody levels to measles, which have come across the placenta from mum. These gradually wane in the first year, giving sufficient protection for vaccination not to be advised until after the first birthday. Vaccination is part of the MMR vaccine given for protection against measles, mumps and rubella and is by simple injection. It is administered at around 13 months and again at around 4 years.

Vaccination is usually without side effects. A few children (10–15 per cent) will suffer with a slight fever about 10 days after the injection when the vaccine takes hold. Some of these children even have a mild measles-like rash. In these instances, it is best to give the child paracetamol to ease the symptoms.

Meningoccocal infection

The meningococcus bacterium is relatively common, found in the back of the nose and throat of healthy people. Why it infects some people and not others is a mystery. It is spread by close person-to-person contact and by droplets spread when an infected person breathes, coughs or sneezes.

Initially meningococcus causes a mild illness with a fever and often a fine rash. But this can progress rapidly to meningitis (inflammation of the tissue that covers the brain), septicaemia (infection of the blood), disability and death. The rapid progression of this disease is what is so frightening and has drawn much publicity in the media. A child who is infected can appear well in the morning but have spiralled rapidly downward only a few hours later. Treatment is by intravenous antibiotics that must be administered in a hospital, which is why it is vital for any person with the symptoms of meningococcal infection to seek medical attention urgently.

There are a number of different sorts of meningococcus. A vaccine against a dangerous strain (Serogroup C) is a primary immunisation given to babies when they are 3 and 4 months old, with a dose of the combined Hib/MenC vaccine being given at 12 months.

Mumps

Mumps is a viral infection which affects the glands that produce saliva. The glands usually affected are those that lie just below the ear. Symptoms include pain and swelling of the glands, along with a fever, a dry mouth and pain when opening the jaw or chewing. The mumps virus can cause problems when it travels to other parts of the body. It can cause pain and swelling of the testes in males who have been through puberty, very rarely resulting in sterility.

For many years it was debated whether to add mumps vaccine to the current immunisation protocol. It was argued that this is a relatively mild condition and not worth the expense of routine vaccination. Following successful programs in the United States and Canada, however, it is now believed to be worthwhile and is given at the same time as the measles and rubella vaccination (MMR). Given as part of the combined MMR injection at around 13 months and around 4 years, it is simple and safe.

Pneumococcal infection

Pneumococcal disease is the common term for a number of conditions caused by the pneumococcal bacterium (Streptococcus pneumonaei). This bacteria is the largest cause of meningitis, pneumonia septicaemia in Australia. It is also a common cause of middle ear infections and sinusitis.

Pneumococcus is carried in the upper respiratory tract and back of the nose and throat of healthy people, especially young children. It is spread by droplets breathed from the respiratory tract and close person-to-person contact.

There are certain types of people who are at increased risk of pneumococcal infection. All otherwise healthy children under the age of 2 are at risk, particularly those who attend day care and come into close contact with infected children. Adults at risk include those with weakened immune systems, who have had their spleens removed, who have diabetes, chronic heart, lung or kidney disease, smokers and all those over the age of 65.

Pneumococcal disease occurs most commonly in the colder winter months in Australia. Symptoms depend on the site of infection but are not the same as meningococcal disease and do not commonly include a rash. It is important to learn the signs of pneumococcal disease and how to identify them.

The vaccine is offered to children at 2, 4 and 13 months, with people older than 65 being routinely offered the vaccine to proect against pneumococcal disease. The vaccine not only reduces your child's chance of suffering the devastating symptoms of septicaemia and meningitis, it also protects them against middle ear infections and pneumonia.

Polio

This viral disease often causes permanent paralysis. It is still common in many overseas countries that experience the devastating problems that were seen here before a safe vaccine was made available.

Polio immunisation is part of the DTaP/IPV/Hib vaccine and is given at 2, 3 and 4 months of age, with another dose at around 4 years. A booster should be given at 13–18 years.

Tetanus

Tetanus, or lockjaw, is caused by an organism that is frequently found in the dirt in our streets, gardens and paddocks. It enters the body through a dirty wound, later to release poisons that cause severe spasms and eventually respiratory failure with a high risk of death.

Every child should be vaccinated. The tetanus vaccine is included as part of the DTaP/IPV/Hib vaccine, which also protects against diphtheria and pertussis. It is given at 2, 3 and 4 months, with another dose at around 4 years. A booster should be given at 13–18 years.

Whooping cough (pertussis)

This illness is very unpleasant although usually not fatal. Those at greatest risk are little babies. About one in 100 of these will die or suffer brain damage from whooping cough. By way of contrast, fewer than one in every 100,000 children given the whooping cough vaccine suffer these symptoms.

Whooping cough is caused by the organism Bordetella pertussis. The Chinese talk of whooping cough as 'the cough of 100 days'. The child gets into a spasm of coughing, loses breath, whoops as he tries to get air into the lungs, spasms again and often ends up vomiting. It is all extremely distressing for the child, as well as for the parent watching.

Whooping cough vaccine is the preparation least liked by doctors. It only gives complete protection to between 80 and 90 per cent of those who are vaccinated. In the past, almost 50 per cent would also get a mild reaction that caused fever or a little irritability. (Such a reaction is usually nothing to worry about and can be relieved with a small dose of paracetamol.) However, since 1997, we have been using a vaccine (DTPa) in Australia that causes far fewer reactions.

The main concern with the whooping cough vaccine debate is the much publicised danger of permanent brain damage. This is exceptionally rare, occurring less frequently than one per million children, but it is still of great concern to the medical profession and all childcare workers.

It is important to see the whooping cough vaccine in proper perspective. If the vaccine is not given, the majority of children will contract natural whooping cough. For most, this will be a really unpleasant and long illness. For a few there is a risk of residual brain damage or even death. The chances of these serious complications alone are at least 100 times greater than the risk of problems due to the vaccine.

Vaccination is given via the DTaP/IPV/Hib vaccine at 2, 3 and 4 months and again at around 4 years.

Common questions

Q. What medicine do you give for a child with fever following immunisation?

A. Paracetamol.

Q. If the baby has a cold or flu, with a fever, should he be immunised?

A. No, not until he has recovered.

Q. If you believe there has been a major illness or reaction to a particular vaccine, is further immunisation to be given?

A. Any severe reactions must be reported to your family doctor. If these fit certain criteria, it is possible the doctor may recommend omitting one part of the vaccine.

Q. When do premature babies get their vaccines?

A. If they are healthy, immunisation should start at the same time after birth as it would for any other child.

Q. If I miss one vaccine do I need to start all over again?

A. No! You need no extra shots. Start where you left off and continue at the original spacing.

Q. If the vaccines are commenced at an older age than suggested, do you use the same spacing?

A. Yes.

Q. If a young child has a bad cut or is bitten by a dog, does he need a tetanus shot?

A. Not if he has had a tetanus immunisation in the previous two years. Check with your doctor.

Q. If a child has been sick with measles in his first year of life, does this mean that no measles vaccine should be given?

A. Studies show that most rashes diagnosed as measles in the first year of life are, in fact, misdiagnoses. There is no harm giving the vaccine to a child who has already had measles, so if in doubt, please vaccinate.

Q. What ever happened to smallpox and tuberculosis vaccinations that many of us were given as children?

A. A worldwide vaccination program for smallpox seems to have eradicated the disease and so it is no longer needed. Tuberculosis vaccine is only given in special instances where there is a risk of contracting TB from someone close to your family who is known to have the condition.

Q. If a child is allergic to eggs, should the measles vaccine (which is egg-cultured) be given?

A. Most doctors would now say yes, but with care.

Q. Does MMR (for measles, mumps and rubella) vaccine increase the risk of autism?

A. There was concern that MMR vaccination miay increase the risk of autism. This was because the age when autism is usually diagnosed is after the first MMR vaccination is given. There was also an increased incidence of autism but this increase predated the introduction of the MMR vaccine. It is thought that MMR vaccination and diagnosis of autism is purely coincidental.

Immunisation schedule – a checklist for parents

WHEN TO IMMUNISE	WHAT IS GIVEN	HOW IT IS GIVEN
2, 3 and 4 months old	Diphtheria, tetanus, pertussis (whooping cough), polio and Hib (DTap/IPV/Hib)	One injection
	MenC	One injection
Around 13 months old	Measles, mumps and rubella (MMR)	One injection
3 years and 4 months to 5 years old	Diphtheria, tetanus, pertussis (whooping cough) and polio (dTap/IPV or DTap/IPV)	One injection
	Measles, mumps and rubella (MMR)	One injection
10 to 14 years	BCG (against tuberculosis)	Skin test then, if needed, one injection
13 to 18 years old	Diphtheria, tetanus, polio (Td/IPV)	One injection

2, 3 and 4 months old

When your baby is 2 months old, you will be asked to bring them for their first DTaP/IPV/Hib injection against diphtheria, tetanus, pertussis (whooping cough), polio and Hib.

They will also be offered the Meningitis C vaccine, which can be given at the same time.

They will then be asked to come back for another 2 doses of both DTaP/IPV/Hib and Men C when they are 3 and 4 months old.

With their vaccination at 2 and 4 months they will also be offered vaccinaton against pneumococcal infection (PCV).

Around 12 months old

Your baby will be offered a final booster dose for protection against Hib and MenC. This is given as a single injection.

Around 13 months old

When your baby turns one, they will be offered their first dose of the triple MMR vaccine against measles, mumps and rubella. This is given as a single injection.

3 years and 4 months to 5 years old

Before your child starts school, they will be offered the dTaP/IPV or DTaP/IPV vaccines which protect against diphtheria, tetanus, pertussis (whooping cough) and polio. This is given as a single injection.

They will also be offered a booster dose of MMR against measles, mumps and rubella, which is also given as a single injection.

13 to 18 years old

13 to 18 year olds are offered Td/IPV at school. It is given as a single injection in the upper arm and protects against diphtheria, tetanus and polio.

APPENDIX IV
Heights from 1 year to 4 years

Height in cm – girls (boys)

Age yrs mths		Average height		Lower average 3% will be shorter 97% will be taller		Upper average 3% will be taller 97% will be shorter	
1	0	74.3	(76.1)	69.0	(71.0)	79.6	(81.2)
1	1	75.5	(77.2)	70.1	(72.1)	80.9	(82.4)
1	2	76.7	(78.3)	71.2	(73.1)	82.1	(83.6)
1	3	77.8	(79.4)	72.2	(74.1)	83.3	(84.8)
1	4	78.9	(80.4)	73.2	(75.0)	84.5	(85.9)
1	5	79.9	(81.4)	74.2	(75.9)	85.6	(87.0)
1	6	80.9	(82.4)	75.1	(76.7)	86.7	(88.1)
1	7	81.9	(83.3)	76.1	(77.5)	87.8	(89.2)
1	8	82.9	(84.2)	77.0	(78.3)	88.8	(90.2)
1	9	83.8	(85.1)	77.8	(79.1)	89.8	(91.2)
1	10	84.7	(86.0)	78.7	(79.8)	90.8	(92.2)
1	11	85.6	(86.8)	79.5	(80.6)	91.7	(93.1)
2	0	84.5	(85.6)	78.5	(79.6)	90.5	(91.6)
2	1	85.4	(86.4)	79.2	(80.3)	91.5	(92.5)
2	2	86.2	(87.2)	80.0	(81.0)	92.4	(93.5)
2	3	87.0	(88.1)	80.7	(81.7)	93.4	(94.4)
2	4	87.9	(88.9)	81.4	(82.4)	94.3	(95.3)
2	5	88.7	(89.7)	82.2	(83.1)	95.2	(96.2)
2	6	89.5	(90.4)	82.9	(83.8)	96.0	(97.1)
2	7	90.2	(91.2)	83.6	(84.5)	96.9	(97.9)
2	8	91.0	(92.0)	84.3	(85.2)	97.7	(98.8)
2	9	91.7	(92.7)	84.9	(85.8)	98.6	(99.6)
2	10	92.5	(93.5)	85.6	(86.5)	99.4	(100.5)
2	11	93.2	(94.2)	86.3	(87.1)	100.1	(101.3)
3	0	93.9	(94.9)	86.9	(87.8)	100.9	(102.1)
3	1	94.6	(95.6)	87.6	(88.4)	101.7	(102.9)
3	2	95.3	(96.3)	88.2	(89.0)	102.4	(103.7)
3	3	96.0	(97.0)	88.8	(89.6)	103.1	(104.4)
3	4	96.6	(97.7)	89.4	(90.2)	103.9	(105.2)
3	5	97.3	(98.4)	90.0	(90.9)	104.6	(106.0)
3	6	97.9	(99.1)	90.6	(91.5)	105.3	(106.7)
3	7	98.6	(99.7)	91.2	(92.0)	105.9	(107.4)
3	8	99.2	(100.4)	91.8	(92.6)	106.6	(108.2)
3	9	99.8	(101.0)	92.3	(93.2)	107.3	(108.9)
3	10	100.4	(101.7)	92.9	(93.8)	107.9	(109.6)
3	11	101.0	(102.3)	93.5	(94.4)	108.6	(110.3)
4	0	101.6	(102.9)	94.0	(94.9)	109.2	(111.0)

Reference: World Health Organization Standards.
Note: The ideal relationship of height and weight is to be in proportion (e.g. if the child is of upper average height, his weight should also be upper average).
Note: 1 cm = 0.3937 inches. 1 inch = 2.54 cm

APPENDIX V
Weights from 1 year to 4 years

Weight in kg – girls (boys)

Age yrs mths		Average weight		Lower average 3% will be lighter 97% will be heavier		Upper average 3% will be heavier 97% will be lighter	
1	0	9.5	(10.2)	7.6	(8.2)	11.5	(12.2)
1	1	9.8	(10.4)	7.8	(8.5)	11.8	(12.5)
1	2	10.0	(10.7)	8.0	(8.7)	12.0	(12.8)
1	3	10.2	(10.9)	8.1	(8.8)	12.3	(13.1)
1	4	10.4	(11.1)	8.3	(9.0)	12.5	(13.3)
1	5	10.6	(11.3)	8.5	(9.1)	12.7	(13.6)
1	6	10.8	(11.5)	8.6	(9.3)	13.0	(13.8)
1	7	11.0	(11.7)	8.8	(9.4)	13.2	(14.0)
1	8	11.2	(11.8)	8.9	(9.5)	13.4	(14.2)
1	9	11.4	(12.0)	9.1	(9.7)	13.6	(14.4)
1	10	11.5	(12.2)	9.3	(9.8)	13.9	(14.6)
1	11	11.7	(12.4)	9.4	(9.9)	14.1	(14.8)
2	0	11.8	(12.3)	9.6	(10.2)	14.4	(15.5)
2	1	12.0	(12.5)	9.7	(10.3)	14.8	(15.7)
2	2	12.2	(12.7)	9.9	(10.4)	15.1	(15.9)
2	3	12.4	(12.9)	10.1	(10.6)	15.4	(16.1)
2	4	12.6	(13.1)	10.2	(10.7)	15.7	(16.4)
2	5	12.8	(13.3)	10.4	(10.8)	16.0	(16.6)
2	6	13.0	(13.5)	10.5	(10.9)	16.2	(16.8)
2	7	13.2	(13.7)	10.6	(11.0)	16.5	(17.0)
2	8	13.4	(13.9)	10.8	(11.1)	16.8	(17.2)
2	9	13.6	(14.1)	10.9	(11.3)	17.0	(17.4)
2	10	13.8	(14.3)	11.1	(11.4)	17.3	(17.6)
2	11	13.9	(14.4)	11.2	(11.5)	17.5	(17.8)
3	0	14.1	(14.6)	11.3	(11.6)	17.8	(18.0)
3	1	14.3	(14.8)	11.5	(11.7)	18.0	(18.2)
3	2	14.4	(15.0)	11.6	(11.9)	18.3	(18.5)
3	3	14.6	(15.2)	11.7	(12.0)	18.5	(18.7)
3	4	14.8	(15.3)	11.8	(12.1)	18.7	(18.9)
3	5	14.9	(15.5)	12.0	(12.2)	18.9	(19.1)
3	6	15.1	(15.7)	12.1	(12.4)	19.1	(19.3)
3	7	15.2	(15.8)	12.2	(12.5)	19.4	(19.5)
3	8	15.4	(16.0)	12.3	(12.6)	19.6	(19.7)
3	9	15.5	(16.2)	12.4	(12.7)	19.8	(19.9)
3	10	15.7	(16.4)	12.5	(12.9)	20.0	(20.1)
3	11	15.8	(16.5)	12.6	(13.0)	20.2	(20.3)
4	0	16.0	(16.7)	12.8	(13.1)	20.4	(20.5)

Reference: World Health Organization Standards
Note: The ideal relationship of weight and height is to be in proportion (e.g. if the child is of lower average height, his weight should also be lower average).
Note: 1 kg = 2.2 1bs; 1 lb = 0.45 kg

APPENDIX VI
Home safety checklist

This checklist is adapted from Child Accident Prevention Foundation of Australia information. It is for general reference only. Please consult a medical professional or child safety organisation for specific information relating to your circumstances and your child.

Through the home
- Are floors free of trip hazards?
- Are floor coverings such as rugs and mats secure and anti-slip?
- Are there barrier gates on stairs to prevent falls?
- Do railings prevent children from climbing them?
- Do power points have covers?
- Have safety switches been installed to prevent electrocution?
- Are blind and curtain cords out of a child's reach?
- Is furniture arranged to prevent collisions?
- Do ceiling fans have guards?
- Are the correct number of working smoke alarms installed?
- Are glass doors and large windows installed with safety glass or film?
- Are there stickers or frosting on sliding glass doors to prevent collisions?

Kitchen
- Can access to the kitchen be restricted?
- Is a fire blanket/fire extinguisher handy?
- Is there a lockable cupboard for cleaning products?
- Have poisons and alcohol been placed out of reach?
- Is the stove firmly fixed?
- Are curtains, blinds and other hanging objects away from the stove?
- Are knives, other sharp objects and matches out of reach?
- Are power cords and appliances such as the kettle out of reach?
- Are saucepans placed on rear hotplates with the handles turned to prevent them being pulled down?

Living room
- Are heating appliances out of reach of children?
- Are electric leads and cables shortened and arranged to prevent a child's reach?
- Are large objects such as televisions, bookcases or entertainment units secured to prevent them falling on children?
- Are sharp edges on furniture covered to prevent injury?
- Are glass objects or items with small pieces kept out of reach?
- Are handbags and wallets kept out of reach?

Dining room
- Are hot drinks placed out of reach?

- Are there non-slip tablemats in use instead of tablecloths?
- Is the child's high chair stable and the wheels locked when in use?
- Does the high chair have a five-point harness?

Bedrooms

- Is furniture located away from windows, electrical switches and ceiling fans?
- Are cot rails 50–85 mm apart?
- Is the cot free of soft toys when the child is sleeping?
- Is the child's bed safe (bunk beds not recommended)?
- Are supplies kept close to the change table to avoid reaching or moving around the room while changing the child's nappy?
- Are toys kept where children can reach them without climbing?
- Are toys in good condition and suitable for the child's age?
- Is there a night light in the room?

Bathroom

- Has the delivery temperature of the hot water service been turned down?
- Is the hot water from the tap no hotter than 50°C?
- Have devices been fitted to bath and basin spouts to prevent scalds?
- Is medicine stored in a lockable cabinet?
- Are razors and other hazardous items stored out of reach?
- Are electrical appliances such as hair dryers stored out of reach?
- Is the room heater out of reach of children?

Laundry

- Is access to the laundry restricted?
- Are poisons such as washing powders stored out of reach?
- Does the nappy bucket have a firm fitting lid and is it stored up high?
- Are the doors or lids to washing machines and dryers kept closed?

Outside

- Is the shed kept locked?
- Can access to the garage be restricted?
- Are poisons, paints and pesticides, etc, stored out of reach and labelled correctly?
- Have drowning hazards such as ponds or water features been removed or made child-safe?
- Has the pool been fenced with child-proof fencing and access gates?
- Is the property securely fenced to restrict access to roads or the driveway?
- Is play equipment in good condition and located in a stable position?
- Is there a soft surface under play equipment to cushion falls?
- Are pathways clear of trip hazards?
- Have all branches at child's eye level been removed?
- Are gardening tools and hoses stored out of reach of children?

APPENDIX VII
Useful Names and Addresses

Action for Sick Children
36 Jacksons Edge Road, Disley, Stockport SK12 2JL
Tel: 0800 0744519
Website: www.actionforsickchildren.org

Child Accident Prevention Trust
4th Floor, Cloister Court, 22-26 Farringdon Lane, London EC1R 3AJ
Tel: 020 7608 3828
Fax: 020 7608 3674
Email: safe@capt.org.uk
Website: www.capt.org.uk

Child Poverty Action Group
94 White Lion Street, London N1 9PF
Tel: 020 7837 7979
Fax: 020 7837 6414
Website: www.cpag.org.uk

Citizens Advice Bureau
Found in most towns and cities – telephone numbers in local telephone book.
Website: www.citizensadvice.org.uk

Department of Health
Richmond House, 79 Whitehall, London SW1A 2NS
Tel: 020 7210 4850
Website: www.dh.gov.uk

Disabled Living Foundation
380-384 Harrow Road, London W9 2HU
Tel: 0845 130 9177
Email: info@dlf.org.uk
Website: www.dlf.org.uk

Down's Syndrome Association
Langdon Down Centre, 2a Langdon Park, Teddington TW11 9PS
Tel: 0845 230 0372
Fax: 0845 230 0373
Email: info@downs-syndrome.org.uk
Website: www.downs-syndrome.org.uk

Gingerbread
307 Borough High Street, London SE1 1JH
Tel: 020 7403 9500
Fax: 020 7403 9533
Email: advice@gingerbread.org.uk
Website: www.gingerbread.org.uk

The Hyperactive Children's Support Group
71 Whyke Lane, Chichester, West Sussex PO19 7PD
Tel: 01243 539966
Email: hyperactive@hacsg.org.uk
Website: www.hacsg.org.uk

Mencap
123 Golden Lane, London EC1Y 0RT
Tel: 020 7454 0454
Fax: 020 7608 3254
Email: information@mencap.org.uk
Website: www.mencap.org.uk

National Association for Gifted Children
Suite 14, Challenge House, Sherwood Drive, Bletchley, Bucks MK3 6DP
Tel: 0870 7703217
Fax: 0870 7703219
Email: amazingchildren@nagcbritain.org.uk
Website: www.nagcbritain.org.uk

National Association of Toy and Leisure Libraries
68 Churchway, London NW1 1LT
Tel: 020 7255 4600
Fax: 020 7255 4602
Email: admin@playmatters.co.uk
Website: www.natll.org.uk

National Childminding Association
Royal Court, 81 Tweedy Road, Bromley, Kent BR1 1TG
Tel: 0845 880 0044
Email: info@ncma.org.uk
Website: www.ncma.org.uk

National Institute for Health and Clinical Excellence
MidCity Place, 71 High Holborn, London WC1V 6NA
Tel: 020 7067 5800
Fax: 020 7067 5801
Email: nice@nice.org.uk
Website: www.nice.org.uk

One Parent Families
255 Kentish Town Road, London NW5 2LX
Tel: 020 7428 5400
Fax: 020 7482 4851
Email: info@oneparentfamilies.org.uk
Website: www.oneparentfamilies.org.uk

Parentalk
115 Southwark Bridge Road, London SE1 0AX
Tel: 020 7450 9072/3
Fax: 020 7450 9001
Email: info@parentalk.co.uk
Website: www.parentalk.co.uk

Pre-school Learning Alliance
The Fitzpatrick Building, 188 York Way, London N7 9AD
Tel: 020 7697 2500
Fax: 020 7700 0319
Email: info@pre-school.org.uk
Website: www.pre-school.org.uk

Royal Society for the Prevention of Accidents
RoSPA House, Edgbaston Park, 353 Bristol Road, Edgbaston, Birmingham
B5 7ST
Tel: 0121 248 2000
Fax: 0121 248 2001
Email: help@rospa.com
Website: www.rospa.co.uk

Which? (consumer association)
2 Marylebone Road, London NW1 4DF
Tel: 0207 7770 7000
Fax: 020 7770 7600
Website: www.which.net

REFERENCES

Pages 38–9 (re New York Longitudinal Study)
Chess et al., *Behavioural Individuality in Early Childhood*, New York University Press, 1963.
Chess, *Temperament and Development*, Brunner Mazel, New York, 1977.

Pages 40–41 (re The Chamberlin Study)
Chamberlin, *Paediatric Clinics of North America, Vol. 21, no. 1, February 1974.*

Page 146 (re a study of children sleeping)
Anders, *Paediatrics*, Vol. 63, pp.860-4, 1979.

Pages 147–8 (re table 'A profile of some sleeping habits')
Beltramini, et al., *Paediatrics* Vol. 71, no 2, 1973.

Page 150 (re 'The Controlled Crying Technique')
Green, *The Journal of Maternal and Child Health*, United Kingdom, February 1980.

Page 200 (re WHO obesity figures)
Lobstein, Baur, Uary for the IOTF Childhood Obesity Working Group, 'Obesity in children and young people: A crisis in public health.' *Obesity Reviews* 2004.

Page 201 (re Australian obesity rates)
Margrey, Daniels, Boulton, 'Prevalence of overweight and obesity in Australian children' and 'Adolescents: reassessment of 1985–1995 data against new standard international definitions', *MJA*, 174: 561-564, 2001.

Page 300 (re Australian day care attendance)
Australian Bureau of Statistics, Child Care Survey, 2002.

Page 337 (re effects on children of working parents)
Harvey, *The Journal of Developmental Psychology*, March 1998.
Rutter, *Scientific Foundations of Developmental Psychiatry*, Heinemann, 1980.

INDEX

BY DR CHRISTOPHER GREEN
ALSO AVAILABLE FROM VERMILION

☐ Toddler Taming Tips	9780091889678	£5.99
☐ Beyond Toddlerdom	9780091816247	£10.99
☐ Beyond Toddlerdom Tips	9780091900069	£5.99
☐ Understanding ADHD	9780091817008	£9.99

FREE POSTAGE AND PACKING
Overseas customers allow £2.00 per paperback

ORDER:

By phone: 01624 677237

By post: Random House Books
c/o Bookpost
PO Box 29
Douglas
Isle of Man IM99 1BQ

By fax: 01624 670923

By email: bookshop@enterprise.net

Cheques (payable to Bookpost) and credit cards accepted

Prices and availability subject to change without notice.
Allow 28 days for delivery.
When placing your order, please mention if you do not wish to
receive any additional information.

www.rbooks.co.uk